AI-FOCUSED PM

(Project Management in the AI Era)

Dr. C S Rayudu, Sushma Cirigire,
Sugun Cirigiri & Susheel Cirigiri

Dr. C. Subbarayudu

Title: 'AI-Focused PM (Project Management in the AI Era)'
Authors: Dr. C Subbarayudu, Sushma Cirigire, Sugun Cirigiri and Susheel Cirigiri
Cover Design: Sugun Cirigiri

ISBN: ISBN 978-93-344-2814-8
Publisher: Dr. C. Subbarayudu
First Edition: 2025
Printed in India

For permissions and others, contact: Dr. C.S. Rayudu
drcsrayudu@gmail.com

DEDICATION

This manuscript, 'AI-Focused PM (Project Management in the AI Era),' is a tribute—a salute to the source of its energy.

Dedicated to the Stalwarts and Leaders of our communities, and to the Fellow Travelers and Mentors whose daily grit and inspiration provided the bedrock for these very pages.

It belongs to the Guild of Builders—to the Project Managers who know that innovation is not an accident. To the dreamers who dare to manage the unmanageable, navigating the future's fog with nothing but courage, sharp focus, and a flash of creative fire.

Finally, it is a whispered charge to the Changemakers to Come: May you find within these lines the spark to harmonize the human heart with the silicon mind, crafting a legacy of projects that serve, elevate, and make a better world.

CONTENTS

PREFACE

Project management has long represented a compelling intersection of structure and creativity, discipline and adaptability. Through our collective journey in academia, research, and professional practice, we have come to regard project management not merely as a collection of tools and techniques but as a mindset—one that harmonises vision with execution and balances people's needs with the demands of processes. This understanding has been the central inspiration for writing *AI-Focused PM (Project Management in the AI Era)*.

The purpose of this book is to provide readers with a comprehensive perspective on project management in general, and software project management in particular, that is both grounded in established foundations and responsive to future developments. While existing literature extensively documents traditional and agile methodologies, few works attempt to integrate these approaches with the emerging influence of artificial intelligence in reshaping leadership, collaboration, and decision-making. Our objective is to bridge this gap by presenting project management as a dynamic discipline—one that evolves alongside technological innovation while remaining firmly rooted in enduring human values.

Professional contexts initiated our engagement with this subject, which we further reinforced by actively participating in software industry projects. Over time, we observed the limitations of traditional project planning models in rapidly changing environments, the resilience fostered by agile practices, and the transformative impact of intelligent tools such as Copilot and GPT-5 in supporting planning, monitoring, and delivery. These experiences have reinforced our conviction that future project managers must be adept not only in established frameworks but also in AI-enabled practices that augment, rather than replace, human leadership.

Our ability to contribute to this work is grounded in a combination of rigorous academic study, research, hands-on experience, mentoring, and collaboration with project management professionals in the software industry. Through these engagements, we have developed an in-depth appreciation for the challenges, ambitions, and evolving methodologies that define contemporary project environments. Rather than presenting prescriptive rules, our goal is to offer a structured framework that enables readers to navigate uncertainty with confidence, drawing on enduring principles while leveraging the capabilities of modern tools.

This book is therefore both reflective and forward-looking. It is dedicated to current and aspiring project managers who seek to understand the full breadth of their profession—from traditional planning models and agile practices to the transformative potential of artificial intelligence. If it succeeds in cultivating both competence and curiosity among its readers, then it will have achieved its purpose.]

Dr C. S. Rayudu

Sushma Cirigire

Sugun Cirigiri

Susheel Cirigiri

INTRODUCTION

Project management has always been about more than schedules, budgets, and checklists—it is about creating order from complexity and guiding diverse teams toward a shared vision. From the construction of ancient monuments to the execution of modern software solutions, the discipline has continually adapted to meet the evolving needs of organizations and societies. In today's digital economy, the pace of change is faster than ever, requiring project managers not only to master traditional practices but also to embrace agile thinking and harness the transformative power of Artificial Intelligence (AI).

This book, *AI-Focused PM (Project Management in the AI Era)*, is designed to provide readers with both foundational grounding and forward-looking insights. It begins with the essentials: defining project management, understanding how projects differ from ongoing operations, and recognising the value of structured approaches. Readers are introduced to traditional methods such as the waterfall model, contrasted with agile principles that have reshaped industries like software development. Through comparative discussions and real-world case studies, the book highlights when each approach—or a hybrid—delivers the greatest value.

As projects take shape, planning becomes central. The text explores critical steps such as defining goals aligned with strategy, gathering and validating requirements, estimating costs, and developing budgets. The text unpacks quality planning, procurement strategies, resource allocation, and scheduling methods with clarity, ensuring that readers develop both conceptual understanding and practical skills. Any professional navigating the planning and initiation stages of a project can use these chapters as a toolkit.

Execution and monitoring demand a different set of competencies. Here, readers will encounter frameworks for tracking progress through Key Performance Indicators (KPIs), Earned Value Management (EVM), and agile metrics [CK1] such as velocity and burndown charts. Leadership, communication, and cultural sensitivity are emphasised as central to project success, alongside tools for scaling methodologies to projects of varying complexity. The role of software applications—MS Project, Jira, Trello, Asana, and others—is addressed through simulations and examples, offering readers a hands-on appreciation of modern project ecosystems.

The book's final section turns decisively toward the future. Artificial intelligence, embodied in tools like Copilot and GPT-5, is no longer a distant possibility but an active force reshaping project management. These systems analyse vast amounts of data, surface insights in real time, and provide contextual intelligence that empowers leaders to make sharper decisions. They also function as mentors and collaborators, augmenting human leadership with predictive analysis and adaptive recommendations. Through case scenarios and industry examples, the book explores how AI is redefining agile leadership, scaling strategies, and even the ethical responsibilities of project managers.

Ultimately, *AI-Focused PM* presents a vision of project management where tradition, agility, and AI converge. For current project managers, it offers strategies to remain relevant and resilient in a changing landscape. For aspiring professionals, particularly in the software industry, it provides both the theoretical foundations and the forward-looking skills necessary to lead projects in an era empowered by AI.

PART I

FOUNDATIONS OF PROJECT MANAGEMENT

CHAPTER 1: DEFINING PROJECT MANAGEMENT

1. Project Management

Project management is the practice of leading a team's work to achieve a set of specific goals within defined constraints, such as scope, time, and budget. It involves applying knowledge, skills, tools, and techniques to project activities from beginning to end.

1.1 Understanding the Concept of a Project:

The Project Management Institute (PMI), widely regarded as the leading global authority on project management, defines a project as "a temporary endeavour undertaken to create a unique product, service, or result." This definition highlights two crucial aspects: temporariness and uniqueness. Temporariness means that every project has a defined start and end point. Unlike operations, which continue indefinitely, projects are bound by time and conclude once objectives are met or deemed unattainable. Uniqueness signifies that each project creates something new—whether it be a product, a system, or an improved process—even if it shares similarities with past projects.

A project typically unfolds through a structured sequence

of tasks, activities, and deliverables, each linked to broader organisational goals. For instance, the construction of a hospital necessitates a range of distinct tasks such as architectural design, procurement, staffing, and commissioning, all of which come together to create a unique healthcare facility. Likewise, a software upgrade may follow repeatable steps, but the end solution is tailored to a specific set of users and objectives, ensuring that each project remains distinct.

1.2 What is Project Management?

If a project is the *what*, then project management is the *how*. It represents the application of knowledge, skills, methodologies, strategies, and techniques to execute a project effectively. The goal of project management is not only to meet deadlines and budgets but also to align outcomes with strategic objectives and stakeholder expectations.

A disciplined approach to project management provides structure to what might otherwise be an uncoordinated collection of activities. It transforms ideas into tangible outputs—products, services, or deliverables—while balancing competing constraints such as scope, time, cost, and quality. Project management methodologies, such as PRINCE2, and Agile, provide frameworks for organising and guiding these processes.

Today, project management has evolved from a specialised function to a mainstream practice across industries. From startups launching new apps to governments implementing infrastructure megaprojects, organizations adopt structured project management not only to boost efficiency and reduce risks but also to drive innovation and competitiveness in an increasingly dynamic marketplace.

1.3 Importance of Project Management:

Project management is not merely a supporting function—it is a strategic enabler of business success. Its importance can be explained through the following dimensions:

1.3.1. Improved efficiency:

A structured approach ensures that tasks are well-defined, timelines are realistic, and resources are allocated appropriately. This reduces redundancy and wasted effort, allowing teams to focus on what matters most. For instance, in construction, clear sequencing of tasks prevents costly delays due to resource clashes.

1.3.2. Better organisation:

Project management creates a roadmap for teams, ensuring that responsibilities are clear and tasks are prioritised. This minimises the risk of critical tasks being overlooked, especially in complex, multi-phase projects.

1.3.3. Enhanced communication:

By establishing regular updates and transparent channels, project management minimises misunderstandings and aligns expectations between stakeholders. In Agile software development, for example, daily stand-ups ensure that team members remain synchronised.

1.3.4. Risk reduction:

Projects are inherently uncertain. Through structured risk identification, assessment, and mitigation, project management reduces the likelihood of unexpected setbacks derailing progress. This proactive approach can save organizations millions in avoided rework or crisis management.

1.3.5. Measurable outcomes:

By setting clear goals and performance metrics, project managers enable organizations to track progress objectively. This provides accountability and generates valuable data for future learning.

1.3.6. Increased client satisfaction:

Delivering projects on time, within scope, and within budget strengthens client trust and satisfaction. Whether in IT or healthcare, successful delivery often translates into repeat business and long-term partnerships.

1.4 Benefits of Project Management:

*P*roject management offers a structured framework for planning, executing, and completing projects, delivering a chain of interconnected benefits. These benefits progress in a logical order—efficiency, organisation, communication, risk mitigation, measurable outcomes, and client satisfaction—each building upon the other to enhance overall project success.

1.4.1. Efficiency:

Project management enhances efficiency by streamlining processes, defining clear objectives, and optimising resource allocation. It minimises duplication of effort, reduces wasted time, and ensures that team members focus on high-priority tasks, leading to faster and more cost-effective outcomes.

1.4.2. Organisation:

Efficiency naturally leads to better organisation. By breaking down projects into phases, tasks, and responsibilities, project management creates clarity and order. This structured approach helps teams coordinate effectively, stay aligned with goals, and manage complex activities without confusion.

1.4.3. Communication:

With organisational structures in place, communication improves significantly. Project management establishes formal communication channels—through regular meetings, reports, and collaborative tools—ensuring that stakeholders and team members remain informed, aligned, and engaged throughout the project lifecycle.

1.4.4. Risk Mitigation:

Strong communication and organisation support proactive risk management. By identifying potential risks early and planning mitigation strategies, project management reduces the likelihood of unexpected disruptions. This approach safeguards both project timelines and quality.

1.4.5. Measurable Outcomes:

Risk mitigation lays the foundation for measurable outcomes. Defined milestones, performance metrics, and evaluation tools allow progress to be tracked objectively. This ensures accountability and enables decision-makers to assess success using tangible data.

1.4.6. Client Satisfaction:

All these benefits culminate in enhanced client satisfaction. By delivering projects efficiently, with clear communication, minimised risks, and measurable success, project management ensures that outcomes meet or exceed client expectations—building trust, credibility, and long-term relationships.

In essence, the benefits of project management form a chain reaction where each element strengthens the next, ultimately driving successful project delivery and stakeholder satisfaction.

Figure 1.1

The Benefits of Project Management

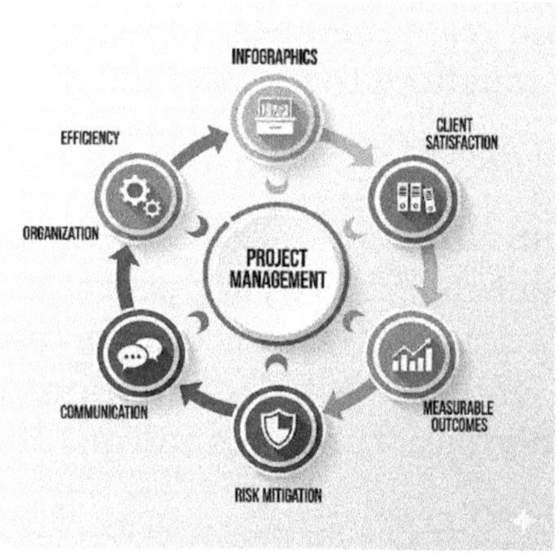

1.4.7. Description of the Figure:

The diagram illustrates six interconnected benefits of project management, showing how they collectively contribute to successful project delivery.

Project management delivers a range of interconnected benefits that collectively strengthen project success. It enhances *efficiency* by streamlining processes, defining clear tasks, allocating resources effectively, and reducing redundancies, ensuring timely and cost-effective completion of work. This naturally fosters *organisation*, as activities are structured into phases, roles, and responsibilities, providing clarity and order for managing complex tasks with discipline. Strong organisation also improves communication, establishing transparent channels that keep stakeholders, team members, and clients aligned on goals, progress, and challenges throughout the project lifecycle. With communication and structure in place, project management supports *risk mitigation* by proactively identifying potential issues, planning contingencies, minimising disruptions, thereby safeguarding outcomes. These practices further enable the achievement of measurable outcomes, as defined objectives, performance metrics, and tracking tools allow progress to be assessed against benchmarks, ensuring accountability and data-driven decisions. Ultimately, these combined benefits lead to client satisfaction, with projects delivered efficiently, transparently, and reliably, fostering trust and long-term partnerships.

Together, these six benefits form an interconnected system, reinforcing one another to create a holistic framework that enhances both the process and results of project management.

1.5 Project Management Across Industries:

The universality of project management lies in its adaptability across diverse domains. Regardless of the sector, the fundamental processes—initiating, planning, executing, monitoring, and closing—remain constant, though tailored tools and techniques may differ based on industry requirements. This universality makes project management not only a methodological discipline but also a professional competency that drives efficiency, innovation, and risk control across organisational contexts.

Construction: *Managing Design, Procurement, and Site Execution for Complex Structures:*

In the construction industry, project management plays a

pivotal role in orchestrating the delivery of highly complex and capital-intensive projects such as bridges, skyscrapers, and transportation infrastructure. Each construction project is unique, constrained by budget, timelines, and stringent safety standards. The project manager is responsible for harmonising design considerations, procurement logistics, and on-site execution while navigating the challenges of labour management, regulatory compliance, and environmental factors. For instance, the successful delivery of the Burj Khalifa in Dubai required the meticulous coordination of international design teams, suppliers, and construction crews across multiple time zones. Here, project management methodologies such as the Critical Path Method (CPM) and Earned Value Management (EVM) were instrumental in ensuring timely delivery while managing the complexities of scale and scope.

Healthcare: *Implementing Electronic Health Record Systems or Constructing New Hospitals:*

In healthcare, project management ensures that highly sensitive initiatives, such as the implementation of Electronic Health Record (EHR) systems or the development of new medical facilities, are executed effectively. Healthcare projects differ from other industries due to their emphasis on patient safety, confidentiality, and regulatory compliance. For example, the rollout of an EHR system requires coordination between IT teams, clinicians, administrators, and regulatory bodies, while managing resistance to change from healthcare professionals who are accustomed to traditional practices. Project managers in this sector often use frameworks like PRINCE2 or Agile Health methodologies to ensure adaptability while maintaining strict compliance with laws such as HIPAA in the United States. A real-world example is the United Kingdom's National Programme for IT (NPfIT), one of the world's largest healthcare IT initiatives, which highlighted both the opportunities and challenges of project management in such complex, multi-stakeholder environments.

Aerospace: *Coordinating Large-Scale, High-Risk Projects like Satellite Launches:*

The aerospace industry represents one of the most demanding environments for project management due to its high-risk, high-stakes nature. Projects in this domain, such as satellite launches, defence systems, or interplanetary missions, require extensive planning, rigorous risk management, and precise execution. These projects often involve budgets running into billions of dollars, international collaborations, and strict safety requirements where even minor errors can lead to catastrophic consequences. For instance, NASA's Mars Rover missions demonstrate the effectiveness of project management in coordinating scientists, engineers, and contractors worldwide under stringent deadlines and performance metrics. Tools such as risk registers, Failure Mode and Effect Analysis (FMEA), and systems engineering frameworks are widely employed to ensure both technical accuracy and mission success. The aerospace sector underscores project management as a discipline of precision, resilience, and innovation.

Software Development: *Delivering Applications, Platforms, and Digital Products Using Iterative Methods:*

In the software industry, project management has evolved significantly, shifting from traditional linear models to more adaptive approaches such as Agile, Scrum, and DevOps. Software projects are characterised by their dynamic nature, where requirements can evolve rapidly due to market feedback, emerging technologies, or user demands. Here, project managers serve as facilitators, enabling cross-functional teams to collaborate iteratively and deliver value incrementally. A well-known case is Microsoft's transition to Agile practices in the development of Windows 10, where iterative delivery cycles allowed the company to release continuous updates rather than rely on monolithic version launches. Project management tools such as Jira, Trello, and Kanban boards exemplify how digital platforms facilitate real-time communication, sprint planning, and progress tracking, making adaptability a central theme in software project management.

1.5.1. Project management is a transferable discipline:

These diverse examples demonstrate that project management transcends sectoral boundaries, functioning as a versatile and transferable discipline. While construction emphasises structural integrity and procurement, healthcare prioritises compliance and patient safety, aerospace relies on risk precision, and software development thrives on iterative adaptability, the foundational principles of project management remain consistent. Whether the goal is building skyscrapers, enhancing healthcare delivery, exploring space, or creating digital innovations, project management ensures that resources are optimised, risks are managed, and objectives are achieved. This adaptability underscores why project management continues to be an indispensable competency in the global economy.

1.6. Who Uses Project Management?

Project management, though often associated with specialised certifications and formal roles, has evolved into a universal competency that extends far beyond professional project managers. In contemporary organizations, the discipline is recognised as a shared framework that guides decision-making, coordinates collaborative tasks, and aligns diverse stakeholders toward common objectives. This diffusion of project management principles across various levels of an organisation reflects its adaptability and relevance in addressing challenges of scale, complexity, and uncertainty.

1.6.1. Project Managers:

At the heart of structured project execution are certified or formally designated project managers. They function as the custodians of project success, overseeing the intricate interplay between people, processes, and resources. Their role is not limited to scheduling or budgeting; rather, they act as orchestrators who balance competing demands, resolve conflicts, and safeguard the project's alignment with organisational strategy. In industries such as construction, healthcare, or aerospace, project managers ensure that critical paths are adhered to and that risk management frameworks are embedded into every phase. Their professional training equips them to anticipate disruptions, mitigate risks, and facilitate seamless communication across diverse teams.

1.6.2. Team Leads:

While project managers maintain a panoramic view, team leads often focus on ensuring that departmental contributions align with broader organisational goals. They translate high-level project objectives into actionable tasks tailored to their team's strengths and resources. For example, in a marketing campaign project, a creative lead may manage designers and content developers while ensuring cohesion with the overall brand strategy. Team leads serve as intermediaries who bridge the gap between the technical details of execution and the overarching objectives, thus reinforcing accountability within their domains.

1.6.3. Software Developers and Product Managers:

In the domain of software development and digital product delivery, project management principles are seamlessly woven into day-to-day practices. Agile methodologies empower software developers and product managers to work in iterative cycles, known as sprints, which prioritise incremental delivery and responsiveness to change. Developers employ project tracking tools to manage bug fixes, feature enhancements, and releases, while product managers align backlogs with customer needs and organisational strategy. This experiment demonstrates how project management, in its Agile form, becomes embedded in operational workflows rather than existing as a separate managerial layer.

1.6.4. Marketing Teams:

Marketing departments also rely heavily on project management practices, though their objectives differ from technical or engineering projects. Campaigns often involve cross-channel coordination, from digital outreach and social media promotion to event management and stakeholder engagement. Each campaign functions as a project, complete with defined goals, timelines, budgets, and deliverables. By applying project management tools, marketing teams can schedule tasks, track dependencies, and evaluate campaign performance. This enhances collaboration among creatives, analysts, and strategists while ensuring consistency in brand messaging across platforms.

1.6.5. Executives: Strategic Stewards:

Even at the highest levels of leadership, project

management principles serve as a guiding compass for strategy execution. Executives adopt these practices to monitor progress on strategic initiatives, allocate resources effectively, and ensure alignment with corporate vision. Large-scale transformations, such as digital modernisation or sustainability initiatives, often comprise multiple projects that require oversight at the portfolio or programme level. By integrating project management dashboards and Key Performance Indicators (KPIs), executives gain visibility into organisational progress and make data-informed decisions that shape the long-term trajectory of the enterprise.

1.6.6. Shared Tools and Collective Outcomes:

Perhaps the most significant feature of project management's universality lies in the use of shared tools and frameworks. Cross-functional teams benefit from common platforms—such as Kanban boards, Gantt charts, or digital project management software—that provide transparency into each other's work. This shared visibility reduces silos, enhances accountability, and fosters alignment across roles and functions. Whether it is a project manager orchestrating tasks, a team lead supervising outputs, or executives tracking organisational initiatives, these tools create a collaborative ecosystem where priorities are synchronised and outcomes are collectively driven.

1.7 The Project Manager: Roles and Responsibilities:

A project manager is a professional responsible for the planning, execution, and completion of projects. They are the central figure who coordinates all project activities, ensuring that the work stays on time, within budget, and meets the specified goals.

In the vast ecosystem of project management, the Project Manager (PM) occupies a central and indispensable role.

Acting as both strategist and executor, the project manager is entrusted with the responsibility of guiding a project from its conceptualisation through to completion. Unlike many other roles, which focus on specific technical or departmental contributions, the PM must integrate diverse inputs, mediate between stakeholders, and ensure that the project adheres to time, cost, and quality constraints. This dual role as a leader and a coordinator makes the project manager the pivotal figure in determining project success.

1.7.1. The Project Manager: Defining scopes and objectives:

At the outset of any project, clarity of purpose is essential. The project manager ensures that the scope—what the project will and will not deliver—is defined and agreed upon. This involves collaborating with stakeholders to establish measurable objectives, deliverables, and success criteria. For instance, in a construction project, the PM must determine whether the scope includes only the structural framework of a building or also the finishing interiors. Scope definition prevents "scope creep", a phenomenon where uncontrolled changes expand the project's boundaries, often leading to cost overruns and delays.

1.7.2. The Project Manager: Planning costs and adhering to budgets:

Financial stewardship is a cornerstone responsibility of a project manager. They prepare detailed budgets that forecast material, labour, and operational expenses while also planning for contingencies. Effective cost management requires continuous monitoring, comparing actual expenditures against planned budgets, and recalibrating when deviations occur. In industries such as healthcare IT, where implementing an Electronic Health Record (EHR) system can involve millions in licensing, integration, and training costs, the PM's ability to balance financial prudence with technological ambition is crucial.

1.7.3. The Project Manager: Assigning Tasks and Delegating Responsibilities:

No project succeeds without effective task distribution. The project manager breaks down the work into smaller, manageable units, often through a Work Breakdown Structure (WBS). Assigning responsibilities involves more than allocating tasks; it requires aligning tasks with team members' skills and strengths. For example, in a software development project, a PM might assign backend integration tasks to senior developers while delegating UI/UX enhancements (for a website, app, or a document/figure layout) to designers, ensuring optimal use of expertise. Successful delegation also involves empowering team members to take ownership of their responsibilities while maintaining accountability.

1.7.4. The Project Manager: Managing Resources—Human and Material:

Resources extend beyond people; they encompass tools, technologies, equipment, and infrastructure essential for project execution. The project manager balances human resources—such as developers, engineers, or marketing specialists—with material needs like machinery, software licences, or raw materials. In aerospace projects, resource management may involve coordinating specialised equipment for testing rocket engines while also scheduling highly skilled scientists and technicians. The PM ensures that these resources are neither underutilised nor overextended.

1.7.5. The Project Manager: Communicating Effectively with Stakeholders:

Communication is arguably the most critical skill in the PM's toolkit. Project managers act as the communication hub between team members, clients, vendors, and executives. They must tailor their messaging—technical details for engineers, progress updates for executives, and milestone reports for clients. Effective communication builds trust, manages expectations, and prevents misunderstandings. For instance, during the rollout of a marketing campaign, a PM must communicate timelines to the creative team, coordinate with media partners, and update executives on campaign impact—all while ensuring consistent alignment across channels.

1.7.6. The Project Manager: Assessing Risks and Troubleshooting Issues:

Every project carries risks, whether technical, financial, or operational. The project manager identifies potential risks during planning and creates mitigation strategies. Such strategies could include contingency budgets, backup suppliers, or alternative timelines. When unforeseen challenges emerge—such as a supply chain disruption in construction or a cybersecurity breach in software projects—the PM must act swiftly to resolve the issue, ensuring minimal disruption to progress. Risk management, therefore, blends foresight with adaptability.

1.7.7. The Project Manager: Ensure quality standards are met:

Deliverables are only valuable if they meet agreed-upon quality standards. Project managers establish quality benchmarks at the start and ensure that deliverables undergo rigorous Quality Assurance (QA) checks. In healthcare projects, where software failures can have life-or-death implications, QA is especially critical. The PM ensures compliance with regulatory standards, such as HIPAA

(Health Insurance Portability and Accountability Act) in the U.S. or GDPR (General Data Protection Regulation) in Europe, while also meeting customer expectations for usability and performance.

1.7.8. The Project Manager: Documenting Progress and Closing Projects Formally:

Project closure is often underestimated, yet it is as important as initiation. The project manager oversees final documentation, compiling lessons learnt, project performance data, and stakeholder feedback. A formal closure ensures that all contractual obligations are met, resources are released, and the organisation benefits from knowledge transfer. For example, in aerospace launches, documenting technical insights and troubleshooting logs is vital for informing future missions and avoiding repeated errors. Closure also reinforces accountability and celebrates team achievements, which enhances morale.

1.7.9. The Project Manager: Balancing Competencies and Soft Skills:

While technical expertise forms the backbone of a PM's effectiveness, soft skills elevate their leadership. Required skills include mastery of project management methodologies (e.g., Agile, PRINCE2), proficiency in tools like MS Project or Jira, and knowledge of scheduling, budgeting, and risk analysis. Soft skills—leadership, emotional intelligence, decision-making, negotiation, and adaptability—are equally indispensable. A PM must not only design a flawless plan but also inspire a team to execute it, mediate conflicts, and maintain motivation through challenges.

1.7.10. Case Example 1:

Consider a project manager overseeing the development of a new mobile banking app. Important skills enable the PM to create sprints, manage code repositories, and track timelines. However, when developers disagree over architectural decisions, it is the PM's soft skills—facilitating dialogue, fostering compromise, and motivating the team—that keep the project on course.

1.8. The Role of Project Management Tools and Software

Digital tools deeply support modern project management, enabling teams to plan, execute, and monitor work more effectively. Software platforms such as Jira, Trello, Asana, and Microsoft Project provide powerful features:

a. Gantt charts to visualise timelines and dependencies.

b. Kanban boards for managing workflows.

c. Dashboards to track progress against milestones.

d. Reporting tools for stakeholder communication.

These tools enhance efficiency and facilitate collaboration, ensuring that diverse teams—from developers to marketers—remain aligned. For example, Jira allows software developers to manage sprint backlogs, QA teams to track testing processes, and marketing teams to schedule product launches, all within a single platform.

1.9 The Project Management Life Cycle and Universal Phases of Project Management:

One of the most fundamental contributions of the *Project Management Body of Knowledge (PMBOK)* and the Project Management Institute (PMI) delineate the life cycle into five foundational phases: initiating, planning, executing, monitoring and controlling, and closing. Although these phases are constant, their depth, flexibility, and application differ depending on the chosen methodology and the context of the project. This framework is not merely theoretical; it provides a practical roadmap that helps managers, teams, and organizations ensure that objectives are systematically pursued, resources are efficiently used, and risks are anticipated and managed. The diagram below (Figure 1.2) illustrates the universal phases of project management."

Figure 1.2

Universal Phases of Project Management

The Project Management Body of Knowledge (PMBOK),

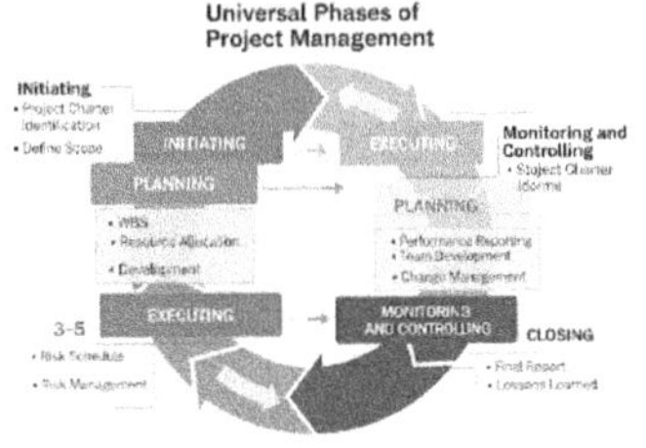

developed by the Project Management Institute (PMI), clearly delineates the project life cycle into five foundational phases, making it one of the most fundamental contributions. These phases—*initiating, planning, executing, monitoring and controlling, and closing*—are considered universal because they provide a structured framework applicable across industries, sectors, and project types. While individual projects may differ in scope, complexity, and methodology, these phases ensure that every project follows a logical and disciplined path from conception to completion.

1.9.1. Initiating:

The initiation phase establishes the foundation of the

project. It involves defining the project's purpose, identifying key stakeholders, and determining feasibility. During this stage, project charters are developed, and high-level goals are articulated to align expectations and secure approval. A strong initiation phase ensures that projects are launched with clarity of vision and adequate stakeholder buy-in.

1.9.2. Planning:

Once initiated, the project moves into the planning stage, which is often the most comprehensive and resource-intensive. Here, detailed objectives are set, work breakdown structures are created, timelines are established, and budgets are allocated. Risk management strategies, quality standards, and communication frameworks are also outlined. Effective planning minimises uncertainties and serves as a roadmap that guides the team through the project's execution.

1.9.3. Executing:

The execution phase is where plans are transformed into action. Resources are mobilised; tasks are performed, and deliverables are developed according to the project scope. Strong leadership, coordination, and communication are vital to ensure that team members remain aligned with objectives. This phase is typically the most visible to stakeholders, as it involves tangible progress and measurable outputs.

1.9.4. Monitoring and Controlling:

Running parallel to execution, this phase ensures that the project remains on track. Monitoring involves systematically tracking progress against the project plan, while controlling allows managers to identify deviations and implement corrective measures. Key Performance Indicators (KPIs), progress reports, and quality checks are employed to maintain alignment with scope, time, cost, and quality requirements. Effective monitoring and controlling enable project managers to anticipate challenges and respond proactively.

1.9.5. Closing:

The closing phase marks the formal completion of the project. Deliverables are handed over, final documentation is prepared, and resources are released. Importantly, this stage also includes evaluating project outcomes against initial objectives and conducting post-project reviews to capture lessons learnt. Proper closure ensures accountability, acknowledges team contributions, and offers helpful tips for future projects.

Together, these five phases embody a universal framework that transforms project management from a reactive process into a disciplined practice. By adhering to these stages, organizations enhance efficiency, mitigate risks, and increase the likelihood of delivering successful outcomes.

2. Projects vs. Operations

Projects:

Projects are temporary endeavours undertaken to create a unique product, service, or result. They have a defined beginning and end, specific objectives, and constraints in terms of scope, time, cost, and resources. A project's primary purpose is to bring about change or deliver something new, making it distinct from routine organisational activities.

Operations:

Operations, in contrast, are ongoing and repetitive activities that sustain an organisation's business. They focus on maintaining efficiency, stability, and continuity in producing goods or delivering services. Unlike projects, operations have no defined end point; they are continuous processes designed to support day-to-day functioning and long-term organisational objectives.

2.1. Key Characteristics of Projects vs. Operations:

2.1.1. Projects are temporary, while operations are ongoing:

The most fundamental distinction lies in their time-bound nature. A project is a temporary endeavour undertaken to create a unique product, service, or result. It has a clearly defined start and end point, and its conclusion is marked by the achievement of objectives or the formal termination of efforts. For instance, designing and launching a new software platform would be considered a project, as it culminates in a finished deliverable. Operations, in contrast, are continuous and repetitive in nature. They encompass the day-to-day activities that keep an organisation running, such as maintaining IT infrastructure, processing payroll, or providing customer service. These tasks have no predetermined end date and persist for as long as the organisation exists. This distinction is critical because project teams often disband after completion, while operational teams remain permanent.

2.1.2. Projects are unique, while operations are repetitive:

Another defining characteristic is uniqueness. Every project, regardless of similarities with past initiatives, presents distinct conditions, deliverables, and challenges. For example, constructing two residential apartment complexes may seem similar in scope, yet each project will involve unique design requirements, site conditions, local regulations, stakeholder demands, and technology choices. These variables make projects inherently non-repetitive. In contrast, operations focus on routine and repeatable processes aimed at achieving consistency and efficiency. Manufacturing a product on an assembly line, for example, is an operational activity—highly standardised, predictable, and designed to deliver uniform outcomes. This uniqueness of projects necessitates tailored planning and execution, while operations rely on established workflows and process optimisation.

2.1.3. Projects are change-driven, while operations are stability-driven:

Projects inherently exist to bring about change, whether in the form of innovation, transformation, or expansion. They act as vehicles for organizations to adapt to evolving markets, adopt new technologies, or introduce new products and services. For example, a company implementing an artificial intelligence system to enhance customer service is undertaking a project that drives technological and organisational change. On the other hand, operations aim to sustain stability by ensuring that existing processes, products, and services run smoothly and consistently. Operations maintain organisational equilibrium by focusing on reliability, efficiency, and predictability. When integrated effectively, projects and operations strike a balance: projects enable organizations to evolve, while operations ensure continuity. This synergy allows organizations to be both innovative and resilient.

2.1.4. Projects are measured by success criteria, while operations are measured by efficiency.

The metrics used to evaluate projects and operations also differ significantly. Projects are typically assessed against success criteria such as adherence to scope, schedule, budget, and quality standards. For example, if a construction project is completed within the agreed timeline, budget, and specifications, it is deemed successful, even though the project ends once the deliverable is handed over. Operations, by contrast, are measured by their efficiency, productivity, and long-term sustainability. An operational process such as order fulfilment would be evaluated based on speed, accuracy, cost-effectiveness, and service quality over time. This distinction in measurement reinforces the idea that while projects are designed to achieve defined goals and then conclude, operations are geared toward maximising performance on an ongoing basis.

2.1.4.1. Synthesis:

These distinctions clarify why project management requires specialised methodologies that differ from those used in routine operations. Projects, by their very nature, require structured frameworks, tools, and adaptive leadership to navigate uncertainty, manage unique challenges, and deliver change. Operations, conversely, thrive on consistency, standardisation, and process optimisation. By recognising and respecting these differences, organizations can allocate appropriate resources, assign skilled personnel, and apply the right strategies to each domain. Failure to do so risks inefficiencies—such as treating projects like routine tasks, which can undermine innovation and lead to costly delays or failures.

The following professional comparison Table 1 presents a dual-column comparison of 'Projects' and 'Operations', with arrows illustrating how the two complement one another. While the table offers a clear, quick-reference snapshot, the accompanying paragraphs provide the detailed narrative and deeper insights.

Table 1

Projects vs. Operations – Key Characteristics

Dimension	Projects	Operations
Nature	Temporary, with a defined start and end date.	Ongoing, continuous activities with no predetermined end.
Objective	To deliver a unique product, service, or result.	To sustain and optimize existing processes, services, or outputs.
Uniqueness	Each project is distinct, shaped by specific goals, stakeholders, and conditions.	Activities are repetitive, standardized, and designed for consistency.
Focus	Change-oriented—introduces innovation, transformation, or expansion.	Stability-oriented—ensures reliability, efficiency, and continuity.
Measurement	Success judged by meeting scope, schedule, budget, and quality criteria.	Performance judged by efficiency, productivity, and service quality.
Team Structure	Temporary, cross-functional teams formed for project duration.	Permanent teams organized around functional or operational roles.
Examples	Developing a new software platform, constructing a bridge, launching a marketing campaign.	Maintaining IT servers, running payroll systems, manufacturing products.

End Point	Concludes once objectives are met or project is terminated.	Has no fixed end point; continues as long as the organization exists.

Moreover, the figure below compares 'Projects' and 'Operations' in dual columns, illustrating their complementary relationship and offering a clear quick-reference snapshot.

Table 2

	Projects	Operations
Nature	Temporary and Unique Endeavors	
Objective	Projects aim for	Ongoing are Repettive Activities
Objective	Specific Outcome or Product	Ongoing Ourtettive Activities
Uniqueness	Distinct and Novel	Sustatined Output or Service
	Distiont and Novel	Standardized and Routie
Focus	Projects empthielaizes	Efficiency and Stability
	Change and Innovation	
	Projects use Change and Innovation	
Measurement	Deliverable Completion, Budget, Schedule	Temporary, Cross-functional
Measurement		Permanent, Functional Teams
Team structure	Projects have Temporary, Cross-functional Teams	Building a New Hospital, Developing New Software Product
Examples	Concerty Venule Management	Hospital Patient Care, Software Mainterence

CHAPTER 2: TRADITIONAL VS. AGILE PROJECT MANAGEMENT

1. Overview Of Traditional (Waterfall) Project Management

Project Management Life Cycle

The project management life cycle and its five universal phases, such as initiating, planning, executing, monitoring and controlling, and closing project management, serve as a disciplined and structured framework for managing projects of diverse scale and complexity. Collectively, these phases promote clarity, accountability, and efficiency, empowering organizations to achieve successful outcomes while continuously learning and refining practices throughout the project cycle. Although the five foundational phases remain consistent across methodologies, their application varies considerably.

1. In *predictive models* such as the waterfall approach, the phases are carried out sequentially, with each stage being fully completed before progressing to the next.

2. In *adaptive models* such as Agile, the same phases are

enacted iteratively, with each development cycle (or sprint) incorporating aspects of all five phases.

This divergence in application underscores the two dominant paradigms of project management—predictive and adaptive—and establishes the conceptual basis for comparative analysis.

***Project Management Models:* Waterfall and Agile**

Project management models provide structured approaches that govern the planning, execution, and oversight of projects. They serve not only as operational roadmaps but also as mechanisms for accountability, efficiency, and alignment with organisational objectives. By systematising project activities from initiation to completion, these models create consistency and reduce ambiguity across complex undertakings.

The selection of an appropriate project management model is a strategic decision that hinges on numerous variables: the complexity and scale of the project, the stability of stakeholder requirements, compliance and regulatory considerations, risk tolerance, and the collaborative dynamics of the team. The chosen model directly influences how resources are allocated, how risks are managed, and how outcomes are measured.

Among the earliest and most influential approaches to emerge in the discipline is the Waterfall Model, a methodology rooted in engineering traditions that emphasises linearity, predictability, and comprehensive documentation. Although modern practice often prioritises adaptive and iterative models such as Agile, the Waterfall methodology continues to hold enduring relevance, particularly in domains where compliance, traceability, and risk minimisation are paramount.

A. Traditional (Waterfall) Project Management

WATERFALL PROJECT MANAGEMENT

Definition:

The traditional or waterfall model is a linear, sequential project management approach with distinct phases—requirements, design, implementation, testing, deployment, and maintenance. It ensures predictability, documentation, and control, making it ideal for projects with stable requirements. However, it lacks flexibility, as late-stage changes are difficult, costly, and disruptive.

The Waterfall Model is a phase-orientated, sequential methodology developed in the mid-20th century and widely applied in large engineering and manufacturing contexts. The model organises project execution into a series of distinct stages—requirements, design, implementation, testing, deployment, and maintenance—that must be completed in strict succession. Each stage generates formal deliverables, and progression to the next stage is contingent upon official approval of the previous one.

This structured approach fosters clarity and accountability. Every participant is aware of the objectives, activities, and expected outputs of each phase. The emphasis on upfront planning and rigorous documentation minimises the risk of ambiguity, while the structured progression enables strong governance and compliance. However, this rigidity also presents challenges, particularly in dynamic environments where requirements may evolve over time. Attempting to revisit earlier phases once a project has advanced often entails significant disruption, cost escalation, and schedule delays.

The Waterfall model remains especially effective in safety-critical and regulated industries, such as aerospace, defence, construction, and healthcare, where requirements are relatively stable, and the cost of late-stage modifications is prohibitively high.

Core Principles of the Waterfall Model

The Waterfall model operates on five foundational principles that define its logic and application:

1. Sequential Flow:

Activities progress in a strictly linear manner through the stages of requirements, design, implementation, verification, and deployment. This orderly progression reduces ambiguity and enforces discipline.

2. Phase Gates:

At the conclusion of each stage, formal checkpoints—known as phase gates—validate deliverables and determine whether the project is ready to proceed. These reviews serve as control mechanisms that safeguard scope, quality, and resource allocation.

3. Baseline Management:

Core parameters such as requirements, budgets, and schedules are baselined at the project's outset. Any proposed deviations are subjected to rigorous change-control procedures, ensuring predictability and disciplined execution.

4. Documentation-Driven Execution:

Comprehensive documentation is central to Waterfall's

effectiveness. Requirement specifications, design blueprints, and testing protocols serve as authoritative sources of truth, enabling clear communication, traceability, and auditability.

5. Predictability:

By emphasising detailed upfront estimation and critical-path scheduling, the model seeks to minimise uncertainty and create reliable forecasts. This predictability is particularly valuable in projects with low tolerance for risk.

Standard Phases of the Waterfall Model

The standard phases of the Waterfall Model are illustrated in Figure 1 below.

Figure 1: Standard Phases of the Waterfall Model

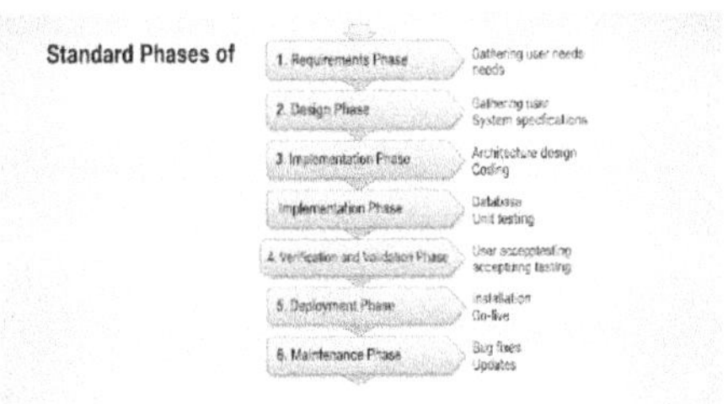

The waterfall lifecycle comprises six sequential phases, each with its objectives, activities, deliverables, and criteria for completion:

1. Requirements Phase:

The objective is to capture and formalise stakeholders' needs, constraints, and expectations. Activities include stakeholder interviews, domain analysis, feasibility studies, and preliminary risk assessments. Artefacts typically include a Business Requirements Document (BRD), a System Requirements Specification (SRS), and a Requirements Traceability Matrix (RTM). Exit is achieved once requirements are validated, testable, and formally approved.

2. Design Phase:

Requirements are translated into a technical blueprint. Activities include architectural modelling, data modelling, interface specifications, and user experience design. Deliverables include High-Level Design (HLD) documents and Low-Level Design (LLD) specifications. Exit criteria involve design peer reviews, validated feasibility, and stakeholder approval.

3. Implementation Phase:

The implementation phase involves building the system or solution based on design specifications. Activities include coding, module integration, configuration, and unit testing. Artefacts consist of source code repositories, build scripts, and unit test results. Completion requires meeting coding standards, coverage targets, and defect resolution thresholds.

4. Verification and Validation Phase:

The system undergoes rigorous testing to ensure both correctness (verification) and alignment with stakeholder needs (validation). Activities include system testing, integration testing, performance evaluation, and User Acceptance Testing (UAT). Deliverables include test plans, test reports, and defect logs. Completion is marked by stakeholder sign-off and closure of critical defects.

5. Deployment Phase:

The *Deployment Phase* solution is transitioned into operational use. Key activities include release planning, data migration, system configuration, user training, and contingency preparations. Deliverables include release notes, deployment guides, and training materials. Successful completion is defined by a smooth go-live and formal handover to operations.

6. Maintenance Phase:

The *Maintenance Phase* or post-deployment phase ensures system sustainability and adaptability. *Maintenance a*ctivities include monitoring performance, managing incidents, applying patches, and planning enhancements. Deliverables include service reports, change requests, and post-implementation reviews. Exit criteria involve stabilised operations and readiness for future upgrades or decommissionings.

Planning and Scheduling Mechanisms:

Waterfall projects rely on analytical techniques to structure and manage time, cost, and resources. The Work Breakdown Structure (WBS) decomposes project deliverables into manageable tasks. The Critical Path Method (CPM) identifies dependencies and schedule bottlenecks, while Gantt charts visually represent project timelines and dependencies. Estimation evolves from top-down approximations in early phases to bottom-up detail in later planning. Risk management is integrated through probability-impact matrices and contingency strategies to mitigate disruptions.

Governance and Control Mechanisms:

The Waterfall model enforces governance through formalised oversight structures. Phase-gate reviews (e.g., System Requirements Review, Critical Design Review) ensure readiness for progression and alignment with project goals. Change Control Boards (CCBs) adjudicate scope or requirement modifications to maintain baseline integrity. Performance is tracked using tools such as Earned Value Management (EVM), which measures cost and schedule efficiency, and Requirements Traceability Matrices (RTMs), which ensure bidirectional linkage between requirements, design, implementation, and validation.

Roles and Responsibilities in the Waterfall Model

The waterfall model is characterised by a linear, sequential flow of activities, where each phase must be completed before moving on to the next. To ensure discipline and accountability throughout this structured process, distinct roles such as Project Manager, Business Analyst, systems architect, developers or engineers, Test Lead, Compliance Officer, and Operations Lead, are assigned to individuals and teams. These roles define responsibilities and establish clear ownership of deliverables across the project life cycle. The following sections elaborate on the key roles within a waterfall-driven project.

1. Project Manager:

The Project Manager plays a central leadership role, overseeing the overall scope, schedule, and budget of the project. In the waterfall model, predictability and documentation are prioritised, and the project manager is responsible for developing detailed project plans, allocating resources, and monitoring adherence to milestones. They also serve as the primary point of contact for stakeholders, ensuring that expectations are managed and communication channels remain transparent. Their authority is critical in approving the completion of each phase before progression to the next stage.

2. Business Analyst:

The Business Analyst (BA) acts as a bridge between stakeholders and the technical team. They are responsible for eliciting, analysing, and documenting functional and nonfunctional requirements. Since requirements in the Waterfall model are gathered comprehensively at the outset, the BA ensures that all business needs are captured with precision and remain traceable throughout the project. They play a vital role in reducing ambiguity by maintaining requirement specifications, which become the foundation for system design and development.

3. Systems Architect:

The systems architect is tasked with creating and safeguarding the structural design of the system. Once requirements are finalised, the architect converts them into system architectures and design blueprints. Their role emphasises ensuring scalability, performance, and security of the solution. In the Waterfall model, where design must be finalised before development begins, the architect's responsibility is to maintain the integrity of the design and minimise risks of rework later in the project lifecycle.

4. Developers and engineers:

The developers or engineers are responsible for constructing the actual solution in accordance with approved specifications. The systems architect and business analyst create detailed design documents that form the foundation of their work. In the Waterfall model, development begins only after requirements and design are locked, which requires developers to adhere strictly to predefined guidelines and avoid deviations. Their accountability lies in translating documentation into functioning software, ensuring compliance with coding standards, and producing deliverables that are consistent with the initial plan.

5. QA/Test Lead:

The Quality Assurance (QA) or Test Lead is responsible for upholding testing rigour and quality standards. Once the development phase concludes, the QA team systematically verifies whether the system meets requirements and functions as intended. In the Waterfall framework, testing is typically a distinct phase that follows development. The QA/Test Lead organises test planning, defines acceptance criteria, and coordinates defect resolution processes. They ensure that all errors are documented and resolved before the system advances to deployment.

6. Compliance Officers and Change Control Boards (CCBs):

In projects subject to regulatory, contractual, or industry standards, Compliance Officers and Change Control Boards (CCBs) play an essential oversight role. They are responsible for ensuring that the system adheres to relevant laws, policies, and contractual obligations. In addition, the CCB evaluates and approves any proposed changes, maintaining discipline in scope control. Such oversight is particularly critical in the Waterfall model, where changes after the requirements phase can be disruptive and costly.

7. Operations Lead:

The Operations Lead is accountable for maintaining the

system's sustainability, reliability, and continuity post-deployment. Once the project transitions into the maintenance phase, the Operations team ensures smooth day-to-day functioning, manages incident responses, and implements necessary updates or patches. Their responsibility is to preserve the long-term value of the system while minimising downtime and ensuring business continuity.

In essence, the Waterfall model relies on well-defined roles and linear accountability. Each participant has a distinct responsibility that aligns with a specific project phase, ensuring clarity, discipline, and structured progress from initiation to maintenance.

V-Model Extension:

The V-Model is an adaptation of the Waterfall model that explicitly pairs each development activity with a corresponding testing activity. For example, system requirements are validated through acceptance testing, high-level design through system testing, and detailed design through integration testing. This symmetry enhances quality assurance, enforces traceability, and reduces the likelihood of late-stage defects.

Strengths and Limitations of the Waterfall Model

1. Strengths:

One of the most significant strengths of the Waterfall Model lies in its high predictability, discipline, and structure. Because the model follows a linear and sequential process, every phase—requirements, design, implementation, verification, and maintenance—is defined and documented before moving on to the next. This structured approach makes it easier for teams and stakeholders to forecast timelines, costs, and deliverables with a high degree of accuracy. It provides a sense of order that can be especially valuable in projects where discipline and clarity are paramount.

Another strength is its ability to ensure strong auditability and compliance support. Since each stage produces detailed documentation, organizations can easily trace decisions, design rationales, and test outcomes. This is highly beneficial for industries that must adhere to strict regulatory or compliance requirements, such as aerospace, defence, or healthcare, where traceability and accountability are non-negotiable.

Contractual fixed-price projects, where requirements are well-understood and unlikely to change significantly, also find the Waterfall model suitable. Its emphasis on upfront planning allows vendors and clients to agree on deliverables, timelines, and costs with minimal ambiguity. This makes the waterfall approach highly effective in environments where financial predictability is critical.

Finally, the model demonstrates exceptional effectiveness in large-scale, safety-critical environments. In projects such as nuclear systems, aviation software, or medical devices, failure is not an option, and changes during development could introduce risks. The waterfall approach ensures careful planning, documentation, and systematic testing that align well with the stringent safety and reliability standards in such domains.

2. Limitations:

Despite these strengths, the Waterfall Model also presents several limitations.

The most notable is its rigidity and high cost of adapting to changing requirements. Because requirements are locked in during the early phases, accommodating changes later in the process often requires extensive rework, which can lead to cost overruns and schedule delays. This rigidity makes it less suitable for dynamic environments where stakeholder needs or market conditions evolve rapidly.

Another significant drawback is the delayed feedback due to late-stage testing. Since verification and testing occur after implementation, defects or misalignments with user expectations are often discovered only at the end of the development cycle. This late discovery can be costly and may result in products that fail to meet actual user needs.

The model also suffers from limited stakeholder engagement until the later phases. Clients or end-users typically see the product only after development is nearly complete, which can lead to dissatisfaction if the outcome differs from expectations. Unlike iterative models such as Agile, where stakeholders are continuously involved, Waterfall's delayed engagement poses communication risks.

Lastly, the reliance on big-bang testing approaches can introduce risks of integration issues. We often develop components independently and integrate them at a late stage, which increases the likelihood of discovering compatibility or interoperability problems. This approach can cause significant delays if major integration challenges arise just before delivery.

Metrics and Reporting in the Waterfall Model

1. Earned Value Management (EVM):

Performance monitoring in waterfall projects often relies

on Earned Value Management (EVM), a robust method for measuring cost and schedule performance. EVM uses indicators such as the Schedule Performance Index (SPI) and the Cost Performance Index (CPI) to assess whether the project is on track in terms of budget and timelines. For example, a CPI value less than one indicates cost overruns, while an SPI below highlights schedule delays. This allows managers to take corrective actions early before problems escalate.

2. Metrics:

Another critical aspect of reporting is the use of defect metrics, which track quality and stability throughout the testing phase. Metrics such as defect density (defects per unit of code), detection rate, and Mean Time to Repair (MTTR) offer details about software reliability and testing effectiveness. High defect density or long MTTR values may indicate weaknesses in design or development processes that require attention.

3. Variance Analysis:

Waterfall projects also employ variance analysis to detect deviations from planned baselines in terms of cost, scope, or schedule. By comparing actual performance against planned performance, project managers can identify areas of concern, such as overspending or delays, and implement mitigation strategies. Variance analysis thus functions as an early warning system, preventing small deviations from snowballing into major project risks.

4. Audits and Quality Gates:

Finally, the Waterfall approach ensures compliance and transparency through audits and quality gates. At the end of each phase, deliverables undergo thorough reviews to verify adherence to predefined standards, requirements, and quality benchmarks. These checkpoints act as control mechanisms, ensuring that errors or non-compliances are detected early before the project proceeds to the next stage. This structured audit process builds confidence among stakeholders and supports regulatory obligations in highly controlled industries.

The Waterfall model remains a cornerstone of project management theory and practice, particularly in regulated and safety-sensitive environments where predictability, control, and documentation are paramount. Although it lacks the adaptability demanded in fast-paced or uncertain contexts, its disciplined governance and structured execution make it invaluable in industries such as aerospace, defence, and construction. In modern practice, the model's utility is maximised, not as an exclusive approach but as a component of hybrid methodologies that combine Waterfall's strengths with the flexibility of adaptive models like Agile, thereby striking a balance between stability and responsiveness.

B. Overview of Agile Model of Project Management

AGILE PROJECT MANAGEMENT

Definition:

Agile Project Management (APM) is a flexible, iterative, and people-focused approach to managing projects that prioritises adaptability, collaboration, and continuous value delivery. Unlike traditional project management, which relies on rigid, sequential phases such as planning, execution, and delivery, Agile divides projects into smaller, manageable cycles called *sprints* or *iterations*. Each sprint produces a usable outcome—such as a feature, prototype, or product increment—that can be tested, reviewed, and refined.

The core philosophy of Agile is to embrace change rather than resist it. By involving stakeholders regularly and focusing on delivering functional solutions instead of excessive documentation, Agile ensures that projects remain aligned with customer needs. It empowers self-organising teams, fosters transparent communication, and encourages continuous improvement through regular reflection and adaptation.

To better understand the difference between waterfall and Agile, consider the example of building a car:

a) In a traditional (waterfall) approach, the process is rigid and linear—you design the entire car first, then build all the parts, and finally assemble them. If a flaw is discovered midway, fixing it becomes costly and complex.

b) In an Agile approach, the car is built in stages. The first sprint might deliver a working chassis and engine. Feedback is gathered, improvements are made, and the next sprint adds body panels and interiors. At each stage, there is a working, testable version of the car. This allows issues to be identified early, new ideas to be integrated quickly, and the final product to meet the customer's expectations precisely.

In essence, Agile Project Management is about responding quickly to change, delivering incremental value, and keeping people at the heart of the process. It transforms projects from rigid plans into adaptive journeys that evolve in collaboration with stakeholders.

Simple Visual Analogy:

Agile project management is like sailing a boat rather than riding a train.

a) On a train (traditional or waterfall project management), the path is fixed—you cannot change direction once the journey starts.

b) On a sailboat (Agile), you adjust the sails based on the wind and weather (customer needs and market changes), constantly steering toward your destination while making course corrections along the way.

) On a train (traditional project management)

(b) On a sailboat (Agile)

Core Principles of Agile Project Management:

Agile project management is guided by a set of core principles that prioritise adaptability, collaboration, and value delivery. These principles stem from the Agile Manifesto and are widely used across industries—from software development to education and even policy design. Table 1 presents a detailed breakdown tailored to integrative style:

Table 1: Agile Project Management is built on core principles

Principle	Detailed Explanation	Visual Analogy
1. Customer Satisfaction through Early and Continuous Delivery	Deliver valuable features early and often to keep stakeholders engaged and confident. This builds trust and allows for real-time feedback.	Like watering a plant regularly—it grows healthier with consistent care.
2. Welcome Changing Requirements, Even Late in Development	Agile embraces change as a source of innovation. Late-stage feedback is not a disruption but a refinement opportunity.	Think of sculpting clay —adjustments shape the final masterpiece.
3. Deliver Working Software Frequently	Frequent releases (e.g., every 2–4 weeks) ensure progress is visible and usable. This reduces risk and improves alignment.	Like publishing chapters of a book serially—readers stay engaged and authors adapt.
4. Close, Daily Collaboration Between Business and Developers	Cross-functional teams work together daily to ensure alignment and shared understanding.	Like musicians in a jazz band—improvising together in sync.
5. Build Projects Around Motivated Individuals	Empower teams with autonomy, trust, and support. Motivation drives creativity and accountability.	Like a research lab —freedom fuels discovery.
6. Face-to-Face Conversation is the Best Form of Communication	Direct communication reduces misunderstandings and speeds up decision-making.	Like a Socratic dialogue—clarity emerges through live exchange.
7. Working Software is the Primary Measure of Progress	Functioning deliverables matter more than documentation or promises. Tangible output is key.	Like a prototype—it speaks louder than a plan.
8. Sustainable Development, Able to Maintain a Constant	Avoid burnout by maintaining a steady	Like a marathon—not a sprint.

Pace	rhythm. Long-term productivity beats short-term sprints.	
9. Continuous Attention to Technical Excellence and Good Design	Quality is not an afterthought. Clean code, scalable architecture, and elegant design are essential.	Like Japanese calligraphy—precision and beauty in every stroke.
10. Simplicity—the Art of Maximizing the Amount of Work Not Done	Focus only on what adds value. Eliminate unnecessary features, meetings, and documentation.	Like Zen minimalism —less is more.
11. Best Architectures, Requirements, and Designs Emerge from Self-Organizing Teams	Teams that manage themselves often produce more innovative and resilient solutions.	Like a beehive— order emerges from collective intelligence.
12. Regularly Reflect and Adjust Behavior to Become More Effective	Teams hold retrospectives to learn, adapt, and improve continuously.	Like tuning an instrument— refinement leads to harmony.

The core principles of agile project management are further discussed as hereunder:

1. Customer Satisfaction through Early and Continuous Delivery:

Agile projects prioritise delivering working features quickly and consistently rather than waiting until the very end of their lives. By giving customers early access to tangible results, they feel involved and valued. This keeps stakeholders engaged and creates trust where customers know their needs are being heard. Early delivery also helps organizations discover potential issues before they escalate.

Visual 1:

Visual Analogy: Imagine caring for a plant—you water it regularly instead of dumping a bucket of water once a month. With consistent care, the plant thrives, just like customer relationships flourish with regular progress and attention.

2. Welcome to changing requirements, even late in development:

Traditional and waterfall project models resist late changes because they disrupt rigid timelines and budgets. Agile flips this mindset by recognising that markets, technologies, and customer needs constantly evolve. Late-stage changes, instead of being considered setbacks, are embraced as opportunities to refine and enhance the product, often leading to innovation that keeps the project competitive.

Visual 2:

Visual Analogy: Imagine an artist creating sculptures out of clay. Each adjustment, even at the final stage, refines the masterpiece. Similarly, late feedback can turn a good product into a great one.

3. Frequently deliver working software:

Rather than long waits for a "big launch", Agile teams deliver working increments every few weeks (often 2–4 weeks). This keeps progress transparent, reduces the risk of failure, and ensures that stakeholders always have something usable in their hands. These frequent iterations help course-correct quickly if expectations are not being met.

Visual 3:

Visual Analogy: It is like publishing a novel chapter by chapter in a magazine. Readers remain engaged and provide feedback, and the author can adjust future chapters accordingly—ensuring the final book resonates with its audience.

4. Close, Daily Collaboration Between Business and developers:

Agile thrives on teamwork where business stakeholders and developers interact daily. This reduces silos, aligns goals, and ensures quick clarification of doubts. The continuous conversation fosters a shared sense of ownership where everyone is working toward the same vision.

Visual 4:

Visual Analogy: Like a jazz band, where musicians improvise and listen to each other in real time, the outcome is harmonious, fluid, and innovative. Collaboration makes the team's "music" richer.

5. Build Projects Around Motivated Individuals:

Agile places strong emphasis on the human element. Teams thrive when they receive motivation, trust, and empowerment to make decisions. Providing autonomy, resources, and recognition unlocks creativity and drives accountability. When people feel ownership, they put forth their best ideas.

Visual 5:

Visual Analogy: Imagine a research lab where scientists enjoy freedom and resources. Their curiosity and motivation fuel discoveries, often leading to breakthroughs that rigidly managed environments cannot achieve.

6. Face-to-Face Conversation is the Best Form of communication:

Despite technological advances in communication tools, Agile emphasises direct, human interaction as the most effective. Real-time discussions reduce delays, misinterpretations, and the loss of nuance that written communication may cause. This ensures clarity and faster decisions.

Visual 6:

Visual Analogy: Like a Socratic dialogue where truths emerge through live questioning and reasoning, face-to-face conversations create clarity, foster trust, and move the team forward quickly.

7. Working Software is the Primary Measure of Progress:

In Agile, progress is not measured by the number of documents, reports, or plans created, but by working features delivered. Tangible output demonstrates actual advancement and provides stakeholders something they can use and test immediately.

Visual 7:

Visual Analogy: A working prototype talks more about a design's success than a hundred blueprints. Similarly, software in action speaks louder than promises on paper.

8. Sustainable Development: Maintaining a Constant Pace:

Agile promotes an indefinite pace that discourages "crunch time" and burnout. Overworked teams may achieve short bursts of productivity, but quality and morale drop over time. A steady rhythm ensures long-term creativity, energy, and effectiveness.

Visual 8:

Visual Analogy: Think of a marathon runner—success comes not from sprinting all out but from maintaining a consistent, sustainable pace that carries them to the finish line strong.

9. Continuous Attention to Technical Excellence and Good Design:

Agile is not only about speed; it is about quality. Agile emphasises well-written code, scalable architecture, and elegant design at every stage, thereby preventing technical debt and ensuring long-term maintainability. As the project progresses, technical excellence lays the groundwork for adaptability.

Visual 9:

Visual Analogy: Like Japanese calligraphy, where each stroke must be executed with precision and artistry, Agile demands elegance and discipline in every line of code and design choice.

10. Simplicity—the Art of Maximising the Amount of Work Not Done:

Agile teams avoid over-engineering by focusing only on features and activities that directly add value. Agile teams eliminate unnecessary meetings, documents, and extra features. This principle encourages prioritisation and sharpens focus on essentials.

Visual 10:

Visual Analogy: Like Zen minimalism, where beauty lies in simplicity, Agile's power is in delivering less but making that "less" truly impactful. Less clutter means more clarity.

11. The best architectures, requirements, and designs emerge from self-organisational teams:

Agile trusts teams to organise themselves rather than rely on strict, top-down control. When people collaborate organically, diverse perspectives lead to innovative solutions. Self-organisation fosters adaptability, resilience, and collective accountability.

Visual 11:

Visual Analogy: Like a beehive, where no single bee commands but the colony thrives through collective intelligence, agile teams naturally create order and achieve excellence.

12. Regularly reflect and adjust behaviour to make it more effective:

Agile projects include regular retrospectives where teams reflect on what went well, what did not, and what can improve. This continuous cycle of learning and adapting builds resilience and efficiency over time, preventing stagnation.

Visual 12:

Visual Analogy: Like a musician tuning an instrument before each performance, Agile teams refine their practices regularly. Small adjustments ensure harmony and peak performance.

Sequential Phases of Agile Project Management

Agile project management, though adaptive and iterative in nature, also follows a structured sequence of phases to ensure clarity and progress. Unlike traditional linear models, these phases are cyclical and flexible, allowing for continuous feedback and adjustment. The process typically moves through conception and initiation, planning, execution through sprints, monitoring and adaptation, and closure with reflection. Each phase builds upon the previous one while leaving room for revisiting earlier steps, ensuring that teams remain responsive to change and focused on delivering value.

The core of the Waterfall Model is its rigid, step-by-step structure. Think of it like building a house: you cannot start laying the foundation until the architectural blueprints are complete, and you cannot install the windows until the walls are up. Here are the key phases:

1. Requirements Gathering & Analysis:

This is the most critical phase. All project requirements are meticulously gathered, documented, and approved upfront. For our house, this means deciding on everything—the number of rooms, the square footage, the type of flooring, and the style of the roof—before any work begins.

2. System Design:

With the requirements locked in, the team creates a detailed blueprint for the system or product. This includes hardware, software, network, and data design. In our house analogy, this step is when the architect turns the wish list into a precise, detailed set of blueprints and structural plans.

3. Implementation:

This phase is known as the actual "building" phase. Developers write codes, builders lay bricks, and so on, strictly following the design documents. There is little interaction with the customer, as all decisions were made in the first two phases.

4. Verification & Testing:

Once the product is fully implemented, it is rigorously tested against the original requirements to ensure it functions as intended. In our house analogy, this is the final inspection—checking that the electrical outlets work, the plumbing is sound, and the paint is the correct colour. Any issues found here can be extremely difficult and costly to correct.

5. Maintenance:

After delivering the product to the customer, this phase encompasses ongoing support, bug fixes, and minor enhancements. This is when you would handle any issues that come up after the new homeowners move in. Further, the sequential phases of the Agile Model are illustrated in Figure 2 below.

Figure 2: Sequential Phases of Agile Project Management

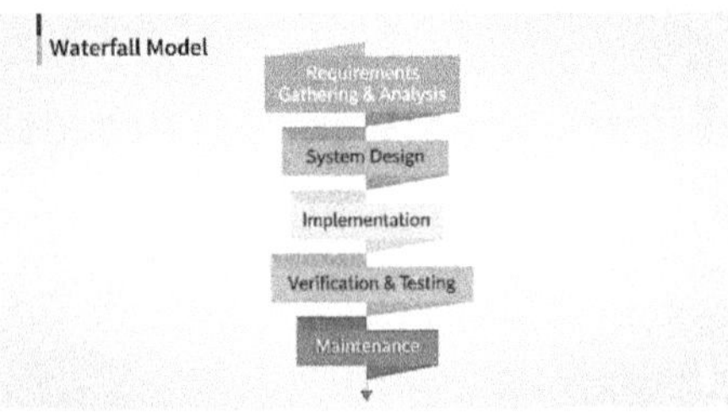

The operating model and lifecycle of agile project management

An Agile lifecycle is cyclical rather than linear. Work begins with a product vision and a prioritised backlog of outcomes, framed as user-centric items (e.g., user stories). Teams deliver in short, time-boxed sprints (commonly 2–4 weeks). Each sprint yields a potentially shippable increment—a cohesive, tested slice of functionality. Planning is progressive elaboration: near-term items are specified enough to build; distant items remain coarse to avoid waste. In flow-based variants such as Kanban, fixed time boxes are replaced with continuous pull and explicit Work-In-Process (WIP) limits; the governing mechanism is queue management and cycle-time control rather than sprint cadence. In both modes, observation and adaptation occur continuously through structured events and transparent artefacts.

Agile Model Process:

The Agile Model is a cyclical and iterative approach to project management. Unlike the rigid, linear nature of the Waterfall model, Agile is a continuous loop of development and feedback, allowing teams to adapt to changing requirements and deliver value incrementally.

Figure 3: Agile Model Process

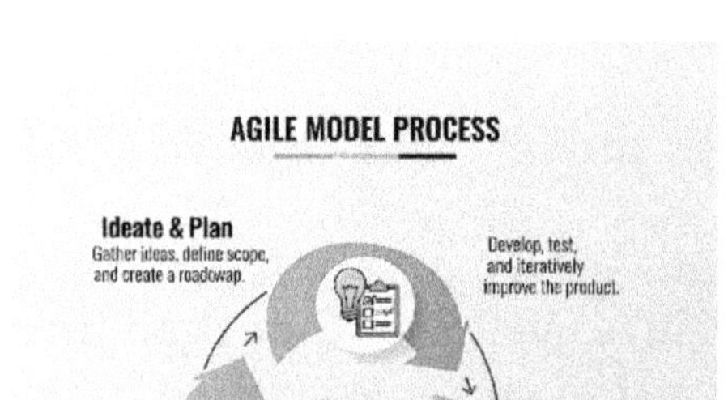

The Agile model is a cyclical and adaptive approach to software development and project management. It is characterised by short, time-boxed development phases known as *sprints* or *iterations*, which typically last one to four weeks. Each sprint is a mini-project in itself, involving planning, development, testing, reviewing, and releasing functional increments of the product. Unlike traditional linear models, Agile is iterative in nature, allowing teams to adapt quickly to feedback, evolving requirements, and market dynamics. The essence of Agile lies in delivering value continuously while fostering collaboration and transparency among stakeholders.

1. Ideate & Plan:

The *Ideate & Plan* stage marks the beginning of each sprint and establishes the foundation for all subsequent work. In this phase, the development team collaborates with the product owner to determine which items from the product backlog—a prioritised list of features, tasks, or user stories—will be selected for the upcoming sprint. The chosen items form the sprint backlog, representing the commitment for that iteration. Effort estimation techniques such as story points, planning poker, or T-shirt sizing are commonly used to gauge the workload and ensure realistic capacity planning.

This stage is crucial because it provides clarity and shared understanding of what needs to be achieved, aligning the team with the overall project goals and business priorities. It fosters ownership, as all team members contribute to the planning and commit to delivering agreed-upon outcomes. In essence, the planning process serves as the blueprint for the sprint, much like an architect's drawing guides the construction of a building. Without a well-defined plan, the risk of misalignment and wasted effort significantly increases.

2. Build & Code:

The *Build & Code* phase represents the heart of the sprint, where ideas are translated into functional software. During this stage, developers focus on writing, integrating, and configuring code that implements the user stories selected during planning. Agile encourages technical excellence and quality by incorporating practices such as pair programming, Test-Driven Development (TDD), and Continuous Integration (CI). These practices ensure that code is not only functional but also maintainable and resilient.

Daily stand-up meetings, also known as daily scrums, play a pivotal role during this stage by providing a forum for team members to synchronise efforts, identify dependencies, and quickly address impediments. Unlike traditional models where development is a lengthy, isolated activity, Agile promotes incremental progress. The team delivers working pieces of functionality that can be integrated into the larger product. This approach is akin to constructing a house room by room, allowing stakeholders to see tangible progress and adjust requirements, if necessary, rather than waiting until the entire structure is built.

3. Test & Refine:

Once features are built, they enter the *Test & Refine* phase, where quality and performance take centre stage. Agile places strong emphasis on testing throughout the sprint rather than treating it as a separate, end-of-project activity. Developers and Quality Assurance (QA) engineers collaborate to conduct unit tests, integration tests, and acceptance tests to ensure the software works as intended. Any bugs, defects, or inconsistencies identified during testing are addressed promptly to prevent technical debt from accumulating.

In addition to functional testing, Agile teams often perform usability testing to evaluate how well the product aligns with user expectations. Refinement is an iterative process: feedback from testing may prompt developers to adjust code, improve performance, or enhance user experience. This approach mitigates risks by catching problems early, much like inspecting and test-driving a car after each repair rather than waiting until all repairs are finished. The focus is on delivering not just functional but reliable, high-quality software.

4. Review & Launch:

At the conclusion of each sprint, the team moves into the *Review & Launch* phase, where the completed increment of the product is showcased and released. The Sprint Review is the central event here: developers demonstrate the new features to stakeholders, who provide feedback and validate whether the outcomes align with business needs. Following this, the team conducts a sprint retrospective, reflecting on the sprint's successes, challenges, and areas for improvement.

The ultimate goal of this stage, *Review & Launch,* is to ensure continuous value delivery. Unlike traditional release models that wait until project completion, Agile enables the release of functional increments after every sprint. These increments can be deployed to production or shared with customers to gather real-world insights. This phase enhances transparency, builds trust between stakeholders and the development team, and ensures that customer expectations remain at the heart of delivery. It resembles showing a prototype to a client—feedback informs future iterations and prevents misalignment.

Continuous Feedback Loop of Agile Project Management

The defining strength of Agile lies in its continuous feedback loop, which connects the *Review & Launch* phase of one sprint back to the *Ideate & Plan* phase of the next. This cyclical approach ensures that every sprint benefits from lessons learnt, stakeholder feedback, and evolving business priorities. As a result, the product grows incrementally, shaped by real-world insights rather than rigid specifications locked at the start of the project.

This adaptability is what distinguishes Agile from traditional methodologies such as the Waterfall model. Whereas Waterfall freezes requirements early on, Agile welcomes change, treating it as an opportunity to maximise value. The iterative cycle enables teams to adapt swiftly to technological discoveries, customer preferences, or market shifts, ensuring that the final product is not only functional but also relevant and competitive.

Advantages & Disadvantages of Agile Project Management

Advantages

1. Flexibility and adaptability:

One of the core strengths of Agile is its ability to adapt to change. Unlike traditional project management, which locks in requirements early, Agile welcomes evolving needs. This makes it especially effective in dynamic industries such as IT, software development, and digital transformation, where client demands and market conditions can shift rapidly. Teams can reprioritise tasks and adjust goals without derailing the project.

2. Faster Delivery of Value:

Agile emphasises iterative development through short cycles (sprints). This allows teams to deliver working increments of the product quickly rather than waiting until the end of the project. Clients or stakeholders can start using and benefiting from early versions while improvements continue, ensuring a faster return on investment.

3. Customer-Centric Approach:

Continuous stakeholder engagement is a hallmark of Agile. Regular feedback loops ensure that the final deliverable aligns closely with customer needs. This reduces the risk of developing a product that looks impressive on paper but fails to meet user expectations in practice.

4. Improved Collaboration and Communication:

Agile thrives on teamwork. Daily stand-ups, sprint reviews, and retrospectives foster open communication, shared accountability, and transparency. This collaborative environment not only boosts productivity but also guarantees the early identification and resolution of potential problems.

5. Higher Product Quality:

Since Agile emphasises testing throughout the development cycle, defects are detected and fixed earlier. This continuous integration and quality assurance reduces the risk of large-scale failures at the end of the project and results in a more robust, reliable product.

6. Better Risk Management:

Agile projects progress in small increments, enabling the identification and mitigation of risks before they escalate. By delivering features in stages, teams can continuously evaluate the project's viability, making it easier to pivot or stop if necessary—before too much time or money is invested.

7. Increased Transparency and Visibility:

Agile practices such as task boards, burn-down charts, and regular progress updates give stakeholders real-time insights into project status. This visibility builds trust and enables more informed decision-making by project sponsors and managers.

8. Motivated and Empowered Teams:

Agile promotes self-organising teams, where members are given autonomy to manage their work. This empowerment boosts morale, creativity, and accountability. Team members feel ownership of the project's success, which often leads to higher productivity and job satisfaction.

9. Continuous Improvement:

Agile encourages reflection through retrospectives at the end of each sprint. Teams identify what worked well and what needs to improve, fostering a culture of ongoing learning and efficiency. Over time, this procedure leads to stronger processes and higher performance.

Thus, the Agile Project Management offers flexibility, faster value delivery, customer alignment, stronger collaboration, higher quality, better risk control, and motivated teams. These advantages make it a powerful methodology for complex, uncertain, and innovation-driven projects.

Disadvantages :

Agile Project Management (APM) has gained popularity for its flexibility, adaptability, and iterative approach. However, like any methodology, it is not without disadvantages. Its effectiveness depends heavily on the project type, organisational culture, and team dynamics. Below are the key disadvantages of Agile Project Management, discussed in detail:

1. Lack of Predictability:

Agile thrives on adaptability, but this flexibility often comes at the expense of predictability. Since requirements evolve during the process, it becomes difficult to forecast timelines, costs, and deliverables with precision. Stakeholders accustomed to fixed budgets and schedules in traditional (waterfall) approaches may consider this uncertainty uncomfortable, especially for large-scale projects with strict contractual obligations.

2. Scope Creep:

Because Agile encourages frequent changes and continuous stakeholder feedback, there is a higher risk of scope creep —the uncontrolled expansion of project objectives. Without strict discipline, projects may keep evolving indefinitely, stretching beyond deadlines, resources, and budgets. This issue is particularly problematic in organizations that lack strong product ownership or governance frameworks.

3. Resource Intensity:

Agile requires continuous involvement from stakeholders, product owners, and customers. Teams need frequent meetings (daily stand-ups, sprint reviews, and retrospectives), active collaboration, and high levels of engagement. For organizations with limited time and manpower, this intensity can be burdensome. Moreover, stakeholders may struggle to consistently dedicate time to iterative feedback cycles.

4. Difficulties in Scaling:

Agile works best with small, cross-functional teams. Scaling it to large, complex projects or across multiple teams in an enterprise setting introduces significant challenges. Coordination across distributed teams, maintaining consistent communication, and ensuring alignment with overall strategic goals can be difficult. Frameworks like SAFe (Scaled Agile Framework) attempt to address this, but implementation is complex and resource-heavy.

5. Dependence on Team Maturity:

Agile requires a high degree of discipline, collaboration, and self-organisation. discipline, collaboration, and self-organisation that struggle with communication may find it difficult to deliver quality results. Poorly trained teams might misuse Agile as an excuse for lack of structure, resulting in chaos instead of efficiency.

6. Documentation Challenges:

Agile emphasises working software and collaboration over comprehensive documentation. While this accelerates development, it can lead to insufficient records of project requirements, design, or decision-making. This becomes a major drawback in industries where compliance, auditing, and detailed documentation are critical (e.g., healthcare, aerospace, or government projects).

7. Unclear Roles and Responsibilities:

Unlike traditional project management with well-defined roles (project manager, developer, tester, etc.), Agile blurs some of these boundaries. While this flexibility empowers teams, it can also cause confusion in organizations not fully accustomed to Agile practices. Lack of clarity can dilute accountability, resulting in conflicts or inefficiency.

8. Challenges with Long-Term Planning:

Agile is iterative and short-term focused, making it harder to see the "big picture" at early stages. While stakeholders may appreciate working software delivered in increments, executives often need long-term roadmaps, cost-benefit analyses, and ROI estimates to make strategic decisions. Agile's adaptive approach does not always align well with these business needs.

9. Customer or Stakeholder Dependency:

Agile relies heavily on active customer involvement throughout the development cycle. If stakeholders are unavailable, indecisive, or provide inconsistent feedback, the entire project can suffer. In many real-world cases, clients expect involvement only at the beginning and end, making it difficult to sustain Agile principles effectively.

10. Risk of Fragmentation:

In fast-moving Agile cycles, teams may deliver functional increments, but if integration across modules is not carefully managed, the final product may lack cohesion. Continuous integration practices can reduce this risk, but they require additional technical expertise and robust infrastructure.

Agile's disadvantages stem from its flexibility, reliance on stakeholder engagement, and team maturity. While Agile works well in dynamic environments requiring innovation and adaptability, it may not be the best fit for projects needing strict predictability, regulatory compliance, or large-scale coordination.

C. Agile Methodology

The Agile Manifesto and Core Principles:

The Agile methodology is not a single, rigid framework but rather a collection of project management frameworks built on a set of core values and principles. It was a direct response to the shortcomings of traditional, plan-driven models like Waterfall, particularly in dynamic, complex environments. The philosophy is codified in the Agile Manifesto, which outlines four core values:

1. Prioritise individuals and their interactions over processes and tools. This value critiques the excessive bureaucracy and heavy documentation of traditional models, instead prioritising direct, face-to-face communication as the most effective method for a development team.

2. Working software over comprehensive documentation. Agile teams prioritise building and testing usable products rather than producing lengthy reports and detailed documents. Progress is primarily measured by the delivery of a working solution.

3. Customer collaboration over contract negotiation. This value emphasises continuous discussions with customers to adjust work as needed. It is an approach of co-creation, working with the customer rather than just for them.

4. It prioritises adapting to changes rather than adhering to a rigid plan. This is the central tenet that directly opposes the inflexibility of predictive models. Agile processes are

designed to harness change for the customer's competitive advantage.

Agile project management is grounded in twelve core principles that underpin its values and practices. These principles emphasize delivering customer satisfaction as the highest priority through early and continuous delivery of valuable outcomes. They encourage welcoming changing requirements, even in later stages of development, and promote building projects around motivated, self-organizing individuals who thrive in a supportive environment.

A fundamental distinction in the debate between traditional and agile approaches is the definition of "discipline". Traditionalists view discipline as adherence to a formal process, while Agile practitioners define it as the self-discipline of an empowered, decentralised team. The Agile model does not lack discipline; it simply uses a different, more organic approach where reviews and decisions are pushed down to the team level.

Agile Methodologies:

Navigating the landscape of modern project management and business process improvement requires a deep understanding of various methodologies, each with its own philosophy and toolkit. While some are structured and prescriptive, others are flexible and adaptive. Here is a detailed introduction to some of the most influential frameworks:

Scrum, Kanban, and Lean:

The term *"agile"* represents a mindset and set of guiding principles that emphasize flexibility, collaboration, and responsiveness to change. Within this overarching philosophy, several widely adopted frameworks—such as

Scrum, Kanban, and Lean—have emerged to provide structured approaches for applying Agile practices in diverse project contexts.

Scrum:

Scrum is a framework designed for developing, delivering, and sustaining complex products. At its core is the Sprint, a short, time-boxed iteration—typically lasting one to four weeks—during which a self-organising team works to deliver a usable product increment by completing tasks drawn from a prioritised product backlog. Scrum is highly prescriptive, defining specific roles (Product Owner, Scrum Master, Development Team), events (Sprint Planning, Daily Scrum, Sprint Review, Sprint Retrospective), and artefacts (Product Backlog, Sprint Backlog, Increment). Its strength lies in its adaptability, enabling teams to respond to changing requirements while ensuring that a working increment of the product is produced at the end of each sprint.

Scrum: A Framework for Agile Practice:

Scrum has emerged as one of the most widely adopted frameworks for implementing the principles of Agile, providing teams with a structured yet flexible approach to managing complex projects. It is particularly effective for teams that are new to Agile methodologies, as its well-defined practices serve as a set of "training wheels", guiding them towards developing collaborative, adaptive, and self-organising behaviours. At its core, Scrum is grounded in two key theoretical underpinnings: empiricism and lean thinking. Empiricism emphasises the reliance on observation, evidence, and experiential learning as the basis for decision-making, while lean thinking underscores the elimination of waste, continuous improvement, and the delivery of maximum value in the shortest possible time. Together, these principles ensure that Scrum teams deliver value incrementally, adapting to change while continuously refining their processes.

Accountabilities in Scrum:

Scrum defines three distinct accountabilities within the Scrum Team, which collectively establish responsibility, ownership, and collaboration.

1. Product Owner:

The Product Owner holds the primary accountability for managing the Product Backlog, which is the evolving list of features, enhancements, and fixes required to improve the product. Acting as a bridge between stakeholders and the development team, the product owner ensures that the team consistently works on the most valuable and strategically aligned tasks. Prioritisation is central to this role, as not all items in the backlog are equally important. By continuously refining and prioritising backlog items, the product owner maximises return on investment, ensuring that customer and organisational needs are addressed effectively. Unlike traditional managers, the Product Owner does not dictate how the work should be done but rather clarifies what should be achieved and why it matters.

2. Scrum Master:

The Scrum Master functions as a servant-leader, a concept that emphasises support, facilitation, and coaching rather than command and control. Unlike traditional project managers who direct teams and assign tasks, the Scrum Master nurtures an environment where the team can thrive by removing obstacles, promoting collaboration, and safeguarding adherence to Scrum values and practices. The

Scrum Master's role also extends to educating stakeholders about Scrum and mediating organisational resistance to change. In essence, the Scrum Master champions the framework itself, ensuring that the team is not only following Scrum principles but also internalising its mindset of continuous learning and adaptation.

3. Developers:

The developers form the cross-functional unit responsible for delivering a potentially shippable increment of the product at the end of each sprint. This group embodies the Agile philosophy of self-organisation, meaning they decide collaboratively how best to accomplish their work without external micromanagement. Developers in Scrum are not confined to a narrow set of skills; instead, they combine diverse expertise—such as programming, design, testing, or documentation—so that the team collectively possesses all capabilities needed to deliver value. We measure their success not just by task completion, but by the tangible delivery of increments that meaningfully contribute to the product vision.

Sprint:

In Scrum methodology, a sprint is defined as a fixed, time-boxed iteration during which a Scrum team works to create a usable and potentially shippable product increment. Typically lasting between one and four weeks, a sprint establishes a predictable rhythm for planning, execution, and delivery, ensuring that progress is incremental and measurable.

A sprint begins with sprint planning, where the team defines the sprint goal and selects items from the product backlog to commit to the sprint backlog. Throughout the sprint, the team conduct daily scrums to inspect progress and adapt their plans. At the end, the sprint concludes with a sprint review, where stakeholders provide feedback on the increment, followed by a sprint retrospective, where the team reflects on their processes and identifies improvements for the next cycle.

The defining characteristics of a sprint are its time-boxed nature, focus on delivering value, and adherence to the principles of transparency, inspection, and adaptation. By providing a consistent cadence, sprints enable teams to manage complexity, respond to change, and deliver meaningful progress in short, iterative cycles.

Sprint and Scrum Events:

The Sprint, a time-boxed iteration typically lasting between one and four weeks, is the core of Scrum. Each sprint provides a structured rhythm for planning, execution, review, and improvement, ensuring that teams remain focused and adaptable. Within this cadence, Scrum prescribes four formal events, each with a distinct purpose in maintaining transparency, alignment, and adaptability.

1. Sprint Planning:

Sprint planning marks the beginning of each sprint, where the team collectively decides what they aim to achieve and how they will accomplish it. The session centres on the sprint goal, a concise statement that articulates the value to be delivered in the iteration. From the Product Backlog, the team selects items that best align with the Sprint Goal and commits them to the Sprint Backlog, which serves as their tactical plan. This collaborative activity ensures alignment between the product owner's vision and the developers' execution strategy, setting a clear direction for the upcoming sprint.

2. Daily Scrum:

The Daily Scrum is a short, time-boxed meeting—typically 15 minutes—that enables developers to synchronise their activities and plan the next 24 hours. It is not a status update for managers but rather an opportunity for the team to identify obstacles, adjust strategies, and maintain progress toward the sprint goal. The brevity and regularity of the daily scrum encourage accountability and foster a habit of continual inspection and adaptation, ensuring the team stays focused and cohesive.

3. Sprint Review:

At the conclusion of each sprint, the team holds a sprint review to inspect the completed increment and discuss progress with stakeholders. This is not merely a demonstration of completed work but a collaborative session aimed at gathering feedback, re-evaluating priorities, and adapting the product backlog based on new insights. By actively involving stakeholders, the Sprint Review ensures that the product evolves in line with user expectations and market realities, thereby reinforcing Scrum's emphasis on transparency and value-driven delivery.

4. Sprint Retrospective:

The Sprint Retrospective serves as a dedicated space for reflection, improvement, and team growth. In this meeting, the Scrum Team candidly examines what went well, what challenges arose, and how processes and interactions can be improved in the next sprint. The retrospective strengthens team cohesion and fosters a culture of continuous improvement, reminding the team that agility is not only about product delivery but also about evolving practices and relationships.

Core Artefacts in Scrum:

To support its empirical approach, Scrum prescribes three central artefacts: the *Product Backlog*, the *Sprint Backlog*, and the *Increment*. Together, these artefacts ensure that work is visible, priorities are clear, and progress is transparent.

1.*Product Backlog*: The Product Backlog embodies the product's long-term vision, encompassing all necessary improvements. Market needs and stakeholder feedback drive its dynamic evolution.

2. *Sprint Backlog*: The Sprint Backlog narrows the focus, containing the set of Product Backlog items selected for the Sprint along with the team's plan to deliver them.

3. *Increment:* The Increment is the actual output of the sprint —a concrete step toward the final product that must meet the team's agreed-upon definition of "done".

These artefacts, coupled with events and accountabilities, embody the three pillars of Scrum—transparency, inspection, and adaptation.

Transparency ensures that all stakeholders have a clear and shared understanding of work and progress.

Inspection provides regular checkpoints to evaluate outcomes against goals.

Adaptation allows the team to refine strategies, processes, and priorities in response to new knowledge and changing circumstances.

Kanban:

Originating from the Toyota Production System, Kanban is a visual workflow management method. It is less prescriptive than Scrum and focuses on a continuous flow of work. The key principles of Kanban are to visualise the workflow (often with a board with columns like "To Do", "In Progress", and "Done"), limit Work in Progress (WIP) to prevent bottlenecks, and manage flow to ensure tasks move smoothly. Kanban is highly flexible and can be overlaid on existing workflows, making it popular for teams that have a constant stream of incoming work, such as maintenance or support teams.

Kanban is a visual, flow-based system for managing work that draws heavily on the principles of lean thinking. Its primary purpose is to optimise efficiency, reduce waste, and improve predictability by ensuring that tasks progress through a system in a smooth and controlled manner. Unlike prescriptive frameworks, Kanban emphasises starting with the current processes in place, making incremental changes, and fostering leadership across all organisational levels. This evolutionary approach makes Kanban both flexible and non-disruptive, as it integrates seamlessly into existing workflows. One of Kanban's greatest strengths lies in its visualisation techniques, which allow teams to easily see the state of work, identify bottlenecks, and collaborate more effectively toward continuous improvement.

Kanban's strengths:

1. Visualise Workflows:

A core practice of Kanban is the visualisation of workflows through tools such as the Kanban board. Typically, the board is divided into columns that represent different stages of a process—commonly "To Do," "In Progress," and "Done." By externalising tasks in a visible format, teams can quickly assess progress, identify delays, and adjust priorities. This transparency reduces ambiguity, fosters accountability, and enhances collaboration, as all stakeholders can see exactly where tasks stand at any given moment. For distributed teams, digital Kanban boards (such as Trello, Jira, or Azure Boards) offer the same level of clarity, making visualisation a universal practice in modern project management.

2. Limit Work in Progress (WIP):

One of Kanban's most distinctive features is the use of Work-in-Progress (WIP) limits. These are caps placed on the number of tasks that can be in progress simultaneously. By restricting multitasking, WIP limits encourage team members to focus on completing current work before starting new tasks, thereby reducing context-switching and inefficiencies. This practice not only improves productivity but also reveals underlying process constraints—such as bottlenecks or resource shortages—that may otherwise remain hidden. In effect, WIP limits act as a mechanism for maintaining a steady, sustainable pace of work while protecting teams from overcommitment and burnout.

3. Manage Flow:

Kanban prioritises the smooth and predictable flow of work items across the system. The goal is to achieve a rhythm where tasks move consistently from initiation to completion without undue delays. Managing flow involves monitoring task progress, identifying bottlenecks, and taking corrective actions to restore balance when issues arise. Metrics such as cycle time (the time it takes for a task to move from start to finish) and throughput (the number of tasks completed in a given period) are often used to track flow performance. By analysing these patterns, teams can continuously refine their processes, improving both predictability and delivery speed.

4. Make Process Policies Explicit:

A fundamental aspect of Kanban is the explicit articulation of process policies. These policies define how work is prioritised, when tasks can move between stages, and what criteria must be met for completion. By making such rules visible and transparent to all stakeholders, Kanban fosters a shared understanding of responsibilities and expectations. Explicit policies reduce ambiguity, support fairness in decision-making, and promote consistency in execution. Importantly, they also provide a baseline for improvement, as any changes to policies can be tested and refined over time in a controlled and collaborative manner.

5. Implement Feedback Loops:

Feedback loops are crucial for ensuring continuous improvement within the Kanban system. Regular reviews —whether through team meetings, retrospective sessions, or performance metrics—allow teams to reflect on what is working well and what needs adjustment. Feedback loops also create opportunities to experiment with new ideas, test hypotheses, and validate improvements without overhauling the entire process. In this way, Kanban aligns with the principles of organisational learning, where iterative reflection and adaptation drive gradual but sustainable change. The frequency and format of feedback loops can vary, but their purpose remains constant: to promote adaptability, resilience, and performance growth over time.

Kanban and Scrum Integration:

Kanban and Scrum are not mutually exclusive methodologies; in fact, they complement each other effectively. A Scrum team, for example, can incorporate a Kanban board to visualise work items and apply WIP limits within its sprint cycles. This hybrid approach, often referred to as Scrumban, combines the iterative, time-boxed discipline of Scrum with the flow-based flexibility of Kanban. By doing so, teams benefit from enhanced visibility, improved efficiency, and reduced risk of work overload without undermining the structural integrity of the Scrum framework. This adaptability illustrates the versatility of Kanban, which can function as a standalone method or an enhancement to existing agile practices.

Lean:

Also rooted in the Toyota Production System, Lean is a philosophy focused on eliminating waste to deliver maximum value to the customer. Lean identifies seven types of waste: defects, overproduction, waiting, non-utilised talent, transportation, inventory, and motion. It is not a rigid methodology but a set of principles that emphasise continuous improvement and respect for people. Both Scrum and Kanban are often seen as ways to apply Lean principles in an Agile context.

The Lean philosophy is a comprehensive approach to business and project management, originating from the Toyota Production System (TPS) in the mid-20th century. While its roots lie in manufacturing, Lean has since evolved into a universal management philosophy applicable across industries, from healthcare to software development. At its core, Lean emphasises delivering maximum customer value with minimal waste, thereby ensuring efficiency, adaptability, and sustainability in organisational practices. Importantly, Lean has served as the conceptual foundation for Agile methodologies, offering the guiding principles of waste elimination, continuous improvement, and value creation, which frameworks like Scrum and Kanban operationalise in practical project environments.

Unlike rigid methodologies, Lean is not prescriptive but principle-driven, encouraging organizations to cultivate a mindset of learning and respect for people. Lean project management frames projects not simply as processes to be executed but as knowledge-creating initiatives, where learning, innovation, and human decision-making drive outcomes. The success or failure of projects, therefore, rests largely on the individuals involved—their collaboration, problem-solving skills, and ability to make informed decisions that add value to the customer.

Lean Principles:

1. Identify Value:

The first principle of Lean is to define value from the customer's perspective. This involves clearly articulating what outcomes or features customers consider meaningful and worthwhile. By identifying value, organizations ensure that resources are directed toward activities that fulfil actual customer needs, rather than wasting effort on unnecessary features or processes. In project management, this step requires rigorous stakeholder engagement, user research, and market analysis to align the project's deliverables with real-world expectations. Prioritising value not only increases customer satisfaction but also reduces the risk of project failure by preventing the delivery of outputs that do not resonate with end users.

2. Map the Value Stream:

Once value is defined, the next step is to map the value stream, which involves visually representing all the actions, processes, and workflows necessary to deliver a product or service. This mapping exercise distinguishes between value-adding activities (those directly contributing to customer outcomes) and non-value-adding activities (often categorised as waste). For example, unnecessary approvals, rework, and delays may not contribute to value creation and thus can be streamlined or eliminated. Value stream mapping is a powerful diagnostic tool, providing clarity on how work moves through the system, where inefficiencies occur, and where improvements can generate the greatest impact.

3. Create a Continuous Flow:

A central goal of Lean is to establish continuous flow, ensuring that tasks progress smoothly from one stage to the next without interruption. Bottlenecks, idle time, and uneven workloads are major sources of inefficiency that disrupt flow and slow down delivery. To create a continuous flow, organizations must optimise processes, balance workloads, and remove obstacles that hinder progress. In practice, this could involve reorganising team responsibilities, simplifying communication channels, or adopting automation tools. A well-designed flow allows for faster delivery cycles, greater adaptability to change, and improved customer responsiveness.

4. Establish a Pull System:

Unlike traditional "push" systems where work is assigned based on forecasts or assumptions, Lean emphasises a pull system—initiating work only when there is actual demand from the customer. This principle minimises overproduction, reduces inventory (or in knowledge work, backlog accumulation), and ensures that teams are not burdened with unnecessary tasks. In project management, a pull system translates into delivering features or outputs based on validated customer needs, rather than speculative assumptions. By doing so, teams remain agile and responsive, producing only what adds value and avoiding wasteful resource allocation.

5. Pursue Continuous Improvement:

The final principle of Lean is a commitment to continuous improvement (Kaizen), which involves making small, incremental changes that collectively lead to substantial long-term gains. Continuous improvement is both a philosophy and a practice, requiring organizations to foster a culture of learning, experimentation, and reflection. Regular reviews, open communication, and the encouragement of employee input are central to this principle. By continually assessing performance and seeking opportunities for refinement, organizations not only enhance efficiency but also build resilience in the face of changing conditions. This principle ensures that Lean is not a one-time implementation but an ongoing journey of adaptation and growth.

Lean in the Context of Projects:

When applied to project management, Lean shifts the perspective from rigid task execution to knowledge creation and value generation. Projects, particularly those undertaken under conditions of uncertainty, are treated as platforms for learning and innovation rather than as linear processes with predetermined outcomes. The emphasis on people as the creators of value highlights the human dimension of Lean, where trust, respect, and empowerment of individuals are paramount. By aligning efforts with customer value, streamlining processes, and fostering a culture of continuous improvement, Lean enables organizations to deliver outcomes that are not only efficient but also deeply impactful.

PRINCE2 ***(Projects IN Controlled Environments)****:*

This is a widely used, process-based project management method. PRINCE2 emphasises dividing a project into manageable stages, with defined roles, responsibilities, and control points. Its strength is in its structured approach, which ensures that a project has a solid business justification, is planned in detail, and remains on track through constant monitoring and control. PRINCE2 is often favoured for government and large-scale, complex projects where clear accountability and documentation are critical.

PRINCE2 (PRojects IN Controlled Environments) is a structured, process-based project management methodology that emphasises organisation, control, and accountability throughout the project lifecycle. Originally developed by the UK government for IT projects, PRINCE2 has since evolved into a globally recognised standard for managing projects across diverse industries, ranging from construction and engineering to finance, healthcare, and software development. Its widespread adoption is largely due to its scalability, structured governance model, and emphasis on clearly defined processes.

Unlike purely sequential models such as the traditional Waterfall approach, PRINCE2 applies the concept of "management by stages", which divides projects into smaller, more manageable phases. Each stage concludes with a review, enabling decision-makers to assess progress, evaluate risks, and determine whether the project should proceed, be adjusted, or be discontinued. This balance of structure and flexibility makes PRINCE2 particularly well-suited for complex, high-stakes projects where clear accountability and continuous oversight are critical.

The PRINCE2 methodology is underpinned by seven key principles, which ensure that projects remain viable, structured, and outcome-driven.

1. Business Justification:

Every PRINCE2 project must begin with and maintain a clear business case. This ensures that resources are only invested in initiatives with well-defined objectives, measurable benefits, and alignment with organisational strategy. The business case is not static; it is continually reviewed at each stage to confirm that the project remains worthwhile and aligned with evolving business priorities. This principle safeguards against wasted investment in projects that no longer serve organisational goals.

2. Continuous Learning:

PRINCE2 places strong emphasis on learning from experience. Lessons are systematically sought, recorded, and applied throughout the project lifecycle—from initiation to closure. This learning culture not only improves the chances of current project success but also contributes to organisational knowledge management, creating a repository of insights that inform future projects. By embedding reflective practices, PRINCE2 ensures that mistakes are not repeated and best practices are institutionalised.

3. Defined Roles and Responsibilities:

Clarity in roles and responsibilities is a cornerstone of PRINCE2. Everyone involved in the project knows precisely what is expected of them and to whom they are accountable. The governance structure includes roles such as the project board (providing strategic direction), the project manager (responsible for day-to-day delivery), and the team manager(s) (handling work packages). This clear delineation prevents overlap, reduces conflict, and enhances accountability across all levels of project execution.

4. Manage by Stages:

Projects under PRINCE2 are divided into discrete stages, each of which is planned, monitored, and controlled independently. At the conclusion of every stage, the project board conducts a review to assess performance against the business case, risks, and objectives. This staged approach enables flexibility, as the project can be adjusted based on new information, lessons learnt, or shifting business needs. It also creates natural checkpoints for accountability, ensuring that stakeholders can make informed decisions about continuing or terminating the initiative.

5. Management by Exception:

To promote efficiency, PRINCE2 operates under the principle of management by exception. This means that the project board sets tolerances (for time, cost, scope, quality, and risk) within which the project manager can operate autonomously. The board only intervenes if these thresholds are breached. This principle prevents unnecessary micromanagement, empowers project managers, and ensures that senior leaders only engage when strategic adjustments are necessary, thereby conserving organisational resources.

6. Focus on Products:

PRINCE2 is fundamentally deliverable-orientated, with a strong emphasis on ensuring that outputs meet pre-defined quality standards. A quality register is used to specify requirements, acceptance criteria, and quality control measures. This product-focused approach ensures that the project does not become consumed by activity for its own sake but remains centered on producing tangible deliverables that align with customer expectations and organisational objectives.

7. Tailor to the Project Environment:

PRINCE2 is designed to be scalable and adaptable. The methodology encourages practitioners to tailor its processes, roles, and documentation to the size, complexity, and context of the project. For example, a large, multinational project may require extensive governance structures, whereas a smaller internal initiative may apply PRINCE2 in a lighter, more flexible manner. This adaptability ensures that PRINCE2 remains relevant and practical across a wide range of organisational contexts.

PRINCE2 Process Model:

The PRINCE2 process follows seven distinct phases: *starting up a project, directing a project, initiating a project, controlling a stage, managing product delivery, managing stage boundaries, and closing a* project. This structured lifecycle ensures comprehensive oversight while maintaining adaptability. The "Manage by Stages" principle allows for a built-in decision framework: at the end of each stage, the project board evaluates whether the initiative should proceed, be modified, or be terminated.

This staged, iterative quality differentiates PRINCE2 from rigid sequential models such as Waterfall, offering a more adaptive and risk-sensitive approach to project management. Its combination of structure, governance, and flexibility has made PRINCE2 a globally recognised best practice methodology, particularly valued in industries and sectors that demand high accountability, traceability, and stakeholder confidence.

Six Sigma:

A data-driven methodology, Six Sigma is a process improvement approach aimed at reducing defects and minimising variability in processes. Its name is derived from the statistical term *'sigma'* (19σ), which measures process deviation. The goal of Six Sigma is to achieve a level of quality so high that there are only 3.4 defects per million opportunities. It uses a structured problem-solving approach, most famously the DMAIC cycle (Define, Measure, Analyse, Improve, Control), to identify and address the root causes of process failures. Six Sigma is often paired with Lean (Lean Six Sigma) to combine a focus on waste elimination with data-driven quality improvement.

Six Sigma: The Data-Driven Approach:

Six Sigma is a data-driven methodology that focuses on improving quality by identifying and removing the causes of defects and minimising variability in processes. The core philosophy is to better understand customer requirements and eliminate waste through a profound knowledge of statistics, engineering, and project management. While it is not a project management model in the same vein as Waterfall or Agile, it is a powerful tool that can be applied to project management to enforce rigour in the quadruple constraints of scope, time, cost, and quality.

Six Sigma Project Phases:

Six Sigma projects follow two distinct methodologies, each with five phases:

1. *DMAIC (Define, Measure, Analyse, Improve, Control):* Used for projects aimed at improving an existing business process. The process involves defining goals, measuring the current process, analysing data to find the root cause of defects, improving the process, and implementing controls to sustain the improvement.

2. *DMADV (Define, Measure, Analyse, Design, Verify):* Also known as Design for Six Sigma (DFSS), this methodology is used for creating new product or process designs.

The application of Six Sigma in project management means enforcing clear requirements, rigorous change management, and strict controls on time and cost to reduce waste and enhance financial performance.

The choice of methodology depends entirely on the project's unique characteristics, the organisation's culture, and the desired outcome. Whether a team is building a rocket ship or designing a mobile app, selecting the right framework is the first crucial step toward success.

***Comparative Insights: A Cross-Methodology Analysis*:**

Each project management model and framework has unique characteristics that make it suitable for different types of projects and organisational cultures. The following table 2 provides a high-level comparison across key criteria.

Table 2: A Cross-Methodology Analysis of project management models

Feature	Waterfall	Agile	PRINCE2	Lean	Six Sigma
Paradigm	Predictive/Sequential	Adaptive/Iterative	Structured/Controlled	Adaptive/Flow-based	Data-driven/Process-focused
Core Goal	Deliver a fixed, predefined outcome.	Deliver customer value quickly and continuously.	Ensure project control and business justification.	Eliminate waste and maximize customer value.	Minimize defects and process variability.
Flexibility	Rigid. Difficult to change requirements late in the process.	Highly flexible. Welcomes and harnesses change.	Structured but can be tailored to the project.	Flexible. Focuses on continuous flow and pull.	Rigid. Depends on strict processes and data.
Documentation	Extensive, detailed upfront documentation is essential.	Minimal documentation. Focus is on working solutions.	Detailed, but emphasizes learning and review at each stage.	Minimal documentation. Focus on visual process mapping	Extensive. Relies on data analysis and formal documents.
Customer Involvement	Limited. Usually occurs at the beginning and end.	High. Continuous collaboration is a core value.	High. Clear roles for stakeholders in reviews.	High. Value is defined from the customer's perspective.	Strong. Focuses on understanding customer requirements.
Ideal Project Type	Projects with fixed, well-defined requirements, such as construction.	Projects with evolving requirements and a need for quick delivery, such as software development.	Projects with complex, diverse, or large-scale requirements that need a high degree of control.	Manufacturing, process optimization, and projects focused on efficiency.	Large-scale projects focused on quality improvement and defect reduction.

D. Agile Ecosystem: Key Frameworks

'Agile' is an umbrella term encompassing a variety of frameworks that operationalise its principles. The Agile ecosystem is a collection of frameworks and methodologies designed to manage projects and product development with a focus on flexibility, collaboration, and continuous improvement. The various frameworks within this ecosystem offer a spectrum of approaches, balancing the need for structure and governance with the freedom of flexibility and autonomy.

The Agile Spectrum: From High Structure to High Flexibility:

Think of the Agile ecosystem as a continuum. On one end, you have frameworks with a high degree of structure, designed for large enterprises that require robust governance and alignment. On the other end, you have more lightweight, minimalist frameworks that prioritise team autonomy and rapid adaptation.

1. High Structure:

SAFe (Scaled Agile Framework) is at this end of the spectrum. It is a comprehensive framework that provides extensive guidance for scaling Agile to the enterprise level. SAFe is ideal for large organizations that need to coordinate many teams working on complex systems, where consistency and alignment are paramount.

2. Balanced Approach:

Scrum@Scale and DAD (Disciplined Agile Delivery) sit in the middle. Scrum@Scale uses a fractal scaling pattern to connect multiple Scrum teams, creating a "Scrum of Scrums" that balances the adaptability of small teams with the need for organisation-wide coordination. DAD, on the other hand, is a "toolkit" approach. It provides a flexible set of practices that can be tailored to an organisation's specific needs, offering a customisable blend of structure and flexibility.

3. High Flexibility:

On the opposite end of the spectrum, you find frameworks like LeSS (Large-Scale Scrum) and Nexus, which are more minimalist. They aim to scale Scrum by applying its principles to a larger group of teams with minimal new rules. This approach prioritises simplicity and transparency, empowering teams to find the best way to work together without the overhead of a prescriptive framework.

4. Culture-Driven Agility:

The Spotify Model is not a traditional framework but a culture-driven approach to scaling Agile. It emphasises team autonomy, communication, and innovation, organising teams into "squads", "tribes", "chapters", and "guilds". This model prioritises flexibility and a focus on culture over a rigid process, allowing for greater innovation and adaptability.

E. The Agile Ecosystem and The Imperative for Scaling

1. Defining the Enterprise Agile Ecosystem:

An enterprise agile ecosystem is a sophisticated organisational construct designed to effectively manage product and service lifecycles by supporting a seamless integration between technical capabilities and business opportunities. This ecosystem is not a static state but a dynamic environment that must be maintained to meet evolving business needs. Modern technological capabilities, such as cloud computing, social computing, big data analytics, and embedded systems, are instrumental in enabling these agile solutions.

The foundation of this enterprise ecosystem reference model rests on several key concepts. The first is Drivers, which involves structured processes for identifying new opportunities and evaluating emerging technologies. Enterprises must be able to assess how these trends will impact their resources and to justify investment decisions based on the ability to deliver promised performance levels. Next is the

Enterprise Portfolio, which involves applying suitable funding models and governance processes to track opportunities and address gaps in capabilities. Business development focuses on assessing the impact of emerging trends to define the right approach, including evaluating risks that could create unfavourable results and eliminating barriers to success. Finally, Enterprise Services emphasises building competence around modular, service-based architectures. This approach allows for a "plug-and-play" enterprise ecosystem that can quickly leverage, modify, and implement new capabilities, which dramatically reduces cost and mitigates the high risk associated with investing in emerging technology.

2. The Inherent Challenge of Scaling Agile:

Agile methods, such as Scrum and Extreme Programming, were initially conceived for small, co-located, and self-organising teams. While highly effective at this level, these foundational methods often provide insufficient guidance for typical enterprises. The need for scaling arises from the complexities inherent in large organizations, including large team sizes, geographic distribution, regulatory compliance, domain and technical complexity, and the intricate web of organisational dependencies. These factors create a significant chasm between team-level agility and enterprise-wide business agility.

This imperative to scale gives rise to a central paradox in agile adoption. Traditional agile philosophy is predicated on simplicity, autonomy, and the minimisation of formal process. However, the act of scaling to address enterprise complexity often necessitates the introduction of structure, roles, and ceremonies to facilitate coordination and alignment. This structural addition, while necessary for managing a large system, can be viewed as moving away from the core values of simplicity and autonomy. The core dilemma of scaling agile lies in an organisation's willingness to either add a new, often heavy, layer of process to manage this complexity or to embrace a more minimalistic approach that forces the organisation to confront its deep-seated, painful dysfunctions. The choice between these two paths —prescription versus minimalism—is the fundamental differentiator between the frameworks, and it reflects a more profound decision about an organisation's readiness for change.

Frameworks

1. THE SCALED AGILE FRAMEWORK (SAFe)

SAFe

1. Foundational Principles and Core Values:

The Scaled Agile Framework (SAFe) is a comprehensive knowledge base of organisational and workflow principles, practices, and competencies designed to help large enterprises implement an agile model at scale. Created by Dean Leffingwell in 2011, SAFe emerged to address the inefficiencies of traditional project management by improving the speed, quality, and customer focus of large-scale software development.

The framework is built upon four core values that leaders must foster to enable a successful cultural transformation:

1. *Alignment*: SAFe ensures that all teams work toward a common goal by synchronising efforts to deliver business value. This is achieved through tools and practices like Program Increment (PI) Planning, roadmaps, and backlogs, which ensure timely flow of information and shared objectives across all levels of the organisation.

2. *Built-in Quality*: The framework insists that agility must never compromise quality. It encourages teams to bake quality into their development practices from the outset, rather than checking it only at the end of a project.

3. *Transparency*: SAFe fosters trust by ensuring all stakeholders have access to reliable information about

programme execution, progress, and challenges. Practices such as visual management, frequent reviews, and open communication channels are used to maintain this openness, which minimises misunderstandings and supports data-driven decision-making.

4. *Programme Execution*: This value is the heart of the framework, emphasising the fundamental requirement for teams and programmes to deliver quality, working software and business value on a regular, predictable basis.

These values are underpinned by a set of eleven Lean-Agile Principles, which include foundational concepts such as "Take an economic view", "Apply systems thinking", "Build incrementally with fast, integrated learning cycles", and "Unlock the intrinsic motivation of knowledge workers". These principles provide the intellectual foundation for the framework's practices, creating an integrated system to improve employee engagement, time-to-market, solution quality, and team productivity.

2. Configurations and Layers:

SAFe provides a structured, hierarchical approach to scaling, which is visually represented in its "Big Picture" model. This model offers a comprehensive view of how various organisational components, from individual teams to entire portfolios, interact to deliver business value. The framework is designed to be composable and scalable, offering different configurations to suit varying organisational needs.

Essential SAFe: This is the foundational building block and simplest configuration. It focuses on coordinating teams at the team and programme level to ensure efficient delivery of value. A key concept at this level is the

Agile Release Train (ART), which is a "virtual organisation" of agile teams that spans geographical and organisational boundaries. The ARTs align these teams toward a common goal, accelerating value delivery by eliminating unnecessary handoffs.

1. *Large Solution SAFe:* This configuration extends Essential SAFe by incorporating additional competencies for building large, complex solutions that require multiple ARTs.

2. *Portfolio SAFe:* This layer addresses portfolio-level concerns by aligning an organisation's strategy with its execution. It includes features like participatory budgeting and Lean Portfolio Management (LPM) to ensure resources are efficiently allocated and projects are aligned with overall strategic goals.

3. *Full SAFe:* This is the most comprehensive configuration, encompassing all aspects of the other layers. It is ideal for organizations implementing large, complex projects that span numerous portfolios.

3. Key Ceremonies and Artefacts:

SAFe's structured nature is most evident in its defined ceremonies and artefacts, which serve as the engine of synchronisation and collaboration. The most pivotal of these is the

Program Increment (PI) Planning ceremony, a time-boxed, typically two-day event held quarterly that is considered essential for the framework's implementation.

The PI Planning agenda is meticulously structured to ensure all participants are aligned and committed to the upcoming development cycle. Day one typically begins with an executive briefing on the business context, followed by a presentation of the product/solution vision from product management and an overview of the architecture vision by a system architect. The core of the event is the Team Breakouts, where teams break down features into user stories, create iteration plans, and identify dependencies and risks. The first day concludes with a draft plan review and a management review & problem-solving session, where leadership and teams address critical concerns.

Day two continues with additional team breakouts, culminating in a final plan review and a crucial programme risks session, where potential risks are deliberated and mitigated. The ceremony concludes with a Confidence Vote, where each team votes on its confidence in meeting the PI Objectives, and a final retrospective. Key roles in this ceremony include the Release Train Engineer (RTE), who acts as the servant leader and driver of the event, and the Product Owners and Scrum Masters, who facilitate their respective teams.

4. Strengths and Criticisms:

SAFe's structured, prescriptive approach provides numerous benefits. It facilitates faster time to market, better products, and increased productivity by aligning cross-functional teams around value delivery. Its emphasis on collaboration, particularly through PI Planning, ensures that teams, stakeholders, and product owners are synchronised and working toward common goals. This structured nature is often cited as a key strength, as it provides a clear, detailed roadmap that can be implemented in large, complex organizations with predefined roles and responsibilities.

However, this very structure also attracts significant criticism. Some agile practitioners argue that SAFe is highly prescriptive and can be viewed as "training wheels" for agile transformations. A key critique is that organizations may become so focused on adhering to the framework's detailed processes and ceremonies that they fail to cultivate a genuine culture of continuous learning and adaptation. This can lead to what critics describe as "a better waterfall", where teams work in increments but the organisation's overall business agility does not significantly improve.

The high market share and broad adoption of SAFe are not coincidental. The framework's prescriptive nature and clear, top-down implementation model provide a sense of control and predictability that traditional, hierarchical, and often risk-averse organizations find appealing. 6 For these organizations, the formality of SAFe is a feature, not a flaw. It provides a formal, low-risk roadmap for change that is palatable to a leadership accustomed to command-and-control structures and concerned with compliance and predictable outcomes. This structured approach enables a large-scale agile transformation by mitigating the perceived risk of a more organic, bottom-up change. In this context, SAFe's rigidity, often criticised by pure agile advocates, is precisely what makes it a pragmatic and viable solution for a specific market segment.

2. LARGE-SCALE SCRUM (LeSS)

LeSS

1. Core Principles and Philosophy:

Large-Scale Scrum (LeSS) is a minimalist, lightweight framework designed to scale Scrum to multiple teams working on a single product. Its central and most critical principle is encapsulated in the statement, "Large-Scale Scrum is Scrum." This principle emphasises that LeSS is not an entirely new or improved version of Scrum but rather a set of rules and guides for applying the existing Scrum framework in a multi-team context. This philosophy stands in direct opposition to frameworks that add new layers, roles, and processes to Scrum.

The LeSS framework is guided by principles drawn from Lean and Systems Thinking. A key principle is empirical process control, which involves inspecting and adapting the product, processes, and organisational design, rather than following a rigid formula. The More with LeSS philosophy aims to achieve more learning with less process, more value with less waste, and more ownership with fewer roles and artefacts. This is rooted in the belief that removing complexity will expose systemic problems. LeSS also places a strong emphasis on Whole-Product Focus and Customer-Centricity, ensuring that all teams are aligned on a single Product Backlog, one Definition of Done, and one Product Owner.

2. The LeSS and LeSS Huge Frameworks:

The LeSS framework is structured into two distinct configurations to accommodate different scales. The basic LeSS framework is designed for adoptions with two to eight teams. For larger-scale adoptions, LeSS Huge is the second framework, designed for more than eight teams and scaling to up to a few thousand people on a single product.

LeSS Huge maintains the core elements of the smaller framework—a single product owner, one common sprint, and one shippable increment—but introduces a few key concepts to manage the additional scale. The primary additions are the introduction of requirement areas and the area product owner role. These areas allow for more focused management within a massive product while maintaining overall cohesion and a single, overarching product owner. The core idea is to add as few new elements as possible, preserving the simplicity and value of Scrum at a greater scale.

3. Foundational Elements:

The simplicity of LeSS is deceptive, as its implementation requires a fundamental shift in organisational design. Central to this is the single product backlog, which ensures a unified view of the work for all teams, regardless of their number. This consolidation enhances collaboration and simplifies prioritisation. Furthermore, LeSS mandates one definition of done for all teams, ensuring a single, shared understanding of what it means for work to be complete. Coordination among teams is not handled by a separate layer of management, as in other frameworks, but is the responsibility of the teams themselves through shared events such as overall retrospectives and cross-team daily scrums.

4. Benefits and Challenges of Adoption:

LeSS offers a minimalistic approach that closely adheres to the core principles of Scrum, avoiding unnecessary complexity and making it easier for teams to understand and implement. By maintaining a single product backlog and encouraging deep collaboration, it fosters a shared understanding of the product and customer needs, leading to higher quality outcomes.

However, the framework presents a significant challenge by intentionally exposing deep-seated organisational problems. LeSS operates on the principle of "lowering the water level" to make the "rocks"—systemic weaknesses in organisational design related to structure, processes, and rewards—visible. The simplicity of the framework acts as a diagnostic tool, forcing the organisation to confront the root causes of its dysfunction rather than layering new processes on top of them. This means that a successful LeSS adoption requires a profound and often difficult cultural and structural transformation, necessitating strong executive sponsorship and a commitment to radical change. Because the framework itself does not provide a prescribed solution to these exposed problems, it demands a much higher level of organisational maturity and a greater willingness to endure the discomfort of fundamental change compared to a more prescriptive model.

3. DISCIPLINED AGILE DELIVERY (DAD)

DAD

1. Historical Context and Evolution:

Disciplined Agile Delivery (DAD) has a history rooted in filling the process gaps left by early agile methodologies like Scrum. The approach began at IBM Rational in 2008 as Disciplined Agile Delivery (DAD), a people-first, learning-orientated hybrid software process framework. The DAD framework was co-created by Scott Ambler and Mark Lines to provide a more cohesive and comprehensive approach to IT solution delivery that addressed the full delivery lifecycle, from project initiation to deployment.

Over time, DAD evolved into the broader Disciplined Agile (DA) toolkit. In August 2019, the Project Management Institute (PMI) acquired DAD, recognising its value as a flexible, context-sensitive framework for optimising an organisation's way of working. This evolution reflects a shift from a singular hybrid framework to a more comprehensive decision toolkit that can be applied across the entire enterprise, not just in software development.

2. The DAD Toolkit and its Core Philosophy:

Disciplined Agile is a comprehensive "process-decision toolkit" and knowledge base designed to guide individuals, teams, and organizations in optimising their ways of working (WoW) in a context-specific manner. Its core philosophy is empowerment through informed choice, rather than mandating a single, rigid process. This pragmatic approach allows organizations to leverage a blend of proven practices from diverse sources, including Agile, Lean, Scrum, Kanban, and even traditional methods, selecting the most effective strategy for a given situation.

DAD operates on the principle that "context counts", acknowledging that every organisation and every project is unique. The toolkit's guidance is designed to help users move beyond the simplistic notion of "best practices" and make choices that are truly "fit for purpose". This goal-driven approach makes it clear what decisions need to be made, what the viable options are, and what trade-offs are associated with each choice.

3. Process Goals and Decision Points: The Mechanics of Pragmatism:

At the heart of the DAD toolkit are process goals and decision points, which are visually represented in goal diagrams. Process goals are high-level objectives that guide teams in their pursuit of delivering value, such as "Explore Scope" or "Address Changing Stakeholder Needs". Within each goal are various decision points, which are critical junctures where teams must choose the most appropriate practices or techniques for their specific situation.

For each decision point, the toolkit provides a curated range of options and illuminates the trade-offs associated with each. For instance, a decision point under the "Address Changing Stakeholder Needs" goal might involve selecting a method for handling changing requirements, with options ranging from backlog refinement sessions to formal change management boards. 30 This approach takes the guesswork out of extending agile methods and makes it clear what risks are being taken with each choice. The goal diagrams not only provide improvement guidance but also enable teams to assess their current processes and identify areas for enhancement, fostering continuous improvement.

4. Strengths and Drawbacks:

The primary strength of Disciplined Agile is its exceptional flexibility and adaptability. It provides a comprehensive framework that supports teams of all types and sizes, from small to large, and can be applied across the entire business, not just in software development. By focusing on optimising the end-to-end flow of value, DAD helps organizations identify bottlenecks and streamline their processes from initial concept to customer delivery. It is particularly well-suited for organizations that want to customise their agile practices to fit their unique context rather than adopting a one-size-fits-all solution.

However, the very flexibility that defines DAD is also its potential drawback. The toolkit's non-prescriptive, hybrid nature can be difficult to handle for teams and organizations that are new to agile ways of working. For a traditional, command-and-control organisation, the responsibility of making a multitude of informed choices and understanding the associated trade-offs can be overwhelming. Unlike a prescriptive framework that provides a clear "what to do", DAD provides a comprehensive guide for "how to choose". This places a significant cognitive load on practitioners and requires a high degree of maturity and self-discipline. While this makes DAD a powerful tool for building a learning organisation over time, it can be a challenging starting point for those lacking agile experience and an ingrained culture of continuous improvement.

4. KANBAN IN SCRUM

1. Synergy of Scrum and Kanban:

The application of Kanban principles within a Scrum framework is a pragmatic and increasingly common approach to enhancing a team's efficiency and predictability. While Scrum is a prescriptive framework centered on a time-boxed, iterative process with defined roles and events, Kanban is a flow-based strategy focused on visualising work, limiting work in progress (WIP), and continuously optimising the flow of value. The synergy between these two approaches allows teams to leverage Scrum's structure and cadence while benefiting from Kanban's emphasis on continuous delivery and flow metrics.

When Kanban practices are integrated, they serve to enhance the Scrum framework, not to replace it. This hybrid model, often referred to as "Scrumban", maintains all of Scrum's core accountabilities, events, and artefacts but adds a focus on improving the flow of value through the feedback loop.

2. Core Kanban Practices in a Scrum Context:

The integration of Kanban principles within Scrum is achieved through the application of four core practices:

1. *Visualisation of the Workflow*: A Scrum team can enhance transparency by visualising its Sprint Backlog workflow on a Kanban board. This board, configured with columns representing the stages of the workflow (e.g., To Do, In Progress, In Review, Done), provides real-time visibility into the work and helps teams identify bottlenecks.

2. *Limiting Work in Progress (WIP)*: Teams must explicitly limit the number of work items they have in progress at any given time. This practice creates a "pull system", where new work is only started when there is clear capacity to do so. The primary effect of limiting WIP is to reduce multitasking, decrease cycle time, and improve focus, ultimately leading to faster and more efficient completion of tasks.

3. *Active Management of Work Items in Progress*: This involves actively managing the flow of work items as they move through the workflow. The team works to resolve any impediments or blockages that are preventing an item from progressing, ensuring a smooth and continuous flow of value.

4. *Inspecting and Adapting the Team's Definition of Workflow*: Teams should regularly inspect their workflow and adapt it based on feedback and learning. This practice, aligned with Scrum's retrospective ceremony, ensures that the team's process is continuously optimised for flow and efficiency.

3. Key Flow Metrics for Predictability:

The application of Kanban principles provides Scrum teams with a set of key flow metrics that help in understanding and improving their performance:

1. *Work in Progress (WIP):* The number of work items that have been started but are not yet finished. This metric provides transparency into the team's workload and helps reinforce WIP limits.

2. *Cycle Time*: The elapsed time from when a work item is started until it is finished. Reducing cycle time is a core objective of Kanban and is directly correlated with a reduction in WIP.

3. *Work Item Age*: The amount of time that an item has been in progress. This metric helps identify items that may be stalled or blocked, prompting the team to take action.

4. *Throughput*: The number of work items finished per unit of time. This metric provides a measure of the team's delivery rate and predictability.

These metrics are governed by Little's Law, which states that the more things a team works on at a given time, the longer it will take for each of those things to finish. This principle provides a quantitative basis for the practice of limiting WIP, solidifying its importance in improving flow.

4. Benefits of the Combined Approach (Scrumban):

The hybrid model of Kanban in Scrum offers several significant benefits. It provides improved workflow efficiency by visually clarifying bottlenecks and allowing teams to focus on completing tasks rather than overloading themselves. The continuous delivery model and a focus on flow metrics lead to enhanced predictability and a more streamlined process. Furthermore, this approach provides greater flexibility to adapt to changing priorities since new work can be pulled as soon as capacity becomes available, rather than waiting for the end of a time-boxed sprint.

The application of Kanban practices within a Scrum context represents a tactical, rather than a strategic, approach to scaling. While frameworks like SAFe, LeSS, and DA are designed for large-scale, enterprise-wide transformations, the Kanban/Scrum hybrid focuses on optimising the internal processes and flow of a single team. Its value lies in providing a low-risk, low-overhead method for improving the predictability and efficiency of an existing Scrum team, which is a necessary but not sufficient condition for achieving macro-level organisational agility. It addresses the "how" for a single team's workflow, whereas the other frameworks address the "how" for an entire organisation's strategic portfolio.

F. Comparative Analysis and Strategic Synthesis

1. A Multi-Dimensional Comparison of Frameworks:

The analysis of SAFe, LeSS, DAD, and Kanban in Scrum reveals that there is no single dominant framework in all dimensions. The choice of a framework is not a matter of selecting the "best" but of identifying the one that provides the optimal fit for a given organisational context, culture, and strategic objective. A comparative analysis across significant dimensions brings to light the core differences, as shown in Table 3.

Table 3:

Comparative Analysis Across Significant Dimensions

Framework	Core Philosophy	Ideal Organizational Size	Approach to Scaling	Key Roles	Core Artifacts/ Concepts
SAFe	Prescriptive Blueprint	50-125+ members	Top-Down	Release Train Engineer (RTE), Product Owner, Scrum Master, Solution Architect	Agile Release Train (ART), Program Increment (PI) Planning, SAFe Big Picture
LeSS	Minimalist Scrum	2-8 teams (LeSS), 8+ teams (LeSS	Bottom-Up	Product Owner, Area Product Owner (Huge), Scrum	Single Product Backlog, One Definition of Done,

		Huge)		Master, Teams	Requirement Areas (Huge)
Disciplined Agile Delivery (DAD)	Contextual Toolkit	Any size/ complexit y	Contextual /Adaptive	Disciplined Agile Scrum Master, Team Member, Product Owner, Stakeholder	Process Goals, Decision Points, Goal Diagrams, Way of Working (WoW)
Kanban in Scrum	Flow Optimization	Single Team	Tactical	Scrum Master, Product Owner, Development Team	Kanban Board, WIP Limits, Cycle Time, Throughput, Work Item Age

To elaborate on the table more, *SAFe's* philosophy is rooted in providing a comprehensive, top-down roadmap for change. It introduces a layer of management between distinct agile teams and the organisational hierarchy, extending the agile framework from a single-team level to "teams of teams". This structured approach is highly effective for large organizations with complex product portfolios that require a high degree of governance and alignment.

LeSS, in contrast, is a minimalistic framework that is a scaled-up version of Scrum. It rejects the addition of new roles and processes, instead focusing on exposing organisational dysfunctions that are often masked by complex structures. This bottom-up approach to scaling requires deep cultural and organisational design changes.

Disciplined Agile Delivery (DAD) is a pragmatic, goal-driven toolkit for optimising an organisation's way of working. Its strength lies in its ability to support informed choices based on a given context, rather than a predefined script. This makes it ideal for organizations that value flexibility and have a higher degree of agile maturity.

The Kanban Scrum hybrid is not a scaling framework in the same vein as the others. Its value is tactical, not strategic. It is a set of practices designed to improve a single Scrum team's workflow, predictability, and efficiency by introducing concepts like WIP limits and flow metrics. While essential for high-performing teams, it does not provide the enterprise-level guidance of the other frameworks.

G. Waterfall (Traditional) Vs. Agile Project Management

Project management methodologies serve as frameworks for structuring, planning, and executing projects. Among the most widely debated approaches are the Waterfall model, often referred to as traditional project management, and the Agile methodology, which represents a modern, adaptive approach. While both aim to deliver successful projects, they differ significantly in philosophy, process structure, adaptability, and stakeholder involvement.

1. Philosophical Foundations:

The Waterfall methodology is based on a predictive and linear philosophy, where projects are assumed to progress through sequential stages—requirements, design, development, testing, and deployment. The underlying belief is that careful upfront planning, thorough documentation, and strict adherence to timelines will minimise uncertainty and maximise control.

In contrast, Agile is rooted in an iterative and adaptive philosophy. Emerging from the Agile Manifesto in 2001, it emphasises collaboration, responsiveness to change, and customer involvement. Agile assumes that uncertainty is inherent in projects—especially in dynamic environments like software development—and thus embraces flexibility and incremental delivery rather than rigid upfront planning.

2. Structure and Process:

The waterfall approach follows a sequential structure: one phase must be completed before the next can begin. This rigid process provides clarity and predictability but leaves little room for revisiting earlier decisions once a phase is closed.

Agile, by contrast, is iterative and incremental. Work is divided into small, manageable units called sprints (in Scrum) or iterations, each typically lasting 1–4 weeks. At the end of each cycle, a potentially usable product increment is delivered. This cyclical process allows teams to continually refine outputs, incorporate feedback, and adapt to emerging requirements.

3. Flexibility and Adaptability:

Waterfall is best suited for projects where requirements are well-defined and unlikely to change, such as construction or manufacturing. Changes during execution are costly, as they often require revisiting completed stages. This rigidity can create challenges in fast-changing environments.

Agile thrives in contexts where requirements evolve over time. Its iterative model enables teams to adapt to changes mid-project without derailing the overall timeline. Agile teams actively welcome changes—even late in development—as opportunities to enhance customer value, making it ideal for software development, product design, and research-driven projects.

4. Stakeholder Involvement:

In Waterfall, stakeholder involvement is front-loaded. Clients or users are heavily engaged during the requirements-gathering and design phases but have limited interaction once execution begins. This often results in deliverables that may not fully align with evolving customer expectations.

Agile fosters continuous stakeholder engagement. Customers, end users, and sponsors collaborate throughout the project, providing feedback during sprint reviews and planning sessions. This constant interaction ensures alignment with customer needs and reduces the risk of delivering misaligned or obsolete products.

5. Documentation and Planning:

Waterfall places strong emphasis on comprehensive documentation. Detailed requirements, specifications, and design documents are created at the start and serve as reference points throughout the project. While this ensures accountability and clarity, it can lead to rigidity when changes arise.

Agile values working solutions over extensive documentation. While documentation is not ignored, it is kept lightweight and flexible, with greater emphasis placed on collaboration and adaptive planning. Plans are revisited frequently to incorporate learning, feedback, and changes, reflecting Agile's dynamic nature.

6. Risk Management:

In Waterfall, risks are typically addressed during the planning phase. Because changes are difficult to accommodate later, unforeseen issues can become major setbacks if not anticipated early.

Agile manages risk through short feedback loops and iterative delivery. By delivering increments regularly, risks are identified and addressed early in the process. This minimises the likelihood of catastrophic failures at the project's end and allows teams to pivot when necessary.

7. Measurement of Success:

Waterfall projects are often judged by adherence to the iron triangle of project management: delivering on time, within budget, and to specification. Success depends on compliance with predetermined plans.

Agile measures success primarily by customer satisfaction and value delivered. A project may deviate from original plans, but if it delivers a high-quality product that meets evolving customer needs, it is considered successful. This customer-centric metric contrasts with the plan-centric measure of Waterfall.

A comparison between Waterfall (Traditional) and Agile Project Management is presented in Table 4.

Table 4:

Comparison and Contrast of Waterfall and Agile Project Management

Dimension	Waterfall (Traditional)	Agile Project Management

Philosophy	Predictive, linear, control-oriented	Adaptive, iterative, change-embracing
Process Flow	Sequential phases, no overlap	Iterative cycles (sprints/ iterations)
Flexibility	Low; changes are costly and difficult	High; welcomes change, even late in development
Stakeholder Involvement	Primarily at start and end	Continuous throughout the project
Documentation	Heavy, detailed, and formal	Lightweight, flexible, secondary to collaboration
Risk Management	Managed during upfront planning	Managed through iterative feedback and adaptation
Success Metric	On-time, on-budget, within scope	Customer satisfaction and value delivered
Best Suited For	Stable, well-defined projects (e.g., construction)	Dynamic, uncertain projects (e.g., software)

Conclusion

The key distinction between Waterfall and Agile lies in their approach to uncertainty and change. Waterfall assumes that predictability is achievable through thorough upfront planning, making it well-suited for stable, repeatable projects. Agile, however, assumes that change is inevitable and therefore embraces flexibility, iterative delivery, and continuous stakeholder involvement to ensure relevance and value creation.

In practice, many organizations adopt hybrid approaches, blending Waterfall's structure and governance with Agile's adaptability. For instance, large-scale infrastructure projects may follow Waterfall for overall planning but integrate Agile practices for software components or innovation-driven tasks. This synthesis illustrates the value of selecting methodologies not as rigid prescriptions, but as adaptable frameworks tailored to the unique context of each project.

The Modern Synthesis:

HYBRID PROJECT MANAGEMENT

The debate between traditional and agile models has largely come to an end. The modern perspective is that a single, dogmatic approach is rarely optimal. The future of project management lies in a hybrid approach, which strategically combines the strengths of both traditional and agile methods to create a more robust and adaptable practice. This approach recognises that projects vary in their predictability and that the best methodology is a customised one that fits the unique context of the project, team, and organisation.

The Agile-Waterfall Hybrid:

The most common hybrid model, the Agile-Waterfall Hybrid, uses a traditional, linear approach for high-level, upfront planning and a flexible, iterative approach for the execution of the work. The Waterfall part of the model is used to define key project frames, such as final deadlines, high-level deliverables, and fixed budgets, which are often required for contractual agreements. Once the high-level plan is approved, the project transitions to an Agile approach for the actual execution. The work is broken down into smaller tasks, prioritised in a backlog, and completed in short, time-boxed sprints, with continuous feedback and adaptation. This allows teams to deliver value incrementally and respond to change while still adhering to a structured, predefined overall plan.

This synthesis of methods provides the benefits of both worlds: the predictability and control of Waterfall in the planning phase and the speed and flexibility of Agile in the execution phase.

Key Drivers for Adoption of the Agile-Waterfall Hybrid:

Several scenarios make an Agile-Waterfall hybrid model the optimal choice:

1. *Mixed Hardware and Software Projects*: For products with both physical and digital components, the linear, sequential nature of hardware development can be managed with a Waterfall approach, while the software development can benefit from an Agile methodology. The two teams can work independently, with a clear handoff between them.

2. *Fixed-Scope and Contractual Projects*: Many clients require a detailed upfront plan and a fixed budget before a project begins. A hybrid model allows for a rigorous, data-driven planning phase that can satisfy these requirements while still allowing the development team to benefit from iterative execution.

3. *Cultural Transition*: The hybrid model can be a valuable stepping stone for organizations with a traditional culture that are seeking to adopt Agile practices. It allows teams to gradually gain experience with Agile techniques like sprint planning and backlog prioritisation without the shock of a full, top-to-bottom cultural transformation.

H. Real-World Application and Strategic Case Studies

The selection of a project management model is not an academic exercise; its effectiveness is measured by real-world outcomes. The analysis of case studies reveals that project success or failure is often less about the methodology itself and more about the cultural and contextual fit of the approach.

***Case of Mayden* -The Waterfall Trap:**

The case of Mayden, a company that initially operated in a traditional, waterfall-based environment, illustrates the pitfalls of applying a rigid model to a dynamic context. Despite a reputation for being responsive to customer needs, the company's linear project execution created an "illusion of progress" where a backlog of work piled up, and very little was ever truly completed. The rigid structure also led to a lack of a team environment, with individual developers becoming single points of failure, which resulted in low morale and poor skills coverage. The company's subsequent successful transition to Scrum highlights how the right methodology, aligned with a need for flexibility, can dramatically improve outcomes.

The limitations of the predictive paradigm also contribute to other notable project failures. Overambitious goals and a fundamental misunderstanding of the market led to the commercial failure of the Concorde supersonic jet, a marvel of engineering. Similarly, the Australian Securities Exchange's failed blockchain-based CHESS replacement project, which was pronounced dead after seven years, demonstrates the high risk of a long-term, linear approach when requirements are not fully understood from the outset.

The Agile Transformation:

In contrast, numerous companies have leveraged Agile to achieve remarkable success. The toy company LEGO, faced with declining sales and a bloated product portfolio, adopted Agile methodologies to become more responsive to market trends. By focusing on iterative development and cross-functional teams, LEGO was able to release new products like LEGO Friends and LEGO Ninjago on shorter timescales, leading to a significant increase in operational efficiency and market responsiveness.

Other success stories include Spotify and Microsoft. Spotify adopted an Agile way of working to scale its teams without losing speed, and Microsoft implemented Agile and DevOps principles for its Azure cloud business, leading to accelerated development and better quality through continuous integration and testing. The banking giant ING saw similar results after an Agile transformation, achieving a shorter time to market for new features, increased client satisfaction, and higher employee engagement.

The Pitfalls of "Fake Agile"

However, not every Agile story is a success. The research highlights a counternarrative of projects that fail despite an attempt to "go agile." A crucial observation is that these failures are rarely due to the methodology itself but rather to a poor or "forced" implementation where the organisational culture, contracts, or leadership do not support the Agile mindset. Simply adopting an Agile framework without embracing its core values and principles can lead to administrative overhead and a misaligned approach. For example, a project with "contractually set in stone" deliverables and due dates is fundamentally incompatible with an Agile approach that welcomes changing requirements. This illustrates that adopting Agile is a cultural transformation, not just a process change, and that without a clear understanding of its purpose, the results can be counterproductive.

I. The Future of Project Management: Trends and Outlook:

1. The AI and Automation Imperative:

The future of project management is inextricably linked to technological advancement. Artificial intelligence is no longer an emerging trend but an enduring factor, poised to bring profound changes to the field. AI is taking over routine tasks, freeing up project managers for more strategic work. AI can learn from historical data to create more realistic plans for duration, effort, and costs. It can also automate administrative tasks such as generating status reports, identifying risks, and suggesting appropriate actions.

The emergence of AI agents, which act as digital assistants to perform complex instructions and interact with other systems, is particularly exciting. These agents can automatically compile important information from emails and documents before a meeting, streamlining the project manager's workflow and enabling them to focus on more complex, human-centric challenges. The demand for automated data consolidation is also growing, as teams are no longer willing to manually compile and re-enter data for reports.

2. Evolving Skill Sets and the Strategic PMO:

In this dynamic environment, the role of the project manager is also evolving. The increasing complexity of projects and the rise of remote work are causing "overstrain" among project participants. To combat this, a new emphasis is being placed on human-centric "power skills", such as effective communication, change management, and team leadership. The project manager's role is shifting from a taskmaster to a facilitator, focusing on building a transparent and positive culture of change.

Concurrently, the Project Management Office (PMO) is transitioning from a purely administrative function to a more strategic role. A modern PMO is involved in coordinating resource management, working with decision-makers to provide forward-looking capacities, and leading the implementation of change management and transparency initiatives. The PMO's evolution reflects a broader organisational need for a strategic partner who can navigate complexity and uncertainty.

3. Strategic Recommendations:

The comprehensive analysis of project management models demonstrates that no single methodology is a panacea for all projects. The choice between Waterfall, Agile, PRINCE2, and other specialised frameworks is not a matter of a single correct answer but rather a strategic alignment of the model with the project's unique characteristics.

The report offers the following strategic recommendations for executives and project leaders:

1. *Adopt a Hybrid Mindset:* The debate between traditional and agile is over. The most effective approach is a hybrid one that leverages the predictable, controlled planning of a traditional model for a high-level roadmap while embracing the flexible, iterative execution of an adaptive framework.

2. *Align Methodology with Project Context*: Before selecting a model, conduct a diagnostic assessment. For projects with fixed requirements, clear deadlines, and strict compliance needs, a more traditional or controlled approach may be best. For projects with evolving requirements, high uncertainty, and a need for continuous customer feedback, an Agile framework is ideal.

3. *Invest in Cultural Transformation*: Adopting an agile framework is a cultural change, not just a process change. Ensure that the organization's culture is prepared to support decentralised decision-making, empower teams, and embrace transparency.

4. *Embrace AI and Automation*: The future of project management involves a blend of human leadership and technological support. Invest in tools and AI agents that can automate routine tasks, provide data-driven insights, and free up project managers to focus on strategic initiatives and human-centric challenges.

5. *Prioritise Continuous Learning*: The project management landscape is constantly changing. Organizations must foster a culture of continuous learning and provide ongoing training for their teams to ensure they can adapt to new tools, methods, and a dynamic world of work.

J. Agile Workflows

Creating Agile Workflows for Enhanced Project Management:

Project management in contemporary organizations increasingly depends on structured workflows that balance clarity, efficiency, and adaptability. A workflow, in its simplest form, delineates the sequence of tasks, responsibilities, and processes required to achieve project outcomes. While workflows can take many forms across different management methodologies, Agile workflows have become particularly significant in contexts where flexibility, responsiveness, and iterative progress are critical to success.

Figure 4: Agile workflows for Enhanced Project management

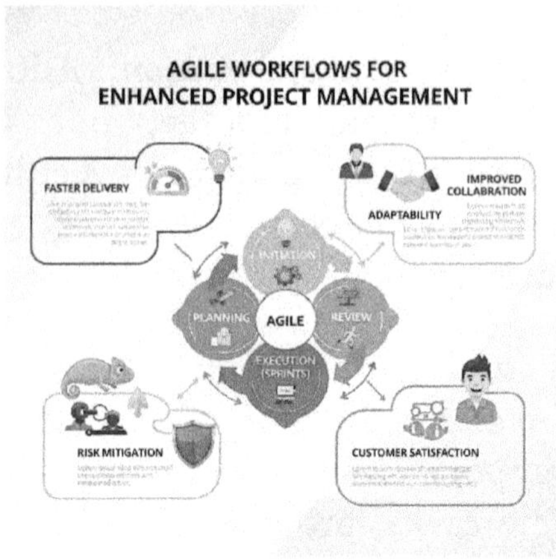

The figure and the discussion define workflows and their variations, situates Agile workflows within the broader landscape of project methodologies, outlines the key phases of project workflows, and offers structured guidance on how organizations can design and refine Agile workflows for optimal performance.

Understanding Workflows:

A workflow is more than a list of tasks; it is a structured representation of how work is initiated, organised, executed, and completed. It sets out the logical sequence of activities, clarifies who is responsible for each step, and provides a temporal framework that guides project teams toward a common goal. By making the invisible processes of coordination visible, workflows serve both as a communication tool and as a control mechanism, ensuring accountability and predictability in project delivery.

Different methodologies conceptualise workflows differently. In Waterfall, tasks are executed in rigid, sequential phases, such as design, development, and testing, with little scope for revisiting earlier steps. Kanban and Lean, by contrast, prioritise continuous flow by limiting work-in-progress to maximise efficiency. DevOps extends the workflow to include operations, promoting integration and rapid deployment. Hybrid models combine predictive elements of traditional frameworks with adaptive practices from Agile. Amid these models, agile workflows stand out for their adaptability: they emphasise iteration, customer feedback, and the ability to change course when conditions shift.

Why Agile Workflows Matter:

Agile workflows matter because they transform abstract principles of agility into actionable processes that teams can follow. By organising work into smaller increments, typically delivered through time-boxed sprints, Agile workflows allow teams to move forward steadily while remaining open to change.

One key benefit is timeliness. Rather than waiting until the end of a lengthy project cycle to deliver results, Agile workflows enable consistent progress by producing usable deliverables in shorter intervals. This incremental delivery reduces uncertainty and provides stakeholders with regular progress visibility.

Second, agile workflows promote effective resource allocation. By breaking large projects into smaller units, managers can align tasks with specific skill sets and adjust workload distribution as conditions evolve. This reduces inefficiencies and prevents burnout.

Third, agile workflows facilitate early risk identification. Because feedback is incorporated continuously, potential obstacles are uncovered before they escalate into crises. This reduces technical debt and enhances resilience.

Finally, agile workflows cultivate transparency and

collaboration. Practices such as daily stand-ups, sprint reviews, and retrospectives ensure open communication and shared ownership of outcomes. In this way, workflows act not just as operational guides but as cultural enablers of agility.

Phases of a Project Management Workflow:

Although methodologies differ, most project workflows encompass four foundational phases:

1. Initiation:

This phase establishes the foundation of a project by defining objectives, scope, and constraints. Stakeholder expectations are clarified, feasibility is assessed, and permission is granted to move forward. In Agile contexts, initiation may be lighter and more flexible, often focusing on developing a product vision and identifying high-level goals rather than fixed requirements.

2. Planning:

In traditional methods, planning involves comprehensive forecasting, scheduling, and risk management. Agile reframes planning as an iterative process: tasks are prioritised in a product backlog, sprints are planned incrementally, and resource allocation adapts to emerging needs. Planning becomes a continuous dialogue rather than a one-time exercise.

3. Execution:

Execution is the stage where plans materialise into deliverables. In Agile, execution occurs within sprints, with cross-functional teams collaborating to complete user stories or features. Daily meetings, collaborative tools, and real-time adjustments ensure that execution aligns with goals while remaining responsive to change.

4. Monitoring and control:

This phase ensures that execution remains on track. Agile integrates monitoring directly into its cycles: velocity charts, burndown graphs, and sprint reviews offer immediate information about progress and challenges. Unlike traditional methods where control may feel hierarchical, Agile monitoring is participatory, empowering teams to self-correct.

Agile embeds learning and improvement throughout the project lifecycle by ensuring that workflows are dynamic rather than static.

Designing an Agile Workflow:

Designing an Agile workflow requires a deliberate process to ensure alignment between organisational strategy and day-to-day operations.

Figure 5: Agile workflow

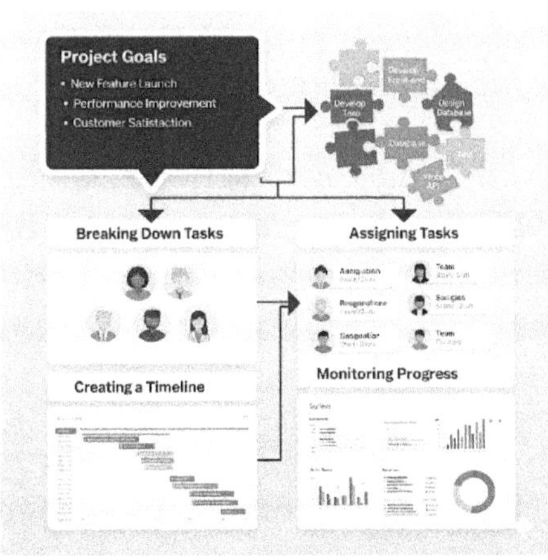

1. Define Project Goals:

Goals should be co-created with stakeholders to ensure they reflect business priorities and customer needs. Rather than rigidly defining outputs, Agile goals emphasise value delivery and adaptability, making them flexible enough to accommodate evolving insights.

2. Break Down Tasks and Milestones:

Large, complex initiatives are decomposed into smaller, actionable components. This makes progress more visible, reduces cognitive load for teams, and ensures that milestones are achievable within short timeframes. In agile contexts, the work breakdown structure often translates into product backlogs organised by epics and user stories.

3. Assign Tasks and responsibilities:

Tasks are allocated to team members based on expertise and availability, but Agile also promotes cross-functionality. Teams are encouraged to share knowledge and collaborate, reducing bottlenecks and creating redundancy that protects against delays if key individuals are unavailable.

4. Create a Timeline and Schedule:

Rather than fixed long-term schedules, Agile emphasises sprint cycles, which are usually one to four weeks long. Dependencies are identified early, and schedules are revisited frequently, allowing for recalibration as conditions evolve.

5. Monitor Progress and adjust:

Continuous monitoring is central to Agile workflows. Teams use tools such as Kanban boards or digital dashboards to visualise progress, while retrospectives at the end of each sprint provide structured opportunities to adjust practices and priorities.

Best Practices for Agile Workflows:

Agile workflows function most effectively when guided by principles of simplicity, transparency, and adaptability.

Figure 6: Best Practices for Agile Workflows

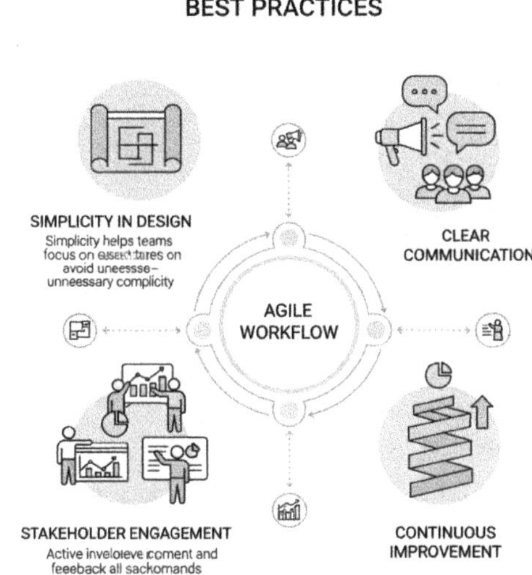

1. *Simplicity in Design:* Overly complex workflows can confuse teams and slow progress. Instead, workflows should reflect essential states—such as *To Do*, *In Progress*, *Code Review*, *Awaiting QA*, and *Done*—that map directly to the team's delivery cycle.

2. *Clear Communication*: Agile depends on open dialogue. Mechanisms such as daily stand-ups, sprint reviews, and stakeholder demos foster collective awareness of progress and obstacles.

3. *Stakeholder Engagement*: Agile thrives when stakeholders are consistently involved. Their feedback shapes priorities, prevents misalignment, and increases confidence in project outcomes.

4. *Continuous Improvement*: Retrospectives institutionalise learning, encouraging teams to identify small, incremental improvements that cumulatively enhance performance.

The use of automation tools such as Jira or Trello amplifies these practices by reducing administrative overhead, enabling real-time visibility, and supporting scalability across multiple teams or projects.

Agile Epics and User Stories:

Agile organises work hierarchically through epics and user stories.

1. An epic represents a significant body of work, often linked to a strategic objective. Epics are too large to complete within a single sprint, so they are decomposed into smaller, testable units.

2. User stories represent these smaller units, framed from the perspective of end-users. They ensure that development is customer-centric, focusing not merely on technical tasks but on delivering tangible value.

For example, an epic such as “Enhance customer onboarding experience” might break down into user stories like “As a new user, I want a guided tutorial so that I can quickly learn the platform’s features.” Epics provide long-term direction, while stories operationalise strategy in daily work, ensuring that tactical tasks serve strategic aims.

Agile Epics: Organising Large Bodies of Work:

In Agile, an epic is a large body of work that can be divided into smaller, manageable tasks known as user stories. Epics often span multiple sprints and may involve several teams. Unlike rigid project phases, epics remain flexible, evolving through customer feedback and ongoing team collaboration.

For example, a fictional "March 2050 Space Tourism Launch" epic might include stories from multiple teams, such as ticketing software updates, propulsion system adjustments, and customer experience enhancements. This structure allows teams to maintain a connection between daily tasks and broader strategic goals.

User Stories: Putting People at the Centre:

User stories represent the smallest unit of Agile work. Written from the end-user's perspective, they articulate needs in simple, non-technical language. A common format is:

"As a specific user type, I want to achieve a particular goal so that I can receive a specific benefit."

For instance:

As a customer, I want to save my payment details so that I can check out faster in future purchases.

User stories keep development focused on real user needs, encourage collaboration, and build momentum as small wins accumulate. Collectively, stories roll up as epics, and epics roll up as large initiatives, ensuring alignment with organisational goals.

Agile vs. Waterfall Workflows:

A critical distinction lies between Agile and Waterfall workflows.

1. Waterfall offers linearity and predictability, making it suitable for industries like construction, where requirements are stable and revisions are costly. However, its rigidity creates risks in dynamic environments, as late-stage changes are difficult to accommodate.

2. Agile, by contrast, embraces iteration and flexibility. Its feedback-driven loops allow teams to pivot as user needs and technological contexts evolve. This makes Agile particularly effective in software development, digital services, and innovation-driven sectors.

Thus, Agile does not simply replace Waterfall; rather, it offers a paradigm shift from predictability to adaptability. In practice, some organizations adopt hybrid approaches, combining Waterfall's upfront structure with Agile's iterative responsiveness.

Agile Metrics and Continuous Learning:

Metrics are central to sustaining Agile workflows. Tools such as burndown charts track how much work remains, velocity charts measure team capacity across sprints, and work-in-progress limits prevent overloading the system. These metrics enhance transparency, allowing both teams and stakeholders to monitor progress objectively.

Yet metrics alone do not guarantee improvement; they must be embedded within a culture of trust and learning. Agile emphasises psychological safety, where teams can acknowledge challenges without fear of blame. Continuous learning occurs through structured reflections, experimentation, and adaptation, ensuring that workflows remain not only efficient but also resilient.

Agile workflows represent more than procedural guides; they embody a mindset of adaptability, customer orientation, and continuous improvement. By breaking projects into iterative increments, embedding stakeholder feedback, and cultivating team autonomy, Agile workflows enable organizations to deliver value consistently in fast-changing environments.

Compared to traditional models such as Waterfall, Agile workflows offer responsiveness over rigidity, learning over prediction, and collaboration over control. For organizations facing complex and evolving challenges, adopting Agile workflows is not merely an operational choice but a strategic imperative to remain competitive and innovative.

Similarities, Differences, and Hybrid Approaches:

Despite their apparent contrasts, both traditional and Agile methodologies share the same overarching purpose: delivering projects successfully within defined constraints of scope, time, cost, and quality. Both approaches emphasise communication, stakeholder involvement, and the importance of leadership in guiding project teams. However, their divergence lies in philosophy and execution. Traditional approaches prioritise stability, structure, and predictability, whereas Agile prioritises adaptability, customer engagement, and rapid value delivery. For instance, in the Waterfall method, success is often measured by adherence to the original plan, while in Agile, success is gauged by the value delivered to the customer and the ability to pivot when conditions change. Acknowledging the intricacies of contemporary projects, numerous organisations are progressively embracing hybrid approaches.

Hybrid project management combines the rigour and documentation of traditional methods with the adaptability and stakeholder-centricity of Agile. This allows organizations to tailor methodologies depending on the project's nature—using waterfall elements for predictable, compliance-driven components and agile techniques for innovative, uncertain aspects.

K. Case Studies

Real-World Case Study: Structured vs. Agile Execution in Practice:

The execution phase of project management reveals its greatest diversity when examined across industries. While the principles of execution—task assignment, quality assurance, stakeholder communication, and team collaboration—remain universal, the ways in which they are applied differ profoundly depending on the nature of the project. Two contrasting examples—the Apollo/Artemis space programmes at NASA and the Agile execution model at Spotify—highlight how structured and adaptive approaches to execution can both deliver transformative outcomes.

NASA Apollo and Artemis: Structured Execution at Scale:

The Apollo programme (1961–1972) and the contemporary Artemis missions epitomise execution in large-scale, high-risk aerospace projects. Once planning established ambitious goals, such as landing astronauts on the Moon, execution demanded precise coordination across hundreds of thousands of contributors.

Task assignment was executed with military-grade discipline. Specialised teams worked on discrete components: propulsion systems for the Saturn V rocket, life-support systems in the Lunar Module, or navigation computing. Each unit operated within a tightly defined scope, contributing to a collective outcome. Similarly, Artemis today relies on global partnerships, including contributions from the European Space Agency and private contractors, making execution a matter of international collaboration.

Quality assurance was uncompromising. Every rocket engine, heat shield, and onboard computer underwent exhaustive testing to simulate real-world conditions. Failures were expected, documented, and treated as learning opportunities. The Apollo tragedy, though devastating, led to enhanced safety standards that defined all subsequent missions. Artemis continues this legacy with rigorous stress testing of the Space Launch System (SLS) and Orion capsule to minimise risks.

Stakeholder communication was centralised yet formalised. Information flowed through strict hierarchies, from NASA's mission control to contractors and suppliers. Weekly integration reviews and systematic reporting ensured that thousands of moving parts aligned into one synchronised mission.

Team performance thrived on a unifying vision—fulfilling Kennedy's promise for Apollo and establishing a sustainable human presence on the Moon for Artemis. Engineers, scientists, and contractors often worked around the clock, bonded by a sense of history in the making. The culmination of execution came with Apollo 11's first lunar landing in 1969, and Artemis seeks to replicate that success by returning humans to the Moon with greater inclusivity and advanced technologies.

Spotify: Agile Execution in the Digital Era:

In contrast, Spotify demonstrates how execution thrives in a fast-paced digital innovation environment. Unlike the rigid hierarchies of NASA, Spotify's model emphasises agility, autonomy, and rapid iteration.

Task assignment occurs within small, cross-functional teams known as "squads." Each squad owns a feature of the platform—such as playlists, search, or recommendation algorithms—and operates almost like a mini start-up within the company. Execution happens in parallel across squads, enabling speed and innovation at scale.

Quality assurance relies less on exhaustive pre-launch testing and more on continuous integration and real-time feedback. New features are tested incrementally with subsets of users, allowing flaws to be identified and corrected quickly. This contrasts with NASA's exhaustive simulations, reflecting the lower-risk, higher-iteration environment of digital products.

Communication at Spotify balances autonomy with alignment. Squads belong to "tribes" that share related missions, while "chapters" and "guilds" foster knowledge-sharing across functions. This structure prevents silos while preserving the agility of small teams, ensuring that execution aligns with strategic goals.

Team performance is driven by ownership and accountability. Squads decide how they work, fostering creativity and motivation. Collaboration is emphasised through rituals like sprint reviews and retrospectives, reinforcing continuous improvement. The result is a platform that evolves rapidly while maintaining high reliability for over 500 million global users.

Contrasting Lessons from Both Worlds:

These two cases illustrate the spectrum of execution approaches:

1. NASA's Apollo and Artemis missions showcase how execution in high-stakes, capital-intensive projects requires structured hierarchies, exhaustive testing, and strict coordination to ensure safety and reliability.

2. Spotify's Agile model highlights how execution in fast-moving industries depends on autonomous teams, iterative delivery, and adaptive communication to achieve speed and innovation.

Despite their differences, both contexts underscore the essence of execution: turning plans into reality through disciplined task management, rigorous quality control, clear communication, and effective team collaboration. Whether building rockets to reach the Moon or deploying algorithms to enhance music discovery, success lies in how well execution bridges vision and reality.

CHAPTER 3: UNDERSTANDING PROJECT STAKEHOLDERS

In the discipline of project management, stakeholders represent one of the most critical variables influencing success or failure. The Project Management Institute (PMI) defines stakeholders as individuals, groups, or organizations that may affect, be affected by, or perceive themselves to be affected by the project's decisions, activities, or outcomes. Unlike static project inputs such as budget or technology, stakeholders are dynamic entities with evolving expectations, varying levels of influence, and diverse interests. Consequently, effective stakeholder management is not merely a support function—it is an essential strategic capability that determines whether a project can achieve its intended objectives.

Stakeholder management involves three interconnected processes: identifying who the stakeholders are, analysing their relative power and interest, and designing engagement strategies that ensure collaboration and alignment throughout the project lifecycle. This chapter discusses the types of stakeholders, introduces analytical tools for stakeholder assessment, and presents practical strategies for stakeholder engagement.

1. Types of Stakeholders

Stakeholders are not a homogeneous group; they differ significantly in their relationship to the project, the nature of their influence, and their degree of involvement. Understanding these categories allows project managers to prioritise interactions, design tailored communication strategies, and allocate resources efficiently. A failure to properly classify and understand stakeholders can result in missed expectations, resource conflicts, or even complete project failure. Stakeholders can be classified based on their relationship to the project, the nature of their influence, and their level of involvement. A nuanced understanding of these categories helps project managers allocate time, communication, and resources proportionately.

Figure 1 presents the various categories of stakeholders involved in a project and highlights their relationship to the project's objectives, processes, and outcomes. It illustrates how each stakeholder group—ranging from internal participants such as project managers and team members to external entities like clients, suppliers, regulatory bodies, and the wider community—interacts with and influences the project. The figure emphasizes that stakeholders are not isolated, but interconnected, with their roles, expectations, and levels of influence shaping the direction and success of the project.

Figure 1
STAKEHOLDERS

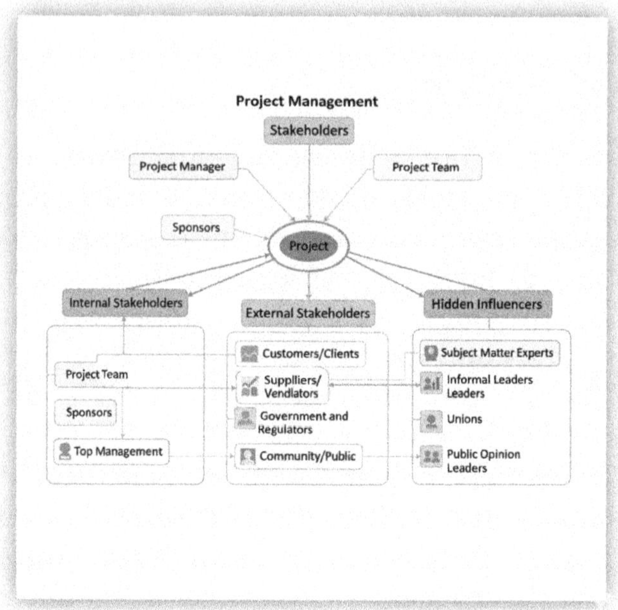

1.1 Internal Stakeholders:

Internal stakeholders are those who operate within the project's executing organisation. Unlike external groups who are primarily recipients or observers of project outcomes, internal stakeholders directly shape the operational mechanics of the project. Their roles are highly interconnected, and the success of one internal stakeholder often depends on the efficiency and collaboration of others.

a. Project Manager:

The Project Manager (PM) is the nerve centre of the project. More than just a coordinator, the PM functions as a strategic leader, risk mitigator, and communication hub. Their responsibilities extend beyond traditional scheduling and budgeting—they must balance the "iron triangle" of cost, scope, and time while safeguarding quality.

i. ***Leadership Style:*** Whether autocratic, democratic, or transformational, the leadership approach directly affects stakeholder morale and productivity. For example, transformational leadership fosters innovation and adaptability, while autocratic leadership might be suitable in high-risk, time-sensitive environments.

ii. ***Risk Management:*** The PM continuously identifies threats (e.g., budget overruns, technical delays) and opportunities (e.g., efficiency gains, process improvements).

iii. ***Stakeholder Bridge:*** They connect strategic visions articulated by top management with the tactical realities faced by team members. In doing so, the PM ensures alignment between the "boardroom" and the "work floor."

b. Project Team:

The project team consists of Subject Matter Experts (SMEs), engineers, developers, analysts, designers, testers, and support staff whose combined skills translate plans into tangible deliverables.

i. ***Role Clarity:*** Lack of defined roles often leads to overlapping responsibilities, duplication of work, or accountability gaps. Tools such as the RACI Matrix (Responsible, Accountable, Consulted, Informed) are critical in clarifying contributions.

ii. ***Access to Resources:*** Teams must have timely access to software, equipment, training, and information. Resource bottlenecks are among the most common causes of delays.

iii. ***Motivation and Environment:*** A psychologically safe and collaborative environment fosters productivity. When team members feel heard and valued, they exhibit higher commitment and innovation.

From a systems perspective, the project team is both the engine (doing the work) and the sensor (identifying emerging issues) of the project lifecycle.

c. Sponsors:

Sponsors are typically executives or senior leaders who provide not only the financial resources but also the political backing required for a project's continuation. Their role transcends funding—they are strategic champions who ensure the project remains visible and prioritised in the organisation's portfolio.

i. ***Financial Authority***: Sponsors unlock budgets and manage funding approvals.

ii. ***Organisational Legitimacy***: They communicate to other executives and departments that the project is strategically vital.

iii. ***Escalation Pathway***: When project conflicts exceed the PM's authority, sponsors intervene to resolve issues at a higher organisational level.

A disengaged sponsor is one of the most common reasons projects stall, while an active sponsor can accelerate decision-making and resource allocation.

d. Top Management:

Top management includes executive directors, vice presidents, and C-level officers who may not be involved in daily activities but play a critical role in shaping project governance and ensuring alignment with long-term organisational objectives.

i. ***Strategic Alignment***: They assess whether the project fits into the company's overall mission and vision.

ii. ***Resource Allocation***: Senior leaders ensure adequate manpower, funding, and technology are allocated, often making trade-offs with other strategic initiatives.

iii. ***Bureaucratic Navigation***: Their authority helps overcome institutional barriers, interdepartmental politics, or bureaucratic slowdowns.

Without top management endorsement, even well-structured projects can suffer from lack of legitimacy, resource starvation, or internal resistance.

Case Example 1:

IT Rollout in a Multinational Corporation:

When a global bank introduced a new core banking system, internal stakeholders played central roles. The project manager acted as the coordinator between IT developers and operations staff. Sponsors in the finance department secured funding, while top management justified the system's alignment with digital transformation goals. Failures in early communication between internal IT teams and branch staff almost derailed adoption. Corrective action involved structured workshops where team members and managers jointly reviewed workflows. This demonstrated the crucial role of active communication with internal stakeholders. When a global bank initiated the rollout of a new core banking system, internal stakeholders became the decisive force behind success and failure:

a. The Project Manager coordinated between IT developers building the platform and operational staff in branches who needed to adopt it. Early misalignment in workflows almost triggered project failure.

b. The Project Team—software engineers and business analysts—faced heavy workloads and pressure. Without clear role division, duplication of tasks created inefficiencies. Only after adopting a RACI framework did performance stabilise.

c. *Sponsors* from the finance department ensured consistent funding and advocated for the project when doubts arose about cost escalations.

d. *Top management* presented the initiative as part of a larger digital transformation strategy, thereby embedding it into the organisation's long-term roadmap.

The project initially suffered delays due to insufficient communication between developers and frontline banking staff. Corrective measures, such as cross-departmental workshops and interactive workflow reviews, allowed stakeholders to co-create solutions. This case illustrates that internal stakeholders are not isolated actors—they form an interdependent ecosystem where effective coordination, transparent communication, and aligned objectives can spell the difference between failure and success.

1.2 External Stakeholders:

External stakeholders exist outside the formal boundaries of the project-executing organisation, but their influence is often decisive. Unlike internal stakeholders, who focus on operational execution, external stakeholders judge the project's outcomes, enforce constraints, or provide critical inputs. Their perspectives are diverse, sometimes conflicting, and must be actively managed to prevent resistance or disruption. A failure to recognise external stakeholder dynamics has historically caused projects to face reputational crises, regulatory shutdowns, or financial overruns.

a. Customers/Clients:

Customers or clients are the primary beneficiaries of a project's deliverables. Their expectations—whether articulated in requirements or unspoken in user behaviour—are the true measure of success.

i. ***Expectation Alignment***: Even if a project meets technical specifications, if it fails to meet customer needs (e.g., usability, affordability, or reliability), it will be deemed unsuccessful.

ii. ***Feedback Loops***: Continuous involvement of customers through user testing, surveys, or pilot programmes ensures the project evolves with their needs.

iii. ***Economic Impact***: Customer satisfaction directly translates into adoption rates, return on investment, and long-term viability.

For instance, in an IT services project, misaligned interfaces or overly complex workflows can lead to rejection—even if the software is technically sound. Similarly, in public infrastructure, commuters measure success not by engineering excellence but by cost, convenience, and safety.

b. Suppliers/Vendors:

Suppliers and vendors provide materials, equipment, technology, and professional services essential for project execution. Their performance directly affects cost, schedule, and quality, making them integral to the project ecosystem.

i. ***Supply Chain Reliability***: Delays in material delivery can halt construction or production.

ii. ***Quality Assurance***: Inferior components (e.g., faulty wiring, substandard concrete, or outdated software) can compromise safety and performance.

iii. ***Strategic Partnerships***: Long-term vendor relationships often provide flexibility and innovation, whereas purely transactional relationships may introduce risks of unreliability.

iv. ***Contractual Risk Management***: Well-defined Service-Level Agreements (SLAs) and penalties for non-compliance help mitigate risks.

In complex projects such as metro rail development, global suppliers (e.g., for rolling stock, signalling systems, or tunnelling machinery) are critical. Their financial stability, logistical capacity, and compliance with technical standards shape the overall success of the project.

c. Government and Regulators:

Government agencies and regulatory bodies act as guardians of compliance. Their role is non-negotiable because they define the legal, safety, and environmental frameworks within which projects must operate.

i. ***Approvals and Licenses***: Construction, environmental clearance, land-use permissions, and operational licenses are granted—or withheld—by regulatory agencies.

ii. ***Oversight and Audits***: Regulators monitor adherence to safety protocols, financial transparency, and environmental sustainability.

iii. ***Penalties and Enforcement***: Non-compliance can lead to stoppages, fines, or even project termination.

iv. ***Policy Influence***: Shifting political priorities or policy reforms (e.g., green building codes, labour regulations) can alter project scope midway.

Engaging regulators proactively—by demonstrating compliance readiness, transparency, and willingness to adapt—reduces adversarial confrontations and accelerates approvals. In infrastructure projects, government agencies often act both as regulators and partners, creating dual roles that must be carefully managed.

d. Community/Public:

Communities represent the social dimension of project stakeholders. While they may not fund or execute the project, they are often the most directly affected by environmental, economic, and cultural impacts.

i. ***Acceptance or Resistance***: Community approval can grant legitimacy, while opposition—through protests, litigation, or activism—can stall progress indefinitely.

ii. ***Environmental and Social Impacts***: Communities are sensitive to issues like noise pollution, traffic disruptions, displacement, and ecological damage.

iii. ***Corporate Social Responsibility (CSR)***: Projects that incorporate community development initiatives (e.g., skill-building programmes and infrastructure upgrades) often earn goodwill that smooths implementation.

iv. ***Reputation and Media:*** Public perception, amplified through media and social networks, can shape investor confidence and political support.

Projects that disregard community concerns risk not only delays but also reputational damage that extends beyond the project itself to the organisation's long-term standing.

Case Example 2:

Urban Metro Rail Project (Delhi Metro):

In the development of the Delhi Metro Rail Corporation (DMRC), external stakeholders were pivotal. Commuters sought affordable, efficient transport. Suppliers provided advanced signalling systems. Regulatory bodies like the Ministry of Urban Development enforced safety compliance. Communities raised concerns about noise, land acquisition, and displacement. The DMRC mitigated these through public hearings, transparent compensation packages, and environmental safeguards, proving that sustained dialogue with external stakeholders can transform public scepticism into widespread acceptance. The Delhi Metro Rail Corporation (DMRC) exemplifies how external stakeholders shape outcomes in large-scale infrastructure projects.

a. *Customers/Commuters*: Millions of daily passengers sought affordable, efficient, and safe transportation. The project team prioritised punctuality, ticketing simplicity, and last-mile connectivity to meet commuter needs. High customer satisfaction later transformed the metro into the preferred urban transport mode.

b. ***Suppliers/Vendors*:** Advanced signalling systems were procured from global vendors, while construction materials came from both local and international suppliers. Early delays in tunnelling equipment procurement created bottlenecks, highlighting the importance of robust vendor contracts and contingency planning.

c. ***Government and Regulators***: The Ministry of Urban Development, municipal authorities, and safety regulators imposed strict compliance requirements. Metro safety certifications were mandatory before operational launch. Close alignment with government agencies enabled DMRC to secure approvals faster than most infrastructure projects of its scale.

d. ***Community/Public***: Local communities raised concerns about land acquisition, displacement, and noise pollution. DMRC engaged in public consultations, provided transparent compensation packages, and implemented environmental safeguards such as noise barriers and tree plantations. This proactive engagement reduced public resistance and built long-term trust.

The success of DMRC was not just an engineering feat—it was a stakeholder management triumph. By balancing commuter expectations, supplier reliability, government regulations, and community interests, DMRC transformed what could have been a politically contested project into one of India's most celebrated infrastructure achievements.

1.3 Hidden Influencers

Unlike formally recognised stakeholders—such as clients, vendors, or regulators—hidden influencers operate outside contractual frameworks and organisational charts. Their impact is often indirect but decisive, shaping project trajectories in ways project managers may underestimate. Ignoring hidden influencers can lead to unanticipated resistance, reputational setbacks, or even project collapse. By contrast, engaging them strategically can convert potential opposition into valuable allies, smoothing implementation.

a. Subject Matter Experts (SMEs):

***Role and Impact*:**

SMEs (Subject Matter Experts) bring deep technical, scientific, or domain-specific expertise critical for addressing complex design, engineering, or compliance issues. Their recommendations often shape core technical decisions, making them silent arbiters of quality and feasibility.

i. ***Technical Accuracy*:** Incorrect or overlooked SME input can lead to design flaws, non-compliance, or performance failures.

ii. ***Innovation Driver*:** SMEs often introduce cutting-edge methodologies or technologies that enhance project outcomes.

iii. ***Risk Mitigation*:** By anticipating potential pitfalls, SMEs reduce costly rework and ensure resilience in project design.

iv. ***Credibility*:** Regulatory bodies and clients may rely on SME endorsements to validate project feasibility, granting implicit authority to their judgements.

For instance, in pharmaceutical R&D projects, SME toxicologists and clinical researchers determine whether a new drug can move from trials to market approval. In infrastructure, structural engineers and geologists can decide the viability of tunnelling methods in metro projects.

b. Informal Leaders:

Role and Impact:

Informal leaders are individuals—within teams, communities, or interest groups—who command respect and influence despite lacking formal authority. Their ability to sway attitudes often surpasses that of official leaders.

i. ***Internal Influence:*** Within project teams, experienced staff or long-serving employees may become "go-to" figures whose support legitimises management directives.

ii. ***Community Impact***: In public projects, respected elders, teachers, or religious figures may shape collective community opinion about land acquisition, resettlement, or environmental disruption.

iii. ***Change Adoption***: Securing informal leaders' backing accelerates acceptance of new processes, technologies, or compensation schemes.

For example, during an IT system rollout in a large organisation, project managers often discover that employees look to senior staff with years of practical experience rather than official managers. Convincing such informal leaders ensures smooth adoption.

c. Unions:

Role and Impact:

In labour-intensive industries such as construction, mining, and manufacturing, trade unions and worker associations wield considerable negotiating power.

i. ***Workforce Stability:*** Strikes, go-slows, or protests can halt project execution, leading to schedule slippage and financial overruns.

ii. ***Negotiation Power:*** Unions influence wages, safety standards, working hours, and grievance redressal, often through collective bargaining agreements.

iii. ***Legal and Political Leverage:*** Well-organised unions may secure political backing, amplifying their influence beyond workplace negotiations.

iv. ***Partnership Potential:*** Constructive engagement with unions can foster collaboration, ensuring smoother project operations and improved worker morale.

For example, in shipyard construction or metro tunnelling projects, unions have demanded additional safety gear and risk allowances. While such demands can raise costs, fulfilling them often prevents prolonged disruptions.

d. Public Opinion Leaders:

Role and Impact:

Public opinion leaders—journalists, activists, academics, or social media influencers—shape how society perceives a project. Their narratives can escalate local disputes into national debates.

i. ***Media Amplification:*** Negative press can damage investor confidence, mobilise political opposition, and attract regulatory scrutiny.

ii. ***Framing of Issues:*** Opinion leaders decide whether a project is seen as a development milestone or an environmental threat.

iii. ***Reputational Risk:*** Social media campaigns, hashtags, and viral videos can rapidly influence perceptions across large audiences.

iv. ***Stakeholder Engagement Strategy:*** Proactively engaging with media and opinion leaders through transparent communication and outreach mitigates hostility.

For instance, in renewable energy projects like wind farms, local environmental activists may highlight ecological disruption, drawing media coverage that pressures developers to adopt additional safeguards.

The following figure 2 further clearly illustrates the different types of stakeholders in project management.

Figure 2:

TYPES OF STAKEHOLDERS

Types of Stakeholders

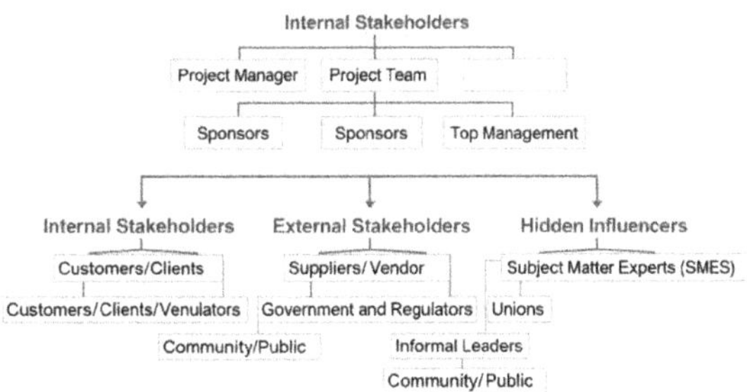

Case Example 3:

Community Infrastructure Development – Large Dam in Andhra Pradesh:

During the construction of a large dam in Andhra Pradesh, hidden influencers became decisive actors. Local environmental NGOs raised concerns over ecological damage. Informal village leaders influenced displaced families' responses to compensation. A popular journalist amplified public opinion against resettlement measures. These stakeholders were not official contracting parties, but their resistance created significant project delays. Only when project leaders engaged SMEs (Subject Matter Experts) to revise environmental safeguards and collaborated with informal leaders to restructure rehabilitation plans did the project regain momentum. This highlights the underestimated power of hidden influencers. The construction of a major dam in Andhra Pradesh illustrates the decisive role of hidden influencers:

1. ***Environmental NGOs (SMEs as Advocates):*** Local environmental organizations, staffed with domain experts, questioned the dam's impact on river ecosystems, fish migration, and downstream agricultural livelihoods. Their technical critiques forced project leaders to revise environmental safeguards, such as fish ladders and water release protocols.

2. ***Informal Village Leaders:*** Traditional village heads and respected elders influenced displaced families' willingness to accept compensation and resettlement packages. Initial resistance stalled rehabilitation efforts until these informal leaders were actively included in negotiations.

3. ***Unions:*** Construction worker unions demanded stricter

safety measures after accidents on-site. Their ability to mobilise labour stoppages compelled project authorities to revise workplace safety standards and invest in protective equipment.

4. ***Public Opinion Leaders:*** A prominent regional journalist amplified stories of displacement and ecological damage, sparking widespread public sympathy for affected communities. Social media campaigns further escalated scrutiny.

The turning point came when project managers shifted strategy:

1. They invited environmental SMEs to co-develop revised safeguards.

2. They collaborated with informal village leaders to restructure rehabilitation packages that respected cultural attachments to ancestral land.

3. They signed binding agreements with unions on worker safety.

4. They held open forums for journalists to access transparent project data.

This transformed adversarial relationships into conditional acceptance, allowing the project to regain momentum. The case demonstrates that hidden influencers, though unofficial, often hold veto power in shaping outcomes.

2. Tools for Stakeholder Analysis

Stakeholder analysis is a systematic decision-support tool that transforms complex social dynamics into structured insights. By categorising stakeholders based on their influence, interests, and expectations, project managers can design targeted engagement strategies instead of treating all stakeholders equally. This ensures efficient resource allocation, minimises conflict, and strengthens alignment between project objectives and stakeholder priorities.

Among the most widely adopted approaches is the Power–Interest Grid, which balances simplicity with practical applicability across industries such as infrastructure, IT rollouts, healthcare, and public policy projects.

2.1 Power–Interest Grid:

The Power–Interest Grid, developed within the broader discipline of stakeholder management, is a two-dimensional mapping framework. It classifies stakeholders by their:

1. ***Power*** – The degree of formal authority, resources, or influence they wield over project decisions.

2. ***Interest*** – The extent to which the stakeholder is affected by, or cares about, project outcomes.

By plotting stakeholders along these axes, project managers identify four strategic engagement zones:

a. High Power, High Interest (Manage Closely):

i. ***Characteristics***: These are stakeholders who both influence outcomes and are deeply invested in project success. They may include project sponsors, funding bodies, regulators, or key clients.

ii. ***Engagement Strategy***: Requires constant involvement, co-decision-making, and transparent communication. Regular progress reviews, governance meetings, and collaborative workshops ensure their continued confidence.

iii. ***Risks if Ignored*:** Loss of trust, funding withdrawal, or strategic derailment.

Technical Note: In complex projects, these stakeholders often form part of the steering committee or governance board, shaping scope adjustments and conflict resolution.

b. High Power, Low Interest (Keep Satisfied):

i. ***Characteristics:*** These stakeholders have the authority to influence or halt projects but are less concerned with daily details. Often senior executives, government oversight bodies, or high-level investors fall in this category.

ii. ***Engagement Strategy*:** Provide strategic briefings, milestone updates, and assurances without overloading them with operational details.

iii. ***Risks if Ignored*:** If their strategic priorities are neglected, they may intervene forcefully, disrupting project flow.

Technical Note: This quadrant often requires political navigation, as these stakeholders may have conflicting agendas across the organisational or governmental spectrum.

c. Low Power, High Interest (Keep Informed):

i. ***Characteristics*:** These stakeholders lack formal decision-making power but have a high degree of personal or professional concern about the project. Examples include frontline employees, community members, or advocacy groups.

ii. ***Engagement Strategy***: Use transparent communication, updates, and feedback mechanisms to sustain their support. For community projects, this could involve public hearings, newsletters, or participatory workshops.

iii. ***Risks if Ignored***: Frustration or alienation can lead to grassroots opposition, damaging reputation or operational stability.

Technical Note[CK1] *:* This group often becomes the voice of end-users and provides feedback loops that improve project design and delivery.

d. Low Power, Low Interest (Monitor):

i. ***Characteristics***: Stakeholders with minimal influence and limited involvement. They may include peripheral regulatory agencies, distant departments, or academic observers.

ii. ***Engagement Strategy:*** Monitor periodically to detect shifts in interest or power. Engagement may remain minimal unless their relevance escalates.

iii. ***Risks if Ignored***: Typically low, but a sudden contextual change (e.g., policy shift, legal action, or public mobilisation) can elevate their importance.

Technical Note*:* The dynamic nature of projects means that today's low-interest stakeholder may become a decisive influencer tomorrow. Continuous reassessment is essential.

Figure 3

Stakeholder Management

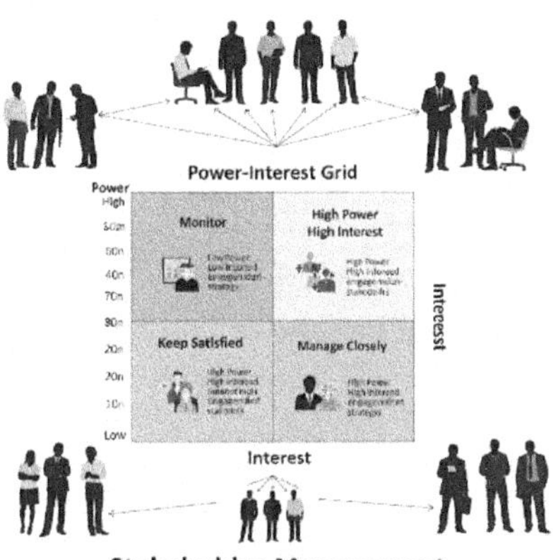

Stakeholder Management

This visual tool serves as an effective means of quickly and comprehensively analysing the entire stakeholder landscape. By mapping stakeholders according to their power and interest, project managers can gain valuable insights that enable them to design a targeted engagement plan. Such a plan maximises support, minimises resistance, and ensures that communication strategies are aligned with the needs and expectations of different stakeholder groups. The grid, in essence, is a straightforward yet powerful matrix that helps prioritise stakeholders and tailor management efforts appropriately.

The first quadrant, High Power, High Interest (Manage Closely), represents the most influential stakeholders in the project. These individuals or groups hold significant authority and deeply invest in the project's outcomes, making them crucial to its success. Project managers must engage actively with them, involve them in decision-making processes, and keep them fully informed of progress and challenges. Their sustained support can determine the overall direction and viability of the project.

In the second quadrant, High Power, Low Interest (Keep

Satisfied), stakeholders hold considerable influence but are not necessarily concerned with the project's operational details. For these stakeholders, it is essential to provide concise, high-level updates that assure them of progress and alignment with strategic goals. By keeping them satisfied without overwhelming them with unnecessary detail, project managers can secure their endorsement while respecting their limited interest in day-to-day activities.

The third quadrant, Low Power, High Interest (Keep Informed), consists of stakeholders who are keenly interested in the project yet lack the authority to exert direct influence. Despite their limited power, they can still play a vital role as advocates and supporters, especially when they feel included and valued. Regular updates, opportunities for feedback, and transparent communication help maintain their trust and engagement, ensuring that they contribute positively to the project environment.

Finally, the fourth quadrant, Low Power, Low Interest (Monitor), includes stakeholders who neither wield much influence nor demonstrate strong interest. While they do not require extensive engagement, it is prudent to monitor their perspectives and provide updates as necessary. Minimal effort should be devoted to this group, but maintaining awareness of their position helps prevent potential issues from being overlooked.

Case Example 4:

Government Digital Identity Rollout (India's Aadhaar Initiative):

In a government digital identity project (such as India's Aadhaar initiative), the grid became a strategic tool. Sponsors and government ministries (high power, high interest) were managed closely with daily updates. Citizens (low power, high interest) were kept informed via mass communication campaigns. Vendors (high power, low interest) were kept satisfied through contracts and audits. Distant academic researchers (low power, low interest) were simply monitored. This structured categorisation ensured that no group was overlooked, reducing implementation resistance. The rollout of Aadhaar, India's biometric-based digital identity programme, demonstrates the practical utility of the Power–Interest Grid:

1. ***High Power, High Interest (Manage Closely)***: Sponsors and central government ministries were deeply invested in Aadhaar's success. They required daily updates, detailed progress dashboards, and integration workshops with IT vendors and policy architects. Their endorsement was essential for sustaining momentum and funding.

2. ***High Power, Low Interest (Keep Satisfied):*** State-level bureaucrats and oversight committees had substantial power to influence adoption but were less concerned with daily technical hurdles. Quarterly review meetings and policy alignment briefings sufficed to maintain their satisfaction.

3. ***Low Power, High Interest (Keep Informed)***: Citizens, particularly those in rural areas, were highly interested, as Aadhaar affected access to welfare schemes. Mass communication campaigns, awareness drives, and grievance redressal systems ensured acceptance and reduced resistance.

4. ***Low Power, Low Interest (Monitor)***: Academic researchers and peripheral NGOs initially had little direct influence. However, as privacy debates intensified, their role shifted, highlighting the importance of continuous monitoring in anticipating new risk vectors.

This structured categorisation ensured balanced attention across groups, preventing neglect of vulnerable but interested stakeholders while avoiding over-engagement with peripheral actors. It illustrates how even a simple two-axis tool can anchor a sophisticated engagement strategy in high-stakes, large-scale projects.

2.2 Salience Model:

The Salience Model, introduced by Mitchell, Agle, and Wood (1997), is a conceptual advancement over simpler stakeholder classification frameworks. While tools like the Power–Interest Grid capture influence and involvement, the Salience Model introduces three interdependent attributes that more accurately reflect the dynamic and political nature of projects:

1. ***Power*** – The stakeholder's capacity to influence project outcomes through authority, resources, or coercion.

2. ***Legitimacy*** – The degree to which the stakeholder's involvement or claim is perceived as appropriate, valid, or justifiable within societal, legal, or organisational norms.

3. ***Urgency*** – The time sensitivity of the stakeholder's claim, defined by both criticality (how essential the issue is) and time pressure (how quickly it must be resolved).

By analysing stakeholders through this triad, the Salience Model classifies them into seven categories, each reflecting different combinations of the three attributes. This taxonomy allows project managers to differentiate between competing claims and to adapt engagement strategies as contexts evolve.

Stakeholder Classes in the Salience Model:

1. Dormant Stakeholders (Power only):

a. ***Characteristics***: They possess influence but lack legitimacy or urgency. Examples include wealthy investors not directly involved in project execution or government agencies with no current jurisdiction over the project.

b. ***Engagement Strategy***: Monitor closely; their influence can quickly escalate if they gain legitimacy or urgency.

2. Discretionary Stakeholders (Legitimacy only):

a. ***Characteristics:*** These stakeholders have a valid claim but no power or urgency to press it. Charitable organizations or interest groups supporting community welfare often fall here.

b. ***Engagement Strategy***: Acknowledge respectfully, but resource investment can remain minimal unless conditions shift.

3. Demanding Stakeholders (Urgency only):

a. ***Characteristics***: They are highly vocal, often creating "noise" without substantive power or legitimacy. Examples include individuals raising isolated complaints or media outlets seeking attention.

b. ***Engagement Strategy***: Monitor and manage expectations to prevent reputational risks.

4. Dominant Stakeholders (Power + Legitimacy):

a. ***Characteristics***: These stakeholders are both authoritative and credible, such as sponsors, regulatory bodies, or executive boards.

b. ***Engagement Strategy***: Provide regular updates and include them in governance mechanisms. They form the backbone of project legitimacy.

5. Dependent Stakeholders (Legitimacy + Urgency):

a. ***Characteristics***: They have valid and urgent claims but lack the power to enforce them. Community groups, environmental activists, or displaced populations often fall in this category.

b. ***Engagement Strategy***: Their concerns must be addressed through advocacy or alliances, as they often rely on external actors (courts, media, NGOs) to amplify their voices.

6. Dangerous Stakeholders (Power + Urgency):

a. ***Characteristics***: Without legitimacy, these stakeholders may resort to coercion, disruption, or even sabotage. Examples include radical activists or labour unions threatening strikes.

b. ***Engagement Strategy***: Requires careful management—addressing their urgency while maintaining legal and ethical boundaries.

7. Definitive Stakeholders (Power + Legitimacy + Urgency):

a. ***Characteristics***: The most critical category. Their claims are powerful, valid, and time-sensitive, meaning they must be prioritised immediately.

b. ***Engagement Strategy***: Allocate maximum resources, co-develop solutions, and ensure trust-building mechanisms are in place. Failure to respond risks legal action, project delays, or reputational collapse.

Distinctive Strength of the Model

The Salience Model recognises fluidity, unlike the Power–Interest Grid, which treats influence and concern as relatively static. A stakeholder initially classified as discretionary (legitimacy only) can become definitive if urgency escalates—for instance, a local community group gaining legal backing during an environmental compliance dispute. This makes the model especially valuable in dynamic environments with multiple, competing interests such as urban infrastructure, healthcare, and IT rollouts.

Case Example 5:

Bangalore's Namma Metro Expansion and Land Acquisition:

During Bangalore's Namma Metro expansion, landowners near construction sites became definitive stakeholders because they had power (legal rights), legitimacy (ownership), and urgency (immediate displacement risk). Environmental activists were dependent stakeholders—they had legitimacy and urgency but lacked direct power, relying on courts or media to amplify their influence. This mapping helped project managers prioritise negotiations with landowners while also devising communication campaigns to address activists' concerns. The Namma Metro expansion in Bangalore illustrates the application of the Salience Model:

1. ***Definitive Stakeholders (Power + Legitimacy + Urgency):***

Landowners whose properties were subject to acquisition. They had legal rights (legitimacy), legal recourse and financial leverage (power), and immediate displacement pressures (urgency). Negotiations, compensation packages, and legal clearances revolved around them.

2. ***Dependent Stakeholders (Legitimacy + Urgency)***: Environmental activists protesting tree felling and ecological disruption. While they lacked formal power, their claims were both valid and urgent. They relied on the media, courts, and NGOs to amplify influence.

3. ***Dominant Stakeholders (Power + Legitimacy)***: The Bangalore Metro Rail Corporation Limited (BMRCL) and the state government. They held both decision-making authority and legitimacy as project executors. Their role was central in balancing competing claims.

4. ***Dangerous Stakeholders (Power + Urgency)***: Disgruntled groups threatening to obstruct construction sites without legal standing. Though lacking legitimacy, their disruptive capacity required preventive measures such as police coordination and grievance redressal cells.

5. ***Discretionary Stakeholders (Legitimacy only):*** Urban NGOs advocating for cultural heritage preservation had valid claims but limited influence. They were acknowledged but not prioritised.

This categorisation allowed BMRCL to sequence stakeholder engagement systematically—first resolving land acquisition disputes with definitive stakeholders, while also addressing environmental groups through public hearings and environmental offset measures. By doing so, the project balanced legal compliance, social legitimacy, and operational continuity.

3. Stakeholder Engagement Strategies

Stakeholder identification and analysis lay the groundwork for project management, but they are merely precursors to the central task: constructive engagement. Engagement is not an isolated or static activity; rather, it is a continuous, adaptive process that evolves alongside project stages, external environments, and shifting stakeholder expectations. A project's technical soundness alone rarely guarantees success—its social acceptance and stakeholder alignment are equally decisive.

Effective engagement strategies encompass structured communication, empathetic listening, proactive conflict resolution, deliberate trust-building, and adaptive mechanisms that evolve throughout the project lifecycle. Each dimension requires deliberate planning, disciplined execution, and context-sensitive tailoring.

3.1 Communication Planning:

Communication represents the lifeline of stakeholder engagement. It ensures that information flows seamlessly across hierarchical levels, geographical boundaries, and interest groups. A robust communication plan does not merely describe "who sends what to whom." It specifies:

a. ***Content***: the type and granularity of information.

b. ***Frequency***: the timing and regularity of dissemination.

c. ***Medium***: channels such as dashboards, town halls, or newsletters.

d. ***Ownership***: clarity on who delivers the message and who is accountable.

The critical principle is audience-tailored communication. For example, project sponsors require aggregated dashboards highlighting cost, schedule, and benefit realisations, while frontline technical teams need task-specific instructions, dependencies, and progress updates. Misaligned communication—too granular for executives or too abstract for operational staff—erodes confidence, breeds frustration, and often manifests as delays, rework, or mistrust.

Case Example 6:

London Crossrail Project:

To mitigate disruptions across London communities, the Crossrail team instituted multi-layered communication strategies. Weekly community newsletters provided layperson-friendly updates on traffic diversions, noise mitigation, and timelines. Simultaneously, interactive dashboards were delivered to government sponsors, displaying progress against key milestones and expenditure forecasts. This structured, yet differentiated approach minimised complaints, bolstered community acceptance, and kept political stakeholders aligned.

3.2 Active Listening:

Stakeholder engagement must be reciprocal, extending beyond broadcasting project messages to carefully listening and responding to concerns. Active listening entails more than hearing—it involves probing for unspoken anxieties, validating perspectives, and incorporating legitimate concerns into project decision-making.

Active listening cultivates:

a. ***Empathy***: strengthening relationships by acknowledging human dimensions of project impacts.

b. ***Risk Discovery***: surfacing latent threats that may not appear in formal reports.

c. ***Collaboration***: fostering shared ownership in solutions.

Case Example:

Canadian Healthcare IT Rollout:

A major Electronic Patient Record (EPR) deployment initially faced strong resistance from medical staff, who feared usability issues and adverse effects on patient safety. Rather than impose top-down directives, project leaders organised listening sessions and focus groups. Physicians voiced concerns about interface complexity, while nurses highlighted patient throughput risks. By revising workflows and customising training modules based on feedback, the project turned sceptics into advocates, transforming potential failure into organisational acceptance.

3.3 Conflict Resolution:

Conflict in stakeholder environments is not anomalous but inevitable. With multiple groups holding divergent values, priorities, and constraints, friction points emerge naturally. What distinguishes successful projects is not the absence of conflict but the capacity to manage it constructively.

Effective conflict resolution relies on:

a. ***Anticipation***: identifying high-risk areas where conflicts are likely.

b. ***Dialogue***: maintaining open channels even under tension.

c. ***Techniques***: applying structured processes such as negotiation, mediation, facilitation, or arbitration.

The objective is not to suppress disagreements but to channel them into win–win outcomes that reconcile project imperatives with stakeholder needs.

Case Example 7:

South African Mining Project:

Conflicts erupted between labour unions pressing for stringent safety measures and management constrained by escalating operational costs. Left unchecked, this could have escalated into strikes and project paralysis. The leadership responded by creating joint health and safety committees, which empowered workers to co-design safety protocols alongside engineers. This shared-problem-solving framework transformed adversarial dynamics into cooperative engagement, preserving productivity while enhancing worker welfare.

3.4 Building Trust:

Trust constitutes the bedrock of sustainable stakeholder engagement. Unlike formal contracts, trust is intangible yet profoundly consequential—it underpins credibility, resilience, and long-term collaboration. Projects earn trust through:

a. ***Transparency***: candidly sharing decisions and rationale.

b. ***Consistency***: delivering on commitments without shifting goalposts.

c. ***Honesty***: acknowledging setbacks rather than obscuring them.

Trust accelerates project momentum because stakeholders, assured of integrity, extend patience and flexibility during inevitable crises.

Case Example:

Dubai Metro Project:

Despite budgetary overruns, the Dubai Metro earned stakeholder confidence by delivering completed sections punctually and maintaining open disclosures about cost escalations. By consistently honouring promises and proactively communicating difficulties, the management preserved trust even amid adversity, ensuring continued government support and public buy-in.

3.5 Adaptation:

Stakeholder engagement is inherently dynamic, shaped by shifting political, social, and technical contexts. Early-stage stakeholders may fade in relevance, while new groups may rise as the project progresses. Engagement strategies that remain static risk obsolescence and resistance. Periodic reassessment enables projects to remain agile, legitimate, and aligned with evolving environments.

Case Example 8:

Global COVID-19 Vaccination Rollouts:

At the outset, regulators, pharmaceutical suppliers, and logistics providers were the most critical stakeholders. As vaccination campaigns scaled, new actors emerged—community leaders, influencers, religious authorities, and educational institutions—whose role in building public trust and increasing uptake became decisive. Governments that adapted strategies from a policy-driven communication model to localised, grassroots engagement witnessed markedly higher vaccination success compared to those that failed to pivot.

Stakeholder engagement lies at the heart of project sustainability. While analytical models such as the Power–Interest Grid and Salience Model offer structured entry points into stakeholder mapping, true engagement transcends categorisation. It resides in the disciplined practice of communication, the empathy of listening, the diplomacy of conflict resolution, the credibility of trust-building, and the agility of adaptation.

Real-world experiences—from London Crossrail to Canadian healthcare IT, from South African mines to Dubai Metro, and from global vaccination campaigns to urban infrastructure expansions—reveal that projects succeed not merely by delivering technical outputs but by nurturing enduring relationships.

Projects that disregard stakeholders often encounter costly opposition or collapse outright. Conversely, those that embed inclusive engagement strategies create not only successful deliverables but also legacies of collaboration, trust, and shared value—an outcome that distinguishes sustainable projects from transient successes.

4. Understanding Project Stakeholders in Software Project Management

In software project management, stakeholders are any individuals, groups, or organizations who may influence, be influenced by, or perceive themselves to be influenced by a project's decisions, activities, or outcomes. They hold a vested interest in whether the project succeeds or fails. Unlike many other industries, software projects often involve a particularly diverse and complex mix of stakeholders, ranging from highly technical professionals to end-users with little or no technical background.

Recognising this diversity is a first step toward managing expectations effectively and ensuring the project delivers value.

The spectrum of stakeholders in software projects is broad. At the core is the project team—developers, designers, testers, and analysts—who are focused on technical feasibility and product quality. The project sponsor provides financial backing and is primarily concerned with return on investment and strategic alignment. End-users, who directly interact with the software, prioritise usability, functionality, and problem-solving, making their acceptance critical for adoption. Management and department heads, though less involved in daily activities, evaluate the project's alignment with organisational objectives and its impact on their teams. Subject Matter Experts (SMEs) contribute specialised knowledge of business processes, ensuring the software meets real-world needs. Beyond the organisation, external stakeholders such as vendors, partners, regulators, or even the public may also influence the project, bringing contractual, compliance, or reputational considerations.

Managing stakeholders effectively is not optional—it is a strategic necessity. Poor stakeholder engagement can result in undocumented requirements, leading to a product that fails to meet user needs. It can also create resistance to change, where even a technically flawless solution is rejected due to a lack of buy-in. Moreover, unconsulted stakeholders often introduce late requirements or conflicting demands, resulting in delays, scope creep, and budget overruns. Effective stakeholder management ensures alignment, reduces risks, and strengthens support across the project lifecycle.

A structured approach to stakeholder management involves four key steps. The first is identification, where the project team and business leaders collaborate to map out all potential stakeholders. Next is analysis, which assesses each stakeholder's level of influence and interest, often visualised in a power/interest grid. High-power, high-interest stakeholders require close engagement, while high-power, low-interest stakeholders need periodic high-level updates. Conversely, low-power but highly interested stakeholders should be kept informed and involved, whereas low-power, low-interest groups require only minimal updates. Engaging involves customising communication strategies for each group, ranging from formal reviews with sponsors to informal user check-ins. Finally, monitoring ensures stakeholder needs and roles are continually reassessed, since interests may evolve as the project progresses.

By proactively identifying, analysing, engaging, and monitoring stakeholder groups, software project managers can foster collaboration, secure critical support, and manage the complex human dynamics that often define project success. Effective stakeholder management transforms potential conflicts into opportunities for alignment, ensuring the software not only functions as intended but also gains acceptance and delivers lasting business value.

PART II

PLANNING AND INITIATING PROJECTS

CHAPTER 4: DEFINING PROJECT GOALS AND OBJECTIVES

1. Project Planning, Goals and Objectives

Project planning and initiation are indispensable phases within the project management lifecycle, as they establish the critical foundation upon which the entire project is constructed. These phases serve not merely as procedural formalities but as strategic cornerstones that shape the trajectory of the project. Defining goals and objectives during this stage ensures clarity of purpose, fosters alignment with broader organisational missions, and secures commitment from key stakeholders. In practice, this means translating the organisation's strategic vision into a set of actionable plans that can be operationalised within realistic constraints. Without well-defined goals and objectives, a project risks becoming directionless, vulnerable to scope creep, and misaligned with stakeholder expectations.

1.1. Project Goals and Objectives:

Goals

Goals represent the broad, overarching aspirations that

articulate what the project seeks to accomplish. They are visionary in nature and reflect long-term outcomes rather than immediate deliverables. For instance, a company may set a project goal such as "expand into new international markets" or "enhance digital transformation to improve operational efficiency". These high-level statements do not prescribe *how* the result will be achieved but instead define the ultimate purpose and intent. In this sense, goals provide the guiding compass that ensures all project activities remain aligned with organisational strategy and stakeholder priorities.

Objectives

Objectives, in contrast, are more precise and operational in scope. They break down aspirational goals into clear, actionable steps that can be systematically executed and evaluated. Objectives must be specific, measurable, and time-bound to serve as effective benchmarks of success. For example, if the goal is to improve customer satisfaction, an objective might be "to reduce average customer complaint resolution time from five days to two days by a specific time (Q2)." This distinction between goals and objectives is crucial, as it balances visionary ambition with practical accountability, enabling project teams to remain both inspired and disciplined throughout the execution phase.

1.2. SMART Objectives and Their Application:

The SMART framework offers a robust methodology for refining objectives into actionable, outcome-focused commitments. Each component of SMART—Specific, Measurable, Achievable, Relevant, and Time-bound—functions as a quality checkpoint to ensure that objectives are neither vague nor unattainable but instead provide a precise roadmap for project execution.

a) ***Specific:*** Objectives must articulate clearly defined outcomes, avoiding ambiguity or generalised aspirations. A specific objective addresses the *who, what, when, where, and why* of the task. For example, instead of setting a broad target like *"improve product quality,"* a specific objective would be *"reduce product defect rates by 15% through the implementation of an enhanced quality assurance process by the end of Q3".* This level of precision ensures shared understanding and reduces the likelihood of misinterpretation among team members.

b) ***Measurable:*** A well-crafted objective must incorporate quantifiable indicators that allow progress to be tracked and validated. Measurability is essential for performance monitoring and evaluation. For example, an objective framed as *"increase website traffic"* is vague, while *"increase website traffic by 25% within six months"* provides a tangible metric against which progress can be gauged. Measurement criteria often include dimensions such as time, cost, quality, and quantity, enabling project managers to apply performance dashboards, KPIs, and reporting systems effectively.

c) ***Achievable:*** Objectives must be realistic within the given constraints of time, budget, resources, and technical feasibility. Overly ambitious targets may demoralise the team, foster burnout, or lead to project failure, while overly modest ones fail to stretch capabilities or deliver meaningful value. An achievable objective finds the balance, ensuring that it challenges the team without exceeding organisational capacity. For example, planning to *"launch ten new international offices in one year"* may be unrealistic for a mid-sized company, whereas setting a target of *"opening two regional offices in strategic markets within 12 months"* may be both challenging and attainable.

d) ***Relevant:*** Objectives should align closely with broader organisational goals and the strategic vision of the project. This ensures that project efforts contribute meaningfully to organisational growth rather than being isolated activities. For instance, a technology firm whose strategic priority is to lead in sustainable innovation should frame objectives that advance eco-friendly solutions, such as *"develop and launch an energy-efficient product line by Q1 of the specific year".* Relevance anchors objectives in organisational strategy and helps justify resource allocation.

e) ***Time-bound:*** Objectives must be grounded in a clear timeframe that defines both deadlines and milestones. Time constraints establish urgency, discipline, and accountability, ensuring that project activities do not drift indefinitely. For example, the objective *"increase market share"* lacks direction, but when specified as *"increase market share by 10% within the next 18 months through targeted marketing campaigns,"* it introduces a clear deadline that motivates timely progress and facilitates performance review.

1.3. Application of SMART Objectives:

Applying the SMART framework transforms abstract ideas into actionable strategies that guide day-to-day project management. This structured approach enhances clarity by eliminating ambiguity, thereby enabling all stakeholders to share a unified understanding of what needs to be achieved. Clear objectives reduce the risk of miscommunication, prevent scope misalignment, and ensure consistent focus across the project lifecycle.

SMART objectives also strengthen accountability by explicitly assigning ownership of tasks to individuals or teams. When responsibilities are clearly tied to measurable outcomes and deadlines, accountability becomes embedded within the project structure. This, in turn, empowers team members to take ownership of their work, fosters trust among stakeholders, and supports transparent performance evaluation.

Furthermore, the SMART approach facilitates effective progress tracking through measurable indicators and milestones. Project managers can leverage these metrics to monitor achievements in real time, identify deviations from the plan, and initiate corrective actions promptly. This data-driven approach not only improves oversight but also enables adaptive management in response to evolving circumstances.

Finally, SMART objectives serve as powerful motivational tools. By providing the team with a clear sense of direction, achievable challenges, and tangible success markers, they foster enthusiasm and sustain momentum throughout the project lifecycle. Team members can experience a sense of accomplishment as milestones are reached, reinforcing commitment and driving continuous improvement. In sum, SMART objectives transform vague intentions into structured, actionable plans that form the backbone of successful project execution.

2. Linking Goals to Organisational Strategy

A project does not exist in isolation; rather, it is part of a larger ecosystem that reflects the priorities, ambitions, and competitive positioning of the organisation. For this reason, a project's success is contingent upon its alignment with the organisation's overarching strategic plan. Establishing this linkage ensures that the project is not perceived merely as an operational exercise but as a deliberate investment that advances the company's long-term vision and strategic objectives. Projects that lack such alignment risk consuming valuable resources without delivering meaningful contributions to organisational growth, thereby undermining both project credibility and overall strategic progress. The process of linking project goals to organisational strategy typically involves three interrelated dimensions: strategic alignment, resource allocation, and stakeholder buy-in.

2.1 Strategic Alignment:

Strategic alignment is the cornerstone of effective project management, as it ensures that project goals are deliberately crafted to reinforce the organisation's mission, vision, and core strategic pillars. Alignment prevents projects from drifting into isolated initiatives that, while operationally sound, fail to deliver real value to the business. Instead, each project should serve as a tactical vehicle for achieving broader strategic priorities.

For example, if an organisation's strategic goal is to *"improve customer service and retention,"* then implementing a new Customer Relationship Management (CRM) system would directly support this objective by enhancing client engagement, streamlining communication, and enabling personalised service delivery. Similarly, a company with a strategic vision centered on sustainability might initiate projects aimed at reducing carbon emissions or improving energy efficiency. In each case, alignment ensures coherence between day-to-day project activities and the organisation's long-term vision.

Strategic alignment also facilitates better communication between project teams and leadership, as it positions the project as a means to fulfil already recognised priorities. This creates a shared language of value and impact, enabling project managers to justify decisions and demonstrate contributions in terms executives and stakeholders can immediately understand.

2.2 Resource Allocation:

Effective linkage between project goals and organisational strategy is also critical for securing and justifying resource allocation. Projects inevitably require investments of financial capital, human expertise, and technological infrastructure, and organizations must make deliberate choices about where to direct these limited resources. A project that demonstrates clear alignment with strategic priorities is more likely to receive funding and personnel support because it is perceived as contributing directly to organisational competitiveness and growth.

For instance, in a technology company aiming to expand its digital transformation strategy, projects focused on developing Artificial Intelligence (AI)-driven analytics tools or cloud-based platforms would be prioritised for investment, as these initiatives underpin the organisation's future market relevance. Conversely, projects that cannot establish a direct link to strategic goals may be deprioritised or even terminated, as they represent misaligned or lower-value efforts.

Moreover, aligning goals with strategy ensures that resources are not wasted on projects that are unlikely to deliver long-term returns. It creates a rigorous justification framework where every dollar, hour, and system invested is tied back to advancing strategic outcomes. This strengthens accountability in project governance, improves portfolio management, and increases the organisation's ability to make evidence-based investment decisions.

2.3 Stakeholder Buy-in:

No project can achieve lasting success without the active support of its stakeholders, particularly senior leadership, decision-makers, and influential sponsors. Linking project goals to organisational strategy provides

3. Examples of Well-Crafted Objectives

The application of the SMART framework transforms broad and often abstract goals into tangible, actionable, and measurable objectives that guide project execution. By integrating the dimensions of Specific, Measurable, Achievable, Relevant, and Time-bound, objectives become more than aspirational statements; they serve as structured commitments that can be systematically tracked and evaluated. To demonstrate the practical utility of this framework, the following examples from a software development project and a marketing campaign illustrate how goals can be translated into SMART objectives that drive organisational success.

3.1 Example 1: Software Development Project:

Goal: To launch a new mobile application.

SMART Objective: *"To develop and deploy a fully functional iOS and Android application with a user rating of 4.5 or higher by the specific time, to increase active users by 20% in the first six months post-launch."*

a) ***Specific:*** The objective clearly defines the deliverable—a mobile application developed for both iOS and Android platforms. By identifying the product scope, it removes ambiguity and sets expectations for the development team, quality assurance specialists, and stakeholders.

b) ***Measurable:*** Progress and success can be evaluated using quantifiable indicators, namely a minimum user rating of 4.5 and a 20% increase in active users within six months. These metrics enable performance tracking through app store reviews, user analytics, and adoption rates, offering objective evidence of value creation.

c) ***Achievable***: The timeline, extending to the end of the particular year, allows adequate scope for coding, design iterations, user testing, debugging, and deployment. This ensures the target is ambitious yet realistic, given the complexity of software development lifecycles.

d) ***Relevant***: The objective directly aligns with the goal of launching a new mobile application. Moreover, it supports organisational priorities such as market expansion, customer engagement, and digital transformation, reinforcing the project's strategic contribution.

e) ***Time-bound:*** A fixed year-end deadline offers a clear and specific time boundary. Additionally, the six-month window for tracking user adoption and satisfaction introduces accountability for post-launch performance, ensuring that success is not measured solely by release but also by market reception.

This example highlights how a broad goal can be refined into a comprehensive objective that integrates development, deployment, and user adoption metrics, thereby ensuring alignment across technical and business dimensions.

3.2 Example 2: Marketing Campaign:

Goal: To increase brand awareness.

SMART Objective: *"To execute a social media marketing campaign that generates 50,000 new followers and a 15% increase in website traffic from social channels within the* *fourth quarter of the specific year, with a budget not exceeding $50,000."*

a) ***Specific*****:** The objective specifies the activity—executing a social media marketing campaign—and clearly identifies its intended impact: follower growth and increased web traffic. By narrowing the scope to social channels, the objective delineates the medium and audience.

b) ***Measurable:*** Success is defined in quantifiable terms: 50,000 new followers and a 15% increase in website traffic. These metrics are trackable using social media analytics tools, web analytics dashboards, and campaign performance reports, making progress assessment objective and transparent.

c) ***Achievable*****:** With a budget cap of $50,000 and a three-month execution window, the objective provides realistic constraints that balance ambition with feasibility. Given the scale of digital advertising and influencer marketing today, these targets can be met without overextending resources.

d) ***Relevant*****:** The objective directly supports the overarching goal of increasing brand awareness, a critical driver of customer acquisition, loyalty, and market competitiveness. It also demonstrates alignment with broader marketing strategies that emphasise digital presence and customer engagement.

e) ***Time-bound:*** The completion deadline—the *fourth quarter of the specific year*—sets a clear timeframe, allowing campaign planners to structure pre-launch, execution, and post-campaign analysis phases. This time constraint enhances accountability and enables the marketing team to synchronise with other organisational initiatives.

This example illustrates how a strategic intent—enhancing

brand visibility—can be operationalised into a concrete objective with clearly defined deliverables, budgetary controls, and timelines.

These examples underscore the transformative value of the SMART framework in project management. By embedding clarity, measurability, feasibility, alignment, and time constraints into objectives, organizations move beyond aspirational goals to actionable commitments. Whether applied to technical domains such as software development or strategic initiatives like marketing, SMART objectives serve as critical tools for ensuring precision, accountability, and strategic impact. They not only provide direction for project teams but also offer tangible benchmarks for evaluating progress and success.

4. Defining Project Goals and Objectives for the Software Project

In software project management, goals and objectives act as the compass that guides decisions from design through deployment. While often used interchangeably, they serve distinct roles. Goals define the broad, long-term ambitions of a project, such as increasing revenue or enhancing customer experience, whereas objectives break these ambitions into specific, measurable steps that drive day-to-day execution. Understanding this distinction ensures teams maintain both clarity of vision and precision in execution, reducing ambiguity and misalignment.

Defining project *goals* and objectives at the outset is critical in the software industry, where complexity, rapid change, and stakeholder expectations are constant. Goals anchor the project to the organisation's broader business strategy, ensuring that the software delivers tangible value rather than becoming a stand-alone technical exercise. Articulated objectives also help prevent scope creep by establishing boundaries that keep features and functionalities aligned with the project's purpose. At the same time, well-defined goals empower the development team. When developers, designers, and testers understand the "why" behind the work, they are more motivated, engaged, and capable of making informed decisions independently. Objectives also provide the metrics for measuring success, ensuring that the project is judged not merely on delivery but on whether it achieved the desired outcomes, such as adoption, efficiency, or customer satisfaction.

A proven approach to defining *objectives* is the SMART framework, which ensures that objectives are specific, measurable, achievable, relevant, and time-bound. For example, instead of stating that the application should be "faster," an objective would specify reducing average page load times by 50 percent. This precision creates accountability and enables progress tracking while aligning with business priorities and deadlines.

Consider a software project aimed at building a new e-commerce website. The overarching goal may be to increase online sales and improve customer satisfaction. To achieve this, the project team might set SMART objectives such as raising the conversion rate from 2.5 to 4 percent, reducing cart abandonment by 15 percent within three months of launch, delivering a minimum viable product with core purchasing functionality in six months, and implementing a customer feedback widget to capture user ratings.

Another objective might ensure that the platform supports at least 100 concurrent users with a response time of under two seconds. By breaking down the broader goal into these targeted objectives, the team gains a clear and actionable roadmap. Each design decision, architectural choice, and feature prioritisation can then be evaluated against the objectives, ensuring the project stays aligned with its purpose and delivers measurable business outcomes.

CHAPTER 5: REQUIREMENT GATHERING STRATEGIES

Requirement gathering, also referred to as requirement elicitation, is a pivotal phase within the project lifecycle, particularly under planning and initiation. This stage defines the "what" of the project, forming the blueprint from which design, execution, and delivery unfold. Inaccurate, incomplete, or ambiguous requirements can result in scope creep, cost overruns, and project failure, while robust requirement gathering ensures clarity, stakeholder alignment, and measurable outcomes.

This chapter explores requirement gathering techniques, documentation and validation processes, and the comparative perspectives of Agile and traditional approaches, emphasising their practical application with examples and structured proformas.

1. Techniques for Requirement Gathering

Requirement elicitation leverages multiple techniques to capture diverse perspectives and insights from stakeholders. No single technique is universally adequate; rather, projects achieve better accuracy and stakeholder satisfaction when multiple methods are employed in combination.

1.1 Interviews:

***Description*:**

Interviews are structured or semi-structured conversations held with stakeholders to elicit their needs, pain points, and expectations. They may be structured (guided by predefined questions), semi-structured (with flexibility to probe deeper), or unstructured (open-ended and conversational). Interviews allow project teams to uncover tacit knowledge —insights that stakeholders may not articulate unless prompted through dialogue.

***Application*:**

Interviews are best suited for key stakeholders, subject matter experts, and end-users. For example, in an ERP system implementation, interviewing finance managers may reveal compliance needs, while interviews with warehouse supervisors uncover operational bottlenecks.

Proforma:

***Interview Guide Example**:*

1. Stakeholder Name: ____________________
2. Role/Department: ____________________
3. Key Questions:

a. What are your primary responsibilities?

b. What challenges do you face in the current process/system?

c. What outcomes would you expect from the new solution?

d. Are there specific constraints (time, budget, regulations) that must be considered?

Mini Case Study 1:

Microsoft Office Product Development:

The evolution of Microsoft Office 365 illustrates how structured stakeholder engagement can directly influence product innovation and adoption. Unlike earlier versions of Microsoft Office, which primarily focused on desktop productivity, Office 365 needed to address the emerging demands of enterprise collaboration, mobility, and cloud computing. To achieve this, Microsoft relied heavily on structured interviews with enterprise clients, particularly IT administrators, CIOs, and business leaders who were responsible for large-scale deployments.

These interviews went beyond surface-level feedback and explored specific pain points with legacy software. Common challenges included version conflicts when multiple people worked on the same file, lack of real-time collaboration tools, difficulties in securing sensitive enterprise data, and limited integration with emerging cloud platforms. Such issues were especially pressing in global organizations with geographically dispersed teams that required seamless digital collaboration.

From these conversations, key requirements were distilled, which directly shaped the development roadmap of Office 365. Among the most critical features identified were:

1. ***Real-time co-authoring*** – allowing multiple users to work

on the same document simultaneously without conflicts.

2. ***Robust data security*** – incorporating enterprise-grade encryption, compliance with international standards, and advanced administrative controls.

3. ***Cloud integration*** – enabling access to documents anytime, anywhere, while ensuring synchronisation across devices and platforms.

By systematically capturing and prioritising these needs, Microsoft ensured that the product aligned with the real-world workflows of enterprises, rather than being a top-down feature push. This user-centred requirements gathering was pivotal to the success of Office 365, allowing it to become the standard platform for enterprise-scale collaboration globally. The case demonstrates the power of structured interviews as a requirements engineering technique, ensuring that business-critical software delivers tangible value to its target users.

Proforma:

Interview Template:

To replicate Microsoft's approach, organizations can use a structured interview template to capture and organise stakeholder insights systematically. Below is a detailed explanation of each element in the provided proforma:

1. *Stakeholder Name & Role*: Identifies who is being interviewed and their position within the organisation. This ensures clarity on the stakeholder's perspective—whether technical, managerial, or operational.

2. *Key Responsibilities*: Outlines the primary duties of the stakeholder. Understanding responsibilities provides context for their needs; e.g., an IT administrator may focus on security and deployment, while a project manager may prioritise usability.

3. ***Current Challenges***: Documents pain points and inefficiencies in the existing system. These challenges often become the foundation for defining requirements that truly address user frustrations.

4. ***Desired Features***: Captures the stakeholder's vision of what improvements or functionalities would enhance their work. This ensures that development is driven by user value rather than assumptions made by the design team.

5. ***Must-have vs. Nice-to-Have Priorities***: Helps in prioritisation by distinguishing between essential requirements and secondary enhancements. This distinction is critical in agile and traditional projects alike, where trade-offs must often be made due to resource constraints.

6. ***Follow-up Action Items***: Ensures continuity by identifying what needs to be clarified, validated, or explored further after the interview. This creates a feedback loop that maintains engagement with stakeholders throughout the project lifecycle.

By employing a template, development teams can systematically capture, analyse, and prioritise stakeholder input, reducing ambiguity and ensuring that products align closely with real-world business needs.

Filled-out sample interview form

Sample Interview Form – Enterprise IT Administrator

Stakeholder Name & Role: Michael Rodriguez – Senior IT

Administrator, GlobalCorp Inc.

Key Responsibilities:

1. Managing enterprise-wide IT infrastructure, including productivity tools and collaboration platforms.

2. Ensuring compliance with company data policies and industry regulations (e.g., GDPR, HIPAA).

3. Supporting over 5,000 employees across multiple global offices.

4. Coordinating with security teams to manage access controls and protect sensitive data.

Current Challenges:

1. Employees working across regions struggle with version conflicts when multiple team members edit Word or Excel files simultaneously.

2. Lack of real-time collaboration tools slows down decision-making, especially for cross-departmental projects.

3. Remote teams often rely on third-party file-sharing tools, raising data security and compliance concerns.

4. Difficulty in maintaining software updates and patching across distributed devices.

Desired Features:

1. Real-time co-authoring in Word, Excel, and PowerPoint.

2. Seamless cloud integration to enable file access from any location and device.

3. Centralised administrative controls for managing user permissions and monitoring usage.

4. Advanced security features, including encryption, multi-factor authentication, and compliance reporting.

5. Mobile app support for employees working on the go.

Must-Have vs. Nice-to-Have Priorities:

1. *Must-Have*: Real-time collaboration, enterprise-grade security, cloud-based file access, administrative dashboards.

2. *Nice-to-Have*: Integration with third-party tools (e.g., Slack, Salesforce), offline editing with auto-sync, advanced analytics on usage patterns.

Follow-up Action Items:

1. Provide Michael with a demo of the current Office 365 beta highlighting real-time co-authoring features.

2. Schedule a security deep-dive session with the compliance team to validate Office 365's encryption standards.

3. Conduct a pilot programme with a select group of 100 employees to test cloud integration and gather feedback.

1.2 Workshops:

Description:

Workshops are structured, collaborative sessions where multiple stakeholders come together in a facilitated environment to define, refine, or validate project requirements. Unlike one-on-one interviews, workshops capitalise on the collective intelligence of diverse participants. They typically include brainstorming exercises, scenario mapping, consensus-building techniques, and even conflict-resolution strategies. A skilled moderator or facilitator ensures that every voice is heard, that discussions remain focused, and that outcomes are documented systematically. This approach allows for the simultaneous elicitation of ideas, clarification of conflicts, and prioritisation of requirements, making workshops highly efficient in complex project settings.

Application:

Workshops are particularly valuable in multi-stakeholder projects where alignment across departments or disciplines is critical. For instance, in designing a new customer service model, input from marketing (who understand customer communication), IT (who manage backend systems), sales (who drive customer relationships), and support teams (who deal directly with customer queries) is equally important. Conducting workshops allows these groups to articulate their perspectives openly, identify overlaps, and reconcile differences in real time. Moreover, workshops foster collective ownership of requirements, reducing resistance to change later in the project lifecycle. They also accelerate decision-making compared to sequential interviews, since competing interests are addressed collaboratively in a shared forum.

Example:

Consider a healthcare project aimed at developing an Electronic Health Record (EHR) system. If requirements are gathered solely from IT staff, the system may end up technically sound but clinically impractical for doctors and nurses. Conversely, focusing only on clinicians might compromise security, regulatory compliance, or data integration. A well-designed workshop that brings together doctors, nurses, IT staff, and administrators allows stakeholders to surface their unique concerns and negotiate trade-offs. For example, doctors may emphasise usability and speed of data entry, nurses may stress the need for bedside access through mobile devices, while administrators may highlight compliance with HIPAA or GDPR. Through structured dialogue, the workshop balances clinical usability with data security and compliance, producing requirements that are comprehensive, realistic, and accepted by all parties involved.

Mini Case Study 2:

Toyota Lean Manufacturing Systems:

When Toyota expanded its Lean Production System across global plants, it faced a significant challenge: aligning practices across different regions, each with unique cultural, operational, and workforce characteristics. To address this, Toyota employed requirement workshops as a central strategy. These workshops brought together plant managers, engineers, and shop-floor workers—ensuring representation from strategic decision-makers to frontline operators.

During the sessions, participants engaged in brainstorming exercises to surface inefficiencies, recurring bottlenecks, and waste within existing workflows. Plant managers highlighted issues of standardisation across international facilities, engineers emphasised the need for robust visual management tools like Kanban boards, and workers contributed practical insights into reducing repetitive tasks and minimising downtime.

The workshops also included group workflow mapping,

where stakeholders visually charted current processes, allowing the identification of overlaps, redundancies, and wasteful steps. Once pain points were clearly visualised, Toyota used consensus-building techniques to prioritise solutions. For example, waste reduction metrics and standardised workflows were elevated as top requirements, while other localised improvements were categorised as region-specific enhancements.

By using this collaborative approach, Toyota ensured that all stakeholders not only contributed to shaping requirements but also felt ownership over the Lean implementation. This method fostered global alignment, minimised resistance to process changes, and facilitated a smooth rollout of the Lean Production System across diverse plants.

Proforma:

Workshop Agenda:

To replicate Toyota's approach, a structured workshop agenda helps ensure productive and outcome-driven sessions. Below is the agenda expanded in detail:

1. Icebreaker and Role Introductions:

Begin with short introductions where participants state their role, responsibilities, and perspectives on the process being discussed. This creates a comfortable environment, reduces hierarchical barriers, and ensures participants understand the diversity of views present.

2. Brainstorming Session (Problem Areas):

Facilitate open-ended discussions to surface pain points,

inefficiencies, or unmet needs. Using techniques such as sticky notes, mind mapping, or digital brainstorming tools, participants list problems without immediately judging or filtering ideas.

3. Group Mapping of Workflows:

Participants collectively draw or model the current workflow, including steps, hand-offs, delays, and decision points. This exercise makes invisible processes visible and uncovers redundancies or waste that individual interviews might miss.

4. Prioritisation of Requirements (MoSCoW Method):

Once requirements or improvements are identified, they are ranked using the MoSCoW method:

1. ***Must-have*** – Essential for success.
2. ***Should-have*** – Important but not critical.
3. ***Could-have*** – Nice-to-have features.
4. ***Won't-have (this time)*** – Deferred for later consideration. This structured prioritisation helps limit resources to the most impactful areas.

5. Consensus-Building and Documentation:

Finally, the group engages in guided discussion to resolve disagreements, build collective ownership, and formally document agreed requirements. A summary report is circulated after the workshop, ensuring clarity and accountability.

Sample Workshop Agenda:

Toyota Lean Manufacturing System:

(This sample illustrates the step-by-step progression of a real workshop, highlighting the capture of varied viewpoints and the conversion of group consensus into concrete actions.)

Project: Global Rollout of Lean Production System
Workshop Date: March 00, 20XX
Facilitator: Kaizen Coach – Lean Transformation Team
Participants:

1. ***Plant Manager:*** (Mr Sato)
2. ***Production Engineer***: (Ms Lee)
3. ***Quality Supervisor:*** (Mr Kumar)
4. ***Line Worker Representative:*** (Ms Hernandez)
5. ***IT Systems Analyst:*** (Mr O'Neill)

1. Icebreaker and Role Introductions

1. ***Mr Sato (Plant Manager)*:** Oversees production operations and is responsible for output and cost efficiency. *Main challenge*: balancing standardisation with local flexibility.

2. ***Ms Lee (Engineer):*** Designs and optimises workflows. *Concern*: lack of uniform visual management across different plants.

3. ***Mr Kumar (Quality Supervisor)*:** Ensures defect-free output. *Challenge*: inconsistent defect reporting methods between regions.

4. ***Ms Hernandez (Line Worker Rep)*:** Represents assembly line staff. *Concern*: repetitive manual tasks leading to

fatigue and errors.

5. ***Mr O'Neill (IT Analyst)***: Supports digital tracking tools. *Concern*: poor integration between local reporting systems and global dashboards.

2. Brainstorming Session (Problem Areas)

Collected Inputs:

1. Lack of standard workflow documentation across plants (Sato).

2. Visual management tools (e.g., Kanban boards) vary—confusing shift handovers (Lee).

3. Defect reporting is inconsistent—each plant has its own coding system (Kumar).

4. Excessive manual logging of tasks; repetitive work wastes time and lowers morale (Hernandez).

5. IT systems fragmented; no central dashboard for real-time monitoring (O'Neill).

3. Group Mapping of Workflows

Visual Mapping Findings (summarised):

1. Step overlap between "inspection" and "quality check" creates redundancy.

2. Material movement from storage to line involves three approvals, delaying flow.

3. Reporting of daily production is paper-based in some plants, digital in others—leading to delayed insights.

4. Prioritisation of Requirements (MoSCoW Method)

Table 1:

MoSCoW Method

Requirement	MoSCoW Priority	Notes
Standardized workflow documentation across all plants	**Must-Have**	Foundational to Lean rollout.
Unified Kanban/visual management system	**Must-Have**	Critical for shift continuity.
Digital defect reporting system with global codes	**Should-Have**	Needed but can be phased in.
Automating repetitive logging tasks (barcode scanners, sensors)	**Should-Have**	Reduces waste but requires upfront investment.
Centralized IT dashboard for real-time monitoring	**Could-Have**	Useful but not urgent in first rollout phase.
Region-specific enhancements (custom reporting formats)	**Won't-Have (this time)**	To be revisited after global rollout.

5. Consensus-Building and Documentation

Agreed Actions:

1. Immediate rollout of standard workflow documentation and Kanban system in all plants.
2. Pilot programme for digital defect reporting in two regions before global adoption.
3. Explore automation solutions for repetitive tasks within

the next quarter.

4. The IT team to design a roadmap for a centralised dashboard (to follow after workflow standardisation).

Closing Statement (Facilitator):

"All participants agree that standardisation and visual management are the highest priorities. By focusing first on must-haves, Toyota ensures consistent practices across regions while building a foundation for future digital enhancements."

1.3 Observation:

Description:

Observation is a requirements elicitation technique that involves directly watching stakeholders perform their day-to-day tasks in their natural work environment. Unlike interviews or workshops, which rely on participants explaining their activities, observation allows analysts to witness actual behaviours and workflows as they occur in real time. This approach helps uncover implicit practices, shortcuts, and workarounds that users often do not articulate because they take them for granted or do not consciously recognise them as noteworthy. For example, a worker may use an unofficial spreadsheet to track progress, or a customer service agent may develop a personal shorthand system to speed up repetitive tasks. By capturing these unspoken practices, observation provides a more authentic and holistic understanding of how processes truly function.

Application:

Observation is particularly effective in workflow-intensive

environments where tasks are complex, repetitive, or highly procedural. In a manufacturing assembly line, for instance, observation might reveal that operators frequently pause work due to unclear visual instructions or that they move tools inefficiently, increasing cycle time. Similarly, in customer service desks, an analyst might notice that representatives spend excessive time on manual data entry across multiple systems, suggesting a clear opportunity for automation or system integration. Observation is also valuable when users struggle to articulate requirements or when analysts want to validate whether stated practices align with actual behaviours. By grounding insights in reality, observation ensures that requirements address not just what people say they do, but also what they actually do.

Proforma:

Observation Notes Template:

1. Process Observed: ____________________
2. Location: ____________________
3. Date/Time: ____________________
4. Observed Activities: ____________________
5. Potential Issues Identified: ____________________
6. Improvement Opportunities: ____________________

Sample Observation Notes:

The filled-out examples below illustrate how structured observation notes capture both visible workflows and hidden inefficiencies, presenting practical improvement opportunities through realistic cases from a manufacturing floor and a call centre.

Sample Observation Notes Form – Manufacturing Floor

1. ***Process Observed:*** Assembly of car door panels

2. ***Location:*** Toyota Manufacturing Plant – Final Assembly Line

3. ***Date/Time:*** March 00, 20XX, 10:00 AM – 12:00 PM

4. ***Observed Activities:***

    a. Workers manually align door panels before bolting them.

    b. Frequent tool switching between pneumatic drill and torque wrench.

    c. Paper-based checklists used to verify torque values.

    d. Operators occasionally wait for parts due to delayed supply cart delivery.

5. ***Potential Issues Identified:***

    a. Manual alignment causes slight delays and ergonomic strain.

    b. Tool switching adds unnecessary seconds to each cycle.

    c. Paper checklists slow down verification and increase the risk of errors.

    d. Just-in-time parts delivery not synchronised with workflow pace.

6. ***Improvement Opportunities:***

a. Introduce alignment jigs to reduce manual effort.

b. Provide multi-functional tools to minimise switching.

c. Replace paper checklists with digital tablets linked to torque sensors.

d. Enhance supply chain synchronisation with automated alerts for cart deliveries.

Sample Observation Notes Form – Call Centre

1. ***Process Observed***: Customer service handling of billing enquiries

2. ***Location***: XYZ Telecom Call Centre, Hyderabad

3. ***Date/Time***: April 00, 20XX, 2:00 PM – 3:30 PM

4. ***Observed Activities***:

a. Agents log into two separate systems: CRM for customer data and Billing Portal for invoices.

b. Repeated copy-pasting of customer ID between systems.

c. Agents put customers on hold while verifying payment histories.

d. Sticky notes on desks used to remember shortcut codes.

5. ***Potential Issues Identified***:

a. Dual-system entry increases handling time per call.

b. Copy-paste errors occasionally result in incorrect account lookups.

c. Hold times frustrate customers and reduce first-call resolution.

d. Reliance on sticky notes suggests poor system usability.

6. *Improvement Opportunities*:

a. Integrate CRM and the billing portal into a single interface.

b. Automate account lookup once customer ID is entered.

c. Add real-time payment history retrieval to reduce hold times.

d. Provide in-system tooltips or reference guides to replace sticky notes.

Mini Case Study 3:

Amazon UX Improvement:

Amazon leverages ethnographic observation to refine its user experience. For example, UX researchers observed customers struggling with the checkout process on mobile devices. These observations revealed unspoken frustrations —such as difficulty toggling between product pages and the cart—that were not articulated in surveys. Amazon responded by simplifying the mobile checkout workflow, adding a one-click buy feature. This small but powerful change contributed to higher conversion rates.

Proforma – Observation Log

1. Date & Context of Observation:
2. User Role and Environment:
3. Tasks Observed:
4. Unspoken Behaviours / Tacit Knowledge:
5. Pain Points Identified:
6. Analyst's Interpretation:

1.4 Prototyping

Description:

Prototyping is a requirements elicitation technique that involves building a preliminary, simplified model of a system to help stakeholders visualise and evaluate potential solutions. These prototypes can vary widely in fidelity—from basic paper sketches or storyboards to interactive digital wireframes and clickable mock-ups. While prototypes may not include full functionality, they provide stakeholders with a tangible representation of the proposed solution, bridging the gap between abstract requirements and practical implementation. By interacting with prototypes, stakeholders can better express their preferences, identify missing elements, and surface usability concerns that might not emerge through documents or verbal descriptions alone. This process significantly enhances clarity and reduces ambiguity in requirements gathering.

Application:

Prototyping is especially valuable in user interface (UI) and user experience (UX)-intensive projects, where design choices strongly influence usability and adoption. For example, mobile applications, websites, and customer portals benefit greatly from prototyping because they require careful attention to navigation flows, screen layouts, and interactive elements. Stakeholders who may struggle to articulate abstract design needs often find it easier to react to something they can see and touch. By enabling early experimentation and adjustment, prototyping helps teams avoid costly redesigns later in the development cycle. It also creates opportunities for iterative feedback loops, where each successive prototype incorporates stakeholder input and converges toward a refined solution.

Example:

Consider the design of an e-commerce website. A team may initially propose a multi-step checkout process, with separate pages for shipping details, payment, and order confirmation. However, when stakeholders interact with a prototype, they may express frustration with the complexity and prefer a single-page checkout that streamlines the process. By testing and refining this requirement during the prototyping phase, the team avoids implementing a workflow that would have been inconvenient for users. Prototyping thus acts as an early detection system for design flaws, allowing developers to make user-friendly choices before full-scale development begins.

Mini Case Study 4:

NASA Aerospace Projects:

A striking example of prototyping in action comes from NASA's spacecraft design efforts. During the development of the Orion spacecraft cockpit, NASA engineers created high-fidelity mock-ups of control panels well before final construction. Astronauts were invited to interact with these prototypes in simulated mission environments, providing feedback on aspects such as control placement, accessibility in zero gravity, and overall usability. For instance, certain switches that seemed logically placed on diagrams turned out to be awkward to reach when astronauts were suited up. By gathering this feedback early, NASA was able to refine cockpit layouts and eliminate design flaws before investing in costly manufacturing. This iterative cycle of prototype–test–refine significantly reduced rework, improved astronaut safety, and ensured that requirements aligned with real-world operational needs.

Proforma – Prototype Feedback Sheet

1. Prototype Version & Date: ____________________

2. Feature Demonstrated: ____________________

3. User Feedback (Usability / Functionality / Aesthetics): ____________________

4. Issues Identified: ____________________

5. Suggested Improvements: ____________________

6. Action Items: ____________________

The following are realistic, filled-out Prototype Feedback Sheets, presented in two variations—one for the e-commerce case and another for the NASA cockpit case—to demonstrate how the template works in practice clearly.

Sample Prototype Feedback Sheet:

E-Commerce Website:

1. Prototype Version & Date: V2.1 – March 00, 20XX

2. Feature Demonstrated: Checkout process (multi-step vs. single-page flow)

3. User Feedback (Usability / Functionality / Aesthetics):

a. Users found the multi-step checkout confusing and time-consuming.

b. Preference for a single-page layout with shipping, payment, and confirmation sections visible at once.

c. Liked the clean design and colour coding for required fields.

4. Issues Identified:

a. Users abandoned the cart when forced to create an account before checkout.

b. The payment gateway button was not clearly visible on mobile screens.

c. Progress bar in multi-step flow caused anxiety ("too many steps").

5. Suggested Improvements:

a. Enable the guest checkout option.

b. Redesign the mobile payment button with a larger touch target.

c. Consolidate steps into a single-page checkout with collapsible sections.

6. Action Items:

a. A UX designer to create a single-page prototype (V2.2) by the specific date.

b. Mobile developer to adjust button size and placement.

c. Product owner to approve guest checkout feature.

Sample Prototype Feedback Sheet:

NASA Orion Cockpit:

1. Prototype Version & Date: High-fidelity Mock-up V3 – July 00, 20XX

2. Feature Demonstrated: Control panel layout and switch placement

3. User Feedback (Usability / Functionality / Aesthetics):

a. Astronauts reported difficulty reaching critical switches while suited up.

b. Positive feedback on touchscreen readability under simulated lighting conditions.

c. Mixed reactions to colour-coded warning indicators —some felt red/amber overlap was confusing.

4. Issues Identified:

a. Switch clusters located near the lower panel created ergonomic strain in zero-gravity training.

b. Touchscreens are prone to accidental activation when brushing against gloves.

c. Emergency override lever not clearly differentiated

from routine toggles.

5. Suggested Improvements:

a. Relocate critical switches to shoulder-height zones.

b. Add glove-sensitive shielding around touchscreens.

c. Redesign the emergency lever with a unique shape and haptic feedback.

6. Action Items:

a. The engineering team is to adjust the panel layout for Prototype V3.1 by August.

b. Human factors specialists to conduct additional glove-use testing.

c. The visual design team to rework the warning indicator colour scheme for clarity.

2. Requirement Documentation and Validation

Once elicited, requirements must be documented and validated to ensure completeness, consistency, and accuracy. Documentation serves as a contract between stakeholders and the project team, while validation ensures alignment with stakeholder expectations.

2.1 Requirement Documentation:

Requirement documentation serves as the backbone of any project, providing a structured record of what the system or product is expected to achieve. This documentation is often formalised through industry-standard templates such as the Software Requirements Specification (SRS) or the Business Requirements Document (BRD). Both documents ensure that project teams, stakeholders, and developers share a common understanding of the goals, scope, and deliverables.

Well-documented requirements are not just lists of features; they are carefully crafted statements that capture stakeholder needs and translate them into actionable technical or business objectives. To achieve this, they must adhere to the following qualities:

1. Unambiguous – Each requirement should allow for only one interpretation, eliminating vagueness or subjectivity. For instance, instead of writing "the system should be fast," a precise requirement would be "the system should process 1,000 transactions per second".

2. Complete – All essential details should be captured without leaving room for assumptions. A complete requirement answers the *what*, *why*, and sometimes the *how*.

3. Consistent – Requirements must be internally coherent and free of contradictions. If one requirement specifies that "all users must log in," another should not state that "guest users can bypass login."

4. Traceable – Each requirement must link back to a business goal or stakeholder need, ensuring relevance and providing a clear path for validation and testing. Traceability allows teams to track requirements from their origin (business case) through implementation and testing.

High-quality requirement documentation reduces misunderstandings, prevents costly rework, and provides a basis for verification and validation throughout the project lifecycle.

Table 2:

Proforma: Requirement Specification

Req. ID	Requirement Description	Priority (High/ Med/Low)	Category (Functional / Non-Functional)	Source / Stakeholder	Traceability (Linked Business Goal / Process)	Acceptance Criteria	Remarks
RQ-001							
RQ-002							
RQ-003							

Table 3:

Proforma – Requirement Specification

Requirement ID	Requirement Description	Priority	Source	Traceability	Status
R-001	System must allow users to reset passwords via email verification.	High	IT Security Lead	Business Goal: Improve User Access	Draft
R-002	Generate monthly financial reports in PDF and Excel formats.	Medium	Finance Dept.	Goal: Regulatory Compliance	Approved

Mini Case Study 5:

Banking Industry (JPMorgan Chase):

The banking sector operates in a highly regulated and risk-sensitive environment, where precision in requirements documentation is not just beneficial but critical. A strong example of this can be seen in JPMorgan Chase's development of a fraud detection system.

To address increasing threats of financial fraud, JPMorgan Chase initiated a large-scale system upgrade aimed at improving detection accuracy, reducing false positives, and maintaining seamless customer experiences. During the requirements gathering phase, the team documented over

500 individual requirements in a comprehensive Business Requirements Document (BRD).

These requirements were organised into two distinct categories:

1. Functional Requirements – These describe what the system should do, such as defining detection thresholds for suspicious transactions, setting reporting frequencies for alerts, and establishing escalation workflows for fraud analysts. For example, a requirement could specify, *"The system must flag transactions exceeding $10,000 conducted outside the customer's usual geography within 2 seconds."*

2. Non-Functional Requirements (NFRs) – These captured system qualities and constraints, such as performance, reliability, and usability. In this case, an important NFR was that the system must respond to suspicious activity in under 2 seconds to ensure real-time fraud mitigation without delaying legitimate transactions. Another NFR addressed system availability, requiring 99.99% uptime due to the mission-critical nature of banking services.

To ensure alignment with business goals, JPMorgan Chase used requirements traceability matrices. These matrices provided a clear mapping between stakeholder needs, regulatory requirements, and system features. For example, a regulatory mandate from the U.S. Office of the Comptroller of the Currency (OCC) requiring real-time fraud monitoring was directly linked to the system's rapid-response requirement. This ensured nothing was overlooked and that compliance obligations were fully met.

The rigour of this documentation approach reduced the likelihood of omissions, duplication, or contradictions across requirements. It also streamlined validation and testing, since each test case could be traced back to a documented requirement. As a result, JPMorgan Chase was able to deliver a system that not only enhanced fraud detection but also maintained customer trust by balancing security with user experience.

2.2 Requirement Validation:

Requirement validation is the critical process of ensuring that the requirements captured and documented are not only technically correct but also genuinely reflective of stakeholder needs and expectations. The purpose of validation is to answer the question, *"Are we building the right system?"* In contrast to verification, which checks whether the system is being built correctly, validation emphasises alignment with business goals, stakeholder expectations, and end-user usability.

For requirements to pass validation, they must meet several key qualities: accuracy, testability, feasibility, and alignment with objectives. Validation prevents the costly problem of developing features that either do not solve the right problem or fail to integrate into real-world workflows.

Techniques of Requirement Validation

1. Reviews and Walkthroughs:

Formal or semi-formal reviews are organised, in which stakeholders—end users, business analysts, developers, and testers—scrutinize the documented requirements. Walkthroughs involve a step-by-step presentation of the requirements, during which stakeholders are invited to critique, identify ambiguities, or highlight contradictions. For example, a finance system requirement that reads *"system shall generate daily reports"* may prompt a stakeholder to question whether weekly or real-time reporting is also needed, preventing downstream conflicts.

2. Prototypes:

Developing prototypes—ranging from low-fidelity sketches to high-fidelity interactive wireframes—helps stakeholders visualise the future system. This is especially useful in projects with a strong UI/UX component. By interacting with a prototype, users can confirm whether the documented requirements match their expectations. For instance, in a retail mobile app project, a prototype might reveal that the checkout flow feels too long, even if the requirements seemed adequate on paper.

3. Test Case Derivation:

A highly practical validation technique is to attempt to create test cases directly from the documented requirements. If test scenarios cannot be derived, this indicates the requirement is vague, incomplete, or unmeasurable. For example, the requirement "system must be user-friendly" is subjective and untestable. A refined, validated requirement would state: "The system must allow first-time users to complete onboarding in under 5 minutes without external assistance." This measurable condition allows testers to design clear acceptance criteria.

Mini Case Study 6:

Healthcare (Electronic Health Records – EHR):

A real-world example of requirement validation can be observed in the healthcare sector during the rollout of Epic Systems Electronic Health Records (EHR) software in U.S. hospitals. EHR systems are highly complex, integrating clinical workflows, administrative tasks, and regulatory compliance into a single platform. If requirements are misaligned, the impact could lead to medical errors, inefficiencies, or compliance failures.

During the Epic implementation, requirement validation was treated as a multi-stakeholder exercise. Physicians, nurses, and hospital administrators were directly engaged in the validation process through walkthrough sessions and scenario testing. For example:

1. ***Patient Intake***: Validation exercises confirmed that the digital intake form captured all necessary demographic and insurance details while remaining user-friendly for front-desk staff.

2. ***Medication Orders***: Test cases were derived from requirements to ensure that physicians could enter, review, and update prescriptions efficiently, with built-in alerts for drug interactions.

3. ***Discharge Summaries:*** Walkthroughs confirmed that summaries generated automatically at patient discharge were aligned with both physician notes and hospital reporting requirements.

The hospitals used test case derivation to confirm that each documented requirement was implementable. A physician might attempt to validate: "The system must support e-prescriptions in under 10 seconds per order." If the prototype or early system iteration took 30 seconds, the requirement would be flagged for revision.

By validating requirements upfront, Epic and its partner hospitals avoided costly redesigns post-deployment. More importantly, this process improved adoption rates, since clinical staff felt their real workflows had been understood and incorporated. Errors that might have occurred if requirements had been ambiguous or incomplete were significantly reduced, directly benefiting patient care and operational efficiency.

In summary, requirement validation acts as a quality gate for requirement documentation. Through reviews, prototyping, and test case derivation, stakeholders confirm that what is written on paper can be built, tested, and used in practice. The EHR case study illustrates how rigorous validation is particularly indispensable in safety-critical domains like healthcare, where alignment with clinical workflows ensures both compliance and patient safety.

The Requirement Validation Checklist is shown in two parts: a proforma template and a completed sample drawn from the Healthcare EHR case.

Table 4:

Requirement Validation Checklist

Proforma (Template)

Validation Criterion	Question to Ask	Status (Pass/ Fail/Needs Revision)	Comments / Notes	Stakeholder Sign-off
Clarity	Is the requirement unambiguous and easy to understand?			
Completeness	Does it include all necessary details for development and testing?			
Consistency	Is it free from contradictions with other requirements?			
Testability	Can clear test cases be derived from the requirement?			
Feasibility	Is it technically and operationally achievable within constraints?			
Traceability	Is it linked to business goals, user needs, or regulations?			
Stakeholder Alignment	Do all relevant			

	stakeholders agree with the requirement?			
Prototyping / Simulation Feedback	Was the requirement validated via a prototype, mock-up, or scenario walkthrough?			
Prioritization	Is the requirement categorized appropriately (e.g., Must-have, Should-have)?			
Approval	Final decision after validation cycle			

Table 5:

Filled-Out Sample – Healthcare EHR Project

Validation Criterion	Question to Ask	Status	Comments / Notes	Stakeholder Sign-off
Clarity	Is the requirement unambiguous and easy to understand?	▯ Pass	Requirement: *"System must allow physicians to generate discharge summaries auto-populated with patient history."* Clear and unambiguous.	Dr. K. Rao (Chief Physician)
Completeness	Does it include all necessary details for development and testing?	⚠ Needs Revision	Discharge summary lacks details on whether it must include lab results. To be clarified in next review.	IT Business Analyst
Consistency	Is it free from contradictions with other requirements?	▯ Pass	No conflicts with patient intake or medication order workflows.	Nursing Supervisor
Testability	Can clear test cases be derived from the requirement?	▯ Pass	Test case: *"Discharge summary must generate in <15 seconds and include diagnosis, treatment, prescriptions, and follow-up plan."*	QA Lead
Feasibility	Is it technically and operationally achievable within constraints?	▯ Pass	Confirmed by development team: achievable within current system architecture.	IT Architect
Traceability	Is it linked to business goals, user needs, or regulations?	▯ Pass	Requirement supports regulatory compliance for patient discharge documentation.	Compliance Officer
Stakeholder Alignment	Do all relevant stakeholders agree with the requirement?	▯ Pass	Physicians, nurses, and admins all agree this is critical.	Project Manager
Prototyping / Simulation Feedback	Was the requirement validated via a prototype, mock-up, or scenario walkthrough?	▯ Pass	Prototype demoed; physicians confirmed usability and layout.	Clinical Validation Team
Prioritization	Is the requirement categorized appropriately (e.g., Must-have, Should-have)?	▯ Pass	Marked as **Must-have** for go-live.	Steering Committee
Approval	Final decision after validation cycle	▯ Approved	Requirement validated, ready for development.	Project Sponsor

3. Agile User Stories vs. Traditional Requirement

Documents

Approaches to documentation diverge significantly between traditional (waterfall) models and agile frameworks, reflecting their underlying philosophies.

3.1. Focus

1. Traditional Documents:

Traditional project documentation, such as the Software Requirements Specification (SRS), serves as a technical blueprint that emphasises functionality, performance parameters, and system constraints. These documents are typically created in the early stages of the project and are intended to capture, in exhaustive detail, what the system must achieve and how it should behave under various conditions.

Such documentation reflects an upfront planning philosophy, where requirements are carefully gathered, analysed, and documented before design or development begins. The goal is to reduce ambiguity and establish a single source of truth for all stakeholders. In this sense, traditional documents are often contract-like in nature, formalising the mutual understanding between clients, developers, and managers. Once approved, they serve as a binding reference point against which progress is measured and deliverables are validated.

While this approach ensures clarity, traceability, and accountability, it can also lead to challenges in projects where requirements evolve rapidly. The rigidity of traditional documentation means that any changes usually require a formal revision process, often resulting in additional costs or delays. Despite these limitations, such documents remain foundational in projects that demand predictability, compliance, and strict adherence to standards, such as government, defence, aerospace, or large-scale engineering projects.

Mini Case Study 7:

Defence Systems (U.S. DoD Projects):

Defence projects, particularly those undertaken by the United States Department of Defence (DoD), provide a classic example of the reliance on traditional documentation practices. Consider a complex system such as a missile defence programme. These systems demand extraordinary levels of precision, safety, and reliability, where even minor deviations can lead to catastrophic consequences.

To address these high stakes, requirements documentation is prepared with meticulous detail. In many DoD projects, specifications extend to thousands of pages, encompassing aspects such as technical performance, system integration, safety regulations, interoperability with allied systems, cybersecurity safeguards, and compliance with federal defence standards. This exhaustive documentation functions as a legal, contractual, and technical foundation, ensuring that every stakeholder—engineers, contractors, government auditors, and defence agencies—shares a common reference point.

The rigidity of this approach serves a critical purpose. Since these systems must undergo rigorous testing, certification, and auditing, traditional requirements provide legal defensibility and traceability. Every requirement can be mapped to a corresponding design, test case, and verification result, which is essential in defending against legal disputes, liability claims, or congressional scrutiny. This traceability is also vital for safety assurance, ensuring that the deployed system performs reliably in combat or national defence scenarios.

However, this rigidity also has drawbacks. Because requirements are contractually locked at the outset, any change requests—whether due to evolving threats, new technology, or shifting policy—necessitate a formal and bureaucratic change management process. These processes are both expensive and time-consuming, often delaying deployment timelines by months or even years. For instance, integrating a new sensor or upgrading a software module may require multiple layers of approval, re-validation of compliance, and extensive re-documentation, all of which inflate costs.

Despite these challenges, traditional documentation remains the cornerstone of defence projects. In domains where failure is unacceptable and accountability is paramount, the benefits of exhaustive requirements, strict compliance, and legal defensibility outweigh the drawbacks of reduced flexibility. The DoD's reliance on traditional documentation demonstrates the enduring relevance of this approach in safety-critical and mission-critical environments, even in an era when many industries are shifting toward Agile and adaptive practices.

***2. Agile Stories*:**

Agile user stories focus on user value, but not on technical details. They evolve iteratively, allowing flexibility as the project progresses. In contrast to traditional documentation, which emphasises exhaustive technical specifications, Agile stories place the user at the centre of requirements definition. A typical Agile user story is expressed in a simple, structured format such as "As a [*type of user*], I want [*a specific feature*] so that [*I achieve a benefit/value*]." For example, "As a student, I want to download lecture notes so that I can revise offline." This framing highlights the value and purpose of the functionality rather than focusing on the technical mechanics of its implementation.

The underlying philosophy of Agile stories is that requirements should evolve over time. Instead of locking in every detail upfront, Agile treats stories as living artefacts. They begin in a simple form and gradually acquire depth through collaboration, sprint planning, backlog refinement, and ongoing team discussions. Technical details are not fixed from the start but are captured progressively, which allows development teams to remain flexible and responsive to new insights, user feedback, or shifting market demands.

Agile stories embody three core principles. *First*, user-centricity, which ensures that requirements are written in the language of the user, making them accessible to both technical and non-technical stakeholders. *Second*, flexibility, which allows stories to evolve iteratively, with acceptance criteria and design specifics refined closer to the point of implementation. *Third*, collaboration, which shifts emphasis away from static documents and toward continuous conversations between product owners, developers, designers, and users.

By adhering to these principles, agile stories help teams stay focused on delivering user value through small, incremental releases. This approach minimises the risk of developing overly complex systems that may not align with user expectations, while fostering a development process that is adaptive, transparent, and driven by actual needs.

Mini Case Study 8:

Spotify Agile Model:

A well-recognised real-world example of agile storytelling in practice is the Spotify Agile Model. Spotify, one of the world's leading music streaming platforms, adopted Agile principles early in its growth to maintain both innovation and responsiveness in a highly competitive digital marketplace. By prioritising adaptability, Spotify was able to deliver continuous improvements and experiment with user-focused features at a pace that outstripped many of its competitors.

At the centre of Spotify's model are squads—small, cross-functional, semi-autonomous teams that operate much like "mini start-ups." Each squad takes ownership of a particular feature or aspect of the user experience, ensuring accountability and focus. These squads rely heavily on user stories as their guiding framework for development. Instead of beginning with highly technical specifications, squads start with simple, user-centred narratives that highlight needs and expected value.

For example, one such story might state, *"As a listener, I want to create collaborative playlists so that my friends and I can add songs together."* This concise expression identifies the user (a listener), the desired functionality (collaborative playlist creation), and the value delivered (shared music experiences with friends). By framing requirements in this way, squads maintain clarity about the purpose of development efforts and avoid being distracted by purely technical considerations.

The details underlying these stories—such as the playlist interface design, permission settings, or real-time synchronisation mechanisms—are not rigidly defined at the outset. Instead, they are worked out iteratively through sprint planning, backlog refinement, and regular team discussions. This allows Spotify to remain flexible, incorporating feedback, adjusting priorities, and refining solutions as development progresses.

This Agile approach enabled Spotify to rapidly prototype and release features in response to emerging user demands, test and refine concepts in real time with actual listeners, and sustain a culture of experimentation and innovation. By embedding adaptability into its development model, Spotify successfully stayed ahead of its rivals in the global streaming market.

Ultimately, the Spotify case demonstrates how Agile user stories empower teams to remain focused on user value while embracing continuous iteration. By linking requirements directly to user needs and outcomes, Spotify created an environment where innovation thrived. The emphasis on value-driven and flexible development practices proved central to the company's rise as a market leader in music streaming.

3.2 Structure:

In traditional (Waterfall) approaches, documentation is formal, detailed, and highly structured, often resembling a contractual agreement. Examples include the Software Requirements Specification (SRS) or the Business Requirements Document (BRD). These documents aim to capture every requirement, assumption, and constraint in exhaustive detail. Their formality serves the purpose of establishing accountability and reducing ambiguity, particularly in projects where compliance, regulation, or legal defensibility is critical. Once finalised, these documents act as an authoritative reference point for the entire project lifecycle, with little room for deviation.

By contrast, Agile takes a more informal and lightweight

approach to structure. Instead of lengthy documents, Agile relies on concise, conversational formats such as user stories. A common method is the Card–Conversation–Confirmation (3Cs) framework, where the "card" captures the initial story, the "conversation" elaborates details through stakeholder interactions, and the "confirmation" defines acceptance criteria to validate success. This approach ensures requirements remain understandable, adaptable, and grounded in dialogue rather than static text. The informality is intentional, as it promotes flexibility and encourages teams to engage in discussions that bring clarity without overburdening them with documentation.

3.3 Level of Detail:

Traditional documentation emphasises comprehensive and prescriptive detail. Requirements are carefully gathered and documented before development begins, often through lengthy analysis phases. The intention is to anticipate all possible scenarios upfront and provide a complete blueprint for developers, testers, and stakeholders. This level of detail ensures predictability and reduces uncertainty, making it especially useful in projects where changes are costly or difficult to accommodate, such as aerospace or defence. However, this rigidity can become a limitation in fast-moving environments where user needs or market conditions shift rapidly.

In Agile, the level of detail is deliberately iterative and evolving. User stories typically begin with a minimal description, capturing only the essence of the functionality and its value to the user. The details are progressively refined during sprint planning sessions, backlog grooming, and ongoing collaboration. This incremental approach avoids the trap of over-specification and keeps requirements flexible. It allows teams to add, remove, or reshape features as priorities change or new insights emerge. The focus is not on predicting every detail in advance but on creating just enough clarity for the team to deliver value iteratively.

3.4 Purpose:

The purpose of traditional documentation is largely contractual and reference-oriented. These documents serve as a baseline against which scope, timelines, and deliverables are measured. Because they are binding in nature, they help minimise scope creep by making changes difficult and costly. This contract-like function ensures accountability and control, particularly in industries where legal or regulatory compliance is non-negotiable. For many stakeholders, such documents provide a sense of security, as they establish clear expectations and limit the risks of misinterpretation.

Agile documentation, on the other hand, serves a collaborative and adaptive purpose. Instead of locking down requirements, it embraces the idea that needs evolve and that the best solutions often emerge through feedback loops. Agile artefacts encourage continuous dialogue among product owners, developers, testers, and end-users, fostering a culture of transparency and flexibility. Rather than minimising change, Agile treats change as an opportunity to refine the product and better align it with user needs. This perspective makes Agile documentation a tool for enabling responsiveness rather than enforcing rigidity. The table compares Traditional Requirement Documents (e.g., SRS) with Agile User Stories.

Table 6:

TRADITIONAL REQUIREMENT DOCUMENTS WITH AGILE USER STORIES

Aspect	Traditional Requirement Docs (e.g., SRS)	Agile User Stories
Focus	Functionality & technical behavior	User value & purpose
Structure	Formal, detailed, contract-like	Informal, concise, conversational
Detail	Comprehensive, upfront	Iterative, evolving
Purpose	Blueprint & legal contract	Collaboration & adaptability

A comprehensive explanation of the table contents, with each aspect elaborated in distinct paragraphs, is provided below.

Focus

Traditional requirement documents, such as the Software Requirement Specification (SRS), primarily focus on functionality and technical behaviour. They aim to capture in detail how the system should perform, including features, constraints, performance criteria, and technical dependencies. The emphasis is on ensuring completeness and precision so that the development team has a definitive blueprint for building the system.

In contrast, Agile user stories focus on user value and purpose. Instead of specifying technical details, they highlight what the user wants to achieve and why it matters. For example, "As a teacher, I want to upload assignments so that students can access them online." This framing ensures that development stays anchored in delivering meaningful outcomes rather than just implementing technical functions.

Structure

Traditional documentation follows a formal, detailed, and contract-like structure. Documents such as SRS or BRD are lengthy, highly structured, and often written in formal language that serves as a legal or contractual reference. Their rigidity provides a sense of control and accountability but often reduces adaptability during execution.

Agile user stories, by contrast, are informal, concise, and conversational. They rely on lightweight formats such as the Card–Conversation–Confirmation (3Cs) model, where the "card" outlines the story briefly, the "conversation" builds shared understanding, and the "confirmation" defines success through acceptance criteria. This flexible structure fosters dialogue and shared interpretation, rather than treating requirements as immutable contracts.

Detail

Traditional requirement documents are typically comprehensive and defined upfront. The expectation is that all requirements should be analysed, documented, and agreed upon before development begins. This prescriptive level of detail reduces ambiguity but often leaves little room for adjustment when user needs evolve or new opportunities emerge.

Agile stories adopt an iterative and evolving approach to detail. They begin with only enough information to capture the essence of the requirement and are progressively refined during sprint planning, backlog grooming, and team discussions. This ensures that details are elaborated just in time, aligning development with the most current user needs and priorities.

Purpose

The purpose of traditional (Waterfall) documentation is to serve as a blueprint and legal contract. It provides a binding reference that defines scope, deliverables, and compliance measures, helping minimise scope changes and protect against misalignment or disputes. In industries like defence, healthcare, or government, this legal defensibility is especially important.

Agile user stories, however, are designed for collaboration and adaptability. Their purpose is not to constrain change but to encourage ongoing interaction among stakeholders. Stories evolve through feedback loops, ensuring that products remain aligned with user needs as they change. In this sense, agile documentation acts less as a rigid baseline and more as a tool to facilitate learning, flexibility, and continuous improvement.

Comparative Insights

Traditional requirement documents are indispensable for projects with regulatory or safety-critical needs, while Agile user stories excel in fast-moving, user-centric industries like software and digital services. Many organizations adopt a hybrid approach—using lightweight user stories for iterative development but maintaining formal documentation for compliance and traceability.

Conclusion

Requirement gathering is not merely a documentation task —it is the cornerstone of project success. By employing a variety of techniques (interviews, workshops, observation, prototyping), rigorously documenting and validating requirements, and choosing the appropriate documentation style (traditional vs. Agile), project teams can ensure that they build the right product, in the right way, for the right stakeholders.

4. Requirements Gathering Strategies for Software Project Management

In software project management, requirements gathering is the cornerstone of successful delivery. It is a structured process of identifying, documenting, and validating stakeholder needs to create a clear and actionable blueprint of what the software must achieve. Because it defines scope, budget, schedule, and quality expectations, this phase directly influences whether a project succeeds or fails. A well-executed requirements process minimises ambiguity and provides the development team with a shared vision aligned with stakeholder expectations.

The primary purpose of requirements gathering is to transform abstract ideas into a concrete set of features and functionalities. By doing so, it ensures alignment between stakeholders and the development team. Strong requirements discipline prevents scope creep by clearly defining what is included and excluded early in the project. It also reduces costly rework by identifying gaps and errors before development begins, when changes are far less expensive to address. Most importantly, well-defined requirements form the basis of customer satisfaction, ensuring that the final product meets both stated and unstated needs.

Key Strategies and Techniques:

Requirements gathering in software projects is rarely accomplished through a single method; instead, project managers and business analysts apply a mix of strategies to capture a 360-degree view of stakeholder needs.

Interviews and surveys are foundational techniques. Interviews—conducted one-on-one or in small groups—allow for in-depth discussions that uncover nuanced requirements and build rapport. Surveys and questionnaires, on the other hand, provide efficient ways to gather broad input from larger audiences, delivering quantitative insights that complement qualitative feedback.

Workshops and brainstorming bring stakeholders and project teams together in structured sessions to collaborate on defining requirements. Skilled facilitation is key to resolving conflicts, encouraging participation, and achieving consensus. Brainstorming sessions, particularly in the early stages, stimulate creative thinking and help identify innovative features that may not surface in formal discussions.

Observation and document analysis provide real-world context. Observing users in their work environment reveals how tasks are actually performed, often highlighting pain points or unmet needs that users themselves may overlook. Reviewing existing documentation—such as business process flows, manuals, and previous project artefacts—can uncover constraints, dependencies, and system rules that must be factored into new requirements.

Prototyping and use cases help stakeholders visualise the product and its functionality. Prototypes—whether low-fidelity sketches or interactive mock-ups—enable early feedback and reduce the risk of misinterpretation. Use cases and user stories, meanwhile, frame requirements from the end-user's perspective, describing goals and interactions in simple, actionable terms that guide both design and testing.

Software Requirements Specification (SRS):

The culmination of requirements gathering is the Software Requirements Specification (SRS), a comprehensive document that serves as the single source of truth for the project. The SRS captures functional and non-functional requirements, defines assumptions and constraints, and clearly outlines project scope. It functions as a formal agreement between stakeholders and the development team, ensuring that every design decision, line of code, and test case can be traced back to an approved requirement.

By consolidating diverse inputs into a structured, unambiguous reference, the SRS reduces risks, aligns expectations, and provides a stable foundation for subsequent project phases. In this way, effective requirements gathering and documentation not only safeguard the project against missteps but also ensure that the final product delivers true business value.

CHAPTER 6: DEVELOPING A PROJECT BUDGET

Project Budget

A project budget is the financial plan that estimates all costs required to complete a project successfully within its defined scope, timeline, and quality standards. It serves as both a forecast of expected expenses and a control tool for managing resources throughout the project lifecycle.

Definition:

A project budget is the total authorised financial allocation for a project, including all projected costs, such as labour, materials, equipment, services, overheads, contingency reserves, and management reserves.

Purpose:

The purpose of a project budget is multi-dimensional. First, it plays a critical role in planning, as it provides a clear roadmap of the funding required and at what stages of the project.

This allows project managers and stakeholders to anticipate financial needs and allocate resources appropriately. Second, it serves as a tool for control, offering a benchmark against which actual expenditures can be compared to planned costs. This guarantees the early detection of any variances and the timely implementation of corrective measures.

Another important function is in decision-making. A well-prepared budget enables stakeholders to evaluate the feasibility of the project, make informed funding decisions, and effectively manage potential financial risks. In addition, the budget ensures accountability by establishing transparency. It connects the money being spent directly with the deliverables and milestones of the project, thereby promoting trust and clarity among stakeholders.

Components:

The components of a project budget typically include several categories of costs. Direct costs, such as labour, materials, and equipment, are directly tied to project tasks and deliverables. Indirect costs, such as administration, utilities, and overhead, represent expenses that support the project but are not directly attributable to specific activities. To address uncertainties, a contingency reserve is often included to cover identified risks, while a management reserve is set aside to handle unforeseen events or scope changes.

In simple terms, a project budget can be considered a complete financial blueprint. It outlines the project's cost, clarifies where the funds will be spent, and establishes a system for tracking funds until the project's successful completion. Several methods are employed in project management to forecast the resources, time, and financial requirements for successful project completion, and these are discussed in the following sections.

1. Cost Estimation Techniques

Cost estimation techniques are methods used in project management to forecast the resources, time, and money required to complete a project successfully. These techniques help project managers plan budgets, allocate resources efficiently, and gain approval from stakeholders.

1.1. Analogous Estimating

Analogous estimating, also known as comparative or top-down estimating, is a technique that leverages historical data from past projects to approximate the costs of a current project. It is most useful during the initiation phase of a project when detailed information on scope, resources, or activities may be limited. The fundamental premise is that if two projects are similar in size, scope, complexity, and execution environment, their costs are likely to be comparable.

For instance, if a software development company previously built a mobile banking application for a financial institution, it might use the actual costs incurred in that project as a baseline to estimate the costs of developing another application of similar scale and functionality. The strength of this approach lies in its speed and simplicity, making it a practical tool for producing quick, high-level estimates. However, its accuracy is often constrained by the degree of similarity between the projects being compared and the reliability of the historical cost records. If there are differences in technology, market conditions, or regulatory requirements, the cost estimate may deviate significantly from actual expenditure, thereby introducing financial risk.

Analogous Estimating – Case Illustration

Case Study 2:

Software Product Launch:

A mid-sized IT company is planning to launch a new e-commerce mobile app. Since it is in the early planning stage, detailed requirements are unavailable. The project manager refers to a similar app developed by the company two years earlier for a retail client. That project cost ₹40 lakhs and took six months. Given the similarity in scope, complexity, and features, the project manager estimates the new app will cost approximately the same, adjusting slightly for inflation and minor scope differences.

***Learning Point*:** While quick and useful, this estimate may overlook hidden differences such as new compliance requirements or higher user load, which can later lead to overruns.

1.2. Parametric Estimating:

Parametric estimation relies on statistical modelling and quantifiable parameters to derive cost estimates with greater precision. By analysing historical data, organizations establish cost relationships between measurable variables and overall project expenditures. These variables may include unit costs, productivity rates, or performance metrics. For example, in telecommunications projects, if the cost of laying one kilometre of fibre optic cable is established as a constant, the total project cost for a 100-kilometre installation can be reliably projected by multiplying the unit cost by the total length. This method is particularly valuable in large-scale or repetitive projects where measurable parameters can be applied consistently. Its accuracy depends heavily on the quality and validity of the underlying data as well as the appropriateness of the statistical model used. When well-implemented, parametric estimating not only provides higher reliability than analogous estimating but also enables scalability, as project costs can be adjusted in proportion to changes in project variables. However, misjudging the linearity of relationships or applying incorrect assumptions can undermine accuracy and lead to significant budget variances.

Parametric Estimating – Case Illustration

Case Study 3:

Fibre Optic Cable Installation

A large telecommunications company is planning to expand its high-speed internet infrastructure by installing 250 kilometres of fibre optic cable. Since this is not the first time the company has undertaken such work, it has access to historical data from past projects. From these records, it is known that the average cost of laying 1 kilometre of fibre optic cable—including trenching, labour, raw materials, and basic installation overhead is ₹250,000.

Using the parametric estimating technique, project managers can multiply the cost per unit length (per kilometre) by the total planned length (250 km) of installation:

Estimated Cost = ₹2,50,000 \times 250

= ₹6,25,00,000\text {Estimated Cost}

= ₹2,50,000 \times 250 = ₹6,25,00,000

Thus, the total project cost estimate is ₹6.25 crore.

Why Parametric Estimating Works Here

1. *Repetitive and Standardised Activity*: Fibre optic installation involves a repeatable process. The unit cost (per kilometre) captures labour, trenching, and material expenses, making the estimate scalable and consistent.

2. *Historical Data Availability*: The company relies on reliable past records, ensuring that the baseline cost per kilometre is validated and realistic.

3. *Quantifiable Metrics*: Since the work is easily measurable in kilometres, it suits parametric models where output per unit can be defined precisely.

Assumptions and Constraints

While parametric estimating provides a quick and reliable cost forecast, it depends on certain assumptions:

1. *Uniform Conditions* – The terrain, soil type, and environmental conditions across the 250 km stretch are assumed to be similar to past projects.

2. *Stable Market Prices* – Costs of fibre, conduit materials, and labour rates are assumed not to fluctuate drastically.

3. *No Extraordinary Risks* – Delays due to regulatory clearances, right-of-way disputes, or unexpected geological barriers are not factored into this estimate.

Any deviation in these assumptions could lead to cost overruns. For example, if a portion of the route passes through rocky terrain, the cost per kilometre may rise significantly.

Learning Point:

The key takeaway is that parametric estimating is most effective when project elements are:

1. Repetitive (e.g., per kilometre, per unit, per square foot),
2. Standardised in execution, and
3. Backed by reliable historical data.

However, project managers must always complement parametric estimates with risk assessments and contingency reserves, especially for large-scale infrastructure projects where external factors may impact costs.

1.3. Bottom-Up Estimating:

Bottom-up estimating is widely regarded as the most rigorous and precise method of cost estimation. It involves decomposing the project into its smallest work packages or activities, as identified in the Work Breakdown Structure (WBS), and individually estimating the cost of each. These granular estimates are then aggregated, or "rolled up," to produce the total project budget. For example, in a construction project, costs may be determined for each floor, room, wall, or material component, factoring in labour, equipment, and overhead costs specific to each unit of work. This approach provides not only a detailed financial blueprint but also a strong foundation for budget tracking and control during project execution. While bottom-up estimating delivers high accuracy and transparency, it is also time-intensive, requiring substantial input from subject matter experts and comprehensive project data. Consequently, it is most effective when a detailed project design and scope definition are available. The high level of granularity also ensures accountability, as each cost element can be traced back to a specific task, making variance analysis and corrective measures easier to implement.

Bottom-Up Estimating – Case Illustration

Case Study 1:

Office Building Construction

In a construction project for a 5-storey office building, the project manager creates a detailed Work Breakdown Structure (WBS). For each floor, costs are calculated for:

1. Materials (cement, steel, tiles, etc.)
2. Labour (masons, electricians, carpenters)
3. Equipment (cranes, lifts, scaffolding)
4. Overheads (permits, insurance, utilities)

Each component is estimated separately and then rolled up:

Table 1:

Sample WBS Cost Sheet (Extract – One Floor)

WBS Code	Task/Activity	Materials (₹)	Labor (₹)	Equipment (₹)	Subtotal (₹)
1.1	Foundation work	4,50,000	3,20,000	1,80,000	9,50,000
1.2	Structural framing	6,00,000	2,75,000	2,00,000	10,75,000
1.3	Electrical works	1,20,000	1,80,000	50,000	3,50,000

1.4	Plumbing works	90,000	1,10,000	40,000	2,40,000
Total	**One Floor**	—	—	—	**26,15,000**

When extended to 5 floors, the rolled-up estimate gives a comprehensive total project cost.

Learning Point: Though time-consuming, bottom-up estimating provides the most reliable basis for budget control.

1.4. Top-Down Estimating:

Top-down estimating begins with an overall cost figure or budget constraint set by management or stakeholders. This amount is then distributed across project components or phases based on priorities, experience, or assumptions. While this method is useful in the early stages of project planning—especially when time is short or only limited data is available—it is less precise than other techniques. Its accuracy is constrained because it may not fully account for task-level details, and it often reflects managerial expectations rather than actual resource requirements.

Top-down estimating starts with a single, overall cost figure — usually a budget cap or high-level estimate set by senior management, financiers, or a feasibility study — and then allocates that total across major project components or phases. Instead of adding up each task, the project manager divides the lump sum proportionally (often by percentage) according to priorities, experience, benchmarks, or strategic constraints. This makes top-down fast and politically useful when a decision must be made quickly (for funding approval or go/no-go), but it can hide task-level detail and therefore understate or overstate specific needs. Because it emphasises an externally set total, its numbers often reflect managerial expectations and strategic trade-offs (what must be preserved Vs where cuts will be taken) rather than a precise resource-based forecast.

1.5. Three-Point Estimating:

Three-point estimating incorporates uncertainty and risk by considering three scenarios: the optimistic estimate (best case), the pessimistic estimate (worst case), and the most likely estimate. Using these three values, a weighted average or statistical calculation is made to provide a more realistic cost forecast. For instance, if a task might cost between ₹8,000 (optimistic), ₹12,000 (most likely), and ₹20,000 (pessimistic), the average gives a balanced figure that accounts for uncertainty factors. This approach reduces the risk of underestimating or overestimating and is especially useful in projects with variable outcomes.

2. Budget Planning and Approval Processes

Budget planning and approval is a systematic, multi-stage process that ensures a project's financial framework is realistic, justified, and aligned with organisational objectives. The process begins with a thorough gathering of project requirements, followed by the development of a detailed Work Breakdown Structure (WBS). The WBS serves as the backbone for applying cost estimation techniques, particularly bottom-up estimating, to determine precise cost components. To safeguard against financial uncertainty, budgets incorporate contingency reserves for known risks and management reserves for unforeseen challenges. Once compiled, the proposed budget undergoes internal reviews with the project team to validate assumptions, reconcile discrepancies, and test its robustness. Subsequently, it is presented to external stakeholders, such as the project sponsor, steering committee, or senior management. This review and approval stage often requires multiple iterations, with revisions made in response to stakeholder feedback, changes in priorities, or resource reallocation. Formal approval not only secures financial authority but also establishes a baseline budget against which future project expenditures are measured and controlled. This budget baseline becomes a critical reference for performance monitoring, variance analysis, and financial accountability throughout the project lifecycle.

Budget Planning and Approval Processes

Case Illustration 2:

Hospital IT System Implementation:

A private hospital plans to implement an Electronic Health Record (EHR) system. The project manager prepares a bottom-up estimate using WBS activities such as hardware purchase, software licensing, training, and data migration. Contingency funds are added for data security upgrades and unexpected regulatory requirements.

The draft budget is then reviewed by the hospital's IT committee, CFO, and board of directors. Feedback leads to adjustments in training costs and licensing fees. After two iterations, the budget is formally approved, creating the budget baseline.

Table 2:

Sample Budget Approval Form (Proforma)

Section	Details (Sample Entry)
Project Name	Hospital EHR Implementation
Project Manager	Dr. S. Rao

Total Estimated Budget	₹2,85,00,000
Contingency Reserve	₹20,00,000
Management Reserve	₹15,00,000
Funding Source	Hospital Development Fund + External Loan
Approval Authority	Board of Directors
Signatures	PM, CFO, Sponsor, Board Chairperson
Approval Date	xxth July 20xx

Learning Point: The approval process formalises accountability and ensures all stakeholders align on financial commitments.

3. Managing Budget Risks

Managing budget risks is a proactive discipline that involves anticipating, analysing, and mitigating financial uncertainties that could undermine a project's success. The process begins with a comprehensive risk assessment, identifying potential cost drivers such as inaccurate estimates, inflation, resource price volatility, regulatory changes, or scope creep. To address these risks, two categories of financial buffers are commonly embedded into project budgets: contingency reserves and management reserves.

Contingency reserves are allocated for known and

anticipated risks, such as the possibility of a key material costing more than projected. Management reserves, on the other hand, are held by senior management to address "unknown unknowns"—risks that were not identified during the planning stage but may surface unexpectedly. Beyond reserves, effective budget risk management also relies on a robust change control process, which ensures that any proposed changes in scope, schedule, or resource allocation undergo formal review and approval. This prevents unanticipated financial disruptions and helps maintain budget integrity. Continuous monitoring of project costs against the baseline budget is equally critical. By using tools such as Earned Value Management (EVM) and variance analysis, project managers can detect early warning signals of overspending and implement corrective measures promptly. Ultimately, systematic risk management not only protects the project's financial viability but also enhances stakeholder confidence by demonstrating fiscal discipline and preparedness.

Managing Budget Risks

Case Illustration 3:

Metro Rail Expansion Project

A metropolitan city's rail expansion project faced risks from fluctuating steel prices and delays in government land acquisition approvals. The project manager included ₹50 crores in contingency reserves for material price hikes and requested a management reserve of ₹100 crores for unforeseen risks, such as political changes or environmental compliance challenges.

Despite careful planning, steel prices rose unexpectedly by 15%, consuming half the contingency reserve. Later, a legal dispute over land ownership delayed construction, triggering the use of part of the management reserve. By having structured reserves and a strong change control system, the project avoided financial collapse and maintained stakeholder trust.

***Learning Point*:** Building structured reserves and monitoring risks proactively enables smoother financial management in volatile environments.

Practical Tools:

The following section presents two comprehensive, professionally formatted proformas designed as ready-to-use practical tools and worksheets, serving as a quick reference and ready reckoner.

Template 1:

Blank WBS Cost Sheet (Proforma):

This template helps project managers and teams systematically estimate costs at the work package or activity level. Learners can fill in each row with details about materials, labour, equipment, and subtotals. Once completed, the values can be rolled up to calculate the overall project budget.

Table 3:

WBS Cost Sheet

WBS Code	Task / Activity	Materials (₹)	Labor (₹)	Equipment (₹)	Subtotal (₹)

Instructions:

1. ***WBS Code*:** Enter the unique identifier for the work package (e.g., 1.1, 1.2.3).

2. ***Task/Activity*:** Describe the specific work item (e.g., foundation work, software module development).

3. ***Materials, Labour, Equipment*:** Record estimated costs for each category.

4. ***Subtotal*:** Add the costs for that activity.

5. ***Total*:** Sum all subtotals to calculate the overall cost estimate.

Template 2:

Budget Approval Form (Proforma):

This template provides a structured document for obtaining formal approval of the project budget from sponsors and key stakeholders. It ensures transparency and accountability.

Table 4:

Budget Approval Form

Section	Details (To be filled)
Project Name	
Project Manager	
Total Estimated	

Budget	
Contingency Reserve	
Management Reserve	
Funding Source	
Approval Authority	
Signatures	
Approval Date	

Illustration:

How to Fill the Budget Approval Form:

Instructions:

Make sure to accurately complete each section of the Budget Approval Form, as it forms an integral part of the official project record. Below are detailed guidelines for each field:

1. ***Project Name:***
   a. Write the full, official title of the project.

b. Avoid abbreviations unless they are widely recognised.

c. This ensures clarity for stakeholders and auditors who may not be directly involved in the project.

2. ***Project Manager:***

a. Record the name, designation, and department of the individual responsible for project execution.

b. This person is responsible for budget utilisation and reporting.

c. Example: *Mr R. Sharma, Senior Project Manager, Infrastructure Division.*

3. ***Total Estimated Budget:***

a. Enter the sum of all projected costs, derived from detailed cost estimation techniques (such as bottom-up or parametric estimating).

b. This should include materials, labour, equipment, overheads, and any other relevant cost categories.

4. ***Contingency Reserve:***

a. Specify the portion of the budget set aside to address **identified risks** (e.g., potential price escalation of raw materials, delays in the supply chain).

b. This reserve is typically calculated as a percentage of the total budget, taking into account the results of the risk assessment.

5. **Management Reserve**

    a. Enter the funds earmarked for unknown or unforeseen risks—issues that cannot be predicted during planning.

    b. It is controlled at the organisational or sponsor level, not directly by the project manager.

6. **Funding Source**

    a. Clearly state the origin of project funds: internal company reserves, external loans, government grants, or private sponsors.

    b. If multiple sources are involved, list each with the proportion contributed.

7. **Approval Authority**

    a. Identify the individual or governing body authorised to approve the project's budget.

    b. This may include a steering committee, board of directors, or senior executive.

    c. Their sanction provides legitimacy and accountability to proceed with financial commitments.

8. **Signatures**

    a. Obtain the necessary signatures to formalise your approval.

    b. This typically includes the Project Manager, the Project Sponsor, and the Chief Financial Officer

(CFO) or an equivalent financial authority.

c. Signatures act as a binding confirmation of roles and responsibilities.

9. **Approval Date**

   a. Please record the exact date when the budget was formally sanctioned.

   b. This date marks the **baseline reference point** for financial tracking and future audits.

***Learning Point*:** Completing the form carefully ensures transparency, accountability, and proper alignment of financial resources with project objectives. Treat this document as both a decision-making record and a compliance artefact in project governance.

Table 5:

Sample (Filled-Out): Budget Approval Form

Section	Details
Project Name	Best Health Multispecialty Hospital Construction (200-bed facility)
Project Manager	Mr. Susheel Rayudu, Senior Project Manager – Infrastructure Division
Total Estimated Budget	₹95,00,00,000 (Ninety-Five Crore)
Contingency Reserve	₹5,00,00,000 (5% of estimated budget, allocated for known risks such as steel price escalation)

Management Reserve	₹3,00,00,000 (Reserved for unforeseen risks – e.g., regulatory delays, unexpected geological issues)
Funding Source	60% Internal Capital (₹57,00,00,000)30% Bank Loan (₹28,50,00,000)10% Government Healthcare Grant (₹9,50,00,000)
Approval Authority	Project Steering Committee (comprising CEO, CFO, and Head of Operations)
Signatures	Project Manager: □ Susheel Rayudu, Project Sponsor: □ Dr. Sugun (Chairperson), CFO: □ Mr. Sugnan
Approval Date	xx September 20xx

Notes:

1. The **budget estimate (₹95 crore)** is rolled up from a detailed **bottom-up estimate**, covering civil works, medical equipment, labour, and overheads.

2. **Contingency Reserve (₹5 crore)** was calculated after a risk assessment highlighting volatile raw material prices.

3. Management Reserve (₹3 crore) was approved by the steering committee to safeguard against *black swan* risks.

4. The approval authority is not a single person but a committee, reflecting the large financial scale.

5. Having multiple funding sources reduces dependency on a

single stream and spreads financial risk.

4. Developing a Project Budget: A Financial Blueprint for Software Projects

A project budget is the financial backbone of any software project. It is more than just a cost estimate—it is a structured financial plan that outlines anticipated expenses, provides a baseline for tracking actual spending, and enables project managers to make informed decisions throughout the project lifecycle. A well-prepared budget ensures that resources are allocated effectively, risks are accounted for, and the project remains financially sustainable while delivering value to stakeholders.

A comprehensive software project budget is built from several key cost categories. The largest and most complex component is labour costs, which include salaries, benefits, and taxes for in-house staff, as well as contractor or consultant fees based on hourly or daily rates. Software and hardware costs cover essential tools and technologies, ranging from licences for development software and third-party APIs to hardware like servers and workstations, as well as cloud services from providers such as AWS, Azure, or Google Cloud. Third-party services and subcontractors represent costs for external expertise, such as consulting, training, or outsourced development for specialised tasks like UX design or security audits. While less common in remote-first teams, travel and miscellaneous costs may still apply, covering stakeholder meetings, training sessions, or team off-sites. Finally, a contingency reserve—typically 10–15% of the total budget—is essential to address unforeseen challenges such as scope creep, unexpected technical issues, or staffing changes.

Several methods are commonly used in software project cost

estimation. Bottom-up estimating provides the most detail and accuracy by breaking the project into small tasks and estimating costs individually, making it especially effective in Agile environments where tasks are defined in sprints. Top-down estimating relies on high-level allocations set by senior management, offering speed but less precision, and is best suited to projects with fixed scopes. Analogous estimating uses data from similar past projects to forecast costs, making it quick but less precise unless the projects closely match. Parametric estimating applies mathematical models based on historical data—such as average cost per feature or per function point—providing scalable and repeatable results when reliable parameters are available.

The budgeting process itself is iterative and dynamic. It begins with defining the project scope, ensuring clarity around deliverables, requirements, and constraints before cost estimation begins. The next step is estimating costs using one or more of the chosen techniques, followed by adding contingency reserves to safeguard against uncertainty. Once prepared, the budget must undergo stakeholder review and approval to secure alignment and commitment. Crucially, the budget does not remain static after approval—it requires continuous monitoring and control. Project managers must track actual spending against planned allocations, generate regular reports, and take corrective action when variances occur.

When developed and managed effectively, a project budget is not merely a financial document but a strategic management tool. It enables proactive decision-making, ensures accountability, and provides a foundation for balancing cost, scope, and schedule. By treating budgeting as a living process, project managers can transform it into a powerful mechanism for ensuring financial discipline and project success.

CHAPTER 7: CRAFTING A QUALITY PLAN: THE BLUEPRINT FOR PROJECT EXCELLENCE

Quality in project management is not simply an aspirational outcome; it is a critical constraint, standing on equal footing with scope, time, and cost. A rigorous commitment to quality ensures that a project not only meets its defined objectives but also delivers tangible value to stakeholders. At the heart of this commitment lies the quality plan—a foundational document that establishes what quality means for a specific project and outlines the systematic approach to achieving it across the project lifecycle. This plan is central to the broader framework of quality management, which encompasses quality assurance, quality control, and continuous improvement.

More than a technical requirement, quality management functions as a strategic imperative for organizations. Research consistently shows that prioritising quality is directly linked to enhanced customer satisfaction, stronger loyalty, and sustained competitive advantage. For instance, methodologies such as Six Sigma enable organizations to better understand customer needs, streamline delivery processes, and secure long-term market positioning. By continuously evaluating and refining processes, companies can achieve greater efficiency, build customer trust, and strengthen overall profitability.

This elevates the quality plan from a procedural checklist to a core strategic document, symbolising an organisation's commitment to excellence, competitiveness, and long-term success. The discussion that follows will first define quality in the context of project management, then analyse the functions of quality assurance and control, and finally explore the practical tools and methodologies that foster a culture of continuous improvement.

1. Foundational Concepts: Defining Quality in a Project Context

1.1 The Multifaceted Definitions of Quality:

Defining quality is the essential first step in any quality plan, yet the concept itself is far from uniform. It is a multifaceted idea that can be interpreted through different lenses. In technical usage, 'quality' often carries two core meanings: first, it represents the set of characteristics of a product or service that enables it to satisfy stated or implied needs; second, it reflects a condition in which a product or service is free of deficiencies. This duality highlights the central focus of quality management—both fulfilling requirements and eliminating errors.

Authoritative sources and key figures in the field have offered distinct but complementary definitions that continue to shape modern quality management:

1. The Project Management Institute (PMI), in its *Project Management Body of Knowledge (PMBOK™ Guide),* defines quality management as "the activity of developing quality (the best possible) products and services required to meet customer expectations using quality (the best possible) processes and procedures." This view underscores the importance of both product and process excellence in fulfilling customer expectations.

2. ISO 9000 provides a precise, technical definition of quality as the "degree to which a set of inherent characteristics fulfils requirements." This perspective ties quality directly to measurable features, documented specifications, and the conformance of outcomes to predefined standards.

3. Joseph Juran famously defined quality as "fitness for use". This customer-centric perspective emphasises how well a product or service performs its intended function for the end user, prioritising utility over mere compliance.

4. Philip Crosby, by contrast, defined quality as "conformance to requirements". His approach is more process-oriented, equating quality with strict adherence to established standards, with the principle of "doing it right the first time."

Synthesising these definitions is a critical step in expert-level quality planning. Juran and PMI present strategic, outcome-oriented views that prioritise customer satisfaction and long-term utility. Crosby and ISO 9000, however, represent tactical, process-oriented perspectives that stress measurable criteria and compliance. A project may fully conform to requirements (Crosby's view) yet fail to be "fit for use" (Juran's view) if the requirements were poorly defined or failed to evolve with customer needs. Thus, a robust quality plan must bridge this gap: it begins with a strategic definition of "fitness for use" and then translates it into tactical conformance through measurable, verifiable standards. The quality plan operationalises this philosophical alignment, ensuring that strategy and execution work in concert.

1.2 The Dimensions of Quality

Beyond formal definitions, quality is best understood as a multi-dimensional construct that captures various characteristics of products and services. These dimensions provide the vocabulary necessary to transform broad stakeholder expectations into concrete, measurable criteria within the quality plan.

Dimensions of Quality for Products:

For products, key dimensions include:

1. ***Performance*** refers to the core operating characteristics of a product, which directly determine whether it fulfills its primary purpose. For example, in a car, performance can be measured by factors such as speed, fuel efficiency, and handling. In consumer electronics, it might relate to processing speed or image clarity. Strong performance establishes the product's credibility and builds customer satisfaction by meeting fundamental expectations.

2. ***Features*** are supplementary attributes that enhance the basic functionality of a product, often distinguishing it from competitors. These might include additional software applications in a smartphone, advanced safety features in a vehicle, or customisation options in home appliances. While not always essential, features add perceived value and can influence a customer's decision to choose one product over another.

3. *Reliability* represents the likelihood that a product will operate consistently and correctly over a defined period. A reliable washing machine, for example, should complete multiple cycles without malfunction, while reliable medical equipment must perform flawlessly under critical conditions. High reliability reduces customer frustration and builds trust in the brand.

4. *Conformance* measures how well a product adheres to established standards, specifications, and regulatory requirements. This includes compliance with industry norms, legal safety requirements, and technical specifications. A smartphone that meets ISO manufacturing standards, or a food product that complies with FDA regulations, exemplifies strong conformance. Failure in this area often leads to recalls, fines, or reputational damage.

5. *Durability* reflects the expected lifespan of a product and its ability to withstand wear and tear. A durable product continues to perform as intended even under heavy or prolonged use. For example, construction tools designed for industrial use are expected to last years, not months. Durability directly affects customer satisfaction, as it reduces the frequency and cost of replacement.

6. *Serviceability* refers to the ease with which a product can be maintained, repaired, or upgraded. A laptop with modular components that can be easily replaced demonstrates high serviceability. This dimension is important not only for minimising downtime but also for extending the overall useful life of the product. It is often tied to after-sales service and the availability of spare parts.

7. *Aesthetics* involve the sensory aspects of a product—how it looks, feels, sounds, or even smells. While subjective, aesthetics significantly influence consumer perceptions and buying decisions. For instance, the sleek design of Apple products, the colour variety of cars, or the ergonomic feel of furniture can create emotional connections with customers.

8. ***Safety*** is the product's ability to prevent harm to users during normal or foreseeable use. This includes compliance with safety standards, the use of non-toxic materials, and built-in protective mechanisms. In industries like automotive, safety features such as airbags and anti-lock braking systems are not optional but expected. A lack of safety undermines trust and exposes companies to liability.

Dimensions of Quality for Services:

For services, the dimensions shift to include factors such as:

1. ***Time and timeliness*** highlight the importance of prompt and punctual service delivery. Whether it is a flight departing on schedule, a doctor seeing patients at the appointed time, or an e-commerce company delivering orders as promised, timeliness strongly influences customer satisfaction. Delays often translate directly into dissatisfaction.

2. ***Completeness*** measures whether the service fulfills all the requirements promised or expected. For example, a banking service that not only processes a loan but also provides clear documentation and ongoing support demonstrates completeness. Similarly, a meal at a restaurant is only "complete" if it includes all ordered items, served correctly.

3. ***Courtesy*** reflects the interpersonal quality of service interactions. Politeness, respect, empathy, and professionalism from staff can significantly enhance the customer experience. In healthcare, for instance, a courteous nurse can ease patient anxiety, while in retail, friendly assistance can build lasting customer loyalty.

4. Consistency refers to the reliability and uniformity of service delivery across different times, locations, or staff members. A global hotel chain, for example, strives to provide the same standard of cleanliness, comfort, and service worldwide. Consistency creates trust, as customers know they can expect the same experience every time.

5. Accessibility concerns how easy it is for customers to obtain a service. This can mean physical access—such as ramps for disabled individuals—or digital access, like user-friendly websites and mobile apps. In the modern era, accessibility is also tied to availability, such as 24/7 helplines or multilingual support options.

6. Accuracy ensures that services are delivered correctly and without errors. For example, an accountant providing tax services must file calculations precisely, while a hospital laboratory must return accurate test results. Mistakes in accuracy can lead to financial, legal, or even life-threatening consequences.

2. The Dual Pillars of Quality Management: Assurance and Control

Quality management in project environments rests upon two interconnected foundations: Quality Assurance (QA) and Quality Control (QC). Though these terms are often used interchangeably in casual conversation, they serve distinct purposes within a project framework. QA is primarily proactive and focused on systems and processes, whereas QC is reactive and centered on deliverables and outputs. Together, they form the structural backbone of any effective quality management system.

2.1 A Nuanced Distinction: Proactive vs. Reactive:

The essential difference between QA and QC lies in their timing, focus, and orientation.

Quality Assurance (QA): The Proactive Approach:

QA represents the proactive, process-driven side of quality management. It comprises “planned and systematic” activities designed to prevent errors and defects before they occur. Rather than inspecting products at the end, QA ensures that the system producing those products is inherently reliable and capable of meeting expectations. QA seeks answers to strategic questions such as *'How will quality be measured?" Who is responsible for measuring it? What standards will define acceptable quality?*

Typical QA activities include:

1. Drafting a quality plan that outlines goals, methods, and metrics:

A quality plan serves as the foundational document for managing quality within a project. It defines the specific quality objectives, the strategies to achieve them, and the metrics by which success will be measured. For example, in a construction project, the quality plan might specify tolerance levels for materials, testing procedures for structural stability, and reporting mechanisms for non-conformities. By clearly articulating these elements at the outset, the plan ensures alignment among all stakeholders and provides a roadmap for consistent monitoring throughout the project lifecycle.

2. Establishing Standard Operating Procedures (SOPs) for consistent work practices:

Standard Operating Procedures (SOPs) are essential for promoting consistency, reliability, and efficiency across processes. SOPs document step-by-step instructions for completing tasks in a way that adheres to established quality standards. For instance, in a pharmaceutical project, SOPs might guide how raw materials are handled, how equipment is sanitised, or how batch records are maintained. This eliminates ambiguity, reduces errors, and ensures that the workforce operates within a controlled framework, thereby safeguarding quality at every stage of production or service delivery.

3. Conducting internal audits to ensure compliance with standards:

Internal audits act as checkpoints within the project's quality management system. These audits systematically evaluate whether processes, practices, and documentation comply with defined standards and the quality plan. For example, in a software development project, an internal audit might assess whether coding practices align with organisational guidelines or whether documentation is up to date. Beyond compliance, audits provide valuable insights into process inefficiencies or recurring issues, enabling corrective and preventive actions. This not only maintains quality but also fosters a culture of accountability and transparency.

4. Implementing supplier quality management to maintain consistent inputs:

The quality of a final product or service is heavily dependent on the quality of inputs, many of which are supplied externally. Supplier quality management involves assessing, selecting, and monitoring suppliers to ensure their materials or services consistently meet required standards. For instance, in the automotive industry, rigorous supplier evaluations ensure that critical parts such as brakes or airbags meet safety specifications. By establishing supplier scorecards, audits, and regular communication, organizations can build strong partnerships, reduce risks of defective inputs, and secure a reliable supply chain that supports overall project quality.

5. Providing training for staff so that quality practices are embedded throughout the workforce:

Training is a proactive measure to instill quality awareness and competence among employees. Well-trained staff are more likely to understand the importance of quality, follow established procedures, and identify potential issues before they escalate. For example, in a healthcare setting, training programs on patient safety protocols, hygiene standards, and reporting practices ensure that staff consistently deliver high-quality care. Ongoing training also keeps the workforce updated on new tools, techniques, and regulatory changes, embedding a culture of continuous improvement that reinforces the effectiveness of the quality management system.

For example, in software development, QA involves establishing coding standards, peer review processes, and continuous integration pipelines that minimise the risk of errors before the code reaches testing.

Quality Control (QC): The Reactive Approach

In contrast, QC operates as the reactive, product-focused counterpart to QA. It involves "operational techniques and activities" aimed at detecting and correcting defects once deliverables have been produced. QC examines outputs after execution to determine whether they conform to specifications and meet stakeholder requirements. Common Quality Control (QC) activities include:

1. Batch inspections in manufacturing to detect non-conforming items:

Batch inspections are a cornerstone of QC in industries such as pharmaceuticals, food processing, and electronics. During this process, finished goods or intermediate products are examined in groups (batches) to identify defects, irregularities, or non-conforming items before they move further along the supply chain. For instance, in a pharmaceutical plant, tablets may be inspected for correct weight, uniformity, and packaging integrity. If defects are detected, the entire batch can be quarantined and investigated, preventing defective products from reaching consumers. This systematic check ensures reliability and safeguards against risks to safety, brand reputation, and regulatory compliance.

2. Sampling and statistical testing to validate production quality:

Rather than inspecting every single product, organizations often use sampling techniques combined with statistical testing to determine whether production quality meets established standards. This approach is cost-effective and time-efficient, especially in large-scale manufacturing. For example, in textile production, random samples of fabric may be tested for strength, colourfastness, and shrinkage resistance. Statistical quality control methods, such as control charts or Six Sigma techniques, provide confidence that the entire production lot maintains consistent quality. This practice ensures balanced oversight while keeping inspection costs manageable.

3. Validation and verification testing in engineering or software to ensure outputs work as intended:

In engineering and software development, QC often centres on validation and verification testing. Verification ensures that the product has been built correctly according to specifications, while validation ensures it fulfills its intended use.

For instance, in software, verification may involve checking that a module's code complies with design documents, while validation may test whether the software performs well under real-world user scenarios. In engineering projects, validation might include stress-testing a bridge design to ensure it can handle projected loads. These activities confirm that deliverables are both technically sound and practically functional, preventing costly failures after release.

4. Corrective actions applied to defective outputs before delivery:

Despite robust systems, defects can occur, and QC includes implementing corrective actions to address them before final delivery. Corrective actions may involve reworking defective items, replacing faulty components, or adjusting production processes. For example, in automobile manufacturing, if an inspection identifies alignment issues in a batch of car doors, technicians may realign or replace the affected parts before the vehicles are released. These actions not only restore the product to acceptable quality levels but also feed back into process improvements, reducing the likelihood of recurrence. Thus, corrective actions serve as both a short-term fix and a long-term preventive measure.

To illustrate, in the context of pharmaceuticals, QC might involve laboratory testing of drug batches to verify chemical composition and potency, ensuring compliance with regulatory standards before distribution.

Although some sources suggest that QC represents an ongoing, long-term process while QA occurs only as a final review, the prevailing consensus in professional practice defines QA as a proactive process design and QC as a reactive product inspection. Together, they form a logical continuum —QA reduces the likelihood of defects by designing strong systems, and QC verifies through inspection that those systems produced satisfactory results.

2.2 A Symbiotic Relationship:

Quality Assurance (QA) and Quality Control (QC) are not stand-alone activities but complementary elements of a larger quality ecosystem. The relationship between them is best understood as a feedback loop that drives continuous improvement.

A QA plan establishes the framework, standards, and procedures to ensure quality is built into the project from the start. Once deliverables are produced, the QC process validates whether those standards have been achieved. Importantly, any issues uncovered by QC serve as feedback for QA.

For instance, if a QC test in a car manufacturing line reveals frequent brake malfunctions, this finding may trigger a Corrective and Preventive Action (CAPA) investigation. QA teams would then analyse root causes—such as supplier defects, process inefficiencies, or inadequate training—and refine procedures to eliminate recurrence. This cyclical relationship ensures that quality management is not a one-time task but a continuous cycle of planning, execution, inspection, and improvement.

The symbiosis between QA and QC underscores the philosophy of continuous improvement (Kaizen, Six Sigma, TQM), where lessons from past inspections reinforce better process designs, creating a culture of excellence over time.

2.3 Roles and Responsibilities in Practice:

The distinction between Quality Assurance (QA) and Quality Control (QC) is reflected in the roles and responsibilities assigned within project teams. Quality Assurance (QA) roles are oriented toward system oversight, governance, and preventive action. They include:

1. A Group Quality Facilitator responsible for developing organisational standards:

The Group Quality Facilitator plays a strategic role in shaping the overall quality framework of an organisation. Their primary responsibility is to design, document, and maintain organisational standards that guide all projects and processes. By developing policies, guidelines, and best practices, they ensure that teams across different departments adhere to consistent approaches toward quality. For example, in a construction company, the facilitator may establish safety and quality benchmarks that must be followed at every site, thereby harmonising practices across projects. Their contribution is preventive in nature, aiming to embed quality into the foundation of every activity before execution begins.

2. A quality assurance manager overseeing compliance and audits:

The Quality Assurance Manager acts as the custodian of compliance, ensuring that all project activities align with internal standards as well as external regulations and certifications. This role involves conducting systematic audits, reviewing documentation, and monitoring adherence to established quality plans. For instance, in pharmaceutical manufacturing, the QA manager ensures compliance with Good Manufacturing Practices (GMP) and regulatory requirements set by authorities such as the U.S. Food and Drug Administration (FDA). Their oversight is crucial in detecting process deviations early and enforcing corrective measures, thereby maintaining both regulatory approval and stakeholder confidence.

3. A quality control reviewer ensuring that processes are applied consistently:

The quality control reviewer is tasked with verifying that the processes established in the quality plan and standard operating procedures are being applied uniformly throughout the project. Unlike the QA Manager, who focuses broadly on compliance and governance, the Reviewer works at a more operational level, cross-checking whether project teams are adhering to documented workflows. For example, in a software development project, the reviewer may confirm that all coding practices follow predefined standards and that peer reviews are conducted consistently. By ensuring process fidelity, this role prevents variations that could compromise the quality of the final deliverables.

4. The Project Manager plays a QA role by ensuring that procedures are implemented properly:

Although the project manager's role spans multiple domains, in terms of quality assurance, they act as the linchpin, ensuring that agreed-upon processes are faithfully implemented. The project manager monitors whether the team follows the quality plan, tracks compliance with SOPs, and ensures corrective actions are taken when deviations occur. For instance, in a civil engineering project, the project manager ensures that site inspections, material testing, and safety protocols are carried out as defined in the QA framework. By bridging governance with day-to-day operations, the project manager helps ensure that preventive measures translate into consistent quality outcomes. These roles focus on building a culture of quality, ensuring that processes are designed to minimise the likelihood of errors.

Quality Control (QC) roles, by contrast, are operational and hands-on, directly tied to the creation, inspection, and correction of outputs. They may include:

a. A designer, responsible for developing products or documents:

The designer plays the first and most critical role in quality control, as they are responsible for producing the initial version of a product, component, or project document. Their work sets the foundation for all subsequent quality checks. For example, in engineering, the designer prepares technical drawings, blueprints, or schematics, while in software development, they create the system architecture or code modules. The quality of their output directly influences the ease of later verification and correction. Since errors at this stage can cascade into later phases, the designer's attention to detail and adherence to requirements are key parts of ensuring overall product quality.

b. A checker, who independently reviews deliverables for accuracy:

The Checker provides an independent perspective by thoroughly reviewing the Designer's work. Their role is to verify that deliverables are accurate, complete, and aligned with specifications or standards. This function creates a safeguard against human error, ensuring that defects are caught before moving forward. For instance, in construction projects, a checker may review design drawings to confirm structural integrity, while in software projects, they might review code for adherence to best practices and absence of logical flaws. By acting as the first line of defence in the QC chain, the checker significantly reduces the risk of errors reaching the final product.

***c. A back-checker, verifying that corrections suggested by the checker are properly applied*:**

The back-checker closes the loop in the correction process by ensuring that any issues identified by the checker have been adequately addressed. This role is particularly important for maintaining consistency and accuracy in evolving deliverables. For example, if a checker flags a calculation error in an engineering design, the back-checker confirms that the designer has corrected the error and that no unintended changes were introduced. In documentation projects, the back-checker ensures that revisions align with the original requirements and improve clarity. This verification step adds a crucial layer of assurance, preventing rework cycles caused by incomplete or incorrect corrections.

d. An updater and re-checker, ensuring ongoing accuracy of evolving project documents or products:

Projects are dynamic, and documents or products often undergo multiple revisions over their lifecycle. The Updater's role is to incorporate these changes accurately, while the Re-checker verifies that updates maintain alignment with requirements and standards. For example, in a long-term infrastructure project, updated blueprints must reflect design changes due to new regulatory requirements, and the re-checker ensures these updates do not introduce conflicts or errors. Similarly, in software development, as code evolves through iterative cycles, the Updater integrates changes from multiple developers, and the Re-checker confirms that these updates function as intended. Together, they sustain quality throughout the project, ensuring that evolving deliverables remain reliable and error-free.

Interestingly, the project manager straddles both QA and QC domains. While they design and oversee processes (QA), they are also ultimately accountable for the quality of final deliverables (QC). This dual responsibility positions the project manager as the nexus point linking proactive system assurance with reactive quality validation.

The dual pillars of QA and QC form the backbone of effective quality management. QA lays the foundation by building robust processes, while QC provides validation through inspection of tangible outputs. Their relationship is symbiotic, creating a continuous cycle of prevention, detection, correction, and improvement. By clearly defining roles and responsibilities, organizations ensure that both dimensions of quality are addressed, reinforcing customer trust, reducing risk, and delivering long-term business value.

A vivid comparative framework between Quality Assurance (QA) and Quality Control (QC) is presented in Table 7.1 below.

Table 7.1:

QUALITY ASSURANCE VS. QUALITY CONTROL: A COMPARATIVE FRAMEWORK

Attribute	Quality Assurance (QA)	Quality Control (QC)
Focus	Process-oriented; ensuring the	Product-oriented;

	process is correct	ensuring the product is correct
Goal	Prevention of defects	Detection and correction of defects
Timing	Proactive; takes place throughout the project lifecycle	Reactive; takes place during or after production
Scope	Systemic: a top-level, planned system of review	Tactical: a hands-on, routine check
Typical Activities	Audits, training, supplier management, documentation	Inspections, testing, sampling, and defect correction

3. Crafting the Project Quality Plan: A Practical Guide

A project quality plan is much more than a formal document—it is the operational blueprint that connects customer expectations with the actual activities, resources, and processes required to deliver the intended outcomes. Unlike static reports, a quality plan is a living, evolving document that must adapt as the project progresses. It serves as both a guidance tool for the project team and an accountability framework for stakeholders, ensuring that quality is not left to chance but built into the fabric of the project lifecycle.

3.1 The Purpose and Core Components:

The primary purpose of a quality plan is to provide a

systematic approach for managing quality by defining the standards, roles, responsibilities, and measures necessary to guarantee success. A well-structured quality plan acts as a reference point for decision-making, ensuring that all project participants work toward the same quality objectives. Below are the core components, each essential to clarity, alignment, and execution:

1. Stakeholder Expectations:

Every project begins with stakeholders, and their definition of "quality" must guide the plan. This component captures customer expectations and any external requirements, such as client specifications, market needs, or regulatory benchmarks. Clearly documenting these expectations ensures alignment between deliverables and what stakeholders actually value. For instance, a hospital construction project may emphasise safety and compliance with health regulations as its foremost quality requirements, while a software project might prioritise usability and data security. By establishing these expectations at the outset, the project avoids the risk of "meeting the wrong standard."

2. Applicable Standards and Specifications:

Projects operate within a framework of internal and external standards that define acceptable practices. These may include organisational quality benchmarks, regulatory compliance requirements (e.g., ISO, ASTM, IEEE), industry standards, and even laws governing safety or data protection. Embedding these standards within the quality plan ensures that deliverables are not only acceptable to the client but also legally defensible and professionally recognised. In highly regulated industries, such as aerospace or pharmaceuticals, adherence to standards is not just desirable but mandatory, making this component central to the plan's credibility.

3. Roles and Responsibilities:

Quality cannot be achieved without clarity on who is responsible for what. This section of the plan defines the division of roles, authority, and accountability for quality-related activities. It ensures that for every task, there is both an executor and a verifier, closing the loop between action and oversight. For example, while a design engineer may be responsible for producing technical drawings, a quality control inspector may be assigned to review and validate them. Clearly defined roles avoid duplication, confusion, and gaps in responsibility, fostering accountability across the team.

4. Processes and Procedures:

At its core, the quality plan must document the step-by-step processes and procedures that will govern project execution. These include methods for creating specifications, conducting tests, performing inspections, managing suppliers, and auditing results. By standardising processes through documented Standard Operating Procedures (SOPs), the plan ensures consistency across teams and project phases. This consistency minimises variation, reduces risks, and creates a predictable environment where outcomes can be confidently anticipated.

5. Quality Control Measures:

This component specifies the inspection and testing activities that will be used to verify compliance with standards and stakeholder expectations. It defines what will be tested, how often, and what criteria will determine success or failure. For example, in construction, this may include regular site inspections and material testing; in software, it may involve code validation and user acceptance testing. Defining these control measures in advance ensures transparency and avoids ad hoc, inconsistent checks later in the project.

6. Continuous Improvement Mechanisms:

A forward-looking quality plan must include mechanisms for continuous improvement, acknowledging that no system is flawless from the outset. This involves embedding policies for regular reviews, lessons learned sessions, and audits that feed back into process refinement. Corrective and Preventive Action (CAPA) systems are a common tool here, ensuring that when problems occur, their root causes are identified and future recurrences are prevented. By institutionalising learning and improvement, the plan transforms quality management from a one-time compliance exercise into a culture of ongoing excellence.

3.2 Linking the Plan to Project Execution:

A quality plan achieves its full potential only when it is integrated into the broader project management framework. It must interact seamlessly with functions like risk management, change control, and configuration management, ensuring that quality considerations are embedded in every decision. For instance, if a design change is proposed, the quality plan provides criteria for assessing how the change affects compliance with standards or stakeholder expectations.

During execution, the quality plan evolves from a planning tool into a record of performance. Inspection logs, statistical process control charts, and audit reports transform the plan into an auditable trail of accountability. This documentation not only validates compliance but also provides evidence for stakeholders, regulators, and auditors that the project has been managed with rigor and transparency. By linking planning with execution, the quality plan ensures that excellence is not aspirational but demonstrably achieved.

4. Essential Tools and Methodologies for Quality Management

A well-crafted quality plan does not exist in isolation; it requires a set of practical tools and methodologies that operationalise its objectives. These instruments act as the hands and feet of quality management—translating theory into action, strategy into practice, and expectations into measurable results. The following tools are widely recognised in professional practice for their ability to ensure that quality is systematically planned, assured, controlled, and improved across the project lifecycle.

4.1 Checklists: Precision and Consistency:

Checklists are one of the simplest yet most powerful tools of quality management. At their core, they are structured documents that guide inspectors, auditors, or project staff through a predefined set of checkpoints aligned with standards or best practices. The strength of a checklist lies in its ability to translate complex requirements into actionable verification points, ensuring consistency and completeness in inspections.

An effective checklist is neither too broad nor too detailed. Best practice recommends beginning with existing templates—often developed from past projects—and tailoring them to the current project scope. Checklists should remain focused, typically containing 10–20 critical items that represent common sources of defects. This ensures that the checklist functions as a practical tool for critical inspection, rather than as a substitute for detailed specifications. Organising items logically, such as by room, process phase, or functional area, maximises efficiency during inspections.

Perhaps the most significant feature of a checklist is its ability to evolve. Through continuous refinement—removing rarely problematic items while adding new checkpoints based on emerging issues—checklists embody the principle of continuous improvement. In this way, they not only ensure precision in current inspections but also act as repositories of organisational learning.

4.2 Quality Audits: Systemic Health Checks:

Quality audits differ from tactical inspections in that they operate at the systemic level. An audit is a structured, independent review designed to determine whether project activities align with organisational policies, regulatory requirements, and project-specific standards. While inspections are backward-looking, verifying whether deliverables meet stated requirements, audits are forward-looking, seeking to uncover weaknesses in processes that may lead to defects in the future.

The purpose of an audit extends beyond fault-finding. It identifies non-conformances, inefficiencies, and systemic risks, but it also highlights best practices that can be replicated across the organisation. In this sense, audits are as much about spreading excellence as they are about correcting flaws. By feeding into the Plan-Do-Check-Act (PDCA) cycle, audit findings provide the evidence base for Corrective and Preventive Actions (CAPA), creating a direct link between observation and process improvement.

For example, a project audit might reveal that outdated work instructions are being used, posing a risk of recurring errors.

Addressing this proactively ensures smoother operations and prevents costly defects downstream. In regulated industries such as pharmaceuticals or aerospace, audits are not only strategic health checks but also compliance imperatives, ensuring organizations maintain their licence to operate.

4.3 Six Sigma: A Data-Driven Approach to Defect Reduction:

Six Sigma is one of the most influential quality methodologies of the modern era, offering a data-driven framework for reducing defects and variability in processes. Originating at Motorola in the 1980s and later championed by companies like GE, Six Sigma emphasises measurable financial returns, statistical rigour, and structured project management. Its goal is ambitious but clear: reduce process variation so that defects occur no more than 3.4 times per million opportunities.

At the heart of Six Sigma is the Define, Measure, Analyse, Improve and Control (DMAIC) framework:

1. Define:

The Define phase sets the foundation for the entire Six Sigma project. At this stage, the team identifies the core problem, clarifies customer requirements, and establishes project goals. This step ensures that the improvement effort is not just about solving an isolated issue but is aligned with the organisation's strategic priorities. Tools such as project charters, stakeholder analyses, and SIPOC (Suppliers, Inputs, Process, Outputs, Customers) diagrams are often used here to map the process and its context. The output of this phase is a clearly stated problem definition, a set of measurable objectives, and agreement among stakeholders about the project's scope and expected outcomes.

2. Measure:

The Measure phase is about turning qualitative assumptions into quantitative insights. Reliable data is collected to determine the magnitude and frequency of the problem. This involves selecting appropriate metrics that reflect both the efficiency of the process and its alignment with customer expectations. Measurement System Analysis (MSA), process capability studies, and baseline performance data are key elements in this stage. By establishing a data-driven picture of the current process, the team gains a factual basis for comparison and future improvement. This phase also guards against "gut-feel" decision-making, ensuring that subsequent analysis and actions are grounded in objective evidence.

3. Analyse:

The Analyse phase digs deep into the data to uncover the root causes of defects or inefficiencies. Rather than stopping at surface-level symptoms, statistical tools such as regression analysis, hypothesis testing, Pareto charts, and cause-and-effect (Ishikawa/fishbone) diagrams are employed to isolate the fundamental drivers of the problem. The focus is on identifying where variability originates and what factors significantly influence performance. This stage requires both analytical rigor and collaborative insight, as data often needs to be interpreted in the light of process knowledge. The goal is to move from "what is happening" to "why it is happening".

4. Improve:

In the Improve phase, solutions are designed, tested, and implemented to directly address the root causes identified in the analysis. This is a creative yet structured stage where brainstorming, Design of Experiments (DOE), and pilot testing are common techniques. The team may run controlled trials of proposed improvements to confirm their effectiveness before rolling them out at scale. The emphasis is not only on eliminating defects but also on optimising the process to enhance overall performance. Improvements must be practical, cost-effective, and sustainable, ensuring they provide long-term value rather than short-term fixes.

5. Control:

The Control phase ensures that the gains made are not temporary but are sustained over time. Successful solutions are institutionalised through monitoring systems, updated Standard Operating Procedures (SOPs), quality control charts, and regular staff training. This stage also includes establishing responsibility for ongoing measurement and integrating improvements into organisational culture. By embedding monitoring mechanisms, the team can detect if performance starts to drift, enabling corrective action before problems escalate. Essentially, the Control phase transforms the project's achievements into permanent organisational assets.

Together, DMAIC provides a disciplined, data-driven cycle of continuous improvement, ensuring that problems are addressed at their root, solutions are validated with evidence, and improvements are embedded into the system for lasting impact.

Six Sigma distinguishes itself from earlier movements like Total Quality Management (TQM) by integrating financial accountability and advanced analytics into its framework. In project management, Six Sigma enforces rigor across the four classic constraints—scope, time, cost, and quality—transforming projects into disciplined, data-driven endeavours. Its structured approach ensures that quality is not aspirational but measurable, scalable, and financially impactful.

4.4 Continuous Improvement: The Engine of Excellence:

Continuous improvement, often referred to by its Japanese term 'kaizen', represents the cultural and philosophical underpinnings of quality management. While tools like checklists, audits, and Six Sigma provide structure, continuous improvement ensures that these tools are applied iteratively and sustainably. It is based on the principle that incremental, ongoing changes yield substantial long-term benefits in efficiency, quality, and customer satisfaction.

PDCA Cycle

The Plan-Do-Check-Act (PDCA) cycle, also known as the Deming Cycle, operationalises continuous improvement.

1. Plan:

The Plan stage is the foundation of the cycle. Here, the organisation identifies a problem or opportunity for improvement and sets specific objectives to address it. This involves gathering baseline data, analysing current processes, and defining measurable goals. The aim is to develop a well-thought-out plan that clearly specifies what needs to be improved, why it matters, and how success will be measured. Planning also includes identifying required resources, assigning responsibilities, and creating a roadmap of activities. For example, a manufacturing team may notice a recurring defect in production and plan to test a new inspection method to reduce errors.

2. Do:

In the Do stage, the planned change or improvement is implemented, but on a small, controlled scale rather than across the entire system. This minimises risk while offering practical guidance on how the proposed solution works in real-world conditions. Teams often pilot-test the idea in one department, on one machine, or with one product line before applying it broadly. During this stage, it is essential to collect detailed observations and data on how the change affects performance. This experimental approach ensures that the organisation is not committing fully to a solution until its effectiveness is validated.

3. Check:

The Check phase is the analytical heart of the cycle. Here, the organisation evaluates the results of a pilot or small-scale test by comparing actual outcomes against the expected objectives defined in the planning stage. Statistical analysis, performance metrics, and customer feedback are used to assess whether the change led to genuine improvements. The emphasis is on data-driven evaluation rather than subjective judgment. For example, if a new inspection method were introduced, the team would analyse whether defect rates decreased significantly and whether the process became more efficient. If the results show little or no improvement, this signals that adjustments—or even a complete rethinking—may be necessary.

4. Act:

The Act phase focuses on decision-making and standardisation. If the proposed change proves successful, it is institutionalised by updating Standard Operating Procedures (SOPs), providing staff training, and integrating them into organisational practices so the benefits are sustained long-term. On the other hand, if the change did not deliver the desired results, the cycle restarts at the Plan stage, using insights from the failed attempt to inform a revised strategy. This makes PDCA a truly iterative and adaptive process, where even unsuccessful trials contribute to learning and eventual success.

In essence, the PDCA cycle is a simple yet powerful framework for embedding continuous improvement into daily operations. By systematically planning, testing, evaluating, and refining, organizations can make incremental changes that, over time, lead to significant enhancements in quality, efficiency, and customer satisfaction.

What makes continuous improvement powerful is its universality—it underpins all other quality methodologies. A checklist evolves through Kaizen; an audit's findings feed into the PDCA loop; even Six Sigma can be seen as a sophisticated application of PDCA. By embedding continuous improvement into organisational culture, quality management transforms from a compliance exercise into a self-sustaining engine of excellence.

5. Conclusion: Integrating Quality into the Project Lifecycle

Quality management is not a discrete function but a strategic imperative woven throughout the project lifecycle. This chapter has emphasised that achieving quality requires not only clear definitions and structured plans but also the systematic application of tools and methodologies. Checklists ensure precision at the operational level, audits safeguard systemic integrity, Six Sigma provides a rigorous, data-driven framework, and continuous improvement binds them all under a philosophy of ongoing excellence.

For project managers, the essential lesson is that crafting and implementing a quality plan is the starting point, but its success lies in execution and culture. A proactive mindset, leadership commitment, robust measurement, and relentless pursuit of improvement turn quality from an aspiration into a competitive advantage. When integrated effectively, these tools enable organizations to deliver projects that not only meet requirements but also exceed expectations, ensuring sustained success in an increasingly competitive environment.

6. Crafting a Quality Plan: The Blueprint for Project Excellence in Software Project Management

In software project management, a quality plan serves as the blueprint for ensuring that every deliverable—whether it is a single code module or the final product—meets clearly defined standards of excellence. It transforms quality from an abstract aspiration into a measurable, actionable objective. Rather than being an afterthought, the quality plan is a core component of the project management lifecycle, providing structure and clarity for all quality-related activities.

A quality plan is indispensable because it underpins several critical aspects of project execution. *First*, it emphasises defect prevention, shifting the focus from fixing bugs late in the cycle to designing and developing with quality in mind from the outset. By setting standards early, issues can be identified at the requirements or design stage, where resolution is significantly less costly. *Second*, it enables stakeholder alignment by establishing a shared definition of "quality." This ensures that developers, project managers, clients, and end-users have consistent expectations, minimising the risk of misunderstandings. *Third*, a quality plan supports risk mitigation by identifying potential quality-related risks—such as complex integrations or untested technologies—and outlining proactive strategies to address them. *Finally*, it fosters continuous improvement, creating a feedback loop where lessons learnt can be applied to refine practices in future projects.

A comprehensive software quality plan typically contains several key elements. It begins with quality goals and metrics, defining success in objective, measurable terms, such as defect density thresholds, test coverage percentages, or performance benchmarks. It then specifies standards and procedures, including coding conventions, documentation practices, and protocols for version control, code reviews, and change management. The plan also clarifies roles and responsibilities, ensuring accountability by outlining the contributions of project managers, QA leads, developers, and other stakeholders. At its core, the quality plan describes Quality Assurance (QA) activities, which span the entire development lifecycle—from requirements and design reviews to unit, integration, system, performance, and user acceptance testing. Each activity is designed to validate that deliverables meet both functional and non-functional requirements. Additionally, the plan defines the defect management process, establishing how issues are reported, prioritised, tracked, and resolved, supported by metrics such as bug severity levels and resolution rates.

The process of developing a quality plan is inherently collaborative. It requires early engagement between the project manager, QA lead, and key stakeholders to identify client-specific quality requirements, define measurable objectives, and adapt organisational standards to fit the unique context of the project. Quality assurance activities must then be integrated into the project schedule, with appropriate resources allocated to support their execution.

By treating the quality plan as a living document, the project team ensures it remains relevant throughout the lifecycle, guiding decisions and enabling adjustments as conditions evolve.

Ultimately, a quality plan is not just documentation—it is a strategic tool for ensuring project excellence. It establishes the foundation for proactive quality management, aligns all participants around shared expectations, and embeds continuous improvement into the development process. When executed effectively, it ensures that quality is not left to chance but is deliberately planned, measured, and achieved.

CHAPTER 8: STRATEGIC PROCUREMENT AND RESOURCE PLANNING

This chapter presents a comprehensive analysis of procurement and resource planning from both strategic and operational perspectives. It emphasises that modern procurement is not merely a tactical support function but a strategic value driver that directly influences project success and organisational competitiveness. Effective procurement today extends well beyond cost-saving measures, requiring informed decision-making, meticulous process management, and uncompromising ethical standards.

The central argument is that procurement is a strategic endeavour designed to generate long-term value, mitigate risks, and strengthen supply chain resilience. A cornerstone of this approach is the make-or-buy decision, which balances financial metrics with broader strategic considerations. Equally critical is the selection of contract type, which serves as a risk-allocation mechanism—whether through fixed-price, cost-reimbursable, or time-and-materials contracts —aligned with the project's scope certainty and the distribution of risk between buyer and seller. Finally, the chapter underscores that ethical integrity is non-negotiable: lapses in ethics can cause systemic failures, expose organizations to legal liabilities, and erode reputation and financial stability.

The recommendations advocate for adopting a robust procurement framework that integrates structured make-or-buy analysis, systematic contract selection, and a comprehensive ethical compliance programme. When implemented effectively, such a framework transforms procurement from a traditional cost centre into a sustainable source of competitive advantage.

1. Procurement Processes and Strategies

1.1 Defining Procurement in the Project Context:

In the realm of project management, procurement refers to the structured process of acquiring and managing goods, services, and resources essential for project completion. It goes beyond simple purchasing transactions to encompass activities such as needs assessment, vendor selection, contract negotiation, and performance monitoring. Effective procurement ensures that project requirements are delivered on time, within budget, and to the expected standard of quality.

Over time, procurement has evolved from a transactional cost-focused activity into a strategic function that delivers value across the organisation. This evolution reflects a shift from concentrating solely on price reduction to a broader, long-term view that prioritises supplier collaboration, innovation, and risk minimisation. Strategic procurement today is concerned with maximising return on purchasing power while reducing risks that could derail project timelines or inflate budgets. Achieving this transformation requires cross-departmental cooperation and the alignment of procurement activities with broader business goals, thereby embedding procurement within the organisational strategy.

1.2 The PMBOK Framework for Procurement Management:

The Project Management Body of Knowledge (PMBOK) integrates procurement into the four main phases of project management: planning, execution, control, and closure. Each phase addresses different but interconnected aspects of acquiring and managing external resources:

1. Planning Phase:

This is the foundation of procurement, where needs are defined and strategies formulated. Project managers prepare the Procurement Management Plan, outlining policies, procedures, and contract types, and the Statement of Work (SOW), which specifies the contractor's deliverables in detail. Precision at this stage prevents costly disputes and scope creep later.

2. Conducting Procurements (Execution Phase):

In this stage, procurement strategies are executed through bid solicitations (e.g., RFQs, RFPs). Proposals are evaluated against pre-established criteria—technical, financial, and operational—and negotiations finalise pricing, terms, and deliverables. The outcome is a signed contract that formalises vendor engagement.

3. Controlling Procurements (Monitoring and Controlling Phase):

Once the contractor is engaged, active oversight ensures compliance with the contract terms, adherence to schedules, and delivery of expected quality. This may involve performance reviews, site inspections, and change management processes to address deviations. Poor subcontractor management at this stage can jeopardise the entire project, even if other tasks are progressing smoothly.

4. Closing Procurements (Closure Phase):

Procurement formally concludes when the contractor's obligations are met, often certified by an acceptance certificate. Final activities include reconciling costs, resolving outstanding claims, and compiling lessons learnt to guide future procurement activities.

1.3 Key Procurement Strategies and Strategic Procurement Activities:

Strategic procurement rests on a set of structured activities that ensure project resources create maximum value.

1. Defining Project Requirements:

A clear, comprehensive, and unambiguous Statement of Work (SOW) is essential. It provides specifications for goods, services, timelines, and budgets. Inadequately defined requirements lead to ambiguity, scope creep, and financial overruns.

2. Sourcing and Vendor Selection:

Effective procurement begins with rigorous market research and supplier evaluation. Vendor selection must be based not only on price but also on quality, reliability, financial stability, and reputation. Objective criteria and due diligence reduce risks and help identify suppliers capable of delivering consistent value.

3. Contract and Relationship Management:

Beyond the transactional exchange, strategic procurement emphasises long-term supplier relationships. Collaborative partnerships can improve service delivery, enhance reliability, and open opportunities for innovation. Such relationships often yield preferential terms and foster mutual trust, reinforcing procurement's role as a driver of organisational resilience and competitiveness.

2. The Make-or-Buy Analysis: A Cornerstone of Strategic Planning

2.1 Principles of the Make-or-Buy Decision:

A make-or-buy analysis is a structured, evidence-based process used to determine whether a product, service, or function should be developed internally ("make") or sourced externally ("buy"). This decision is not merely operational; it is a cornerstone of the Plan Procurement Management phase and has far-reaching implications for cost efficiency, resource allocation, and strategic alignment.

At its core, the analysis involves comparing the total costs of internal production against those of external procurement. However, effective decision-making extends well beyond financial metrics. A truly strategic make-or-buy analysis also considers organisational competencies, long-term sustainability, and qualitative factors that shape competitive positioning. In this sense, the decision is not simply about "cheaper versus costlier" but about "strategically aligned versus misaligned".

2.2 A Framework for Quantitative Analysis:

A robust quantitative analysis requires a detailed breakdown of direct and indirect costs for both alternatives:

1. *Make* ***(in-house production):*** Costs include raw materials, labour, equipment, maintenance, and facility overheads.

2. Buy (external sourcing): Costs typically include supplier pricing, logistics, customs or shipping charges, and contract management expenses.

Indirect costs, such as shared administrative support or overheads, must also be accounted for, as they influence the true financial picture.

To strengthen decision accuracy, organizations often employ advanced financial tools:

a. ***Break-Even Analysis:*** Determines the production volume at which making internally becomes more cost-effective than outsourcing.

b. ***Marginal Cost Analysis:*** Examines the incremental cost of producing one additional unit in-house versus purchasing it externally.

c. ***Opportunity Cost Evaluation:*** Assesses the value of alternative uses of internal resources that would be sacrificed if the firm chooses to produce in-house. For example, dedicating staff and facilities to manufacturing may divert resources from high-value R&D activities.

A critical insight revealed through this analysis is the relationship between production volume and cost viability. "Make" options often carry high fixed costs (e.g., machinery investments), which only become economical at higher volumes. Conversely, "buy" options usually involve relatively stable per-unit costs, making them preferable at lower volumes. The intersection point between these cost curves represents the break-even threshold where the financial advantage shifts.

2.3 A Framework for Qualitative Analysis:

While quantitative factors are important, they alone cannot dictate a sound make-or-buy decision. Organizations must weigh a set of strategic and operational considerations:

1. ***Core Competencies and Strategic Fit:*** Does internal production align with the firm's unique strengths and long-term goals, or would outsourcing free resources for higher-value activities?

2. ***Quality Control and Intellectual Property:*** In-house manufacturing may ensure stricter quality standards and safeguard proprietary knowledge. However, specialised vendors may offer superior technical expertise.

3. ***Operational Flexibility and Scalability:*** Outsourcing often provides agility to ramp production up or down without major capital investment, a key advantage in volatile markets.

4. ***Supply Chain and External Risks:*** Buying externally introduces dependency risks, such as supplier instability, geopolitical disruptions, or logistical challenges.

5. ***Employee Morale and Resource Utilisation:*** In-house work may boost workforce engagement by linking employee contributions directly to organisational outcomes.

6. ***Sustainability and Ethical Goals:*** Firms committed to sustainability may prefer in-house production to maintain control over environmental practices and ethical standards.

2.4 Integrated Decision-Making and Documentation:

The make-or-buy decision is ultimately an integrated judgment call, balancing both hard financial data and soft strategic considerations. Over-reliance on a single metric, such as cost savings, risks oversimplification and long-term misalignment.

Best practice involves using a structured evaluation template that documents cost comparisons, qualitative assessments, and identified risks. This systematic approach ensures transparency, provides a defensible rationale for stakeholders, and minimises the influence of bias or short-term pressures.

By integrating quantitative rigour with qualitative insight, organizations can transform the make-or-buy decision from a cost-driven calculation into a strategic lever for efficiency, competitiveness, and sustainable growth.

3. Navigating Contract Types: Fixed-Price, Cost-Reimbursable, and Time & Materials

3.1 Contract Types as Risk-Allocation Mechanisms:

The choice of contract type is the primary means by which risk is distributed between the buyer and the seller. Each contract exists along a risk continuum—from scenarios where the seller assumes most of the risk to those where the buyer carries the greater burden. The decision depends heavily on project complexity and the degree of scope certainty. A poorly defined scope, regardless of contract structure, heightens risks for both parties, making thoughtful contract selection indispensable.

3.2 Fixed-Price Contracts (FP): Certainty and Risk Transfer:

3.2.1 Characteristics and Use Cases:

Fixed-price contracts, often referred to as lump-sum agreements, establish a single, predetermined price for a clearly defined deliverable. They are most effective in projects with a stable scope, accurate cost estimates, and low likelihood of change.

a. ***Firm Fixed-Price (FFP):*** The most common form, transferring maximum cost and performance responsibility to the seller.

b. ***Fixed-Price with Economic Price Adjustment (FPEPA):*** Allows price adjustments based on pre-defined contingencies, such as inflation, material cost fluctuations, or labour market volatility—making it suitable for long-duration projects subject to changing conditions.

3.2.2 Advantages and Disadvantages of :

1. Buyer Perspective:

a. *Advantages:* High cost predictability, reduced exposure to overruns, and simplified administration.

b. *Disadvantages:* Typically higher upfront prices, as sellers incorporate risk premiums; potential quality compromises if sellers attempt to protect profit margins.

2. Seller Perspective:

c. *Advantages:* Opportunity for higher profits if costs

are well managed; limited administrative oversight compared to cost-based models.

d. *Disadvantages:* Maximum exposure to cost overruns or unforeseen challenges; underestimation can cause financial strain or losses.

A critical nuance is that fixed-price contracts do not eliminate risk—they reallocate it. Sellers often build in a risk premium of 10–20%, meaning buyers ultimately pay for uncertainty. Furthermore, shifting cost risk to the seller may introduce new risks for the buyer, such as delayed schedules, reduced quality, or even seller default if financial pressures mount. Thus, these contracts demand careful judgment from project managers to balance apparent cost certainty with hidden risks.

3.3 Cost-Reimbursable Contracts (CR): Flexibility and Oversight:

3.3.1 Characteristics and Use Cases:

Cost-reimbursable contracts reimburse the seller for all allowable expenses, plus an additional fee for profit. They are particularly suitable for projects with uncertain, evolving, or high-risk scopes where costs cannot be reliably estimated upfront.

a. ***Cost-Plus-Fixed-Fee (CPFF):*** Covers all costs plus a negotiated fixed fee; best suited for R&D or feasibility studies.

b. ***Cost-Plus-Incentive-Fee (CPIF):*** Links the seller's fee to cost efficiency through a pre-defined sharing formula, encouraging cost control.

c. ***Cost-Plus-Award-Fee (CPAF):*** Provides a base fee

plus performance-based awards, often determined subjectively by the buyer to reward excellence in quality, innovation, or responsiveness.

3.3.2 Advantages and Disadvantages of Cost-Reimbursable Contracts (CR):

1. Buyer Perspective:

a. *Advantages:* Flexibility in scope, adaptability to changes, and potential for higher quality outputs due to use of premium materials and talent.

b. *Disadvantages:* High exposure to cost escalation, significant administrative oversight required, and potential disputes over allowable expenses.

2. Seller Perspective:

c. *Advantages:* Minimal financial risk from overruns, assured profit, and opportunity to use optimal resources without bearing cost penalties.

d. *Disadvantages:* High administrative burden from detailed record-keeping and potential conflict over cost classification and approval.

These contracts are valuable in complex, uncertain projects but demand rigorous buyer oversight to maintain financial discipline.

3.4 Time and Materials Contracts (T&M): The Hybrid Model:

3.4.1 Characteristics and Use Cases:

Time and materials contracts blend elements of fixed-price and cost-reimbursable approaches. The buyer pays for actual time (at pre-agreed labour rates) and materials used. They are well-suited for projects with unpredictable requirements or scope uncertainty, such as consulting, maintenance, or exploratory software development.

To mitigate buyer risk, T&M agreements often include "not-to-exceed" (NTE) clauses, establishing a maximum allowable budget unless explicitly authorised otherwise. This safeguard ensures financial control while retaining flexibility.

3.4.2 Advantages and Disadvantages of Time and Materials Contracts (T&M):

1. Buyer Perspective:

a. *Advantages:* High adaptability to evolving needs, quick initiation, and reduced upfront planning requirements.

b. *Disadvantages:* Cost risk remains open-ended, with potential for runaway expenses and inefficiency unless closely monitored.

2. Seller Perspective:

c. *Advantages:* Guaranteed compensation for time and resources, predictable profit margins, and minimal risk of overruns.

d. *Disadvantages:* Intensive tracking and documentation demands, and potential for disputes if reporting lacks transparency.

T&M contracts offer balance but rely heavily on buyer oversight and governance to ensure efficiency.

3.5 Strategic Selection and Hybrid Approaches:

Contract selection is not a one-size-fits-all decision; it must align with the project's risk profile, scope certainty, timeline, and contractor capabilities. In many cases, the most effective approach is a hybrid strategy:

a. A **fixed-price component** may be used for well-defined deliverables.

b. A **T&M or cost-reimbursable component** may manage exploratory or high-uncertainty phases.

This blended model allows organizations to leverage the stability of fixed-price agreements while retaining the flexibility of adaptive contracts—demonstrating procurement not merely as a transactional activity but as a strategic instrument for risk management and value creation.

4. Ethical Considerations in Procurement: Upholding Integrity

4.1 The Foundational Principles of Ethical Procurement:

Ethical procurement is not simply an aspirational ideal but a fundamental, non-negotiable requirement for building a sustainable and trustworthy business model. At its core, ethical procurement is anchored in fair business practices, respect for human rights, and compliance with all applicable legal and regulatory frameworks. Its foundation rests on three guiding principles: transparency, confidentiality, and fairness. These principles ensure that all suppliers are treated equitably throughout the procurement process.

Beyond the prevention of corruption, ethical procurement

embraces broader dimensions of social responsibility. This includes eliminating forced or child labour, ensuring safe and dignified working conditions, and promoting fair wages across the supply chain. Organizations that prioritise these values not only safeguard compliance but also contribute to long-term sustainability and reputation.

4.2 Identifying and Mitigating Common Ethical Issues:

4.2.1 Bribery and Favouritism:

Bribery—offering or accepting payments, gifts, or favours to influence procurement decisions—remains one of the most damaging threats to ethical practice. Closely related is favouritism or nepotism, where procurement professionals extend undue preference to friends, relatives, or close associates. Such practices distort competition, undermine credibility, and expose organizations to legal liabilities.

Mitigation strategies emphasise a fair and transparent bidding process. This requires pre-defining evaluation criteria, applying consistent weighting, and documenting all decisions clearly. Bid openings, evaluations, and final selections should be communicated openly to stakeholders, leaving no space for subjectivity or hidden influence. In many jurisdictions, bribery constitutes a criminal offence, and international laws increasingly target offshore corruption as well.

4.2.2 Conflicts of Interest:

A conflict of interest occurs when personal relationships or financial stakes compromise—or appear to compromise—a professional's ability to act impartially. For example, an employee might hold shares in a supplier company, or a family member may be employed by a vendor. Such conflicts erode trust and can distort procurement decisions, even unintentionally.

To address this risk, organizations must institute formal procedures for identifying, disclosing, and managing conflicts. Best practices include requiring annual disclosure statements from procurement staff, establishing protocols for reporting new or perceived conflicts, and involving independent oversight in reviewing disclosures. These safeguards ensure decisions remain objective and in the best interest of the organisation.

4.2.3 Social and Environmental Responsibility:

Ethical procurement extends to the social and environmental impacts of sourcing decisions. Organizations must ensure that suppliers comply with labour laws, uphold safe working environments, and provide fair compensation in line with industry standards. Equally important is the responsibility to verify that supply chains are free from forced or child labour.

Proactive engagement with suppliers is critical, particularly in regions where enforcement of labour and environmental regulations is weak. Audits, certifications, and collaborative partnerships can help strengthen compliance and uphold organisational values. Neglecting these responsibilities has systemic consequences: lack of transparency and bias in procurement erodes trust, deters reputable suppliers, and drives up costs, often forcing organizations into partnerships with less reliable vendors. This can result in inflated pricing, substandard services, and reputational harm—directly undermining the strategic objectives of procurement.

4.3 Building a Culture of Integrity:

While written policies form the backbone of ethical

procurement, their true effectiveness depends on consistent leadership, communication, and accountability. Ethical guidelines should be clear and accessible and provide practical direction on sensitive issues such as gift acceptance and personal interests. Senior management must not only endorse but also model ethical conduct to reinforce organisational commitment.

Ongoing training and awareness programmes further strengthen ethical culture, equipping staff to recognise risks and respond appropriately. Monitoring mechanisms —such as compliance questionnaires, independent audits, and whistleblower systems—help ensure accountability. Importantly, organizations must cultivate a culture where employees feel safe to disclose conflicts or report suspected misconduct without fear of retaliation. Such openness fosters a "culture of candour", where integrity is not an obligation imposed from above but a shared value embraced across the organisation.

5. Conclusion and Recommendations for Strategic Excellence

The analysis in this report underscores that modern procurement and resource planning are no longer merely operational necessities but critical strategic functions. They directly shape an organisation's financial performance, competitiveness, and long-term sustainability. Achieving excellence requires a deliberate shift from a narrow, cost-centred mindset to a value-driven approach grounded in informed decision-making, proactive risk management, and uncompromising ethical standards.

To support this transformation, the following recommendations are proposed:

1. Formalise the Make-or-Buy Process:

All significant acquisitions should undergo a comprehensive, documented make-or-buy analysis. This process must go beyond a simple financial cost comparison to include both quantitative and qualitative considerations —such as alignment with organisational competencies, innovation potential, and long-term scalability. By doing so, organizations ensure that sourcing decisions directly reinforce strategic objectives.

2. Adopt a Risk-Based Contracting Model:

A uniform approach to contracting is inadequate for today's dynamic business environment. Organizations should adopt a structured framework that matches contract type—fixed-price, cost-reimbursable, or time and materials—to the unique risk profile and scope of each project. This ensures an optimal balance of risk allocation between buyer and seller while safeguarding project outcomes.

3. Institutionalise Ethical Governance:

Ethical procurement must be embedded in governance frameworks. This involves establishing a clear code of conduct, a mandatory conflict-of-interest disclosure policy, and an independent oversight mechanism. Combined with regular training and a culture that encourages candour, these measures foster transparency and fairness, strengthening organisational reputation and attracting trustworthy suppliers.

4. Invest in Supplier Relationship Management:

Organizations should move beyond transactional cost-cutting and embrace supplier relationship management as a strategic priority. Treating suppliers as long-term partners enables shared innovation, resilience against disruptions, and the development of a sustainable supply chain ecosystem that benefits all stakeholders.

By implementing these recommendations, organizations can elevate procurement from a back-office function to a strategic enabler of competitive advantage. In doing so, procurement becomes not just a support mechanism but a driver of innovation, resilience, and sustainable growth.

6. Strategic Procurement and Resource Planning in Software Project Management

In software project management, strategic procurement and resource planning are interdependent practices that ensure projects are delivered on schedule, within budget, and at the expected quality level. Together, they provide the foundation for operational efficiency and effective risk management, allowing project teams to remain focused on delivering value.

Strategic procurement in software projects goes beyond transactional purchasing. It is a forward-looking, value-driven approach that considers the total cost of ownership and long-term benefits rather than short-term savings. Effective procurement requires careful vendor and partner selection, where technical competence, reliability, scalability, and security practices must be weighed alongside cultural fit. Poor vendor alignment can lead to risks such as technical debt, project delays, or compliance issues. Procurement also involves negotiating favourable contracts and licensing terms, including flexible models, strong service-level agreements, intellectual property protections, and data security clauses. Building strong supplier relationships is equally important, as it can unlock better support, competitive pricing, and opportunities for joint innovation. Finally, procurement strategies must incorporate risk mitigation measures such as vendor diversification, contingency planning, and predefined escalation procedures to safeguard project continuity.

Resource planning complements procurement by ensuring that all human, technological, and financial assets are properly identified, allocated, and managed throughout the project lifecycle. It is a dynamic process that directly affects a project's ability to meet scope, time, and quality goals. Resource identification must go beyond developers to include roles such as designers, testers, analysts, project managers, and supporting infrastructure like cloud services and software tools. Once identified, resources must be allocated strategically, taking into account skill sets, availability, and workload balance. Tools such as Gantt charts, RACI matrices, and scheduling software help maintain visibility and efficiency in allocation. Resource optimisation ensures maximum utilisation without overburdening staff or overspending on technology, often requiring task reprioritisation, deadline adjustments, or additional resource acquisition. Continuous monitoring and control are essential to track utilisation rates, Agile velocity, and cost burn-down, enabling proactive adjustments and accurate forecasting.

The interplay between procurement and resource planning is critical for software project success. Procurement ensures that the right tools, expertise, and services are available, while resource planning determines how those assets are applied effectively. For example, securing a flexible cloud computing contract adds value only if resource planning ensures efficient consumption. Similarly, identifying a skills gap during resource planning may trigger procurement of external consultants or outsourcing partners. Weakness in either area—such as poor vendor contracts or ineffective allocation—can result in cost overruns, delays, or reduced quality. When integrated effectively, strategic procurement secures the “what” a project needs, and resource planning governs the “how,” creating a resilient framework that balances cost, quality, and time to deliver successful outcomes.

CHAPTER 9: DEVELOPING A PROJECT SCHEDULE

Project scheduling lies at the heart of project management. It provides the structure for organising, sequencing, and controlling work while offering a roadmap for balancing competing priorities. A well-crafted schedule is far more than a list of dates—it is a strategic instrument that enables project managers to anticipate risks, allocate resources efficiently, and make informed decisions throughout the project lifecycle.

This chapter explores the essential tools and methodologies that underpin effective scheduling. It begins with the Work Breakdown Structure (WBS), the foundation for defining scope and organising work. From there, it examines network-based scheduling techniques, particularly the Critical Path Method (CPM) and the Program Evaluation and Review Technique (PERT), which provide analytical rigour for sequencing tasks and managing uncertainty. The discussion then turns to the practical toolkit of modern project management, including Gantt charts, Kanban boards, and Agile sprints, highlighting how these approaches can be combined for both strategic and tactical control. Finally, the chapter addresses the triple constraint of time, cost, and scope, demonstrating how scheduling becomes a balancing act that ultimately determines a project's success.

1. Work Breakdown Structure (WBS)

Every successful project begins with decomposition—the deliberate act of breaking down a large initiative into smaller, more manageable components. In software project management, this process is formalized through the Work Breakdown Structure (WBS), a hierarchical, deliverable-oriented model that organizes the total scope of work into progressively smaller units. Unlike a simple checklist, the WBS is a strategic planning tool that provides a structured framework for estimating costs, scheduling activities, and assigning responsibilities. By breaking down complex projects into smaller work packages, managers can create a roadmap that is easier to track, control, and adapt as the project evolves.

1. Strategic Value of WBS:

The WBS holds immense strategic value because it is directly tied to risk management and scope control. One of the biggest challenges in software projects is scope creep—the uncontrolled expansion of project deliverables without proper evaluation or approval. A robust WBS mitigates this risk by clearly defining project boundaries in terms of deliverables rather than activities. In doing so, it ensures that every task performed contributes to a specific output that has been approved and documented. Any work item that does not align with the WBS can be flagged for formal change control, protecting the project from hidden or unplanned requirements. Beyond scope control, the WBS also establishes clear links to cost and schedule baselines, making it a unifying framework that connects the three pillars of project management: scope, time, and cost.

2. Anatomy of a WBS:

The WBS itself is structured as a hierarchy with multiple layers, each offering increasing detail about the project. At the top level, the Project Root Task represents the entire project as a single entity, summarising its total duration, effort, and cost as the sum of all its components. Beneath this, Summary (Container) Tasks act as logical groupings of related tasks, rolling up values from their subtasks to provide mid-level visibility. At the most granular level are the work packages, which represent the smallest units of work that can be realistically estimated, assigned, and tracked. To support this structure, a WBS dictionary is often developed, providing detailed descriptions, required resources, timelines, deliverables, and communication protocols for each WBS element. This ensures that all stakeholders share a consistent understanding of project tasks and responsibilities, reducing ambiguity and miscommunication.

3. Practical Application of WBS:

The process of developing a WBS typically unfolds in three structured steps. The first step is work decomposition, in which the project is progressively broken down from large deliverables into smaller, more manageable components until work packages are defined. This step requires careful thought to balance detail and clarity without overcomplicating the structure. The second step is work scheduling, where durations are estimated, dependencies are established, and start and finish dates are determined within the project calendar. This ensures that work packages are not only defined but also positioned realistically within the project timeline. The final step is cost estimation, where resources such as labour, materials, and overhead expenses are assigned at the work package level. This builds a reliable budget that reflects the actual effort and resources required to deliver each component.

By completing these steps, the WBS becomes far more than a planning artefact—it evolves into a planning and control tool. It anchors the project's scope, informs resource allocation, provides the basis for realistic schedules, and ensures that the project progresses in a consistent, transparent, and predictable manner. In essence, the WBS transforms a complex software project into a structured, manageable, and trackable endeavour.

2. Critical Path Method (CPM) and PERT

Once the project's work is defined through the Work Breakdown Structure (WBS), the next challenge is determining the sequence of tasks and managing the project timeline effectively. This is where two foundational scheduling techniques—Critical Path Method (CPM) and Program Evaluation and Review Technique (PERT)—play a central role. Both methods rely on network diagrams to visualise dependencies between tasks, but they approach scheduling from different perspectives. CPM provides a deterministic framework suited for projects with well-defined activities, while PERT introduces a probabilistic dimension, accounting for uncertainty in task durations. Together, they form a powerful toolkit for managing complex schedules in software and other types of projects.

1. Deterministic vs. Probabilistic Approaches:

Critical Path Method (CPM):

The Critical Path Method (CPM) operates on the assumption

that task durations are fixed and predictable. This makes it ideal for projects where activities are repetitive or standardised, such as construction or implementation of well-understood software modules. CPM excels at analysing time–cost trade-offs, enabling project managers to shorten schedules by "crashing" certain activities—allocating additional resources to reduce task duration without altering the project's scope.

Program Evaluation and Review Technique (PERT):

By contrast, the Program Evaluation and Review Technique (PERT) is designed for projects where uncertainty is high, such as research, product development, or innovative software design. Instead of assuming fixed durations, PERT uses a three-point estimation model—Optimistic (O), Most Likely (M), and Pessimistic (P) times. These values are used to calculate an expected duration and standard deviation for each activity, producing more statistically grounded forecasts. This approach helps managers account for uncertainty, anticipate risks, and prepare contingency plans.

In practice, sophisticated project managers often combine the strengths of both approaches. CPM is used to provide structure and optimise resource allocation, while PERT is applied to assess uncertainty and build resilience into the schedule. This hybrid approach allows teams to stay both efficient and adaptable.

2. The Critical Path Explained:

At the heart of CPM lies the concept of the critical path—the longest chain of dependent tasks that determines the project's minimum completion time. If any task on this path is delayed, the entire project is delayed, since tasks on the critical path have zero float (or slack). This makes identifying the critical path a crucial exercise for project managers, as it pinpoints the activities that demand the most attention and control.

Identifying the critical path typically involves several structured steps. First, activities are listed, usually derived directly from the WBS. Next, dependencies between tasks are defined, ensuring the logical order of execution is clear. Durations for each task are then estimated, followed by the creation of a network diagram to visualise task sequences. Using forward and backward pass calculations, project managers determine the early start, early finish, late start, and late finish for each activity. The path with zero slack is identified as the critical path, establishing the project's shortest possible timeline.

3. PERT and Statistical Forecasting:

While the *Critical Path Method* (CPM) highlights structure and precision, PERT emphasises probability and forecasting. Its use of the three-point estimation model—optimistic (O), most likely (M), and pessimistic (P)—allows managers to calculate expected activity durations using a weighted average formula:

PERT and Three-Point Estimation

For uncertain projects, PERT improves accuracy through a weighted formula:

$$ET = \frac{O + 4M + P}{6}$$

Where:

- **O** = Optimistic time
- **M** = Most likely time
- **P** = Pessimistic time

This not only generates a realistic estimate of task duration but also provides variance and standard deviation measures that quantify uncertainty. By aggregating these across the project, managers can develop probability distributions for overall project completion times. Unlike CPM, which gives a single completion date, PERT allows managers to assess a range of possible outcomes, offering insights into both best-case and worst-case scenarios.

4. Practical Significance:

By integrating CPM and PERT, project managers gain both structure and flexibility. CPM ensures that dependencies are honoured and resources are effectively allocated, while PERT helps in navigating the unpredictability inherent in software projects. Together, they enable proactive decision-making, allowing teams to anticipate risks, test "what-if" scenarios, and build more resilient schedules. In this way, CPM and PERT transform scheduling from a static exercise into a dynamic process that balances precision with adaptability.

3. Gantt Charts, Kanban Boards, and Agile Sprints

While techniques such as CPM and PERT provide the analytical backbone of scheduling, modern project management increasingly relies on visual and adaptive tools that make schedules more actionable and easier to communicate. These tools—Gantt charts, Kanban boards, and Agile sprints—bring clarity, transparency, and flexibility to project execution. Each serves a unique purpose, and when combined, they create a comprehensive scheduling ecosystem that balances long-term planning with day-to-day adaptability.

1. Gantt Charts:

A Gantt chart is one of the most widely used scheduling tools, presenting tasks along a horizontal timeline. Each bar represents the duration of an activity, with dependencies and milestones clearly marked. This visualisation helps managers and teams understand not only what needs to be done but also how different tasks interrelate over time. Gantt charts are particularly effective in high-level planning, where multiple teams, overlapping activities, and complex dependencies must be coordinated.

For stakeholders and clients, a Gantt chart serves as a single source of truth. It provides a snapshot of the project's overall timeline, making it easy to track progress against milestones and deadlines. For project managers, it supports monitoring and control by showing where delays occur and how they affect the broader schedule. Despite their strengths, Gantt charts can become unwieldy for highly dynamic projects, which is why they are often paired with more adaptive tools.

2. Kanban Boards:

In contrast to the timeline-oriented nature of Gantt charts, a Kanban board focuses on the flow of tasks through different stages of work. Typically structured with columns such as "To Do," "In Progress," and "Done," the board provides a clear visualisation of work status at any given moment. This simplicity is its greatest strength—it allows teams to quickly identify bottlenecks, overloaded tasks, or delays that might not be obvious in a traditional timeline view.

The Kanban system also emphasises limiting Work-In-Progress (WIP), which prevents teams from taking on too many tasks simultaneously and encourages completion before new work is started. This principle enhances efficiency, reduces context switching, and fosters a steady rhythm of delivery. Kanban boards are especially valuable in operational or repetitive workflows such as software maintenance, bug fixing, or customer support, where continuous flow and efficiency are more important than rigid deadlines.

3. Agile Sprints:

Agile sprints represent the iterative core of modern software project management. In frameworks like Scrum, work is organised into short, time-boxed cycles—usually lasting one to four weeks—where teams commit to delivering a small but meaningful increment of the product. Each sprint follows a structured rhythm that includes sprint planning, daily stand-ups, sprint reviews, and retrospectives.

This cycle fosters adaptability and responsiveness to change, as priorities can be reassessed at the end of each sprint based on user feedback, evolving requirements, or newly discovered risks. Sprints also promote team focus and accountability, as progress is continuously reviewed in short intervals. Unlike Gantt charts or Kanban boards, which provide structural visibility, sprints emphasise value delivery—ensuring that the project evolves incrementally in alignment with client and user needs.

4. Hybrid Scheduling: Combining Strengths:

In practice, no single tool fully addresses the complexities of modern projects. The most effective schedules are built using a hybrid approach that leverages the strengths of each tool. For instance, a Gantt chart may be used to outline the overall programme timeline and track dependencies across large workstreams. Within that framework, Kanban boards can help teams manage their day-to-day workflow, while Agile sprints ensure that uncertain or complex features are delivered iteratively.

This layered approach strikes a balance between predictability and flexibility. Stakeholders gain confidence from seeing long-term timelines and milestones, while teams retain the agility needed to adapt to change and continuously deliver value. By integrating these tools, project managers not only gain better control over project execution but also create an environment that fosters collaboration, efficiency, and adaptability.

4. The Strategic Balancing Act: Time, Cost, and Scope

1. The Triple Constraint in Software Projects:

At its core, project scheduling revolves around the triple constraint of time, cost, and scope—commonly visualised as a triangle where each side effects the others. In software projects, this interplay is even more pronounced because of evolving requirements, technology uncertainties, and resource limitations. If a team attempts to shorten the project timeline (time), they may need to hire additional developers, use premium tools, or increase overtime costs (raising cost). Conversely, if management imposes strict cost controls, the team may have to extend timelines or reduce the number of features delivered in the release. Similarly, expanding scope—such as adding new modules, features, or integrations—inevitably demands more time and budget. Successful scheduling requires acknowledging that no decision is isolated—changes in one dimension cascade through the others.

2. Fixed Constraints and Trade-Off Decisions:

Not all three constraints are equally flexible in a given project. Some software projects are time-bound (e.g., a product launch aligned with a market event), where deadlines cannot shift, forcing managers to adjust cost or scope. Others are budget-constrained (e.g., startup projects with limited funding), which requires stretching timelines or trimming features to stay viable. In enterprise solutions, scope is often non-negotiable because regulatory or client requirements dictate the deliverables. Recognising which of the three is fixed versus flexible empowers project managers to make informed trade-offs instead of reacting blindly to pressures. This clarity helps teams prioritise efforts, allocate resources effectively, and prevent scope creep from derailing progress.

3. Applying Methodologies to Manage the Balance:

Each project scheduling methodology offers a distinct approach to balancing the triple constraint of time, cost, and scope, making them essential tools in a project manager's toolkit. By strategically applying these methodologies, managers can create schedules that are both realistic and adaptable, enabling them to navigate uncertainties while keeping the project aligned with its goals.

a. WBS:

The Breakdown Work Structure (WBS) is the foundation for managing scope effectively. By decomposing the project into smaller, manageable deliverables, the WBS ensures that every requirement is captured and accounted for. This prevents scope creep by defining clear boundaries and responsibilities. Moreover, it provides a structured framework for assigning tasks, estimating resources, and mapping dependencies, all of which contribute to more accurate scheduling and cost estimation.

b. CPM and PERT:

The Critical Path Method (CPM) and Program Evaluation and Review Technique (PERT) shift the focus to time management. CPM identifies the sequence of activities that directly determine the project's duration, allowing managers to recognise which tasks must be closely monitored to avoid delays. PERT, on the other hand, incorporates uncertainty into scheduling by considering optimistic, pessimistic, and most likely task durations. Together, these methods help project teams foresee risks, anticipate slippage, and allocate buffers, enabling proactive adjustments rather than reactive firefighting.

c. Agile Tools:

In dynamic environments where change is inevitable, Agile methodologies provide the flexibility to balance shifting priorities. Techniques such as sprints, backlogs, and iterative reviews allow teams to adapt scope incrementally while sustaining steady progress. Agile ensures that the most valuable features are prioritised, delivering business value early and often, even if time or cost constraints limit the project's total scope. This adaptability is particularly critical in software and innovation-driven projects where requirements evolve rapidly.

d. Gantt charts:

Gantt charts bring a visual dimension to scheduling by mapping out tasks, dependencies, milestones, and progress in a timeline format. This enhances transparency and communication among stakeholders, ensuring that everyone shares a common understanding of where the project stands. By comparing planned timelines with actual progress, Gantt charts help identify deviations early and provide a basis for corrective actions, thereby maintaining alignment across time, cost, and scope.

When woven together, these methodologies create a robust decision-support framework. Instead of merely responding to problems as they arise, project managers can anticipate potential challenges, weigh trade-offs, and implement mitigation strategies before issues escalate. In this way, the blend of WBS, CPM, PERT, Agile practices, and Gantt charts transforms scheduling from a static plan into a dynamic management process—one that balances constraints while keeping projects resilient and outcome-driven.

By weaving these tools into the schedule, project managers not only manage constraints but also create decision-support frameworks that anticipate challenges rather than merely responding to them.

4. From Rigid Plans to Strategic Advantage:

When time, cost, and scope are treated as competing forces, schedules risk becoming rigid documents that quickly lose relevance in a dynamic software environment. However, by mastering the interplay among the triple constraints, project managers transform scheduling into a strategic advantage. A well-balanced schedule allows stakeholders to trust the roadmap, teams to adapt without chaos, and organizations to maximise value delivery within real-world constraints. Instead of being a straitjacket, the schedule becomes a living instrument for alignment, negotiation, and strategic steering—which is precisely what separates successful software project management from reactive firefighting.

5. Developing a Project Schedule in Software Project Management

1. The Role of a Project Schedule:

In software project management, developing a project schedule is one of the most critical activities that transforms abstract plans and requirements into a tangible roadmap for execution. A project schedule is not merely a timeline; it serves as a structured framework that defines what needs to be done, when it should be accomplished, who is responsible, and how various activities interrelate. Since software projects are inherently complex, iterative, and subject to frequent change, creating a realistic and adaptive schedule becomes a key factor in ensuring successful delivery.

2. Importance of Scheduling:

A well-designed schedule serves as both a management tool and a communication instrument. It enables project managers to allocate resources effectively, monitor progress, identify potential risks early, and maintain alignment among stakeholders. For the development team, it provides clarity on priorities, dependencies, and task responsibilities, while for clients and sponsors, it offers visibility into milestones, deliverables, and deadlines. Without a reliable schedule, projects often face issues such as scope creep, resource bottlenecks, and missed deadlines.

3. Inputs to Scheduling:

The development of a project schedule begins with gathering essential inputs. These include a clear understanding of project scope and requirements, which define the features, modules, and deliverables expected. A Work Breakdown Structure (WBS) helps decompose the project into manageable tasks, while effort estimation techniques—such as function point analysis, story points, or expert judgement —are used to determine task durations. Resource availability also plays a crucial role, taking into account the skills, experience, and capacity of developers, testers, designers, and other contributors. Additionally, external constraints such as budget limits, deadlines, and contractual obligations must be carefully considered.

4. Scheduling Techniques and Tools:

To build an effective schedule, software project managers rely on various techniques and tools. Gantt charts are commonly used to visualise timelines and track task progress. Methods such as the Program Evaluation and Review Technique (PERT) help address uncertain task durations, while the Critical Path Method (CPM) identifies the longest sequence of dependent tasks and the shortest possible project duration. In Agile environments, iterative approaches like sprint planning, release planning, and burndown charts in Scrum or Kanban provide flexibility and adaptability. Popular project management tools such as Microsoft Project, JIRA, Trello, and Azure DevOps further support collaborative task management and progress tracking.

5. Sequencing and Dependencies:

Another important aspect of scheduling is sequencing activities and identifying dependencies. In software projects, certain activities must precede others—for example, system architecture must be finalised before coding begins, and unit testing must be completed before integration testing. Proper sequencing prevents conflicts, ensures smoother workflows, and minimises delays caused by misaligned tasks.

6. Buffering and Risk Considerations:

Since software development is prone to requirement changes, technical challenges, and integration issues, project managers often incorporate buffers and flexible milestones into schedules. Risk assessments are conducted to anticipate potential obstacles, and contingency plans are built into the schedule to account for unforeseen issues. This approach helps maintain stability without compromising adaptability.

7. Monitoring and Adaptation:

Equally important is the ongoing monitoring and adaptation of the schedule. Unlike static plans, project schedules evolve as work progresses. Agile methodologies emphasise continuous rescheduling through sprint reviews and retrospectives, while traditional methods rely on regular status checks and earned value analysis. The central principle is to adapt the schedule in response to changing requirements, delays, or risks while ensuring transparency with all stakeholders.

8. Striking the Right Balance:

One of the most challenging aspects of scheduling is finding the right balance between realism and ambition. An overly optimistic schedule may create unrealistic expectations, leading to stress, burnout, and compromised quality. Conversely, a pessimistic schedule may reduce the project's competitiveness. Striking this balance requires negotiation, the use of historical project data, and iterative refinement of estimates.

9. Conclusion:

In essence, developing a project schedule in software project management is about balancing predictability with flexibility. It transforms project goals into actionable steps, guides resource allocation, and ensures that all participants remain aligned throughout the development lifecycle. By integrating structured planning techniques, risk management, and adaptive practices, project managers can design schedules that not only ensure timely delivery but also enhance team efficiency and client satisfaction.

PART III

EXECUTING AND MONITORING PROJECTS

CHAPTER 10: MONITORING AND CONTROLLING PROJECT PROGRESS

1. Introduction: The Imperative of Project Oversight and Control

1.1 Defining the Monitoring and Controlling Process Group:

The monitoring and controlling process group constitutes the fourth phase of the project lifecycle and operates concurrently with the execution phase. This stage functions as the central oversight mechanism, ensuring that project activities remain consistent with the originally approved scope, schedule, and budget. Its primary purpose is to systematically track progress, detect deviations from baseline plans, and implement corrective measures before such variances escalate into major risks or failures. Unlike discrete milestones, monitoring and controlling is a continuous, iterative loop of data collection, analysis, decision-making, and corrective action that endures throughout the entire project duration.

The iterative nature of this process ensures that project managers, sponsors, clients, and other stakeholders maintain real-time visibility into project performance. Regular reports, dashboards, and key performance indicators (KPIs) provide an evidence-based understanding of progress, enabling informed decision-making. This ongoing oversight not only promotes cost efficiency and optimal resource utilisation but also functions as an early warning system for risks and deviations. By detecting and addressing issues promptly, this process group safeguards project objectives and guides initiatives toward a successful and sustainable conclusion.

1.2 The Dichotomy of Monitoring vs. Controlling:

Although the terms "monitoring" and "controlling" are frequently paired, they serve distinct yet complementary functions within project management. *Monitoring* can be conceptualised as the project's "radar system." It involves the systematic collection of work performance data—such as task completion rates, resource consumption, cost expenditures, and quality outcomes —against baseline expectations. Activities include status reporting, performance reviews, quality inspections, and risk assessments, all of which culminate in the generation of actionable work performance information. Monitoring is primarily diagnostic, providing visibility into current conditions.

By contrast, *controlling* serves as the project's "steering mechanism." It is the active, intervention-orientated process of analysing monitoring data to identify variances and then determining appropriate corrective or preventive actions. Examples of controlling include reallocating resources, modifying timelines, and updating risk mitigation strategies to realign performance with expectations. For instance, if monitoring reveals that a software development initiative is behind schedule, controlling might involve assigning additional developers, reducing scope, or adjusting deadlines to restore equilibrium. Together, monitoring and controlling establish a feedback-control system in which observation informs intervention, thereby enabling adaptive project governance.

1.3 The Role of Baselines and the Change Management Plan:

The foundation of effective monitoring and controlling lies in the establishment of baselines. A baseline is the approved reference point for scope, schedule, and cost, against which all subsequent performance is measured. Without clearly defined baselines, project assessment becomes arbitrary, as progress would be gauged against a shifting target. Baseline development involves decomposing work into tasks, estimating durations and costs, and assigning resources to establish a fixed plan.

Complementing these baselines is the project's change management plan, which operationalises the controlling function. A formalised change management process specifies the criteria for initiating a project change request (PCR), the documentation and approval workflow, and the implementation of authorised adjustments. This framework ensures that variances are handled systematically and transparently, rather than reactively. In mature project management environments, change control is not perceived as a disruption but as a structured process that enables adaptation to unforeseen circumstances while preserving traceability and accountability. Collectively, baselines and change management practices provide both stability and flexibility, striking a balance between disciplined governance and responsive adaptation.

2. Key Performance Indicators (KPIs)

Key Performance Indicators (KPIs) are measurable values

that indicate how effectively an individual, team, or organization is achieving specific objectives. They serve as performance benchmarks, helping managers and stakeholders track progress toward goals, evaluate success, and make informed decisions.

In software project management, KPIs provide a structured way to monitor whether the project is on track in terms of cost, schedule, quality, productivity, and customer satisfaction. For example, metrics like Cost Performance Index (CPI), Schedule Performance Index (SPI), defect density, and customer satisfaction scores can all be considered KPIs.

In simple terms, KPIs answer the question: *"Are we moving in the right direction, and how close are we to achieving our goals?"*

2.1 The Strategic Function of Project KPIs:

Key Performance Indicators (KPIs) are quantifiable measures used to assess the extent to which a project is achieving its strategic and operational objectives. Beyond serving as data points, KPIs function as decision-support instruments that enable project managers to monitor performance, anticipate risks, and demonstrate value creation. Through targeted KPI tracking, project managers foster accountability, enhance transparency, and align project outcomes with organisational strategy.

While traditional project management emphasised schedule and budget adherence as primary measures of success, contemporary practice adopts a more holistic perspective. KPI selection now reflects the unique priorities of the organisation and the strategic context of the project. For example, a cost-constrained project may prioritise budget efficiency, whereas a market-driven initiative may emphasise schedule adherence or product quality. Thus, the choice of KPIs is not arbitrary but an intentional reflection of organisational risk tolerance, priorities, and definitions of success.

2.2 Methodology for KPI Selection:

The selection of KPIs must be deliberate, methodical, and tightly aligned with project objectives. Tracking too many metrics can obscure critical insights and overwhelm stakeholders, while tracking too few may result in blind spots. Therefore, the emphasis should be on a carefully curated set of indicators that provide actionable intelligence.

A widely recognised best practice for designing effective KPIs (Key Performance Indicators) is the application of the S.M.A.R.T. (Specific, Measurable, Assignable, Realistic, and Time-bound) framework, which ensures that performance measures are both meaningful and actionable.

a) Specific:

A KPI should clearly target a defined performance dimension rather than being vague or generalised. For example, instead of setting a broad goal such as "improve engagement," a specific KPI would articulate a measurable target like "increase customer engagement by 20% within six months". This level of clarity eliminates ambiguity, aligns team efforts, and provides a precise focus for performance monitoring.

b) Measurable:

KPIs must be quantifiable to enable objective tracking and evaluation. A measurable indicator allows project managers to collect concrete data, compare performance against established baselines, and determine whether progress is on track. Without measurability, assessments become subjective and inconsistent, undermining the reliability of performance analysis.

c) Assignable:

Responsibility for each KPI should be explicitly allocated to an individual or team to ensure accountability. When ownership is clearly defined, it reduces the likelihood of oversight and ensures that performance reporting is systematic. Assignability also facilitates communication, as stakeholders know who is accountable for tracking progress and providing updates.

d) Realistic:

KPIs must be achievable within the available resources, organisational constraints, and contextual limitations. Targets should be informed by historical data, industry benchmarks, or expert insights to ensure that expectations are ambitious yet attainable. Unrealistic KPIs can demotivate project teams and distort performance evaluations, whereas realistic ones support sustained progress and encourage continuous improvement.

e) Time-bound:

Every KPI should include a defined timeframe for achievement, which establishes urgency and enables regular performance assessment. A time-bound indicator provides checkpoints for evaluating progress and ensures that results are achieved within a meaningful window. This temporal dimension reinforces accountability and helps project managers prioritise tasks to align with overall project schedules.

Engaging stakeholders in the KPI development process is also critical, as it ensures that diverse expectations are addressed and that the selected measures have broad organisational legitimacy. Furthermore, KPIs should not be static; they require periodic review and refinement to remain relevant across the project lifecycle. Metrics that fail to yield meaningful insights should be retired to maintain focus on what truly matters.

2.3 A Typology of Project Metrics:

'Typology of Project Metrics' refers to the systematic classification of project performance measures into distinct categories based on their purpose, scope, and aspect of the project they evaluate. In project management, especially in software project management, this typology helps managers understand not only *what* to measure but also *why* and *how* those measurements contribute to decision-making.

The typology ensures that metrics are not viewed as isolated numbers but as part of a structured framework that reflects different dimensions of project success. Typically, project metrics can be grouped into categories such as:

1. ***Time/Schedule Metrics*** – Measure whether project activities are being completed on time (e.g., Schedule Performance Index, milestone variance).

2. ***Cost Metrics*** – Track financial efficiency and budget utilisation (e.g., Cost Performance Index, cost variance).

3. ***Quality Metrics*** - Assess the reliability, functionality, and defect levels of deliverables (e.g., defect density, test coverage, and mean time to failure).

4. ***Scope/Process Metrics*** – Evaluate whether the defined scope

and processes are followed and managed effectively (e.g., requirements stability index, change request rate).

5. ***Productivity Metrics*** – Measure how efficiently resources are used to produce deliverables (e.g., lines of code per developer per month, story points completed per sprint).

6. ***Customer/Stakeholder Satisfaction Metrics*** – Reflect on how end users and stakeholders perceive the outcomes (e.g., satisfaction surveys, Net Promoter Score).

In essence, the typology of project metrics provides a structured way to select and apply the right set of indicators depending on the project's priorities, enabling balanced monitoring of time, cost, quality, scope, and stakeholder value.

Furthermore, project metrics can be categorised to provide a multidimensional perspective of project performance.

a) ***Traditional Project Health Indicators:*** These include metrics related to scope, schedule, cost, and quality. Scope and quality can be tracked through defect counts, change request volumes, or user satisfaction ratings. Schedule adherence may be assessed using measures such as percent complete, velocity (in Agile contexts), or sprint burndown charts. Cost performance can be evaluated through return on investment (ROI), cost variance, or cost performance indices.

b) ***Leading vs. Lagging Indicators***: Another critical classification is between predictive (leading) and retrospective (lagging) metrics. Leading indicators provide early warning signals by predicting future performance; for example, user feedback scores can forecast customer satisfaction trends. Lagging indicators measure completed performance, such as the number of customer complaints logged after product release. Effective project governance requires a balance of both: leading indicators to enable proactive intervention and lagging indicators to evaluate the outcomes of completed efforts.

By adopting a structured typology of metrics, project managers can generate a balanced and comprehensive view of project health, one that captures both immediate performance and long-term outcomes.

3. Earned Value Management (EVM)

Earned Value Management (EVM) is a project management technique that integrates scope, time, and cost to measure project performance and progress objectively. It compares the planned work with the actual work completed and the resources spent, allowing managers to identify variances early and take corrective actions.

EVM answers three critical questions about a project:

1. ***Where are we?*** (current progress against the plan)

2. ***How are we doing?*** (performance in terms of cost and schedule)

3. ***Where are we heading?*** (future forecast of cost and schedule performance)

The Earned Value Management (EVM) method uses three core data points:

a) ***Planned Value (PV):*** The budgeted cost for the work scheduled up to a specific date.

b) ***Earned Value (EV):*** The budgeted cost of the work actually completed by that date.

c) ***Actual Cost (AC):*** The actual money spent to accomplish the work.

Furthermore, the Earned Value Management (EVM) method is based on three fundamental data points, which are elaborated on and explained below.

a) Planned Value (PV):

Planned Value (PV) refers to the budgeted cost of work that should have been completed by a specific point in time, serving as the financial benchmark against which project progress is assessed. It represents the project's time-phased baseline and directly answers the question, *'What is the value of the work that was planned to be completed by now?'* By establishing PV, project managers can evaluate whether the project is progressing in line with its planned schedule. For instance, if a software project had a budget of ₹10,00,000 and aimed to complete 40% of its coding effort by the end of the third month, the PV at that stage would be ₹4,00,000. This structured baseline enables managers to identify variances between planned progress and actual performance, thereby supporting more informed decision-making.

b) Earned Value (EV):

Earned Value (EV) represents the budgeted cost of the work actually completed by a given date, providing a clear link between progress and cost. It answers the critical question: *'What is the value of the work accomplished so far?'* By quantifying how much of the planned budget has been effectively 'earned' through completed tasksSP, EV offers a reliable measure of real progress. For example, if a project was scheduled for 40% completion but only 30% of the work was finished, the EV would equal 30% of the total budget. Unlike measures based solely on time spent or money consumed, EV reflects tangible output, enabling project managers to assess true performance and make more informed decisions.

c) Actual Cost (AC):

Actual Cost represents the total money spent on the work performed by a specific date. Unlike PV and EV, which are based on budgeted estimates, AC reflects real expenditure, including salaries, materials, tools, and overheads. For example, if the team spent ₹500,000 to achieve 30% completion of work, then the AC is ₹500,000. Comparing AC against EV shows whether the project is under or over budget. This distinction is crucial because a project may appear to be progressing well in terms of schedule but may still be consuming more resources than anticipated.

From these three metrics, performance indices such as the Cost Performance Index (CPI = EV ÷ AC) and Schedule Performance Index (SPI = EV ÷ PV) are derived to assess efficiency and predict project outcomes. CPI reveals how effectively the budget is being used—whether the project is spending more or less than planned to deliver completed work. The Schedule Performance Index (SPI), on the other hand, measures adherence to schedule, showing whether the project is ahead, on track, or behind. By combining these indices, project managers gain a comprehensive view of both cost and schedule performance, enabling them to take corrective action early and predict the likelihood of finishing the project within budget and on time.

In software project management, EVM is especially useful because it provides a quantitative, real-time snapshot of progress, highlighting whether the project is on track, over budget, or behind schedule.

3.1 Foundational Components of EVM:

Earned Value Management (EVM) is a rigorous, data-driven methodology that integrates scope, schedule, and cost dimensions to provide a comprehensive assessment of project performance. By synthesising these three perspectives, EVM enables project managers to measure progress objectively, diagnose performance issues early, and make informed decisions based on empirical evidence rather than subjective judgment. The framework is anchored in three foundational variables that collectively form the pillars of EVM.

Pillars of EVM:

1. *Budgeted Cost of Work Scheduled (BCWS):*

Planned Value (PV), also referred to as the *Budgeted Cost of Work Scheduled (BCWS),* represents the authorised budget assigned to the work scheduled for completion at a specific point in time. It is essentially the financial representation of the project's time-phased baseline and answers the question, *"What is the value of the work that should have been completed by this stage?"* The formula for PV is expressed as:

PV=BAC × Planned % Complete

where *BAC* denotes the Budget at Completion.

2. *Budgeted Cost of Work Performed (BCWP):*

Earned Value (EV). commonly known as the *Budgeted Cost of Work Performed (BCWP),* EV reflects the value of work that has actually been completed by a given point. Unlike cost-based measures, EV provides an objective assessment of physical progress, regardless of actual expenditures incurred. It answers the question, *"What is the value of the work that has been accomplished to date?"* The formula is defined as:

EV=BAC × Actual % Complete

3. Actual Cost of Work Performed (ACWP):

Actual Cost (AC), also termed the *Actual Cost of Work Performed (ACWP),* represents the total cost incurred in completing the work up to a specific point in time. It includes all direct and indirect expenditures—such as labour, materials, equipment, and overhead—and answers the question: *"How much did it actually cost to perform the completed work?"*

3.2 Technical Derivation and Interpretation of Performance Indices:

The true analytical power of EVM (Earned Value Management) lies not merely in tracking PV (Planned Value), EV (Earned Value), and AC (Actual Cost) independently but in combining them to generate performance indices that deliver integrated insights. These indices compel managers to assess scope, cost, and schedule simultaneously, thereby avoiding the pitfall of evaluating project health in isolation. For instance, reporting that a project is "on budget" is meaningless if the work completed is substantially less than what was planned at the same point.

Cost Performance Index (CPI):

The CPI measures cost efficiency by comparing the value of work accomplished to the actual expenditure.

CPI = EV/AC

Interpretation: A CPI > 1.0 indicates that the project is under budget; CPI < 1.0 signals overspending; CPI = 1.0 reflects exact alignment with the budget.

Schedule Performance Index (SPI): The SPI measures schedule efficiency by comparing the value of work accomplished to the planned value of work.

SPI = EV/PV

Interpretation: An SPI > 1.0 suggests the project is ahead of schedule; SPI < 1.0 indicates slippage; SPI = 1.0 denotes schedule adherence.

Table 1:

EVM Performance Metrics table

Metric	Formula	Interpretation (Value)
Cost Performance Index (CPI)	CPI=EV/AC	> 1.0: Under budget; 1.0: On budget; < 1.0: Over budget.
Schedule Performance Index (SPI)	SPI=EV/PV	> 1.0: Ahead of schedule; 1.0: On schedule; < 1.0: Behind schedule.

The Cost Performance Index (CPI) is a key efficiency indicator in Earned Value Management (EVM) that evaluates how effectively a project is utilising its budget. It is calculated by dividing the Earned Value (EV), which represents the value of work actually completed, by the Actual Cost (AC) incurred for that work. Mathematically expressed as CPI = EV ÷ AC, the index provides a ratio that compares the value delivered against the expenditure. A CPI greater than 1.0 indicates that the project is operating under budget, meaning it is delivering more value for every unit of cost spent. A CPI equal to 1.0 signifies that the project is precisely on budget, with costs aligning directly to the value earned. Conversely, a CPI below 1.0 reveals inefficiency, as the project is over budget and spending more than the value it is generating. This metric is critical for cost control and informs managers about whether corrective actions are needed to realign financial performance with planned objectives.

Schedule Performance Index (SPI):

The Schedule Performance Index (SPI) is a vital measure of schedule efficiency in EVM, providing insight into how well a project is adhering to its planned timeline. It is derived by dividing Earned Value (EV) by Planned Value (PV), expressed as SPI = EV ÷ PV. The index indicates the rate at which the project is progressing relative to the schedule baseline. An SPI greater than 1.0 demonstrates that the project is ahead of schedule, completing more work than originally planned by the given point in time. An SPI equal to 1.0 reflects perfect alignment with the schedule, where actual progress matches planned progress. An SPI less than 1.0 signifies that the project is behind schedule, indicating inefficiencies in work execution or potential risks of delay. This metric is particularly valuable for proactive management, as it enables the early identification of schedule slippages and supports timely interventions to mitigate risks and realign progress with project goals.

By evaluating CPI and SPI together, managers can achieve a balanced perspective of both cost and schedule performance. This integrated interpretation is what distinguishes EVM from conventional tracking systems that focus on a single dimension in isolation.

3.3 Practical Application and Insights from a Case Study:

To illustrate the practical application of EVM (Earned Value Management), consider a construction project to build a 10-apartment complex with a total budget, BAC (Budget at Completion), of $5,000,000 and a planned duration of two years. At the one-year mark, the project manager is required to assess performance. The following data is available:

a) **Budget at Completion (BAC):** $5,000,000

b) **Planned Work Completion:** 50% (5 of 10 apartments)

c) **Actual Work Completion:** 40% (4 of 10 apartments)

d) **Actual Cost (AC):** $2,200,000

Step 1: Calculate Earned Value (EV):

EV = 0.40 × $5,000,000 = $2,000,000

Step 2: Calculate Planned Value (PV):

PV = 0.50 × $5,000,000 = $2,500,000

Step 3: Calculate Cost Performance Index (CPI):

CPI = EV / AC

=2,000,000 / 2,200,000 = 0.909

Interpretation: The project is operating at 90.9% cost efficiency, indicating a cost overrun.

Step 4: Calculate Schedule Performance Index (SPI):

SPI = EV / PV

=2,000,000 / 2,500,000

=0.8

Interpretation: The project is achieving only 80% of the planned progress, indicating significant schedule slippage.

This case study demonstrates the analytical strength of EVM (Earned Value Management). By integrating scope, schedule, and cost data, the project manager obtains a precise, objective diagnosis of performance: the project is simultaneously over budget and behind schedule. Such insights are indispensable for corrective action planning, whether through resource reallocation, schedule compression strategies, or cost control measures.

4. Variance Analysis and Corrective Actions

Variance Analysis:

Variance Analysis is the process of comparing planned project performance (baseline values such as PV and budget) with actual results (EV and AC) to identify deviations in cost and schedule. It helps determine whether the project is ahead or behind schedule, and under or over budget.

Corrective Actions:

Corrective Actions are the specific measures taken by project managers to address variances identified during analysis. These actions aim to realign the project with its planned objectives, such as reallocating resources, adjusting schedules, revising budgets, or refining processes to improve efficiency and performance.

4.1 The Principles of Variance Analysis:

Variance analysis is a systematic technique used to evaluate the differences between actual and planned project performance. It provides a quantitative basis for identifying deviations from the project baseline and serves as a critical control mechanism throughout the project lifecycle. The two most frequently examined dimensions are cost variance and schedule variance, both of which highlight performance gaps in monetary terms.

1. Cost Variance (CV) measures the difference between the value of work completed (earned value) and the actual cost incurred to complete that work. The formula is expressed as CV = EV - AC. A positive cost variance indicates that the project is under budget, whereas a negative variance reveals that expenditures have exceeded the planned value. This metric provides a direct monetary assessment of cost efficiency.

2. Schedule Variance (SV) evaluates the difference between the value of the work actually completed and the value of the work that was planned to be completed at a given point. It is calculated as SV = EV - PV. A positive schedule variance signifies that the project is ahead of schedule, while a negative variance indicates that the project is lagging behind. Like cost variance, this metric is expressed in monetary terms, allowing integration with financial performance measures.

It is important to note that the magnitude of a variance is as significant as its direction. Small deviations may fall within acceptable thresholds, but large negative variances often point to systemic issues requiring immediate intervention. Continuous monitoring of variances allows project teams to detect emerging risks, identify weak areas in performance, and implement corrective measures before problems escalate.

4.2 The Process of Responding to Variances:

The existence of a variance does not necessarily signify project failure but rather provides an early-warning signal that corrective action may be required. A structured response process ensures that variances are systematically analysed and addressed in alignment with project objectives.

The first step is to establish baselines and thresholds. The project's scope, schedule, and cost baselines must be clearly defined, and predetermined variance thresholds should be set in the change management plan. These thresholds determine the point at which a variance becomes significant enough to trigger a formal response rather than being treated as a routine fluctuation.

Next, it is necessary to conduct a root cause analysis. Before implementing corrective actions, project managers must investigate why the variance occurred. Analytical techniques such as process mapping, causal diagrams, or statistical analysis may be applied to identify underlying issues. Addressing root causes ensures that corrective measures are targeted and effective, rather than superficial adjustments.

Following this analysis, the project team must implement corrective actions. In many cases, this requires formal documentation and approval through a Project Change Request (PCR) process to ensure accountability and transparency. Corrective actions should aim to realign the project with its baseline objectives while balancing the constraints of scope, schedule, cost, and quality.

4.3 A Compendium of Corrective Actions:

When negative variances are identified, a range of corrective actions can be considered to bring the project back on track. Each corrective measure involves trade-offs, and therefore, the choice of strategy must be guided by structured analysis and stakeholder alignment.

1. ***Crashing*** is a time-compression technique that involves assigning additional resources to activities on the critical path to reduce their duration. While this can shorten the project schedule, it usually increases project costs due to overtime, additional labour, or specialised expertise. Hence, crashing is most suitable when early delivery has high strategic or financial benefits that outweigh the increased expenditure.

2. ***Fast-tracking*** reduces project duration by conducting activities in parallel that were originally scheduled sequentially. This method does not necessarily increase direct costs but often elevates the risk of errors, coordination problems, or rework. Effective application of fast-tracking requires robust oversight and strong stakeholder communication to mitigate these risks.

3. ***Resource reallocation*** seeks to optimise project execution by moving resources from non-critical tasks to those on the critical path. This can accelerate project progress without increasing overall costs. However, the risk lies in potential delays to secondary activities and reduced flexibility in managing unforeseen challenges. Resource balancing must therefore be carefully planned to avoid unintended bottlenecks.

4. ***Scope reduction*** is a more drastic corrective strategy

that involves reducing, deferring, or eliminating certain deliverables. While this approach can alleviate cost and schedule pressures, it inevitably reduces the value delivered to stakeholders. Because of its impact on project objectives, scope reduction must be formally approved through the change control process and justified in terms of strategic trade-offs.

*5. **Schedule rebaselining*** is considered a last-resort measure. It involves formally revising the project schedule baseline to reflect the updated reality of progress and constraints. Although rebaselining provides a more accurate framework for future performance monitoring, it signals significant deviation from original plans and may undermine stakeholder confidence. Consequently, this step should only be taken after exhausting all other corrective options.

Ultimately, the selection of corrective actions requires a structured decision-making approach that weighs the impact of each option on scope, schedule, cost, and quality. By applying systematic analysis and engaging stakeholders in the evaluation process, project managers can choose the most appropriate corrective strategies while maintaining project credibility and stakeholder trust.

5. Agile Metrics (velocity, burndown charts):

5.1 The Philosophical Underpinnings of Agile Measurement:

Traditional and agile project management operate on fundamentally different philosophies, which are reflected in their respective approaches to measurement. Traditional methods, with their linear and sequential process, prioritise predictability, control, and efficiency, focusing on adherence to a fixed budget and schedule. In contrast, Agile, with its iterative and adaptive approach, prioritises continuous improvement, adaptability, and the continuous delivery of value to the customer.

This philosophical divergence means that Agile metrics often focus on measuring outcomes—such as customer satisfaction and time to market—rather than just outputs, like completed tasks and budget variance. Agile metrics are also typically leading indicators, providing early insights into a team's performance and capacity. The goal is not to enforce a static plan but to provide the team with the data needed to self-organise and adapt to changing requirements.

5.2 Velocity: Measuring Team Capacity for Forecasting:

Velocity is a key metric in Agile methodologies that measures the average amount of work a team can complete in a single sprint or iteration. This work is typically measured in a relative unit of effort, such as "story points". The Scrum Master is generally responsible for calculating and tracking velocity by summing the points from all stories that were completed and accepted in a given sprint.

Velocity is primarily used as a tool for forecasting and capacity planning, not as a performance indicator to be constantly increased. By tracking a team's historical velocity over several sprints, a project manager or product owner can gain a realistic understanding of the team's capacity and use this information to estimate how quickly they can work through the project backlog. A team's velocity chart should not show a constant increase over time; instead, it should converge on a consistent horizontal line as the team matures. This stable, predictable output is a sign of a healthy and sustainable work rhythm, which is a more valuable indicator of team health than a volatile, ever-increasing output.

5.3 Burndown and Burnup Charts: Visualising Progress and

Scope:

Agile teams utilize visual tools, such as burndown and burnup charts, to track progress and communicate project status to all stakeholders.

a) Burndown Charts:

A burndown chart tracks the work that remains to be completed over a given time period. The horizontal x-axis represents time, while the vertical y-axis tracks the work remaining, typically in story points or tasks. The chart shows an "ideal" burndown line, which is a straight line from the starting point to zero, representing the pace required to finish on time. The team's actual progress line is plotted against this ideal line. If the actual line is above the ideal line, it indicates the team is behind schedule. Burndown charts are excellent for visualising progress toward a sprint goal and are simple for all team members to understand.

b) Burnup Charts:

A burnup chart visualises work that has been completed over time. The key difference between a burnup and a burndown chart is the ability of the burnup chart to account for and visualise scope creep. A burndown chart can be misleading if new work is added mid-sprint, as it will simply show the "work remaining" line increase, making it look as if no progress has been made. The burnup chart addresses this by including a separate line that tracks the size of the project or sprint backlog. This second line moves up when new work is added, providing a clear and accurate picture of both work completed and changes in project scope. The evolution from the simpler burndown chart to the more robust burnup chart is a perfect illustration of how project management metrics adapt to address the real-world complexities and limitations of earlier models.

6. Traditional vs. Agile Project Monitoring: Comparative Analysis

6.1 A Philosophical Divergence:

The choice between traditional and Agile project management methodologies is rooted in a fundamental philosophical divergence. Traditional project management, exemplified by the Waterfall method, is a linear, sequential, and structured process. Its core philosophy is rooted in predictability and control, with a strong emphasis on detailed, upfront planning and rigid adherence to a fixed scope, schedule, and budget. The metrics used in this model, such as budget and schedule variance, are typically lagging indicators that measure adherence to a predefined plan and reflect past performance.

Agile, by contrast, is a circular, iterative, and adaptive approach. Its philosophy prioritises adaptability, continuous improvement, and the frequent delivery of incremental value. Agile methodologies, such as Scrum, are particularly well-suited for projects with evolving or uncertain requirements. The metrics used are often leading indicators that provide early insight into future performance. The core difference is that while traditional metrics aim to enforce stability and control, Agile metrics are designed to embrace and manage change.

Traditional vs. Agile Monitoring Metrics Comparison:

1. Approach:

Traditional project management methodologies, such as Waterfall, follow a linear and sequential approach where project phases—requirements gathering, design, development, testing, and deployment—are completed in a fixed order. This structure provides clarity and predictability but can limit flexibility when changes arise.

In contrast, Agile methodologies adopt an iterative and incremental approach, typically through short cycles known as sprints. Each sprint delivers a potentially usable increment of the product, allowing for regular feedback and adjustments. This flexibility enables teams to respond dynamically to evolving requirements and stakeholder needs.

2. Planning:

In traditional methodologies, project planning is detailed and conducted upfront. Comprehensive documentation, long-term scheduling, and precise resource allocation are emphasised to establish a well-defined roadmap before execution begins. While this approach reduces uncertainty, it also makes adapting to unforeseen changes more difficult.

Agile planning, however, is adaptive and ongoing. Teams plan at multiple levels—such as release planning, sprint planning, and daily stand-ups—allowing for continuous refinement of priorities. This ensures that planning evolves in response to stakeholder feedback and emerging project realities, reducing the risk of misalignment.

3. Scope Management:

Traditional project management typically enforces a fixed scope, where requirements are defined early and modifications are minimised to preserve stability. Any changes usually require formal approval through a change control process, which can slow responsiveness. Agile methodologies, on the other hand, embrace scope flexibility by allowing requirements to evolve over time. Scope adjustments are not seen as disruptions but as opportunities to enhance value delivery.

Agile teams prioritise backlog items iteratively, ensuring that the most valuable features are developed first, even if it means altering earlier assumptions.

4. Metrics:

Traditional metrics emphasise outputs, such as the number of tasks completed, adherence to budget, and conformance to schedule. These indicators measure project efficiency in terms of deliverables but may not reflect whether the end product meets customer expectations or delivers intended business value.

Agile metrics shift the focus to outcomes, emphasising measures such as customer satisfaction, delivered business value, and product usability. Tools like velocity, burn-down charts, and Net Promoter Score (NPS) help assess how effectively the team is delivering value rather than merely tracking activity.

5. Indicator Type:

Traditional methodologies rely heavily on lagging indicators —metrics that measure past performance, such as schedule variance, cost variance, and earned value. While useful for historical reporting, these indicators often identify issues only after they have occurred, limiting the opportunity for proactive intervention.

Agile approaches emphasise leading indicators, which provide early signals of potential problems or success. Metrics such as sprint velocity trends, defect rates, and backlog health help predict future performance and allow teams to take corrective action before risks escalate.

6.2 Mapping Metrics: Identifying Analogous Concepts:

Despite their philosophical differences, some metrics and concepts from the traditional and Agile worlds have natural counterparts. The Project Management Institute (PMI) has explored how traditional Earned Value Management (EVM) can be applied to Agile projects.

1. EVM (PV, EV, AC) vs. Agile Burn Charts:

There is a direct conceptual mapping between these two. A burnup chart, which tracks work completed over time, closely resembles the classical EVM 3-line graph of cumulative Earned Value (EV), Actual Cost (AC), and Planned Value (PV). With some modifications, such as adding a "budget burnt" line to the burnup chart, the visual tool can incorporate traditional cost metrics, bridging the gap between the two worlds.

2. ROI vs. Incremental Value Delivery:

While traditional projects often measure a single, large Return on Investment (ROI) at the end, Agile breaks down value into smaller, frequent increments. This enables a continuous and more frequent evaluation of value delivery throughout the project.

3. Resource Utilisation vs. Velocity:

Traditional approaches measure how efficiently resources are being used, often in terms of hours or tasks completed per employee. Agile's velocity metric, by contrast, reflects the team's output without assigning blame to individuals and is a measure of the team's collective capacity.

6.3 The Hybrid Approach: Integrating Methodologies:

A sophisticated project management organisation recognises that strict adherence to a single methodology is often counterproductive. The most effective approach is a hybrid model that adapts and integrates metrics from both traditional and Agile frameworks as needed. The challenge in this integration is not technical but cultural and educational. Stakeholders accustomed to static, lagging indicators must be educated on how Agile's leading, trend-focused metrics, such as velocity and cycle time, align with overarching business goals.

For example, Earned Value Management (EVM) can be adapted for Agile projects by redefining its components on a per-iteration basis. By establishing planned value (PV) at the beginning of each sprint and tracking Earned Value (EV) and Actual Cost (AC) throughout, a project manager can integrate cost measurement into Scrum to maximise project ROI. This demonstrates that the two methodologies are not mutually exclusive but can be combined to leverage the strengths of each. This integration requires moving beyond simply using dashboards to translate metrics and instead fostering a culture that trusts data from both frameworks.

7. Conclusion and Recommendations

7.1 Synthesising Key Principles for Effective Project Monitoring:

Effective project monitoring and control an imperative for success in today's dynamic business environment. The analysis of traditional and agile methodologies reveals a set of core principles that underpin a mature approach to project oversight:

a) ***A Continuous Process:*** Monitoring and controlling is not a one-time event but a continuous, systematic process that operates in parallel with project execution.

b) ***The Primacy of Baselines:*** All effective monitoring relies on the establishment of clear, agreed-upon baselines for scope, schedule, and cost. Without these fixed points of comparison, all analysis is meaningless.

c) ***The Strategic Function of KPIs:*** The selection of Key Performance Indicators is a strategic exercise that reflects an organisation's priorities and risk tolerance. Metrics must be simple, relevant, and directly aligned with project and business goals.

d) ***The Power of Integration:*** Frameworks like Earned Value Management provide a holistic, integrated view of project health by combining cost, schedule, and scope into a single, objective assessment. Poor performance in one area (e.g., schedule) can render a seemingly favourable metric (e.g., cost) meaningless.

e) ***The Value of Adaptability:*** Agile metrics, such as velocity and burnup charts, provide the tools to manage projects in environments with high uncertainty and frequent change. They shift the focus from strict adherence to a plan toward continuous value delivery and team empowerment.

7.2 Guidance for Selecting the Right Metrics for a Given Project Context:

The choice of which metrics to employ should be a deliberate decision based on the characteristics of the project and the needs of the stakeholders.

a) For **large-scale, long-term projects** with well-defined, stable requirements (e.g., large-scale infrastructure, aerospace), a traditional approach with a comprehensive EVM framework is often the most appropriate choice to ensure tight control over budget, schedule, and scope.

b) For **smaller, cross-functional projects** with evolving requirements and a focus on rapid delivery (e.g., software development, product innovation), an Agile approach using metrics like velocity and burn charts is highly effective.

In practice, a hybrid model is often required. The most effective organizations move beyond rigid adherence to a single methodology and instead cultivate a culture that uses a blend of traditional and Agile metrics to gain a comprehensive view of project health.

7.3 The Future of Project Measurement in a Dynamic Business Landscape:

The future of project management monitoring lies in this ability to adapt and integrate. The discipline is moving toward a metrics-focused culture where data is used to foster trust and guide decision-making, rather than to enforce rigid control. The existence of a formal change management plan, which anticipates and plans for deviation, demonstrates a shift in mindset from control-as-elimination to control-as-management. The most successful organizations will be those that can master this duality, leveraging the predictability of traditional frameworks for stable elements while embracing the adaptability of Agile for the dynamic and uncertain aspects of their projects.

8. Monitoring and Controlling Progress in Software Projects

Monitoring and controlling project progress is a critical phase in software project management, as it ensures that the project stays aligned with its defined scope, schedule, cost, and quality objectives. Unlike traditional projects, software development is often more dynamic, with frequent requirement changes, evolving technologies, and complex stakeholder expectations. This makes continuous monitoring and proactive control mechanisms vital to achieving success. Managers must not only track progress against the baseline plan but also anticipate deviations early and implement corrective actions before they escalate into significant risks.

In software projects, progress monitoring primarily involves comparing the actual performance with the planned performance using various project metrics and tools. Techniques such as Earned Value Management (EVM), burndown charts, and velocity tracking are commonly used to quantify schedule adherence, budget utilisation, and productivity. Regular status meetings, sprint reviews in Agile projects, and automated reporting dashboards provide stakeholders with real-time visibility into the project's health. These mechanisms allow managers to identify whether the team is on track, lagging, or surpassing expectations.

Controlling progress goes beyond tracking—it focuses on taking corrective and preventive actions when variances are detected. For example, if code development is falling behind schedule, the project manager might reassign resources, adjust priorities, or break tasks into smaller increments to improve throughput. Observing budget overruns may necessitate scope negotiation or re-estimation. In software development, control also involves quality aspects, such as monitoring defect density, test coverage, and customer feedback to ensure that the product being delivered meets the required standards.

Another key dimension is risk monitoring and control. Since software projects face uncertainties like requirement volatility, integration challenges, or technology obsolescence, monitoring mechanisms must continuously assess risks and trigger contingency plans. Agile methodologies address this aspect by incorporating iterative reviews and retrospectives, allowing teams to quickly adapt to changes while maintaining control over deliverables. In contrast, traditional models like Waterfall require more formal control measures, such as phase-end reviews and change control boards.

Communication plays a central role in monitoring and controlling project progress. Transparent reporting to stakeholders—whether through dashboards, progress reports, or demos—helps build trust and facilitates timely decision-making. Effective collaboration tools, such as Jira, Trello, or Git-based platforms, provide shared visibility into tasks, code progress, and testing results, making monitoring more integrated and less intrusive. The goal is to maintain alignment between developers, testers, managers, and clients while ensuring issues are addressed promptly.

Ultimately, monitoring and controlling progress in software project management is about maintaining a balance between flexibility and discipline. While software projects demand agility to adapt to evolving requirements, they also require robust control systems to prevent scope creep, cost overruns, and missed deadlines. By combining performance measurement techniques with adaptive control strategies, project managers can guide the team toward successful and predictable project outcomes.

CHAPTER 11: BEST PRACTICES IN PROJECT MANAGEMENT

Project management in the modern era has evolved into a multidisciplinary discipline that integrates leadership, technical expertise, cross-cultural awareness, and continuous learning. While methodologies such as PMBOK, PRINCE2, and Agile provide structured frameworks, successful project delivery depends on a deeper set of practices that balance human dynamics, risk governance, knowledge transfer, and ethical responsibility. The following sections outline four pillars of best practices that serve as critical enablers of project success across diverse industries and contexts.

1. Leadership and communication skills.
2. Risk management and mitigation strategies.
3. Lessons learned and knowledge management.
4. Cultural and ethical considerations.

1. Leadership and Communication Skills

At the heart of effective project management lies the dual

capability of leadership and communication. Complexity, uncertainty, and diverse stakeholder expectations characterise modern project environments, particularly in software development, engineering, and global technology initiatives. Project managers can no longer be considered task schedulers alone; they must act as visionaries, facilitators, and connectors of people. Effective leadership aligns cross-functional teams, executives, and clients toward common objectives, while effective communication ensures that each stakeholder receives relevant, comprehensible, and timely information. This section elaborates on the evolving best practices in leadership and communication, supported by real-world case studies including NASA's James Webb Space Telescope (JWST), Spotify's Agile squads, Siemens' ERP rollout, and Google's cross-functional innovation teams.

1.1 Moving Beyond Command-and-Control Leadership:

Traditional project management models frequently relied on hierarchical authority, emphasising command, compliance, and control. While effective in stable, predictable environments, such approaches tend to falter in dynamic and innovation-driven projects where creativity, adaptability, and stakeholder engagement are crucial. Contemporary leadership emphasises influence, facilitation, and Emotional Intelligence (EI)—qualities that enable leaders to inspire rather than impose (Goleman, 1998).

Emotional intelligence in project leadership involves self-awareness, empathy, and the ability to manage relationships constructively. For example, in Siemens' multinational ERP (Enterprise Resource Planning) implementation, regional divisions often had conflicting requirements due to local regulations and cultural practices. Rather than impose a standardised solution, the project leader relied on empathy and facilitation workshops to negotiate compromises. This approach not only preserved project momentum but also strengthened trust across regions. These cases demonstrate how Emotional Intelligence (EI) - based leadership converts conflict into collaboration, fostering an environment that values and integrates diverse perspectives.

1.2 Communication as a Multidimensional Process:

Communication in project management is not monolithic; it is multidimensional and audience-specific. Effective leaders tailor their messaging depending on whether they are addressing technical experts, senior executives, clients, or policymakers.

1. ***Technical experts*** require communication that is highly detailed, precise, and technically rigorous. Their work depends on access to accurate data such as system architecture diagrams, error logs, performance metrics, and test results. This level of specificity allows engineers, developers, and analysts to diagnose problems, refine solutions, and ensure the integrity of the technical system. When project managers provide experts with transparent and comprehensive technical documentation, they enable informed decision-making and reduce the likelihood of misinterpretations that can compromise quality or timelines.

2. ***Executives and managers*** require communication at a higher level of abstraction, focussing less on technical details and more on strategic alignment and resource utilisation. Dashboards, milestone reports, and performance indicators are critical tools for this audience, as they highlight budget adherence, schedule progress, and overall risk exposure. Unlike technical teams, executives use this information to determine whether the project is on track to deliver value, justify resource allocations, and maintain organisational

confidence. The clarity and conciseness of communication at this level directly influence executive decision-making and support for the project.

3. ***Clients and external stakeholders*** are primarily concerned with the tangible and long-term outcomes of the project. Their focus lies on understanding how the project aligns with their expectations, the potential return on investment, and broader organisational or societal benefits. Effective communication with this group avoids technical jargon and instead emphasises value delivery, the impact on end-users, and strategic advantages. By framing updates around outcomes—such as efficiency improvements, customer satisfaction, or competitive positioning—project leaders ensure that external stakeholders remain engaged and confident in the project's relevance and success.

NASA's (James Webb Space Telescope) JWST project provides a powerful example of this layered communication. Engineers were given detailed reports on cryogenic mirror performance, managers tracked progress via milestone charts, and political stakeholders such as Congress were engaged with simplified narratives highlighting scientific breakthroughs and societal benefits. This differentiated approach ensured alignment across groups with vastly different concerns. Importantly, it allowed NASA to maintain credibility despite cost overruns and delays, showcasing communication as a strategic tool for sustaining trust in high-risk projects.

1.3 Agile Ceremonies and Adaptive Dialogue:

In Agile environments, communication is embedded into structured rituals—daily stand-ups, sprint reviews, and retrospectives—that foster transparency, adaptation, and inclusivity (Schwaber & Sutherland, 2020). These ceremonies streamline task updates and provide forums for addressing technical, process, and human factors simultaneously.

1. ***Developers*** typically concentrate on immediate and tangible technical difficulties that directly influence productivity and software quality. Their discussions often revolve around challenges such as the need for code refactoring, resolving technical debt, improving test automation, or addressing bottlenecks in the Continuous Integration/Continuous Delivery (CI/CD) pipeline. By focusing on these issues, developers ensure that the system remains maintainable, scalable, and reliable, reducing the risk of technical failures that could delay future deliverables. Communication at this level is detail-oriented, highly specific, and grounded in technical problem-solving.

2. ***Scrum Masters*** direct their attention to team collaboration and the overall efficiency of Agile processes. Their role is to facilitate dialogue, remove impediments, and ensure that ceremonies such as daily stand-ups and retrospectives contribute to continuous improvement. Scrum Masters often highlight issues such as imbalances in workload distribution, lack of adherence to Work-in-Progress (WIP) limits, or breakdowns in cross-functional communication. Rather than prescribing solutions, they create a psychologically safe space for open dialogue, guiding the team toward self-organisation and sustainable productivity.

3. ***Product owners and stakeholders*** focus on evaluating whether the team's deliverables align with customer needs and strategic business objectives. Their priority is to assess whether features enhance user satisfaction, generate market competitiveness, and deliver a measurable return on investment. Communication with this audience emphasises outcomes and value creation rather than

technical intricacies. By translating development progress into customer and business impact, product owners ensure that technical achievements are tied to organisational goals, maintaining alignment between day-to-day execution and long-term strategy.

1.4 Leadership through Vision and Motivation:

Leadership in project management requires more than coordination—it involves inspiring purpose, cultivating motivation, and sustaining commitment. A clear vision unites diverse teams, while motivational strategies ensure consistent energy and resilience under pressure. Effective leaders combine active listening, constructive feedback, and recognition of contributions to keep teams engaged.

Motivation often stems from non-financial factors: purpose, autonomy, and mastery. For example, agile leaders motivate teams by celebrating sprint completions, showcasing how delivered features improve user experience, and giving teams autonomy in design decisions. Google applies this philosophy in its cross-functional "moonshot" projects, where psychological safety and encouragement of bold experimentation motivate teams to pursue breakthroughs without fear of failure. These cases show how leadership grounded in vision and intrinsic motivation drives innovation in uncertain and demanding contexts.

1.5. Establishing Formal Communication Channels and Tools:

While adaptive dialogue is essential, projects also require structured communication systems to prevent misalignment and ensure accountability. The best practices emphasise:

1. *Formal communication* plans established at the outset of a project serve as the foundation for effective information flow. These plans define the intended audiences, the methods of communication, and the frequency of reporting, ensuring that every stakeholder receives the right information at the right time. For example, executives may request monthly dashboards summarising progress and financial performance, while development teams may need daily updates on task-level dependencies. By articulating expectations early, communication plans reduce ambiguity, align stakeholder expectations, and prevent gaps or redundancies in the dissemination of critical information.

2. ***Collaboration tools*** such as Jira, Trello, Microsoft Teams, and Slack have become indispensable in modern project management, offering real-time visibility into tasks, milestones, and dependencies. These tools not only enhance transparency but also allow distributed teams to coordinate seamlessly across geographies and time zones. For instance, Jira's sprint burndown charts can provide developers with granular insights into task completion, while executive dashboards can give managers a consolidated view of project health. By centralising communication and documentation, these platforms minimise the risk of miscommunication and enable data-driven decision-making.

3. ***Clear role and responsibility* definitions** are essential for avoiding duplication of effort and preventing critical tasks from being overlooked. Poorly defined roles often lead to inefficiencies, conflicting responsibilities, or neglected deliverables. By contrast, frameworks like RACI (Responsible, Accountable, Consulted, and Informed) provide structured clarity, ensuring that each task has an accountable owner and supporting contributors. This role clarity fosters accountability, enhances productivity, and allows project managers to allocate resources effectively, reducing the likelihood of bottlenecks or gaps in execution.

In large-scale ERP rollouts, for instance, Jira's sprint burndown charts allow technical teams to monitor progress, while executive dashboards consolidate financial and scheduling data for senior decision-makers. Here, the project manager acts as the information hub, ensuring coherence across distributed and functionally diverse teams. Formal structures complement adaptive communication, creating a balanced system that supports both control and flexibility.

1.6 Case Study Synthesis:

The following cases highlight how best practices in leadership and communication play out in diverse industries:

1.6.1.NASA — James Webb Space Telescope (JWST): layered communication for a mega-project:

The JWST programme exemplifies leadership and communication in a high-risk, long-duration, multi-party engineering programme. From concept to launch, JWST involved dozens of contractors (e.g., Northrop Grumman), multiple space agencies (NASA, ESA, and CSA), congressional appropriations, and a global scientific community. The project experienced repeated schedule slips, complex technical integration challenges (e.g., cryogenic performance, sunshield deployment), and large budget escalations—conditions that would rapidly erode support without disciplined communication.

What leaders did: NASA established a multi-tiered communication architecture that deliberately differentiated content, format, and cadence for distinct stakeholder groups. Engineers participated in formal systems-engineering forums (PDR/CDR, integration test reports, anomaly logs) that delivered exhaustive technical evidence for decision-making. Programme and project managers used summarised programme artefacts—Integrated Master Schedules (IMS), Earned Value Management (EVM) reports, risk registers, and mitigation plans—to drive managerial decisions and contract actions. For political stakeholders and the public, NASA translated technical complexity into narratives about scientific value and societal impact, supplemented by compelling visuals and analogies to build political buy-in and public enthusiasm.

Why it mattered: Tailored information preserved technical rigour for engineers, enabled rapid executive decisions, and sustained funding support from Congress. Moreover, NASA coupled transparency with contextualisation: they acknowledged delays and cost growth but framed them against technical milestones and the program's strategic value, which maintained credibility. Independent reviews and formal change control boards provided further assurance to oversight bodies.

Key lessons for project managers: implement stakeholder segmentation and produce role-specific artefacts (detailed technical logs vs. executive dashboards vs. narrative briefs); commit to regular, honest status reports paired with mitigation plans; use independent reviews and formal governance to increase stakeholder confidence; and invest in visual storytelling to explain technical trade-offs to non-technical audiences.

1.6.2. Spotify —Agile squads: adaptive dialogue, psychological safety, and continuous improvement:

Spotify's squad/tribe/chapter model is frequently cited for how organisational design and communication practices enable rapid innovation while maintaining coherence across many small autonomous teams. Squads are cross-functional, own specific features or products, and operate with high autonomy; chapters and tribes provide cross-squad alignment and standards.

What leaders did: Leadership at Spotify emphasises servant leadership, local decision rights, and a cadence of lightweight ceremonies (stand-ups, sprint reviews, and retrospectives). Retrospectives are structured to solicit technical feedback (CI/CD performance, code quality, deployment failures) alongside human factors (team morale, workload imbalances). Spotify also uses "health checks" and team metrics to surface issues without stigmatising failure. Leaders and chapter leads act as coaches—facilitating problem solving, removing impediments, and ensuring that squad autonomy remains aligned with product strategy and company OKRs (Objectives and Key Results).

Why it mattered: This combination of autonomy and alignment—supported by tailored retrospective facilitation —creates psychological safety (so engineers surface real problems), rapid technical remediation (through CI/CD improvements), and cultural cohesion (through rituals and recognition). The result is resilient teams that learn quickly and innovate without sacrificing cross-team standards.

Key lessons for project managers: structure retrospectives to capture both technical and human insights; cultivate coaching-style leadership that removes blockers rather than micromanages; use lightweight metrics plus narratives to guide improvement; and institutionalise rituals and recognition to sustain motivation.

1.6.3. Siemens — Global ERP rollout: emotionally intelligent leadership and stakeholder negotiation:

Large ERP implementations demand reconciling global standardisation with local regulatory, process, and cultural differences. Siemens' multinational ERP programmes encountered friction because regional business units had specific compliance rules, legacy practices, and differing priorities.

What leaders did: Siemens' project leadership prioritised stakeholder engagement early and often. Rather than imposing a single global template, leaders instituted inclusive design workshops and regional steering committees that surfaced local concerns. Project managers used mediated negotiation sessions—combining facilitation, empathy, and data-driven options analysis—to broker compromises (e.g., configurable processes, phased localisation). They coupled these social interventions with technical mitigations such as regional pilot rollouts, parallel run testing, and staged data migration to reduce perceived risk.

Why it mattered: Emotional intelligence in leadership (active listening, respect for local expertise, and reframing conflicts as design constraints) reduced resistance, improved local adoption, and prevented costly rework. Technical choices, such as pilot deployments and robust testing, reinforced the social approach by fostering confidence in the solution.

Key lessons for project managers: invest in early stakeholder mapping and inclusive workshops; use negotiation and mediation to reconcile competing needs; incorporate phased pilots and localised test cycles to lower adoption risk; and align programme governance so regional voices have structured representation without fragmenting global objectives.

1.6.4. Google — Cross-functional Teams: Vision-driven Leadership, Psychological Safety, and Moonshot Thinking:

Google's innovation model centres on cross-functional

teams that combine engineers, product managers, UX researchers, and data scientists to pursue ambitious outcomes. Leadership fosters a clear, aspirational vision while protecting teams' autonomy to experiment.

What leaders did: Google leaders articulate strong missions and measurable Objectives and Key Results (OKRs) that orient teams toward bold goals. They also invest in culture: psychological safety is encouraged so team members expose assumptions, report failures candidly, and iterate rapidly. Communication channels (all-hands, internal documents, peer reviews, and asynchronous forums) ensure knowledge flow across functions. Leaders explicitly tolerate controlled failure—viewing experiments and post-mortems as learning mechanisms—while ensuring that experiments are data-driven and tied to user or business metrics.

Why it mattered: A clear, high-level vision combined with permissive, evidence-based experimentation encourages breakthrough innovation (e.g., multiple Google products emerged from internal experiments). Cross-functional communication ensures that technical choices are evaluated against user needs and market signals, increasing the odds that innovations produce substantive value.

Key lessons for project managers: set concise, measurable objectives that tie work to a compelling mission; design communication patterns that enable rapid cross-functional feedback; institutionalise blameless post-mortems and data-driven decision rules; and balance visionary goals with disciplined experimentation.

1.6.5. Synthesis: Common Patterns and Practical Checklist:

Across these cases, the following patterns recur:

(1) ***Stakeholder Segmentation*** — produce different artefacts

and cadences for technical, managerial, and political audiences;

(2) ***Psychological Safety***—create spaces (retrospectives, mediated workshops, and post-mortems) where issues can be surfaced without fear;

(3) ***Cadenced Transparency*** — consistent reporting combined with mitigation plans;

(4) ***Governance + Autonomy*** — formal controls (change boards, EVM) paired with empowered teams; and

(5) ***Narrative Framing*** — translate technical complexity into value stories for non-technical stakeholders.

Practical checklist for managers: map stakeholders and information needs; design role-specific artefacts and cadences; institutionalise safe forums for candid feedback; adopt governance mechanisms that preserve agility; and use visuals and metaphors to explain technical trade-offs to non-technical audiences.

These examples collectively underscore that leadership and communication are not static competencies but dynamic, context-dependent practices. Successful project managers combine emotional intelligence, audience-specific communication, adaptive dialogue, and formal communication structures to align stakeholders, build trust, and deliver results in complex and uncertain environments.

2. Risk Management and Mitigation Strategies

Risk management is the systematic process of identifying, analysing, and addressing uncertainties that may affect project outcomes. It ensures that potential threats are anticipated and controlled before they escalate into critical issues. Mitigation strategies typically involve four approaches:

i. ***Avoidance***, where risks are eliminated by altering project plans;

ii. ***Mitigation***, which reduces the likelihood or impact through proactive measures such as prototyping or backups;

iii. ***Transference***, where responsibility is shifted to third parties through contracts or insurance; and

iv. ***Acceptance***, where low-impact risks are tolerated without intervention.

By combining structured frameworks like PMBOK with adaptive practices such as Agile retrospectives and iterative reviews, project teams can proactively manage risks, maintain resilience, and increase the likelihood of project success.

2.1 Importance of Risk Management in Project Governance:

Risk management is a cornerstone of effective project governance, providing a structured approach to navigating uncertainty. In software project management, risks are inevitable due to factors such as rapidly evolving technologies, resource dependencies, shifting business priorities, and external market pressures. Frameworks such as PMBOK and PRINCE2 emphasise the importance of systematically identifying, analysing, and responding to risks so that projects remain resilient and adaptable. Effective risk management not only protects projects from potential threats but also positions them to capitalise on emerging opportunities.

2.2 Categories of Risks in Projects:

Risks can manifest in multiple dimensions. Technical risks may arise from adopting untested technologies, integration challenges, or performance bottlenecks. Organisational risks can emerge from resource conflicts, competing priorities, or misalignment between teams. External risks often involve regulatory changes, cybersecurity threats, or vendor dependencies. Each category requires a tailored strategy, as a "one-size-fits-all" approach is ineffective in complex project environments.

2.3 Risk Response Strategies:

Mitigation strategies typically fall into four categories:

1. Avoidance:

Avoidance involves modifying the project scope or plan to eliminate the risk altogether, ensuring that potential issues never materialise. This strategy is often applied when the cost or impact of a risk is deemed too high to justify continuing with the original approach. For example, if a third-party tool is considered unreliable or prone to failure, a project team may decide to exclude it and instead adopt a proven technology. By making this adjustment early, the project avoids exposure to unnecessary instability, even if it means slightly altering the original scope.

2. Mitigation:

Mitigation focuses on reducing either the likelihood of a risk occurring or the severity of its impact if it does. This approach is proactive and aims to minimise disruptions without eliminating the activity that carries the risk. A common technique is early prototyping, where teams build small-scale models or simulations to test the viability of new technologies before full-scale adoption. By doing this, we can clarify uncertainties, identify performance bottlenecks, and implement corrective measures early in the development process.

3. Transference:

Transference shifts the responsibility of managing a risk to another party, usually through contractual agreements or partnerships. This does not eliminate the risk, but it ensures that an external entity with the expertise or resources to handle it bears the consequences. For instance, a company may purchase insurance to cover potential financial losses or outsource certain high-risk tasks, such as cybersecurity testing, to specialised vendors. This strategy is especially useful when the risk lies outside the project team's direct control or competence.

4. Acceptance:

Acceptance acknowledges that some risks are either too small in impact or too costly to address, making it more practical to simply live with them. In these cases, the project team documents the risk, monitors it, and prepares to deal with the consequences should it occur but does not allocate significant resources to preventing it. For instance, the project team may tolerate a minor delay in a non-critical feature if it does not impact the project's overall objectives or delivery timeline. This approach allows teams to focus resources on managing higher-priority risks while maintaining efficiency.

Cybersecurity risks often illustrate the layered use of these strategies. Many organizations employ DevSecOps practices

—such as automated vulnerability scanning and continuous monitoring—to mitigate threats while also outsourcing specialised penetration testing to external vendors.

2.4 Agile Approaches to Risk Management:

Unlike traditional project management, Agile methodologies embed risk management into their iterative cycles. Agile practices like sprint reviews, daily stand-ups, and retrospectives guarantee the early identification, discussion, and resolution of risks. Because Agile projects deliver incrementally, potential failures are contained within smaller, manageable iterations, minimising large-scale impact.

For example, NASA's Jet Propulsion Laboratory (JPL), during the Mars Curiosity Rover project, relied heavily on iterative testing in simulated environments to identify failures before deployment. Similarly, startups often manage funding and market risks by launching Minimum Viable Products (MVPs), testing real-world demand before committing heavy resources. This adaptive responsiveness makes Agile an effective model for managing uncertainty.

2.5. The Risk Management Process:

A systematic process helps project teams manage risks effectively:

1. Risk Identification:

Risk identification is the first step in developing a robust risk management strategy. It involves systematically brainstorming, documenting, and categorising potential threats that could disrupt project success. This process often engages the entire project team, as diverse perspectives help uncover risks that a single viewpoint might overlook.

Typical risks in software projects include the unexpected departure of a critical developer, failures in key technologies such as databases or APIs, and financial challenges such as budget overruns. By creating a comprehensive risk register at the outset, teams can anticipate potential challenges rather than react to crises as they unfold.

2. Risk Analysis:

Once risks are identified, their likelihood and severity must be assessed. This process, often referred to as qualitative and quantitative risk analysis, enables project managers to prioritise risks according to their urgency and significance. For example, the likelihood of a minor user interface delay may be high, but its impact relatively small, while the probability of a database migration failure may be lower, but its consequences far more severe. Through structured tools such as probability–impact matrices, Monte Carlo simulations, or risk scoring methods, managers can ensure that resources and attention are directed toward the risks most likely to jeopardise project objectives.

3. Risk Response Planning:

Risk response planning translates the insights gained from analysis into actionable strategies. Depending on the nature and severity of the risk, managers may choose to avoid it, mitigate its likelihood or impact, transfer responsibility to a third party, or accept it when intervention is impractical. For example, in vendor-dependent projects, a team might mitigate the risk of supplier failure by engaging a backup vendor or building internal fallback capabilities. Similarly, teams can address technology-related risks by developing prototypes or proof-of-concepts prior to large-scale implementation. Effective planning ensures that the project team is not caught off guard but is prepared with predefined strategies when risks materialise.

4. Monitoring and control:

Risk management does not end with planning; it requires ongoing monitoring and control throughout the project lifecycle. Risks evolve as the environment, technologies, and stakeholder expectations change, making continuous vigilance essential. Periodic reviews of the risk register, regular risk workshops, and the use of monitoring tools help identify emerging risks or shifts in existing ones. Agile practices such as sprint retrospectives and daily stand-ups provide built-in opportunities to reassess risks dynamically. By adapting responses as conditions change, project teams maintain resilience, ensuring that risks are not just managed at the beginning but throughout the entire project journey.

2.6 Conclusion: Proactive and Adaptive Risk Management:

Ultimately, risk management is both proactive and adaptive. Traditional frameworks provide the structure necessary for systematic risk governance, while Agile practices introduce flexibility and responsiveness to emerging threats. Effective project leaders do not view risks solely as threats but also as opportunities for learning and innovation. By blending structured methodologies with iterative practices, project teams can maintain resilience, safeguard stakeholder trust, and steer projects successfully through uncertainty.

3. Lessons Learnt and Knowledge Management

Knowledge management transforms project experiences into enduring organisational assets. Without systematic capture and sharing, valuable insights often dissipate at project closure, resulting in repeated mistakes, inefficiencies, and lost opportunities for improvement. Effective practices in this domain go beyond documentation—they embed learning into the organisational culture, ensuring continuous growth and innovation.

3.1 Integrating Lessons Learnt into Training and Onboarding:

The first step in effective knowledge management is ensuring that lessons from past projects directly inform future ones. This is achieved by incorporating findings into structured training and onboarding programmes. For instance, if requirement volatility led to project delays, new team members can be trained on techniques such as enhanced stakeholder engagement, iterative backlog refinement, and improved requirements management. Embedding lessons in this way transforms training from a generic orientation into a targeted learning mechanism that prevents recurrence of past issues.

3.2 Assigning Accountability through a Project Management Office (PMO):

Sustainable knowledge management requires clear ownership. Many organizations assign this responsibility to the Project Management Office (PMO), which acts as the custodian of organisational memory. The PMO ensures consistency in knowledge capture by standardising documentation templates, mandating post-project reviews, and conducting portfolio-level analysis of trends. This accountability mechanism prevents the dispersion of knowledge across departments and systematically consolidates valuable insights.

3.3 Balancing Qualitative and Quantitative Knowledge:

A robust knowledge management system must capture both qualitative reflections and quantitative project metrics. Qualitative insights—such as challenges in cross-cultural collaboration or communication breakdowns in distributed teams—offer context that raw data cannot provide. Meanwhile, quantitative indicators like defect density, cost variance, schedule adherence, or velocity provide objective evidence of project performance. Industry leaders such as Microsoft and IBM employ a blended approach, combining retrospective storytelling with analytics dashboards. This dual perspective ensures that lessons are both actionable and evidence-based.

3.4 Fostering Psychological Safety for Open Reflection:

Knowledge sharing thrives in an environment of psychological safety, where team members feel secure enough to admit mistakes and share candid reflections without fear of blame. Research by Amy Edmondson (2019) and findings from Google's Project Aristotle highlight that teams learn most effectively in cultures that encourage openness. Companies such as Etsy have institutionalised this practice through blameless post-mortems, where the focus is on systemic improvements rather than individual fault. Such practices transform failures into growth opportunities and normalise learning as part of the organisational culture.

3.5 Knowledge Management as a Strategic Enabler:

When integrated into organisational processes, knowledge management goes beyond being a passive archival function. It becomes a strategic enabler of innovation and resilience. Lessons learnt are not just stored—they actively shape decision-making, refine methodologies, and strengthen future project delivery. In industries such as software, where rapid iteration and adaptation are essential, well-structured knowledge management provides a competitive edge by ensuring that each project begins stronger than the last.

4. Cultural and Ethical Considerations

In today's interconnected world, project management extends beyond technical execution to include sensitivity to cultural diversity and ethical responsibility. As projects increasingly involve distributed teams, global stakeholders, and technologies with far-reaching societal impact, project managers must integrate cultural awareness and ethical integrity into their practices. These dimensions not only prevent conflict and misalignment but also build trust, legitimacy, and long-term sustainability.

4.1 Navigating Cross-Cultural Collaboration:

Global projects often involve diverse teams with varied communication styles, work ethics, and decision-making traditions. Without careful adaptation, these differences can create misunderstandings, delays, or stakeholder dissatisfaction. Effective project managers tailor their approach to fit cultural contexts, ensuring inclusivity and clarity.

For example, Infosys's distributed Agile teams working across India, Europe, and the U.S. adjusted communication strategies to align with stakeholder expectations. European clients preferred detailed written documentation to support governance and compliance requirements, U.S. executives valued concise ROI-driven presentations, and Indian developers required deep technical walkthroughs for alignment. By adapting formats and tones, Infosys minimised cross-cultural miscommunication and enhanced collaboration efficiency.

Such practices demonstrate that cultural awareness is not a

peripheral skill—it is central to building trust and sustaining productivity in multinational environments.

4.2 Ethical Responsibility in Project Delivery:

Ethical considerations are equally critical. Projects frequently encompass sensitive data, resource allocation, or environmental impact, requiring managers to uphold principles that go beyond contractual compliance. Ethical lapses can erode trust, damage reputations, and, in some cases, cause societal harm.

For instance, in AI-driven software projects, managers must address issues of algorithmic bias, transparency, and accountability. Without proactive safeguards, systems risk perpetuating discrimination or reinforcing existing inequalities. Similarly, sustainability concerns increasingly shape project decisions, compelling leaders to evaluate environmental footprints in procurement, operations, and lifecycle management. A project that optimises cost at the expense of ecological harm risks long-term reputational and regulatory consequences.

4.3 Professional Codes of Conduct as Guiding Frameworks:

To support consistent ethical behaviour, professional associations, such as the Project Management Institute (PMI), provide formal codes of ethics and professional conduct. These frameworks emphasise responsibility, respect, fairness, and honesty as non-negotiable principles for project delivery.

1. Adherence to professional codes of conduct requires project managers to maintain transparency when reporting risks or setbacks. Instead of concealing potential issues to protect reputations or avoid conflict, ethical leaders communicate openly about challenges. This transparency

enables stakeholders to make informed decisions, allocate resources effectively, and collectively develop solutions before problems escalate.

2. Another essential practice is the ability to resist pressure from stakeholders to manipulate data or conceal challenges. On competitive or politically sensitive projects, managers may face demands to present overly optimistic metrics or suppress unfavourable results. However, ethical stewardship prioritises integrity over convenience. By presenting accurate data, project managers preserve trust and ensure accountability, even if the truth is uncomfortable in the short term.

3. Finally, ethical project management entails prioritising stakeholders' and societal well-being over short-term financial or political gains. Projects exist within larger social, environmental, and organisational ecosystems, and decisions made for immediate profit or expediency can have lasting negative consequences. Ethical leaders take a long-term perspective, ensuring that deliverables contribute positively to communities, safeguard the environment, and respect human rights. This approach transforms project managers into guardians of both professional values and societal interests.

These practices reinforce accountability and align project management with broader professional and societal responsibilities.

4.4 Integrating Cultural Sensitivity with Ethical Integrity:

Ultimately, cultural and ethical considerations are not separate domains but interdependent. Culturally adaptive communication fosters collaboration, while ethical integrity ensures fairness, transparency, and long-term trust. When project managers combine these dimensions, they create environments that are technically competent, socially responsible, and globally adaptive.

For example, multinational development projects funded by international agencies often succeed when leaders balance cross-cultural negotiation with ethical governance. Such approaches build not only successful deliverables but also legitimacy among diverse stakeholders.

The best practices in project management—leadership and communication, risk governance, knowledge management, and cultural-ethical stewardship—form an interdependent framework. Strong leadership ensures alignment, risk management sustains resilience, knowledge management fosters continuous improvement, and cultural-ethical considerations safeguard trust and legitimacy. Together, these practices elevate project management from a mechanical exercise in task execution to a strategic discipline that delivers value, innovation, and sustainability in complex environments.

CHAPTER 12: MANAGING PROJECTS OF DIFFERENT SCALES

Project management is not a "one-size-fits-all" discipline. The scale and complexity of a project—whether small, medium, or large—fundamentally influence the choice of methodologies, governance structures, risk management strategies, and communication mechanisms. A small, focused initiative may thrive with lightweight processes and a high degree of flexibility, while a large-scale, multi-stakeholder program may require rigorous structures, sophisticated tools, and carefully designed governance mechanisms. Understanding these dynamics is essential for project managers seeking to deliver value efficiently while maintaining control over time, cost, and scope.

This chapter explores the differences between small and large project dynamics, examines how methodologies can be tailored to suit varying levels of complexity, and presents real-world case examples of scaling strategies. The goal is to provide project managers with both theoretical insights and practical guidance on how to adapt their approaches when working across projects of different magnitudes.

1. Small vs. Large Project Dynamics:

Small Projects

Small projects typically distinguish themselves from large-scale initiatives due to their limited scope, shorter timelines, and smaller budgets. They thrive on agility, flexibility, and efficient use of resources, as their narrowly focused objectives reduce the need for extensive governance structures and formal documentation. Typically, these projects address specific, well-defined goals with lean teams, which often require individuals to assume multiple roles and responsibilities, making multitasking and resource optimisation critical to success. Their shorter duration demands rapid decision-making, quick iterations, and adaptability, often supported by Agile or Lean methodologies. Stakeholder groups are usually smaller and more focused, allowing for streamlined communication and faster alignment, though limited resources mean even minor setbacks can have significant consequences if risks are not managed effectively. Ultimately, small project dynamics emphasise efficiency, adaptability, and clarity of purpose, enabling organizations to deliver targeted results with minimal bureaucracy.

Large Projects

Extensive scope, longer timelines, and significant budgets characterise large projects, rendering their dynamics fundamentally more complex than those of small-scale initiatives. They often involve multiple teams, cross-functional collaboration, and a wide range of stakeholders, which necessitates formal governance structures, detailed planning, and robust documentation to maintain alignment. The scale of these projects increases interdependencies among tasks, heightening the risk of delays, cost overruns, and scope creep, thereby requiring sophisticated tools and methodologies such as PRINCE2, PMBOK, or advanced project portfolio management systems. Communication and coordination become critical, as misalignment across diverse stakeholder groups can lead to major setbacks. While large projects have the potential to deliver transformative outcomes, their dynamics demand strong leadership, systematic monitoring, and well-defined change management processes to ensure progress and mitigate risks effectively.

1.1 Scope and Objectives:

Small and large projects differ significantly in their scope and objectives. Small projects usually focus on a narrowly defined deliverable, often with a short timeline, fewer resources, and a limited set of stakeholders. Their objectives are precise and relatively easy to monitor. In contrast, large projects encompass broad goals, multiple deliverables, extended timelines, and complex interdependencies between tasks. They typically involve diverse stakeholder groups with varied expectations, requiring extensive planning and alignment efforts.

The scope of a project is the first and most visible differentiator between small and large initiatives. Small projects are often tactical in nature, with narrowly defined deliverables and objectives. For example, updating a company's website interface, conducting a short-term market research survey, or integrating a minor software feature enhancement typically fall under small projects. Their objectives are measurable and limited in time, often allowing managers to monitor progress with straightforward metrics.

By contrast, large projects are inherently strategic and multi-dimensional. They encompass broader goals that often extend across organizational units or geographical boundaries. Consider, for instance, the implementation of a nationwide health information system or the construction of a smart city initiative. Such projects involve multiple deliverables, diverse stakeholders, and extended timelines, with outcomes that must align with both short-term milestones and long-term strategic visions. The scale of objectives creates greater interdependencies, requiring more structured planning and coordination mechanisms.

1.2 Resource Allocation and Team Structure:

Small projects often operate with compact teams where members wear multiple hats, leading to higher flexibility but also increased dependency on individual expertise. In large projects, teams are larger, hierarchical, and often distributed across geographies, with clear role specialization. Resource allocation in large projects is more structured, requiring formal processes for procurement, budgeting, and scheduling to ensure efficiency.

Small projects usually operate with lean teams where members take on multiple roles. This creates agility but also introduces vulnerabilities, since the absence or departure of a single member can significantly disrupt progress. Resource allocation is often informal, relying on the availability and versatility of team members.

Large projects, in contrast, are characterized by distributed teams, often spanning multiple functional areas or geographical regions. Here, specialization becomes essential: project managers oversee dedicated sub-teams for design, development, testing, quality assurance, and risk management. Resource allocation is formalized through budget approvals, procurement processes, and role definitions. This structure enhances efficiency but also introduces challenges of coordination and communication.

1.3 Risk Profile and Uncertainty:

Small projects are usually less risky because their limited scale reduces exposure to uncertainties. However, they are highly vulnerable to resource bottlenecks since they rely on fewer people and technologies. Large projects, on the other hand, face higher levels of uncertainty due to interdependencies, external influences, and long durations. Risks such as scope creep, budget overruns, and stakeholder misalignment are more prevalent, necessitating robust risk management frameworks.

The risk profile of a project is directly linked to its size and duration. Small projects face fewer risks overall but are highly sensitive to changes in resources or stakeholder expectations. A small project with only three key resources may face significant setbacks if one member leaves unexpectedly.

Large projects, on the other hand, face complex and multi-layered risks. Scope creep, cost overruns, delays, and regulatory compliance issues are common. The extended timelines also expose large projects to environmental shifts —such as changes in market conditions, political landscapes, or technological innovations—that can alter assumptions made at the planning stage. Managing such risks requires a structured framework involving risk registers, periodic assessments, and contingency plans.

1.4 Communication and Governance:

Small projects often benefit from direct communication among team members, which fosters agility and quick decision-making. Governance structures are usually lightweight, with the project manager often serving as the main point of authority. Large projects, in contrast, require multi-layered governance mechanisms, involving steering committees, reporting frameworks, and formal communication channels. Effective governance is essential to coordinate decision-making and maintain transparency across different levels of stakeholders.

Communication is another defining aspect of scale. Small projects typically enjoy the advantage of direct and informal communication. Team members often share updates in real-time through daily stand-ups, instant messaging, or co-located meetings. Decision-making is rapid, as fewer stakeholders are involved and governance layers are minimal.

In contrast, large projects require structured governance frameworks to handle complexity. Communication must flow across multiple levels: project teams, program management offices, executive sponsors, and external stakeholders. Governance structures often include steering committees, reporting dashboards, and escalation protocols. Formal communication becomes essential not only for transparency but also for accountability, especially when projects are subject to external audits or political scrutiny.

2. Tailoring Methodologies to Project Complexity

2.1 Agile for Small and Adaptive Projects:

Agile methodologies such as Scrum and Kanban are particularly suited for small projects or projects characterized by evolving requirements. Agile thrives in environments where adaptability, frequent feedback, and rapid delivery cycles are critical. For instance, in software development projects involving feature enhancements, Agile allows small teams to respond swiftly to user feedback and deliver incremental value.

Agile methodologies are particularly suited for small-scale or adaptive projects where requirements evolve dynamically. Frameworks such as Scrum and Kanban emphasize iterative development, continuous feedback, and rapid delivery of value. For instance, a software startup developing a mobile application enhancement may rely on Scrum to deliver incremental updates every two weeks, incorporating user feedback into each iteration.

The lightweight governance of Agile minimizes bureaucratic overhead, allowing small teams to pivot quickly when priorities shift. Moreover, Agile's emphasis on customer collaboration over rigid contract negotiation aligns well with the realities of small projects, where clients may refine their expectations as they see tangible outputs.

2.2 Waterfall and Hybrid Approaches for Large Projects:

Large projects, especially those with regulatory requirements or infrastructure components, often demand structured approaches like the Waterfall. This methodology emphasizes upfront planning, sequential execution, and rigorous documentation. However, due to the dynamic nature of modern projects, hybrid methodologies are increasingly being adopted. Hybrid approaches combine the predictability of Waterfall with the flexibility of Agile, enabling large projects to balance structure with adaptability.

Large projects with high regulatory, technical, or safety requirements often rely on structured methodologies such as the Waterfall. Waterfall's sequential nature—moving from requirements gathering to design, implementation, testing, and deployment—provides the rigor and traceability needed in contexts such as aerospace engineering, infrastructure development, or healthcare IT systems.

However, given the dynamic nature of contemporary environments, many organizations adopt hybrid approaches. These approaches combine the predictability of Waterfall with the flexibility of Agile. For example, an infrastructure project may use Waterfall for compliance-heavy elements such as design approvals and construction, while Agile practices may be employed in the development of digital tools or customer-facing applications that accompany the physical infrastructure.

2.3 Scaling Agile for Enterprise Projects:

Frameworks such as SAFe (Scaled Agile Framework), LeSS (Large-Scale Scrum), and Disciplined Agile Delivery (DAD) are designed to extend Agile practices to large-scale, multi-team environments. These frameworks address challenges such as inter-team coordination, dependency management, and strategic alignment. By tailoring Agile principles to enterprise contexts, organizations can ensure that even large, complex projects retain agility while maintaining cohesion.

In recent years, large organizations have increasingly sought to scale Agile principles to enterprise-wide projects. Frameworks such as the Scaled Agile Framework (SAFe), Large-Scale Scrum (LeSS), and Disciplined Agile Delivery (DAD) provide structured mechanisms for applying Agile at scale. These frameworks address challenges of inter-team dependencies, synchronization, and strategic alignment, ensuring that large initiatives benefit from the adaptability of Agile without losing coherence.

For example, a multinational corporation implementing a global Enterprise Resource Planning (ERP) system may organize multiple Agile Release Trains (ARTs) under SAFe, synchronizing the work of dozens of teams across different regions. This approach ensures that Agile principles of collaboration and incremental delivery are retained while managing the sheer scale of enterprise requirements.

2.4 Methodology Selection Criteria:

Selecting the right methodology depends on several factors:

project size, complexity, stakeholder diversity, regulatory requirements, and risk tolerance. A small, experimental project may benefit from Agile's flexibility, whereas a safety-critical project, such as building a healthcare system, may require the rigor of Waterfall. In many cases, organizations adopt a methodology continuum, where the chosen framework is dynamically adjusted based on project evolution.

The selection of methodologies should never be arbitrary. Instead, project managers must consider criteria such as:

a) *Project Size and Duration* – Short-term projects may benefit from Agile, while long-term strategic initiatives may require hybrid or structured approaches.

b) *Complexity and Interdependencies* – Projects with high technical or stakeholder interdependencies demand structured coordination mechanisms.

c) *Stakeholder Diversity* – Projects with diverse or global stakeholders may require formal governance frameworks to ensure alignment.

d) *Regulatory Environment* – Projects in safety-critical domains must comply with standards, often necessitating Waterfall or hybrid approaches.

e) *Risk Tolerance* – The greater the risk exposure, the more structured the methodology must be.

By systematically evaluating these criteria, project managers can tailor their methodologies to ensure optimal alignment between the project's context and the management approach.

3. Case Examples of Scaling Strategies

3.1 Case Example 1:

Small-Scale Software Enhancement Project:

A local startup developing a mobile application enhancement opted for Agile Scrum. The project involved a five-member team, bi-weekly sprints, and continuous integration practices. With direct communication and daily stand-ups, the team quickly responded to customer feedback, reducing delivery cycles and increasing user satisfaction. The small project scale allowed for rapid iterations and efficient decision-making.

A small e-commerce startup aimed to enhance its mobile application by adding personalized recommendation features. The project involved a five-member team with expertise in front-end development, machine learning, and testing. The team adopted Scrum, with two-week sprints, daily stand-ups, and sprint reviews involving key stakeholders.

The Agile approach allowed rapid experimentation, enabling the team to test recommendation algorithms and gather user feedback continuously. Despite limited resources, the project was completed within eight weeks, significantly boosting customer engagement and sales. This case illustrates how small projects can leverage Agile's adaptability and lightweight governance for swift value delivery.

3.2 Case Example 2:

Large-Scale Infrastructure Project:

A national highway development initiative illustrates the complexity of large projects. The project involved multiple contractors, government agencies, and financial stakeholders. A traditional Waterfall methodology was used to ensure compliance with regulations, safety standards, and budgetary constraints. A centralized Project Management

Office (PMO) oversaw governance, while risk management frameworks addressed delays, cost escalations, and environmental concerns. The structured approach provided accountability and transparency across multiple layers of stakeholders.

A government-led national highway development initiative highlights the complexities of large-scale projects. The project involved multiple contractors, government agencies, financial institutions, and local communities. Due to its scale and regulatory requirements, a traditional Waterfall methodology was chosen.

The project was divided into sequential phases: feasibility study, design, procurement, construction, and handover. Governance was provided by a central Project Management Office (PMO), which coordinated communication, risk management, and stakeholder engagement. Despite occasional delays due to land acquisition challenges, the structured approach ensured accountability, transparency, and adherence to safety standards. This example underscores the necessity of rigorous methodologies for projects with high societal impact and regulatory oversight.

3.3 Case Example 3:

Scaling Agile in a Global IT Program:

A multinational IT company implemented a global Enterprise Resource Planning (ERP) system across several regions. Due to the scale and complexity, a Scaled Agile Framework (SAFe) was adopted. Multiple Agile Release Trains (ARTs) coordinated work across teams in different time zones, ensuring synchronization of deliverables. The hybrid model combined Agile adaptability with Waterfall-style governance to handle compliance, integration, and stakeholder alignment. The scaling strategy allowed the organization to manage complexity without losing agility.

A multinational IT corporation sought to implement a global ERP system to harmonize processes across more than 20 countries. Given the system's complexity, a hybrid approach based on SAFe was adopted. Multiple Agile Release Trains coordinated the work of over 500 professionals spread across different regions.

While Agile teams worked iteratively on specific modules, the overall program maintained Waterfall-style governance to ensure compliance with financial regulations and integration milestones. The scaling strategy enabled the organization to deliver incremental value, adapt to local requirements, and reduce resistance to change, while still meeting overarching global objectives.

Lessons Learned from the Case Studies:

1. Small projects benefit from lean governance and high adaptability.
2. Large projects demand structured planning, stakeholder management, and robust risk controls.
3. Hybrid and scaled Agile approaches offer balance for projects that combine complexity with evolving requirements.
4. Contextual tailoring of methodologies ensures that project management is neither overly rigid nor excessively flexible.

Practical Implications for Project Managers:

1. *Adopt a Contextual Mindset* – Project managers must resist the temptation to apply a single methodology across all projects. Instead, they should analyze project characteristics—scale, risk, stakeholders, and environment—before choosing an approach.

2. *Invest in Governance Structures* – As projects grow in scale, governance must evolve from informal communication to formal reporting, steering committees, and performance dashboards. Project managers must ensure governance is not overly bureaucratic but sufficient to maintain control.

3. *Balance Flexibility and Discipline* – In dynamic environments, even large projects benefit from adopting Agile practices for components requiring adaptability. Project managers should champion hybrid models where appropriate, striking a balance between flexibility and discipline.

4. *Strengthen Risk Management* – Large projects require dedicated risk management frameworks, but even small projects must account for vulnerabilities such as resource bottlenecks. Risk awareness should be embedded in the project culture regardless of scale.

5. *Leverage Technology* – Tools such as project management software, collaboration platforms, and automated reporting systems play a vital role in managing scale. Project managers must adopt digital solutions to maintain efficiency and transparency.

Conclusion

Managing projects of different scales requires a nuanced understanding of dynamics, methodologies, and governance mechanisms. Small projects excel when managed with agility, adaptability, and minimal overhead, while large projects demand structure, formality, and robust risk management. Increasingly, organizations are adopting hybrid and scaled Agile approaches to balance flexibility with control in complex environments.

For project managers, the key lies in tailoring methodologies to the context, ensuring that management practices align with project objectives, risks, and stakeholder expectations. By developing the ability to scale approaches up or down, project managers can enhance efficiency, improve outcomes, and build resilience across a diverse portfolio of projects.

CHAPTER 13: PROJECT MANAGEMENT SOFTWARE IN PRACTICE

In today's dynamic business environment, projects serve as the central mechanism through which organizations deliver innovation, achieve strategic objectives, and sustain competitive advantage. However, projects are no longer confined to small, localised teams; they often involve geographically dispersed stakeholders, compressed timelines, and rapidly changing requirements. As a result, the role of project management software has shifted from being an optional support mechanism to a core enabler of project success. Digital platforms now underpin every stage of the project life cycle—from planning and scheduling to monitoring, communication, and reporting.

This chapter explores the practical applications of project management software by analysing popular tools such as Microsoft Project, Jira, Trello, and Asana, discussing the importance of collaborative platforms and integrations, and emphasising the role of simulation and hands-on practice. Through global and Indian case studies, it illustrates how organizations leverage these platforms to enhance efficiency, agility, and accountability in project delivery.

1. Popular Tools: MS Project, Jira, Trello, and Asana

Modern project management relies on specialised software solutions designed to streamline workflows, enable coordination, and support decision-making. While traditional methods such as spreadsheets remain in use, their limitations in handling complex dependencies, real-time collaboration, and large-scale data have made them inadequate for today's projects. Tools like Microsoft Project, Jira, Trello, and Asana have emerged as leaders, each aligning with distinct methodologies and organisational needs.

1.1 Microsoft Project: A Traditional Powerhouse:

Microsoft Project (MS Project) is one of the most established and widely adopted project management applications, especially in industries requiring precision and detailed scheduling. It provides comprehensive functionality for creating and managing complex project plans with thousands of interrelated tasks.

Its core features include Gantt charts for visualising timelines, Work Breakdown Structures (WBS) for decomposing scope into manageable deliverables, resource levelling to prevent over-allocation, and Critical Path Method (CPM) analysis to identify tasks that directly influence project completion dates. Furthermore, MS Project supports Earned Value Management (EVM), a widely respected performance measurement approach for comparing planned versus actual progress in terms of cost and schedule.

The primary use cases of MS Project are in industries such as construction, engineering, and infrastructure, where projects often extend over several years and involve multiple contractors. For example, in a multi-year construction project, MS Project allows managers to allocate resources across subcontractors, forecast costs, and monitor progress against milestones, thereby ensuring that delays in one workstream do not compromise the entire initiative.

Despite its advantages, MS Project has certain limitations. Its steep learning curve makes it less accessible for smaller teams, and its orientation toward predictive methodologies means it may not align with fast-changing Agile projects.

Case Example 1:

Delhi Metro Rail Corporation (DMRC):

The Delhi Metro Rail Corporation (DMRC) stands as one of the most celebrated infrastructure success stories in India. Constructing and managing a world-class metro system in a city as dense, congested, and logistically challenging as Delhi required not only engineering excellence but also sophisticated project management practices. Among the many tools deployed, Microsoft Project (MS Project) emerged as a critical enabler in orchestrating the complexity of this multi-phase, multi-stakeholder initiative.

Complexity of the Project Environment:

The Delhi Metro project involved thousands of interdependent tasks cutting across civil engineering, electrical systems, rolling stock procurement, signalling and telecommunication, station construction, and safety systems. Each of these domains had its own subcontractors, timelines, and dependencies. Coordinating them within strict budgetary and time constraints required a platform that could both capture complexity and translate it into actionable project schedules.

Delhi's unique challenges—including land acquisition delays, congested traffic corridors, and stringent safety regulations—made it imperative to adopt a structured and predictive project management methodology. Here, MS Project's Gantt charts, Work Breakdown Structures (WBS), and Critical Path Method (CPM) functionalities provided DMRC with the ability to anticipate risks and recalibrate timelines before issues escalated.

Role of MS Project in Planning and Scheduling:

MS Project was extensively used to break down the massive undertaking into a hierarchical Work Breakdown Structure (WBS). Every deliverable, from tunnelling to track laying, was decomposed into sub-tasks with dependencies clearly mapped. This not only created clarity among the project teams but also ensured that no critical element was overlooked.

a) *Dependency Visualisation:* With thousands of tasks interlinked, MS Project's dependency mapping allowed project managers to identify critical paths—those sequences of activities where a single delay could jeopardise the entire schedule.

b) *Milestone Monitoring*: Key construction milestones such as the completion of elevated viaducts, commissioning of stations, or integration of signalling systems were tracked against baseline schedules. Deviations could be flagged early, allowing for immediate corrective action.

c) *Resource Allocation*: By leveraging MS Project's resource levelling features, DMRC could assign labour, equipment, and contractors efficiently, minimising cost overruns and idle time.

Dynamic Control and Risk Management:

MS Project also played a pivotal role in monitoring and control. During execution, DMRC had to constantly adjust schedules due to unforeseen challenges such as monsoon-related delays, utility relocations, and safety clearances. By updating progress in real-time, the software recalculated dependencies and critical paths, enabling managers to re-sequence tasks dynamically.

Moreover, risk scenarios were modelled using MS Project's simulation features. For example, delays in tunnelling due to geological surprises could be mapped to their downstream effects on station construction and rolling stock integration. This capability gave DMRC a robust risk management framework that combined predictive planning with real-time adaptability.

Governance and Stakeholder Coordination:

One of the biggest challenges of the Delhi Metro was coordinating across a multi-stakeholder environment that included the central government, the Delhi state government, international funding agencies like the Japan International Cooperation Agency (JICA), and multiple contractors. MS Project served as a single source of truth, producing detailed reports and visual dashboards that could be shared with stakeholders at different levels of technical expertise.

This transparency was crucial in building trust among stakeholders and ensuring accountability across the project ecosystem. Regular updates generated from MS Project enabled leadership to monitor progress against global benchmarks, reinforcing DMRC's reputation for punctuality and fiscal discipline.

Outcomes and Global Recognition:

The disciplined application of MS Project was one of the reasons why the Delhi Metro became a benchmark for infrastructure delivery in India and abroad. Unlike many Indian public infrastructure projects, which are often plagued by delays and cost overruns, the Delhi Metro phases were consistently completed on or ahead of schedule, with minimal deviation from budget.

The project's success not only transformed urban mobility in Delhi but also positioned DMRC as a model of project governance. International observers—including metro corporations in cities such as Jakarta, Dhaka, and Hanoi—studied the DMRC approach, particularly its use of project management software, to replicate similar practices.

Practical Insights:

From a theoretical perspective, the Delhi Metro Rail Corporation (DMRC) case underscores how project management software is not merely a planning aid but a governance instrument. By integrating planning, execution, monitoring, and stakeholder communication within a single platform, MS Project elevated project management from a supporting role to a strategic enabler.

Practically, the case illustrates that even in resource-constrained and high-risk environments like India, structured adoption of digital project management tools can dramatically improve outcomes. The Delhi Metro demonstrates the importance of aligning technological tools with disciplined processes, strong leadership, and stakeholder collaboration to achieve world-class results.

1.2 Jira: Agile-Centric Flexibility:

In contrast to MS Project's predictive focus, Jira, developed by Atlassian, is the tool of choice for Agile and iterative project environments. It is particularly popular among software development teams where adaptability and rapid delivery cycles are essential.

Jira's core features include customisable Scrum and Kanban boards, sprint planning modules, backlog prioritisation, issue and bug tracking, and visual burndown charts that provide real-time progress monitoring. Its flexibility lies in the ability to adapt workflows to specific team requirements, making it suitable for organizations practicing Agile, SAFe (Scaled Agile Framework), or hybrid methodologies.

For instance, in a fintech company developing a mobile banking app, Jira facilitates backlog organisation, sprint management, and issue resolution, ensuring incremental product releases and alignment with regulatory standards.

Jira's limitations include high configuration requirements and the challenge of adoption for teams unfamiliar with Agile. Without proper training, the platform's extensive customisation options can overwhelm users.

Case Example 1:

Spotify:

Spotify, the global music streaming giant, is widely regarded as a pioneer in leveraging Agile practices at scale to sustain innovation, adaptability, and customer-centric growth. With operations spanning multiple countries and a product serving hundreds of millions of users, Spotify faces the constant challenge of managing large-scale development while maintaining the speed and creativity of smaller teams. To meet this challenge, the company relies extensively on Jira, supported by Confluence for documentation and Slack for team communication. Together, these tools form the backbone of Spotify's project management ecosystem.

The Spotify Model and Agile Squads:

Spotify is credited with popularising the "Spotify Model" of Agile scaling, which emphasises small, autonomous, cross-functional teams known as squads. Each squad functions like a mini-startup, responsible for specific features or services within the larger Spotify platform—such as search functionality, recommendation algorithms, playlist management, or advertising modules.

Jira is the central platform that enables these squads to:

a) *Manage backlogs*: Squads maintain prioritised product backlogs within Jira, ensuring that development efforts align with customer needs and product roadmaps.

b) ***Plan sprints***: Through Jira's Scrum boards and sprint planning features, squads define short, iterative cycles for feature development and bug fixing.

c) ***Track issues and progress***: Bugs, technical debt, and feature stories are logged and tracked within Jira, creating visibility and accountability for every team member.

This use of Jira allows Spotify to balance autonomy at the squad level with alignment at the organisational level, enabling rapid feature delivery without compromising quality or coordination.

Integration with Confluence and Slack:

While Jira handles task management and workflows, Confluence acts as the knowledge repository for documentation. Squad members record technical specifications, sprint retrospectives, and architectural decisions within Confluence, ensuring that critical knowledge is preserved and accessible across teams.

At the same time, *Slack* provides real-time communication and collaboration. Integrated with Jira, Slack channels notify teams of task updates, sprint progress, or blockers. This reduces communication lags and fosters immediate alignment, especially across geographically distributed squads.

Together, this Jira–Confluence–Slack ecosystem embodies the collaborative infrastructure required for global-scale Agile practices. It ensures that while teams operate independently, they remain synchronised through transparent workflows and information-sharing practices.

Maintaining Innovation Velocity:

One of Spotify's most pressing challenges is sustaining its innovation velocity while scaling globally. Jira enables this by providing:

a) Burndown charts and velocity tracking to monitor the pace of feature completion across squads.

b) Dashboards and reports to give product owners and leadership visibility into progress and bottlenecks.

c) ross-team alignment through programme-level tracking that aggregates squad activities into higher-level initiatives.

This structure ensures that new features—such as personalised playlists, real-time lyrics, or integrations with smart speakers—can be rolled out rapidly and iteratively while maintaining consistency across a vast and complex platform.

Outcomes and Global Recognition:

Spotify's disciplined use of Jira, combined with its Agile philosophy, has made the company a global benchmark for Agile-driven innovation. By structuring its work into smaller, manageable units while maintaining organisational coherence, Spotify has achieved:

a) Faster product release cycles compared to traditional software companies.

b) High adaptability to user feedback, allowing continuous improvement of features.

c) A culture of autonomy and ownership, where developers feel empowered to experiment and innovate.

The effectiveness of this approach has not only fuelled Spotify's growth but also influenced how organizations worldwide implement Agile at scale. Many global enterprises, from ING Bank to Lego, have studied and adopted variations of the Spotify Model, often replicating its reliance on Jira as the primary coordination tool.

Practical Insights:

From a theoretical lens, the Spotify case demonstrates the critical role of project management software in enabling scaled Agile frameworks. Jira is not merely a task tracker; it is a strategic coordination platform that aligns decentralised teams with enterprise-level goals.

Practically, the case highlights that while culture and structure (the Spotify Model) provide the foundation for agility, digital tools like Jira, Confluence, and Slack operationalise these principles by embedding them into everyday workflows. This synergy between organisational philosophy and software infrastructure is what sustains Spotify's innovation velocity in a competitive digital economy.

Case Example 2:

Infosys:

Infosys, one of India's largest IT services and consulting firms, has long been a global leader in outsourcing, application development, and enterprise transformation projects. With delivery centres spread across multiple continents and clients that include Fortune 500 companies, Infosys operates in a highly complex, distributed, and client-driven environment. To stay competitive and meet evolving client expectations for faster, more adaptive solutions, Infosys undertook a large-scale Agile transformation. A cornerstone of this transformation was the adoption of Jira as its central project management software, supported by Confluence for documentation and Slack for communication.

The Need for Agile Transformation:

Traditional delivery models in IT services often relied on predictive, waterfall-style approaches, where scope, cost, and timelines were fixed upfront. While effective for certain large-scale system implementations, this approach became increasingly inadequate in an era where clients—particularly global banks, retailers, and digital enterprises—demanded faster time-to-market, continuous iteration, and the ability to pivot quickly.

Infosys recognised that to maintain its competitive edge, it had to shift from rigid project structures to an Agile, client-centric delivery model. This shift required not only cultural and process changes but also the deployment of a robust digital toolset capable of enabling agility at scale.

Role of Jira in the Transformation:

Infosys standardised on Jira as its primary agile project management platform, rolling it out across its global delivery centres in India, the U.S., Europe, and Asia-Pacific. Jira's flexibility and scalability made it well-suited for an organisation of Infosys' size and complexity.

a) ***Workflow Customisation***: Infosys leveraged Jira's customisable workflows to tailor processes for different industry verticals. For example, a global banking client's project emphasised regulatory compliance and audit trails, while a retail client's digital commerce project prioritised speed and feature deployment. Jira allowed these workflows to coexist within the same platform, aligning delivery models with client-specific priorities.

b) ***Backlog Management and Sprint Planning***: Global delivery teams used Jira to manage product backlogs, prioritise tasks, and plan sprints. This ensured that distributed teams remained aligned despite geographical separation.

c) ***Transparency and Visibility***: Jira dashboards provided real-time visibility into project status for both Infosys leadership and client stakeholders. Clients could track the progress of feature development, defect resolution, and release readiness, reinforcing trust and accountability.

d) ***Scalability***: Given Infosys' large workforce, Jira's ability to scale across thousands of users and integrate with other enterprise tools was critical in ensuring consistent adoption.

Integration with Confluence and Slack:

To complement Jira, Infosys integrated Confluence and Slack into its project management ecosystem.

a) ***Confluence*** served as the documentation hub, where teams maintained design documents, sprint retrospectives, decision logs, and client-specific compliance records. This eliminated duplication of knowledge and ensured a single source of truth across projects.

b) ***Slack***, integrated with Jira, enabled real-time communication between globally distributed teams. For instance, when a Jira ticket was updated or a sprint milestone was reached, automated Slack notifications kept team members and clients instantly informed. This reduced email overhead and accelerated decision-making cycles.

Together, this triad of Jira, Confluence, and Slack created a cohesive ecosystem where planning, execution, documentation, and communication seamlessly flowed together.

Outcomes of the Transformation:

The adoption of Jira and its ecosystem yielded measurable benefits for Infosys:

1. ***Enhanced Transparency*** – Clients gained unprecedented visibility into delivery progress through shared dashboards, which improved trust and collaboration.

2. ***Accelerated Delivery*** – Agile sprints managed in Jira

enabled Infosys to deliver incremental value quickly, aligning with client expectations for faster product and feature releases.

3. ***Alignment of Distributed Teams*** – By using common tools across delivery centres, Infosys minimised coordination challenges inherent in global projects, ensuring consistency in delivery standards.

4. ***Client-Centric Flexibility*** – Infosys could adapt project management approaches to different industries and regions without losing standardisation.

Case in Practice 1:

Infosys: Global Banking and Retail Clients:

a) ***Banking Sector***: For a leading global bank, Infosys used Jira to manage a multi-year digital transformation initiative involving core banking modernisation. Jira's traceability features ensured compliance with strict regulatory requirements while enabling iterative delivery of digital products like mobile apps and customer portals.

b) ***Retail Sector***: For a large North American retailer, Infosys employed Jira to coordinate a digital commerce platform revamp. Distributed teams worked on features such as personalised shopping, omnichannel integration, and real-time analytics. Jira's sprint tracking and backlog prioritisation ensured that the client saw incremental improvements every few weeks, rather than waiting months for results.

Practical Insights:

From a theoretical perspective, Infosys' adoption of Jira illustrates how project management software can enable organisational transformation at scale. It highlights the interplay between technology, methodology, and organisational culture in embedding Agile practices across thousands of employees.

Practically, the case shows that tools like Jira are not only beneficial for product companies like Spotify but also highly effective in service delivery organizations, where client-specific demands and global team distribution add additional layers of complexity. Infosys demonstrates how structured adoption of project management tools can bridge geographical divides, enhance client trust, and accelerate enterprise-scale delivery.

1.3 Trello: Simplicity and Transparency:

Where MS Project and Jira are designed for complex environments, Trello appeals to teams seeking simplicity, ease of use, and visual task management. Based on a Kanban-inspired card-and-board system, Trello makes project tracking intuitive even for non-technical teams.

Its core features include boards, lists, and cards that can be moved via drag-and-drop. Cards can contain checklists, labels, attachments, and due dates, making them versatile for task-level tracking. Trello's lightweight design is well-suited to small projects, startups, or marketing campaigns, where flexibility and transparency outweigh formal scheduling needs.

A marketing agency, for example, can use Trello to assign content creation tasks, track approvals, and monitor campaign progress without the overhead of complex project management methodologies.

However, Trello's limitations are evident in large, resource-heavy projects, as it lacks advanced features for dependency management, resource allocation, and cost control.

Case Example 1:

National Geographic's Use of Trello for Editorial Workflow Management:

Context and Challenges:

National Geographic, a globally recognised leader in documentary storytelling, operates with geographically distributed editorial teams. These teams are responsible for producing, curating, and publishing high-quality content across multiple channels—print, digital, and broadcast. Given the scale and diversity of operations, the editorial process often faced delays due to fragmented communication, lack of visibility in task progress, and misalignment across global contributors.

Adoption of Trello as a Workflow Solution:

To streamline these challenges, National Geographic's digital media team implemented Trello as its core project management tool. Trello's visual Kanban-style boards allowed editors, writers, designers, and managers to map the entire content lifecycle—from ideation and draughting to review, approval, and publishing. Each piece of content was represented as a card, which could be moved seamlessly across stages, providing real-time visibility to all stakeholders.

Enhancing Collaboration and Transparency:

One of the critical benefits realised was transparency across distributed teams. Editors in different time zones could instantly view the status of any article, feature, or multimedia project. This reduced the dependency on long email threads or status meetings. Moreover, the tagging and checklist features ensured accountability, as responsibilities for reviews or approvals were clearly assigned.

Efficiency Gains and Reduced Delays:

The introduction of Trello brought measurable efficiency improvements. The content approval cycle shortened significantly, as editors could monitor pending tasks at a glance and prioritise accordingly. Automated reminders and notifications prevented bottlenecks, while integration with cloud storage facilitated instant access to drafts and multimedia assets. The result was a smoother publishing pipeline, ensuring that National Geographic's content maintained both timeliness and quality.

Key Takeaways:

National Geographic's implementation of Trello highlights how visual project management tools can overcome coordination barriers in creative industries. By aligning distributed editorial teams through shared visibility, the organisation achieved a balance between creative freedom and operational discipline.

Case Example 2:

Tata Steel's Innovation Labs and Trello-Slack Integration:

Context and Challenges:

Tata Steel, a global steel manufacturing giant, invests heavily in research and development (R&D) to drive innovation in sustainable materials, manufacturing processes, and product design. Managing innovation projects is inherently complex, involving idea generation, prototype development, and cross-functional collaboration. Traditional project management systems often created friction, with rigid workflows that discouraged dynamic collaboration and slowed decision-making.

Adoption of Trello in R&D Environments:

To address these challenges, Tata Steel's innovation labs adopted Trello as a lightweight and flexible project management platform. Trello's card-based interface suited the dynamic nature of R&D projects, where ideas often evolve iteratively rather than following rigid linear processes. Teams could create cards for new concepts, assign them to researchers, and track their progression from brainstorming to testing and validation.

Integration with Slack for Communication:

Recognising the critical role of real-time communication in innovation, Tata Steel integrated Trello with Slack, a widely used messaging and collaboration platform. This integration meant that any updates in Trello—such as new ideas logged, status changes, or prototype feedback—were instantly communicated to the team via Slack channels. This eliminated the lag associated with email communication and fostered rapid decision-making, an essential factor in competitive R&D landscapes.

Encouraging Idea-Sharing and Knowledge Flow:

The system not only tracked projects but also encouraged a culture of openness and innovation. Researchers felt empowered to contribute ideas without bureaucratic overhead, knowing that their suggestions were visible to peers and decision-makers. The collaborative environment facilitated faster prototyping cycles, as stakeholders could immediately provide feedback and align resources.

Impact on Research-Driven Initiatives:

The Trello-Slack ecosystem transformed Tata Steel's R&D labs into a more agile and adaptive environment. The approach reduced the time taken to move from ideation to prototype, enhanced accountability in experimental tasks, and promoted stronger collaboration between engineers, scientists, and business strategists. By aligning lightweight project management with real-time communication, Tata Steel positioned its innovation labs to respond swiftly to emerging challenges and opportunities in the steel industry.

Key Takeaways:

The Tata Steel case underscores the importance of integrating flexible project management tools with instant communication platforms in research environments. Unlike traditional project structures, innovation requires rapid iteration and feedback, which Trello and Slack jointly enabled, fostering a culture of agility and innovation within a large industrial enterprise.

Together, these two cases illustrate how Trello, either standalone or integrated with tools like Slack, can be adapted to different organisational needs—whether it is streamlining editorial workflows in media organizations or accelerating innovation cycles in industrial R&D labs.

1.4 Asana: Balancing Structure and Flexibility:

Asana positions itself between the rigidity of MS Project and the simplicity of Trello, offering a balanced solution for teams that require both flexibility and structure.

Its core features include task assignments, dependencies, workload dashboards, project timelines, and reporting features. It enables organizations to monitor individual workloads alongside project progress, which is particularly useful in environments with cross-functional teams managing multiple projects.

A healthcare NGO, for example, can use Asana to assign responsibilities across volunteers, visualise timelines for community projects, and ensure that resources are distributed equitably.

While powerful, Asana's broad feature set may overwhelm smaller teams that require only basic task management.

Case Example 1:

Airbnb: Cross-Functional Collaboration through Asana:

Context and Organisational Challenge:

Airbnb is a global online marketplace connecting hosts offering homes with travellers seeking stays. Founded in 2008, it transformed hospitality by enabling unique, affordable, and diverse accommodations. Operating in more than 220 countries, it fosters cultural exchange, empowers hosts with income opportunities, and leverages technology for trust, personalisation, and convenience.

Airbnb, a global leader in the hospitality and travel industry, operates at the intersection of technology, customer experience, and operations. Its success depends on the seamless alignment of product development teams, customer support units, and operational departments spread across multiple regions. However, as the company scaled, silos began to form between departments, leading to communication gaps, delays in decision-making, and inefficiencies in project execution. The lack of a unified platform to track goals and tasks across functions was a critical barrier.

Adoption of Asana as a Central Collaboration Platform:

To address these challenges, Airbnb adopted Asana, a cloud-based project management and work coordination tool. Asana enabled the organisation to create structured project boards and task lists where each function—product, support, and operations—could contribute and align their objectives. The platform's ability to integrate with other tools (Slack, Google Workspace, and data visualisation systems) makes it suitable for Airbnb's complex, technology-driven environment.

Role of Reporting Dashboards:

A pivotal feature leveraged by Airbnb was Asana's reporting dashboards. These dashboards provided a single source of truth for project progress, resource allocation, and bottleneck identification. Instead of relying on fragmented reports from individual departments, managers could access a unified view of milestones, deadlines, and dependencies. These reduced delays caused by siloed reporting and ensured that strategic initiatives—such as rolling out new product features or improving customer service protocols—were executed with cross-functional alignment.

Breaking Down Departmental Silos:

By making workflows visible across teams, Asana facilitated transparency and accountability. For example, if the product team introduced a new feature, the customer support team could simultaneously prepare FAQs and training materials, while operations could plan system rollouts. This parallel coordination minimises downtime and improves responsiveness to market needs.

Efficiency and Cultural Transformation:

The adoption of Asana at Airbnb was not merely a technical upgrade but also a cultural shift towards collaborative execution. Teams became less reliant on email chains and ad hoc meetings, focusing instead on structured workflows with clear ownership. The reduction in duplication of efforts and missed handovers contributed to measurable efficiency gains, enabling Airbnb to maintain agility in a fast-paced global marketplace.

Key Takeaways:

Airbnb's case demonstrates how Asana's dashboards and centralised workflows can dismantle silos in cross-functional organizations. By enabling transparency and shared accountability, the platform supported Airbnb in achieving operational excellence while maintaining customer-centric agility.

Case Example 2:

Tata Consultancy Services (TCS): Hybrid Project Management with MS Project and Asana:

Context and Organisational Needs:

Tata Consultancy Services (TCS), one of the world's largest IT services and consulting firms, manages a diverse portfolio of projects ranging from highly regulated government contracts to innovation-driven digital transformation initiatives. The duality of its work required a hybrid project management approach: while government contracts demanded rigid compliance, documentation, and milestone tracking, innovation projects in artificial intelligence and emerging technologies required flexibility, collaboration, and adaptability.

TCS: Use of MS Project for Government Contracts:

For government contracts, TCS employs Microsoft Project (MS Project), a robust tool suited for large-scale, structured, and compliance-driven projects. MS Project enables granular planning, dependency mapping, and compliance reporting, ensuring that TCS meets strict government requirements related to budgeting, scheduling, and documentation. The platform supports the predictability and rigour demanded in this context.

TCS: Adoption of Asana for Innovation Initiatives:

In parallel, for innovation-driven initiatives—such as AI research, digital transformation projects, and rapid prototyping—TCS uses Asana. The platform's flexibility and ease of use made it ideal for teams experimenting with emerging technologies. Asana's ability to accommodate iterative planning allowed researchers and developers to pivot quickly as new insights emerged.

Leveraging Workload Dashboards for Team Balance:

A defining feature that TCS capitalised on was Asana's workload dashboards. These dashboards provided managers with real-time visibility into how tasks were distributed among innovation teams. By monitoring capacity, TCS ensured that no team member was overloaded while also maximising productivity. This balance was particularly critical in innovation projects, where creativity and problem-solving thrive under manageable workloads rather than pressure-driven environments.

Flexibility and Collaboration in Hybrid Environments:

The dual use of MS Project and Asana exemplifies how TCS strategically differentiates project management tools based on context. While MS Project ensured compliance and predictability in structured projects, Asana fostered collaboration, agility, and cross-functional communication in exploratory initiatives. The integration of both approaches reflected TCS's ability to balance rigour with innovation, aligning with its position as both a government contractor and a leader in digital services.

Strategic Outcomes:

By adopting this hybrid model, TCS enhanced its ability to deliver consistency in regulated environments while also enabling flexibility in fast-moving innovation contexts. This adaptability allowed the company to maintain credibility with public-sector clients while simultaneously pushing the boundaries of digital transformation.

Key Takeaways:

The TCS case highlights how a hybrid approach to project management—leveraging MS Project for structured projects and Asana for innovation—can optimise both compliance and creativity. This demonstrates the strategic importance of tool differentiation in large enterprises that span diverse project types.

Together, these cases illustrate how organizations can tailor project management platforms like Asana to their unique contexts. While Airbnb used Asana to dismantle silos and unify workflows, TCS employed it selectively within a hybrid model to balance compliance-driven rigour with innovation-led flexibility.

1.5 Comparative Reflection: Project Management Tools as Expressions of Philosophy

Introduction: No Universal "Best Tool":

The rapid growth of project management software underscores a fundamental reality: there is no universal tool that suits all projects, organizations, or industries. Instead, each tool embodies a distinct project management philosophy, shaping how teams collaborate, prioritise, and deliver outcomes. The choice of software must therefore be viewed not as a matter of selecting the "best" tool in absolute terms, but rather as aligning the tool's strengths with organisational context, project complexity, and methodological preference.

MS Project:

Precision and Predictability:

MS Project has long been associated with predictive, structured methodologies such as the Waterfall model. It is particularly effective in industries and contexts where:

a) Compliance, documentation, and accountability are paramount (e.g., government contracts, construction, infrastructure).

b) Projects follow clear sequential phases, with milestones, dependencies, and deliverables that must be tracked meticulously.

Its advanced capabilities—such as Gantt charts, dependency

mapping, and resource levelling—offer managers granular control over schedules and budgets. However, this same rigidity makes MS Project less suitable for environments requiring rapid iteration or creative experimentation. In essence, MS Project reflects a philosophy of control, structure, and predictability, ideal for projects where deviation is costly or unacceptable.

Jira:

Agile Iteration and Continuous Delivery:

Jira represents a contrasting philosophy, thriving in agile, iterative environments. It is most widely adopted in software development and IT projects, where requirements evolve continuously, and outcomes are refined through incremental cycles. Jira's strength lies in:

a) Sprint planning, backlog management, and issue tracking, which align with Scrum and Kanban methodologies.

b) Its ability to support Continuous Integration and Continuous Delivery (CI/CD) pipelines, providing transparency into progress at granular levels.

By prioritising adaptability and responsiveness over rigid schedules, Jira enables teams to fail fast, learn quickly, and pivot effectively. This makes it invaluable in industries driven by innovation, speed-to-market, and customer feedback loops. Its philosophy can be summarised as agility, iteration, and continuous value delivery.

Trello:

Simplicity and Visual Collaboration:

Trello epitomises the philosophy of simplicity and visual

clarity. Using a card-and-board system inspired by Kanban, it allows teams to visualise workflows intuitively, making it especially effective for:

a) Creative industries (e.g., media, design, marketing) where clarity and flexibility are more important than strict schedules.

b) Distributed teams, as their interface reduces communication friction and provides immediate visibility into task progression.

The appeal of Trello lies in its lightweight adoption curve—teams can begin using it with minimal training. However, its simplicity also imposes limits for highly complex, multi-stakeholder projects that demand rigorous scheduling and reporting. Trello's philosophy is centered on collaboration through visibility, promoting alignment without overwhelming users with excessive structure.

Asana:

Structured Flexibility and Balance:

Asana occupies a middle ground, blending structured planning with adaptability. It is designed to support both operational and innovation-driven projects by providing:

a) Task hierarchies, workload dashboards, and reporting tools for structured oversight.

b) Flexible workflows and integrations that allow teams to experiment, iterate, and collaborate dynamically.

Organizations such as Airbnb and TCS have demonstrated that Asana works effectively in cross-functional environments where multiple departments must align while still retaining autonomy. Its philosophy is one of balance—offering enough structure to maintain accountability while remaining flexible enough to adapt to changing needs.

1.6 Strategic Implications for Managers:

The comparative analysis of these tools underscores a critical insight: the decision to adopt a project management platform should not be driven by popularity or perceived superiority but by contextual alignment. Managers must evaluate:

1. ***Nature of the project*** – Is it compliance-driven, iterative, creative, or hybrid?

2. ***Organisational culture*** – Does the organisation thrive on control and predictability or agility and innovation?

3. ***Complexity and scale*** – Are projects small and visual (Trello), enterprise-level and regulated (MS Project), or mid-scale with cross-functional teams (Asana)?

By framing the choice of software as a strategic fit rather than a universal standard, managers can maximise efficiency, reduce friction, and align tool usage with both project goals and organisational philosophy.

1.7 Conclusion: Tools as Philosophical Mirrors:

Ultimately, project management tools serve as mirrors of organisational philosophy. MS Project reflects discipline and control; Jira embodies agility and iteration; Trello champions clarity and simplicity; and Asana balances structure with adaptability. For managers, the central task is not simply adopting a tool but adopting the right tool for the right context, thereby ensuring that technology becomes an enabler of strategy rather than a constraint.

This expanded reflection ties the tools to philosophical underpinnings, their practical applications, and their strategic implications for managers, making it suitable for academic and professional book-style writing.

2. Collaborative Platforms and Integrations

Collaborative platforms in project management provide central spaces where teams can plan, track, and execute tasks together. Tools like Microsoft Teams, Slack, Asana, Trello, and Jira integrate communication, file sharing, scheduling, and reporting. Integrations with services such as Google Workspace, Zoom, and GitHub streamline workflows, reduce silos, and ensure real-time collaboration. These platforms enhance transparency, accountability, and decision-making by allowing seamless data flow across applications. Ultimately, they empower distributed teams to work efficiently, maintain project alignment, and adapt quickly to changes, making collaboration and integration vital to modern project management success.

2.1 The Role of Integration in Modern Project Management:

In today's globalised and technology-driven environment, organizations rarely rely on a single tool for project execution. Instead, collaborative platforms and integrations serve as the backbone of modern project management, allowing teams to combine communication, task tracking, and documentation into unified ecosystems. Integration not only reduces duplication of effort but also ensures that geographically distributed stakeholders operate with a shared view of project progress. The following case examples from Indian Railways, Tata Steel, and Infosys Consulting illustrate how strategic integrations of project management tools with collaboration platforms enhance efficiency, accountability, and innovation.

Case Example 1:

Indian Railways – Integrating Teams with Microsoft Teams and MS Project:

Context and Challenge:

Indian Railways, one of the world's largest rail networks, is undergoing modernisation initiatives that include digital ticketing systems, track electrification, high-speed rail corridors, and smart station upgrades. These projects span thousands of kilometres and involve multiple regional offices, contractors, and central authorities. The scale and geographical spread made real-time visibility and accountability a persistent challenge, with progress updates often delayed by layers of reporting.

Adoption of Microsoft Teams and MS Project:

To address these challenges, Indian Railways integrated Microsoft Teams with MS Project. MS Project provided the structured framework for scheduling, dependency management, and milestone tracking, while Teams facilitated seamless communication between regional offices, contractors, and central project managers.

Benefits of Integration:

a) ***Real-Time Updates***: Regional project engineers could log updates into MS Project, which were instantly visible to managers through Teams channels.

b) ***Centralised Reporting***: Consolidated dashboards allowed project managers at headquarters to generate reports for the Railway Board without waiting for manual submissions from regional offices.

c) ***Improved Accountability***: The transparent flow of updates ensured that delays could be traced back to specific tasks or contractors, enhancing accountability.

d) ***Reduced Reporting Delays***: With communication and project data integrated into one ecosystem, the time taken to escalate issues or provide board-level reports was significantly reduced.

Key Takeaway:

For large, government-driven infrastructure projects, the integration of structured planning tools with collaborative platforms is essential. Indian Railways demonstrates how MS Project and Teams together provide a balance of rigour, oversight, and communication efficiency.

Case Example 2:

Tata Steel – Using Trello and Slack for Innovation Projects:

Context and Challenge:

Tata Steel's R&D division in Jamshedpur is tasked with developing sustainable materials, process automation techniques, and energy-efficient practices. Unlike production and supply chain projects that follow structured methodologies, R&D projects are inherently exploratory, demanding creativity, agility, and rapid iteration. Traditional project management tools proved too rigid for the fluid nature of innovation.

Adoption of Trello and Slack:

To address these needs, Tata Steel's R&D teams adopted Trello boards integrated with Slack. Trello's visual, card-based interface provided an intuitive way to organise ideas, prototypes, and experiments, while Slack offered real-time communication to ensure rapid feedback cycles.

Benefits of Integration:

a) ***Encouraging Idea-Sharing***: Trello cards allowed researchers to propose ideas, which could then be tracked through phases of validation, prototyping, and testing.

b) ***Transparency of Prototypes***: Stakeholders could easily visualise progress by monitoring Trello boards, reducing ambiguity in project status.

c) ***Agility through Slack***: The integration with Slack ensured immediate notifications on task changes, enabling faster decision-making—a necessity in research-driven projects.

d) ***Separation of Contexts***: While core operations at Tata Steel still relied on structured methodologies (e.g., MS Project or SAP systems), the R&D team could experiment freely in a lightweight, flexible environment.

*Key Takea**way:***

Tata Steel illustrates how different divisions within the same organisation can adopt tailored platforms. By integrating Trello with Slack, its innovation labs fostered a culture of openness and agility, while the production side continued using structured systems for efficiency and control.

Case Example 3:

Infosys Consulting – Cross-Border Collaboration with Asana:

Context and Challenge:

Infosys Consulting, a global IT and management consulting firm, frequently manages cross-border digital transformation engagements. A typical scenario involves consultants in India working with client teams in Europe or North America. Time zone differences, reliance on emails, and fragmented documentation often created delays, miscommunication, and version-control issues.

Adoption of Asana and Google Workspace:

Infosys addressed these challenges by integrating Asana with Google Workspace (Docs, Sheets, Meet, and Drive). Asana served as the central task management platform, while Google Workspace enabled real-time co-authoring, document sharing, and virtual meetings.

Benefits of Integration:

a) ***Shared Digital Environment***: Clients and consultants worked within the same Asana tasks, linked directly to relevant Google Docs or Sheets, ensuring that deliverables were transparent and version-controlled.

b) ***Reduced Email Dependence***: Updates and discussions were logged in Asana tasks and Google Docs comment, reducing reliance on lengthy email threads.

c) ***Real-Time Collaboration***: Google Meet integration enabled virtual workshops, while Asana ensured that action items were tracked immediately after discussions.

d) ***Cross-Border Transparency***: Clients in Europe could monitor progress overnight, while Indian consultants updated deliverables in their workday, creating a continuous workflow across time zones.

Key Takeaway:

Infosys demonstrates how integrating Asana with Google

Workspace creates a seamless, cross-border collaboration ecosystem. By reducing communication lags and ensuring transparency, the firm was able to deliver digital transformation projects with greater efficiency and client trust.

2.2 Comparative Insight: Integration as a Strategic Choice:

The three cases of Indian Railways, Tata Steel, and Infosys Consulting collectively underscore a crucial principle: integration choices in project management are not universal but context-driven. Organizations select collaborative platforms and integrations not merely for their technical features but because these tools resonate with the specific demands of project type, organisational structure, and strategic priorities. The effectiveness of an integration depends on whether it supports the required balance between control, flexibility, and collaboration.

Indian Railways: Structured Oversight and Accountability:

For Indian Railways, the sheer scale and complexity of infrastructure modernisation projects—spanning track electrification, ticketing systems, and station upgrades—demanded a high degree of control, reporting discipline, and centralised oversight. In this context, the integration of MS Project with Microsoft Teams was a natural fit.

a) *MS Project* offered structured scheduling, dependency mapping, and milestone tracking, ensuring alignment with government reporting requirements.

b) *Microsoft Teams* provided the communication layer, enabling updates to flow seamlessly from regional offices to central authorities.

The integration reflected a strategic choice to prioritise

accountability and compliance in a high-stakes, publicly funded environment. Here, delays or misreporting could have far-reaching financial and political consequences, making structured oversight indispensable.

Tata Steel R&D: Flexibility and Agility for Innovation:

In contrast, Tata Steel's R&D division operated under an entirely different paradigm. Research-driven initiatives such as sustainable materials and process automation require rapid prototyping, constant iteration, and a culture of idea-sharing. For such projects, rigid methodologies risk stifling innovation.

a) ***Trello***, with its lightweight, visual boards, allowed researchers to log ideas and track prototypes without the burden of complex structures.

b) ***Slack*** provided instantaneous communication, ensuring decisions and feedback loops occurred in real time.

This integration supported the division's need for speed, creativity, and transparency, while keeping overhead minimal. The choice reflected a recognition that innovation thrives under agility, not bureaucracy, making Trello–Slack the ideal ecosystem for Tata Steel's research labs.

Infosys Consulting: Cross-Border Collaboration and Transparency:

Infosys Consulting faced a different challenge altogether: the coordination of global consulting teams working across time zones with international clients. Projects often involved digital transformation initiatives where delays in communication or documentation could erode client trust.

a) ***Asana*** provided task management and workload visibility, ensuring that all stakeholders—consultants and clients—remained aligned.

b) ***Google Workspace*** (Docs, Sheets, Meet, Drive) enabled real-time document collaboration and virtual workshops, reducing dependence on fragmented email chains.

The integration reflected a strategic choice to prioritise real-time collaboration and shared transparency. Unlike Indian Railways or Tata Steel, Infosys needed a system that could function as a shared digital workspace across borders, fostering continuous workflows and eliminating version-control issues.

2.3 Strategic Comparison Across Cases:

When examined collectively, the three cases reveal that integration strategies are not uniform but are instead shaped by the intersection of project characteristics and organisational objectives. In the case of Indian Railways, projects were highly compliance-driven and geographically dispersed, which made oversight, control, and accountability the central focus of the MS Project–Teams integration. At Tata Steel's R&D division, projects were exploratory and innovation-oriented, so Trello–Slack integration was adopted to foster flexibility, creativity, and agility in research-driven initiatives. For Infosys Consulting, whose projects are global and client-facing, Asana integrated with Google Workspace provided the transparency and real-time collaboration necessary for cross-border engagements. Together, these examples illustrate that no single platform is inherently superior; instead, success lies in the fit-for-purpose selection and integration of tools that align with organisational goals and the specific demands of the project environment.

The overarching insight is that collaborative platforms

and integrations should be treated as strategic levers, not merely operational tools. Leaders must assess their organisational context—whether it demands control, agility, or collaboration—and adopt integration ecosystems that directly support those priorities. In doing so, organizations can ensure that project management tools are not just enablers of tasks but enablers of organisational strategy and competitive advantage.

2.4 Conclusion: Towards a Unified but Flexible Future:

The collective lesson from these cases is that no single platform can address all project management needs. Instead, organizations must adopt integration strategies that balance structure, agility, and collaboration. Whether it is enabling accountability in large government projects, fostering innovation in industrial R&D, or supporting cross-border consulting, platform integration emerges as the enabler of transparency, efficiency, and adaptability in modern project management.

3. Simulation: Practising with Real Tools

Simulation-based learning has become a powerful approach in project management education and organisational training. Instead of relying solely on theoretical frameworks, institutions and enterprises are increasingly turning to hands-on practice with real tools to bridge the gap between classroom learning and industry application. By engaging with software such as MS Project, Jira, and Asana in sandbox environments, learners and professionals gain the ability to experiment, make mistakes, and refine decision-making skills in a controlled setting before applying them in high-stakes projects. These simulations not only replicate the technical challenges of project execution but also capture the collaborative, cross-functional, and dynamic nature of real-world projects.

Case Example 1:

Indian Institutes of Management (IIMs) – Project Management Labs:

Leading business schools in India, including IIM Bangalore and IIM Ahmedabad, have introduced simulation labs equipped with industry-standard project management tools such as MS Project, Jira, and Asana. Students engage in case-based simulations designed around real-world scenarios like launching a fintech startup, implementing a healthcare IT system, or managing a renewable energy initiative.

Within these labs, students experiment with:

a) ***Resource allocation***: Assigning team members to tasks while balancing constraints of cost and availability.

b) ***Backlog management:*** prioritising features or deliverables in fast-moving projects.

c) ***Stakeholder communication***: Using dashboards and reports to update investors, regulators, and customers.

This experiential pedagogy ensures that students graduate not only with theoretical knowledge but also with practical tool familiarity that employers demand. By simulating the pressures of project deadlines, interdependencies, and scope changes, the IIMs prepare graduates to step seamlessly into industry roles.

Case Example 2:

ISRO – Mission Planning Simulations with MS Project:

The Indian Space Research Organisation (ISRO) exemplifies

the use of simulations in high-stakes engineering environments. Before a satellite launch, ISRO teams conduct detailed mission planning simulations using MS Project. This allows them to model:

a) Resource allocation across engineering, supply chain, and launch site teams.

b) Critical path dependencies, ensuring that activities like payload integration, fuel testing, and trajectory programming are scheduled with no conflicts.

c) Scenario testing, where potential delays (e.g., late component delivery) or resource bottlenecks (e.g., shared use of test facilities) are analysed in advance.

By stress-testing schedules and dependencies before execution, ISRO can anticipate risks, develop contingency plans, and optimise limited resources. This structured approach has contributed significantly to ISRO's reputation for delivering complex space missions within cost-effective budgets, often outperforming international peers in terms of efficiency.

Case Example 3:

National e-Governance Division (NeGD) – Agile Simulations with Jira:

The National e-Governance Division (NeGD), responsible for flagship initiatives such as Unified Payments Interface (UPI) and DigiLocker, uses Jira simulations to train teams in agile practices. Unlike ISRO's predictive planning, NeGD's projects require adaptability to evolving citizen needs, vendor coordination, and regulatory requirements.

Through simulated sprints and backlog management

exercises, participants practise:

a) ***Sprint planning***: Prioritising user stories and tasks for bi-weekly releases.

b) ***Cross-agency coordination***: Managing work shared between government IT teams, private vendors, and regulatory bodies.

c) ***Iterative delivery***: Releasing features in stages and responding to real-time feedback from pilot rollouts.

These simulations allow NeGD staff and partners to build agility into governance projects, ensuring that digital platforms remain relevant, user-friendly, and scalable across India's diverse population. The training also minimises risks of misalignment by familiarising teams with agile methodologies before actual implementation.

Broader Implications of Simulation-Based Learning:

Across these examples, a clear pattern emerges: simulation practices align with project complexity and organisational needs.

a) In academic institutions, simulations prepare students for real-world industry challenges.

b) In aerospace and engineering, simulations de-risk projects where errors are extremely costly.

c) In digital governance, simulations foster adaptability and cross-sector collaboration.

Ultimately, practising with real tools enables teams to internalise both technical proficiency and collaborative behaviours, making simulations an indispensable component of modern project management training and execution.

Conclusion

The practice of project management software is not limited to global corporations; it is equally vital in the Indian context, where organizations such as Infosys, TCS, ISRO, and Indian Railways demonstrate its transformative potential. From the structured precision of MS Project in Smart City initiatives to the Agile adaptability of Jira in Infosys' digital delivery, these case studies highlight how the right tools can be aligned with project scale, methodology, and sector-specific needs.

Simulation and practice with real tools further ensure that professionals are equipped not only with theoretical knowledge but also with hands-on competence to navigate complex, high-stakes environments. As India continues its rapid economic and technological development, mastering project management software will be central to delivering successful outcomes across both private and public sector projects.

PART IV

AI AND THE FUTURE OF PROJECT LEADERSHIP

CHAPTER 14: COPILOT AND GPT-5 IN AGILE LEADERSHIP

The landscape of project management is undergoing a profound transformation. The increasing complexity of digital ecosystems, the globalisation of workplaces, and heightened market volatility have exposed the limitations of traditional leadership and coordination models. In response, agile methodologies—most notably Scrum and the Scaled Agile Framework (SAFe)—have become dominant paradigms for addressing uncertainty, fostering adaptability, and enabling rapid delivery cycles (Leffingwell, 2016; Atlassian, 2023). Nonetheless, despite their widespread adoption, Agile frameworks continue to face persistent challenges, including the coordination of distributed teams, the management of overwhelming volumes of data, and the emergence of decision-making bottlenecks (Modi & Strode, 2020).

Against this backdrop, Artificial Intelligence (AI) has begun to redefine the parameters of project leadership. Advanced tools such as Microsoft Copilot and large-scale language models like GPT-5 represent a significant evolutionary step in augmenting human decision-making capacity. Rather than merely automating routine or repetitive tasks, these AI copilots offer real-time insights, generate context-sensitive recommendations, detect latent patterns in complex data, and simulate potential outcomes. As a result, they extend leadership capabilities beyond tactical execution, enabling a more strategic orientation toward value creation and long-term alignment.

This chapter examines the varied functions of Artificial Intelligence (AI) in agile leadership, with particular attention to its application within SAFe Scrum delivery management. Specifically, it examines how AI supports the evolution of leadership decision-making processes, transforms the facilitation of sprint ceremonies, and augments coordination within large-scale Agile environments. Drawing on academic frameworks, industry case studies, and emerging best practices, the discussion highlights how AI integration is not merely streamlining project workflows but fundamentally reshaping the nature of leadership in contemporary project environments.

1. Role of AI in SAFe Agile Scrum Delivery Management

1.1 The SAFe Framework and Its Core Needs:

The Scaled Agile Framework (SAFe) has emerged as one of the most influential and widely adopted approaches for scaling Agile practices across large and complex enterprises. Whereas methodologies such as *Scrum* and *Kanban* are highly effective for small, cross-functional teams, they struggle to address the coordination challenges that arise when organizations attempt to scale Agile practices across hundreds or even thousands of practitioners. SAFe helps solve the problems that come up when big companies try to use Agile methods by applying Agile ideas to larger areas like portfolios and programmes, creating a clear way to manage everything effectively. Its structured yet flexible design has made it particularly attractive to industries such as finance, telecommunications, government, and IT services, where large-scale coordination and alignment are critical to success.

At the heart of SAFe are Agile Release Trains (ARTs), which serve as the central organising construct of the framework. An ART typically comprises 50–125 individuals from multiple Agile teams who work together in a synchronised manner to deliver continuous value to customers (Leffingwell, 2016). These trains operate as long-lived, cross-functional teams of teams, encompassing roles such as product managers, system architects, Release Train Engineers (RTEs), and business owners. By synchronising planning, execution, and delivery across multiple Agile teams, ARTs ensure that value is delivered predictably and consistently. This synchronisation occurs through Program Increments (PIs)—time-boxed planning cycles that usually last between 8 and 12 weeks. PIs are like the rhythm of the ART, helping teams work together towards shared goals, manage their interdependencies, and allow for regular check-ins and adjustments.

The Scaled Agile Framework itself rests on five foundational pillars, which serve as guiding principles for ensuring alignment, quality, and responsiveness at scale. The framework rests on the following five key pillars:

1. ***Alignment*** – ensuring that teams' work is tied directly to the enterprise strategy.

2. ***Built-in Quality*** – embedding quality into development practices rather than treating it as an afterthought.

3. ***Transparency*** – making progress, risks, and impediments visible across all levels.

4. ***Program Execution*** – synchronising work at the ART level for predictability.

5. *Continuous feedback*—fostering iterative learning loops that adapt to market shifts and customer needs.

First, *alignment* ensures that the work undertaken by agile teams is directly tied to the strategic objectives of the enterprise. In large organizations, there is a constant risk that teams may optimise locally for their own backlog priorities, thereby drifting away from overarching business goals. SAFe mitigates this risk by explicitly connecting team-level activities to portfolio-level strategies, ensuring that every increment of work contributes to the larger mission of the organisation. Mechanisms like PI Objectives, Strategic Themes, and Portfolio Kanbans reinforce this alignment by transforming high-level vision into actionable team deliverables.

Second, *built-in quality* emphasises the need to integrate quality assurance throughout the development lifecycle rather than treating it as an afterthought. In complex enterprise environments, defects and technical debt can accumulate rapidly if quality practices are deferred. SAFe promotes ongoing testing, automated processes, following rules, and managing architecture to make sure that the solutions created not only satisfy customer needs but also meet legal and industry requirements. This principle resonates strongly in regulated industries such as healthcare and finance, where lapses in quality can have significant operational and legal consequences.

Third, *transparency* is fundamental to the functioning of SAFe, as it provides visibility into progress, impediments, and risks across all levels of the organisation. Transparency ensures that decision-makers are not blindsided by hidden problems and that teams are accountable for their commitments. Tools such as PI Planning boards, Scrum-of-Scrums meetings, and Program Kanban boards serve as enablers of transparency by making work visible and traceable. Without transparency, the scaling effort can quickly descend into chaos, with teams working at cross purposes or hiding delays until it is too late to respond effectively.

Fourth, *program execution* underscores the necessity of synchronising work at the ART level to achieve predictable delivery. While individual Agile teams can demonstrate velocity at a micro level, the true value of SAFe lies in its ability to orchestrate these outputs into cohesive solutions delivered at the programme level. This requires rigorous discipline in planning, coordination, and release management. Successful programme execution ensures that value delivery is not fragmented but is instead aligned with customer and business expectations, maintaining trust in the Agile transformation.

Finally, *continuous feedback* ensures that organizations remain adaptable in dynamic and often volatile markets. Traditional project management often delays feedback until the end of long release cycles, resulting in misaligned solutions and costly rework. SAFe embeds iterative feedback loops through system demos, Inspect and Adapt workshops, and regular stakeholder engagement sessions. This allows enterprises to sense and respond to market shifts, customer preferences, or competitive pressures in near real time, thereby fostering a culture of continuous learning and adaptation.

Even though this system is strong, it becomes much harder to manage when SAFe is used by many ARTs working in different parts of the world. For instance, the requirement for continuous alignment often clashes with time zone differences, cultural variations, and fragmented tooling ecosystems. Delayed reporting is common, as manual updates across multiple systems slow down the flow of information to decision-makers. Geographically dispersed teams frequently reveal hidden dependencies, making it challenging to predict cross-team impacts before they become bottlenecks. In addition, risk blind spots are created when programme-level leaders are overwhelmed by fragmented or incomplete data, resulting in reactive rather than proactive management.

The sheer volume and complexity of data further exacerbate these challenges. ARTs and portfolios generate vast streams of information—ranging from backlog items, sprint metrics, and velocity reports to defect logs and customer satisfaction feedback. Without intelligent mechanisms to aggregate, interpret, and contextualise this data, programme managers and RTEs are left struggling to manually consolidate insights—often weeks after events occur. This leads to a disconnect between operational reality and strategic decision-making. Traditional leadership approaches, which rely heavily on manual oversight, spreadsheets, and siloed reporting, are increasingly insufficient in navigating this scale of complexity. As organizations scale Agile to enterprise levels, they require augmented capabilities to manage data overload, anticipate risks, and enable leaders to focus on strategic outcomes rather than administrative burden.

1.2 How AI Tools Respond to SAFe Challenges:

The emergence of AI copilots—such as Microsoft Copilot and advanced large language models (LLMs) like GPT-5—offers a profound shift in how SAFe delivery management is executed. Unlike conventional project management tools, which depend on manual input and static dashboards, AI copilots actively ingest, analyse, and interpret real-time data from platforms like Jira, Rally, and Azure DevOps. They provide decision support that is predictive, adaptive, and context-aware.

Four forms of augmentation stand out:

1. Predictive Metrics:

By analysing historical sprint velocity, backlog growth rates, defect density, and team throughput, AI can forecast the likelihood of ART or PI slippage. This predictive intelligence allows Release Training Engineers (RTEs) and product managers to intervene early, reprioritising scope or reallocating resources before delays become systemic.

2. Dependency and Bottleneck Detection:

According to the Project Management Institute's 2021 publications, including the *PMBOK® Guide – Seventh Edition* and its reports on AI in project management, dependencies between teams represent one of the greatest sources of risk in scaled Agile environments (PMI, 2021). Managing these interconnections effectively is critical, as unresolved dependencies can create cascading delays that compromise delivery timelines and value outcomes. AI offers a powerful solution by automatically scanning work items across backlogs, detecting cross-team linkages, and visualising potential bottlenecks. These data-driven insights equip leaders to anticipate and resolve blockers proactively, reducing systemic risk and ensuring smoother coordination across Agile Release Trains and portfolios.

3. Automated Reporting:

Instead of burdening Scrum Masters and RTEs with manual reporting tasks, AI copilots generate dynamic dashboards and narrative summaries. These can be tailored for executives, product owners, or portfolio managers, ensuring the right level of detail for each stakeholder while freeing teams to focus on delivery.

4. Scenario Simulation:

AI enables “what-if” analysis at scale. For example, delivery managers can model the effects of reallocating capacity from one ART to another, adjusting PI scope, or changing sprint priorities. These simulations allow leaders to explore trade-offs before making commitments, reducing the risks of reactive decision-making.

By enabling these capabilities, AI shifts SAFe delivery management from a reactive paradigm—where leaders respond only after risks materialise—to a proactive paradigm, where they are continuously guided by predictive intelligence and scenario-based foresight.

1.3 SAFe in the Era of AI:

In large-scale implementations, the success of the Scaled Agile Framework (SAFe) relies heavily on the synchronisation of sprints and Program Increments (PIs) across dozens, sometimes hundreds, of distributed teams. Traditionally, this synchronisation is achieved through extensive manual coordination, including PI planning events, Scrum-of-Scrums meetings, dependency mapping exercises, and routine status reporting cycles. While effective in principle, these practices are often labour-intensive and limited by the human capacity to process complex, interdependent data streams in real time. As organizations grow in scale and complexity, manual methods frequently lead to information bottlenecks, delayed responses, and reactive leadership behaviours.

The integration of AI copilots fundamentally changes this dynamic. By automatically gathering data, understanding information from tools like Jira, Rally, and Azure DevOps, and highlighting useful insights, AI builds smart dashboards that update themselves instantly. These dashboards change the role of leaders from just managing tasks to helping teams succeed, letting them concentrate on delivering value and building flexible cultures instead of dealing with scattered data.

1. Real-Time Velocity Predictions:

One of the most valuable contributions of AI in SAFe is the ability to provide real-time velocity predictions for individual teams and Agile Release Trains (ARTs). Velocity, a measure of how much work a team can deliver in a sprint or PI, is often tracked manually and retrospectively. By contrast, AI copilots use historical velocity data, backlog health, and even defect clustering to generate forward-looking forecasts. These predictions highlight teams or ARTs at risk of underperforming against their PI objectives before problems materialise. For leaders, this early visibility enables pre-emptive interventions, such as adjusting scope, reallocating resources, or facilitating targeted coaching. Instead of discovering slippages at the end of a PI, leaders can anticipate and act during execution, increasing the likelihood of predictable delivery.

2. Dependency Heatmaps Across Value Streams:

In scaled agile environments, dependencies between teams and value streams represent one of the greatest risks to delivery. Traditionally, dependency management is handled through spreadsheets or visual boards updated during PI planning, which often become outdated within weeks. AI copilots replace this static approach with dynamic dependency heatmaps. These visualisations map connections across teams, ARTs, and value streams, highlighting where bottlenecks are most likely to occur. For example, if two ARTs in different geographies rely on a shared component team, AI can flag potential scheduling conflicts before they affect delivery. Leaders are no longer reacting to missed dependencies but proactively orchestrating collaboration to avoid downstream disruptions.

3. Automated Risk Alerts:

Risk management in SAFe is often reactive, relying on teams or RTEs to escalate issues during Scrum-of-Scrums or Inspect and Adapt workshops. With AI copilots, risk detection becomes continuous and automated. By monitoring delivery timelines, quality metrics, capacity forecasts, and even team sentiment (through natural language analysis of retrospectives), AI copilots can issue real-time risk alerts. These alerts flag deviations from expected performance—such as a sudden drop in velocity, an increase in defect density, or resource over-allocation—allowing leaders to respond quickly. This level of predictive awareness shifts leadership from firefighting to proactive risk mitigation and improves organisational resilience.

4. Scenario Simulations for Strategic Decisions:

Perhaps the most transformative capability AI (Artificial Intelligence) introduces is the ability to run scenario simulations. During PI planning or portfolio reviews, leaders often face difficult choices: what happens if scope increases unexpectedly, if a high-priority initiative must be fast-tracked, or if capacity is reduced due to external constraints? Traditionally, such "what-if" analyses were speculative and reliant on manual estimates. AI copilots enable leaders to simulate multiple delivery strategies in real time, testing the downstream impacts of changes in scope, capacity, or prioritisation. This empowers decision-makers to base their strategies on evidence-backed forecasts rather than intuition, aligning with the PMI's emphasis on data-informed governance and the Agile Alliance's commitment to adaptability.

1.4 Shifting Leadership Priorities:

The cumulative effect of these AI-driven capabilities is a redefinition of leadership priorities within SAFe organizations. Now, automation handles administrative tasks like compiling reports, chasing dependency updates, and interpreting velocity trends. Leaders, freed from these burdens, can redirect their focus toward higher-order responsibilities: delivering strategic value, engaging stakeholders, and coaching teams. This shift aligns closely with the Agile Alliance's principle of empowering individuals and fostering collaboration, as leaders spend more time enabling people and less time policing processes. AI copilots handle the heavy lifting of data aggregation and interpretation, while human leaders concentrate on areas where uniquely human skills—empathy, creativity, and vision—are indispensable.

1.5 AI as a Cultural Catalyst:

Beyond efficiency, AI acts as a catalyst for cultural transformation in agile leadership. By democratising access to predictive insights and visual dashboards, AI reduces its reliance on hierarchical reporting structures and promotes greater transparency and trust. Leaders trust AI-generated insights to guide strategic decisions, while teams gain confidence in the early detection and resolution of risks. This mutual confidence fosters a culture of empowerment and psychological safety, where teams can focus on delivering value and experimenting with innovation rather than being consumed by reporting overhead.

In this way, AI copilots are not merely tools of operational efficiency but strategic enablers of cultural change, amplifying the human side of leadership within the SAFe framework.

Case Example 1:

Accenture's AI-Enabled SAFe Implementation:

Accenture's collaboration with a global telecommunications provider serves as a compelling illustration of AI's transformative role in scaled Agile delivery. The client sought to extend Agile practices across five continents, managing a technology portfolio that included more than 30 Agile Release Trains (ARTs). Each ART consisted of dozens of teams, operating under unique dependencies, delivery constraints, and regulatory environments. Traditional coordination mechanisms—based largely on manual reporting, weekly synchronisation calls, and fragmented tooling—prove increasingly unsustainable. Leaders struggled to obtain real-time visibility into backlog health, delivery risks, and cross-team dependencies, leading to reactive problem-solving and delayed interventions.

AI-Driven Predictive Analytics in SAFe Ceremonies:

To address these challenges, Accenture deployed AI-driven predictive analytics, deeply integrated into the client's SAFe ceremonies. Specifically, AI copilots were embedded within Program Increment (PI) planning sessions, Inspect and Adapt (I&A) workshops, and system demos. These tools ingested vast datasets from Jira and Azure DevOps, creating unified, predictive dashboards accessible to Release Train

Engineers (RTEs), Product Managers, and Business Owners.

The role of AI in these ceremonies was multifaceted:

1. During PI Planning, predictive algorithms forecasted velocity trends and flagged ARTs at risk of overcommitment, allowing leaders to adjust scope before execution began.

2. In Inspect and Adapt workshops, AI highlighted defect clustering and backlog imbalances, enabling data-driven retrospectives rather than anecdotal feedback.

3. At system demos, copilots provided real-time summaries of delivery performance, linking progress to business objectives and highlighting emerging risks for leadership attention.

This systematic integration of AI ensured that leaders were no longer reliant on lagging indicators; instead, they had access to proactive, data-driven insights that informed both operational adjustments and strategic decisions.

Tangible Outcomes:

The impact of Accenture's AI-enabled implementation was measurable and profound. Three key outcomes stand out:

*1. **85% Accuracy in Predicting PI Slippage:***

By analysing historical velocity, defect density, and backlog health, AI models achieved high accuracy in predicting Program Increment delays. This predictive capability allowed leadership to intervene weeks in advance, reallocating capacity or de-scoping features before risks materialised into missed commitments.

2. ***15% Improvement in Cross-Team Dependency Management:***

One of the most persistent challenges in scaled Agile delivery is managing dependencies between ARTs. AI copilots generated dependency heatmaps that visually mapped potential conflicts and bottlenecks across geographies. This enabled RTEs to negotiate adjustments early in the cycle, reducing late-stage escalations and improving synchronisation across distributed teams.

3. 40% Reduction in Reporting Effort through Automated PI Summaries:

Executive stakeholders typically required extensive manual reporting, which consumed valuable time from RTEs and product managers. With AI copilots, PI summaries were generated automatically, synthesising backlog progress, risk indicators, and delivery outcomes into concise, executive-ready reports. This not only reduced reporting effort by nearly half but also ensured greater consistency and reliability in leadership communication.

Cultural Transformation Beyond Operational Efficiency:

Perhaps the most striking outcome was not merely operational but cultural. As leaders began to trust AI-generated insights, their role shifted from administrative oversight to strategic enablement and facilitation. RTEs, freed from the burden of manual coordination, invested more time in coaching teams, fostering collaboration, and aligning delivery outcomes with enterprise objectives. Teams experienced increased autonomy and empowerment due to the reduction of reporting overhead and the enhancement of transparency and data-driven decision-making.

This cultural transformation reflects a broader shift in the nature of leadership within scaled Agile environments. AI did not replace leadership functions; rather, it augmented human judgement by providing predictive foresight, intelligent recommendations, and automated reporting. As a result, leaders could focus on higher-order responsibilities —guiding vision, enabling innovation, and reinforcing alignment with organisational strategy.

Broader Lessons Learnt:

This case demonstrates that AI is not merely an operational augmentation to SAFe practices but a strategic enabler that redefines leadership in enterprise Agile contexts. By embedding AI into core ceremonies and workflows, organizations can move from reactive coordination to proactive orchestration, ensuring that delivery outcomes are both predictable and strategically aligned.

The Accenture example highlights a broader trend across industries: as enterprises embrace AI within frameworks such as SAFe, leadership roles evolve from transactional reporting to transformational facilitation. This shift illustrates the ability of AI copilots not only to streamline execution but also to reshape the very fabric of Agile leadership in the digital age.

2. From Streamlining Delivery to Strategic Decision-Making

2.1 AI serves as a cognitive partner for leadership:

AI tools such as Copilot and advanced LLMs (e.g., GPT-5) operate less like traditional automation and more like cognitive partners: they intake heterogeneous streams of project data, interpret patterns, and present distilled, actionable knowledge to human leaders. Instead of merely producing status cookies (e.g., "X stories are done"), these systems synthesise context—linking code changes, backlog items, defect clusters, build failures, and stakeholder feedback—so that leaders receive a coherent, prioritised view of what truly matters. In practice, this looks like an AI that not only reports that three teams slowed in the last two sprints but also correlates those slowdowns with increased API latency, a recent change in a shared library, and a spike in customer complaints about a single feature. That multi-dimensional framing enables leaders to diagnose system-level problems quickly and to choose interventions with more confidence.

2.2 Synthesising sprint retrospectives into system-level insight:

When dozens of teams produce independent retrospectives, the raw volume of text and action items becomes noise rather than intelligence. GPT-5–class models can apply advanced natural-language processing and unsupervised clustering to extract recurring themes, rank them by prevalence and impact, and surface root-cause hypotheses. For example, if twenty teams repeatedly mention "build instability" and the AI finds common references to a particular CI (Continuous Integration) job and a shared library, it can elevate that signal as a systemic engineering-practice risk rather than separate, low-priority team issues. The AI can also propose grouped action items (e.g., "stabilise CI pipeline X, add contract tests for library Y, allocate a cross-team spike for two sprints") and estimate likely improvement in velocity or defect reduction if those measures are implemented—thereby converting scattered feedback into coherent, cross-programme improvement plans.

2.3 Simulating trade-offs: time-to-market versus technical debt:

Strategic choices often require evaluating multi-dimensional trade-offs under uncertainty. AI enables precise “what-if” simulations: leaders can pose scenarios such as “If we divert two squads to refactor core authentication for four sprints, how will feature throughput and defect rates change over the next three PIs versus if we instead prioritise feature X for the same period?” Behind the scenes, the AI runs probabilistic models (drawing on historical velocity, defect injection rates, test coverage, and team ramp curves) to project outcomes—presenting confidence intervals, expected cumulative value, and cost-of-delay estimates. This transforms a gut-level debate into an evidence-based decision: leaders can see quantified trade-offs (e.g., 18% lower defects at the cost of 12 weeks of feature delivery) and choose a policy aligned to organisational appetite for risk and long-term maintainability.

2.4 This elevates the project manager to a position of strategic leadership:

With AI automating repetitive coordination and reporting tasks, the role of delivery managers and RTEs becomes more strategic. Rather than spending hours reconciling dashboards or chasing blocked tickets, managers use AI-produced insights to shape portfolio priorities, broker cross-ART trade-offs, and mentor teams on capability gaps revealed by analytics (e.g., persistent test flakiness or architectural bottlenecks). This shift reframes project leadership from task supervision to outcome stewardship—ensuring that day-to-day execution maps to business KPIs such as customer retention, revenue impact, or regulatory compliance. AI becomes an instrument that enables leaders to allocate scarce human and technical capital to the highest-value opportunities.

2.5 Tactical versus strategic leadership in Agile—differentiated:

Tactical leadership in Agile addresses immediate execution concerns: refining backlogs, removing impediments, moderating daily standups, and ensuring sprints close with committed scope. Strategic leadership looks outward and forward: it sets product and portfolio direction, balances investment against technical sustainability, and orchestrates organisational change. AI helps connect tactical and strategic leadership by taking care of routine tasks (like status updates, writing meeting notes, and keeping backlogs organised) and highlighting important trends (such as new market signals, patterns across teams, and return on investment predictions). As a result, leaders spend fewer cycles on micro-coordination and more on shaping portfolio trade-offs, stakeholder alignment, and capability building.

2.6 AI-powered strategic support—methods and outputs:

AI-powered strategic support leverages intelligent methods and actionable outputs to enhance decision-making, optimize processes, and strengthen leadership effectiveness.

1. *Theme synthesis across teams:*

The AI ingests retrospectives, Jira issue descriptions, release notes, and defect reports, then uses topic modelling and entity extraction to identify systemic issues—ranking them by frequency, impact, and propagation. The output is a prioritised list of program-level problem statements (not raw comments), complete with linked evidence and suggested owner roles for remediation.

2. *Trade-off modelling:*

AI applies simulation techniques—Monte Carlo sampling, scenario trees, or discrete event simulation—using inputs like team capacity, historical throughput, and defect rates. Leaders receive comparative dashboards showing expected delivery, variance bands, and sensitivity to changes in scope or staffing. This provides a rigorous basis for decisions such as shifting squads from new features to platform work.

3. *External data integration:*

By ingesting customer feedback (NPS, support tickets, app reviews), market intelligence (release announcements, price changes), and operating metrics, AI correlates external signals with internal backlog priorities. For example, a sudden surge in negative reviews about latency in a specific region can automatically bump performance fixes in the backlog and trigger cross-functional response playbooks.

2.7 Application of AI in decision-making processes:

Here are some concrete examples of the application of AI in decision-making processes:

1. *Synthesising retrospectives:*

GPT-5 can process retrospective notes from fifty teams, cluster sentences that indicate the same underlying problem (e.g., “tests flaky”, “builds fail intermittently”, “integration tests unstable”), and produce a single “root problem” narrative with recommended experiments. It can also draft a prioritised improvement roadmap and estimate the impact on sprint predictability.

2. *Trade-off analysis:*

Suppose leadership is evaluating whether to invest in a major refactor or to push an aggressive new feature roadmap. The AI compares historical metrics from past refactors, models the effect on delivery velocity and error rates, and computes the expected Net Present Value (NPV) of each option considering the cost of delay. Decision-makers receive a ranked recommendation with quantified pros and cons and a sensitivity analysis.

3. *Market responsiveness:*

By continuously scoring customer sentiment and mapping it against planned backlog items, AI can recommend urgent reprioritisation—elevating security patches or usability fixes when the external signal indicates rising customer dissatisfaction and downgrading lower-impact enhancements when market conditions change.

2.8 Limits, risks, and governance considerations:

While AI amplifies strategic capability, it is not infallible. Model outputs depend on data quality, consistent taxonomy (what "story points" mean across teams), and accurate mapping between engineering metrics and business value. Poor data hygiene or biased historical practices can produce misleading recommendations—e.g., penalising teams that tackle complex security work because historical velocity was lower. Therefore, AI should be governed: models must be explicable, forecasts accompanied by confidence intervals and provenance, and humans must retain veto authority. Effective governance also includes continuous model calibration, cross-functional review of AI suggestions, and privacy protections for people analytics.

2.9 Leaders should implement practical best practices to strategically use AI:

AI should be adopted gradually, starting with small pilot projects. The tests should evaluate both predictive accuracy and business value. Clear decision-making protocols are essential, specifying which AI outputs can drive automatic operational changes. operational changes that require human review. To ensure reliable results, organisations must also invest in data quality, establish consistent definitions across teams, and provide AI systems with uniform inputs. This should be done across teams to provide AI systems with uniform inputs. Finally, AI insights should always be combined with human judgement. While AI can reveal options and highlight trade-offs, cross-functional leadership is necessary to interpret cultural, ethical, and market dimensions that models alone cannot address. Additionally, there are market dimensions that models alone cannot address.

Case Example 2:

Spotify's AI-Augmented Tribe Model:

Spotify is well known for its tribe-squad-chapter-guild structure, often cited as a model for scaled, agile organisations. This structure emphasises autonomy, alignment, and cross-functional collaboration. Squads act as small, independent teams focused on specific features or services, while tribes coordinate several squads working toward related objectives. Chapters provide functional alignment across teams, and guilds create opportunities for knowledge sharing across the organisation. This decentralised approach allows Spotify to innovate quickly while maintaining overall cohesion. However, balancing competing priorities such as feature delivery, infrastructure stability, and technical debt presents ongoing challenges for leadership.

To address these challenges, Spotify has recently experimented with AI-powered decision-support tools. These tools use predictive modelling and natural language processing to reinforce strategic decision-making. For instance, tribe leaders often face the recurring decision of whether to assign squads to infrastructure improvements at the potential cost of delaying customer-facing features. Traditionally, leaders made these decisions based on their intuition, anecdotal evidence, and manually compiled data from multiple squads. By contrast, AI-driven analytics now combine historical performance data, current velocity, defect trends, and inter-squad dependencies to estimate opportunity costs and predict downstream effects on delivery.

In practice, AI copilots support tribe leaders by providing scenario simulations that show the trade-offs of different allocation choices. These simulations can forecast delays in feature delivery, anticipate quality impacts, and identify which squads are best suited for certain tasks. An accessible dashboard presents the results, revealing the implications of each decision to both technical teams and business stakeholders. This enables leaders to make evidence-based decisions while respecting the autonomy and agility of individual squads.

The experiment reflects a broader trend: the use of AI in scaled Agile is extending beyond routine tasks to support strategic leadership. AI ensures a closer alignment between squad-level decisions and long-term organisational strategy by quantifying risks, dependencies, and opportunity costs. Leaders are able to balance innovation, stability, and technical debt without undermining delivery speed or team morale.

Spotify's use of AI also strengthens transparency and accountability. Data-driven recommendations help explain the rationale for prioritisation decisions, reducing perceptions of arbitrariness. For example, when a tribe leader slows feature delivery to prioritise infrastructure, the AI dashboard makes clear the projected impacts and reasoning. The result not only improves stakeholder buy-in but also promotes shared organisational goals.

In conclusion, Spotify's experiment demonstrates an important development in agile leadership. AI is no longer limited to forecasting sprint outcomes or automating reporting. Instead, it acts as a strategic co-pilot, enabling leaders to navigate complex trade-offs, allocate resources effectively, and make decisions with greater confidence. This case illustrates how AI can help scaled agile organisations evolve from reactive delivery systems into strategically intelligent enterprises where predictive insight complements human judgement.

3. Case Scenarios of AI in Sprint Planning and Retrospectives

The integration of (Artificial Intelligence) AI-powered copilots into sprint planning and retrospective sessions represents a significant evolution in Agile practices. Traditionally, sprint planning relies heavily on the judgement and experience of Scrum Masters and Product Owners, while retrospectives depend on subjective observations and manually collated feedback. AI systems, particularly GPT-5-class models, offer the ability to objectively analyse large volumes of historical and real-time data objectively, enabling evidence-based planning and actionable insights. By doing so, AI reduces human bias, improves predictability, and allows leadership to focus on facilitation, coaching, and strategic interventions.

3.1 AI in Sprint Planning:

Agile practice often challenges sprint planning with issues like inaccurate estimation, overcommitment, and human bias. AI copilots, such as GPT-5, provide a systematic way to address these challenges by analysing historical performance data and current team capacity to generate realistic, data-driven sprint plans.

The process begins with the examination of historical velocity. AI tools review metrics from past sprints, identifying patterns in throughput, variability, and scope completion. This analysis enables GPT-5 to recommend achievable sprint goals that are grounded in empirical evidence rather than optimistic projections. By providing confidence ranges for expected story completion, AI reduces the likelihood of overcommitment and the stress or rework that often results.

Another important function is the assessment of story complexity and workload optimisation. GPT-5 can evaluate backlog items by considering factors such as story points, technical difficulty, and historical completion times for similar tasks. Based on this, the tool can suggest splitting larger stories into smaller tasks or grouping items in ways that balance workload across the team. This helps prevent individual overload, enhances predictability, and supports team morale by ensuring sprint commitments are feasible.

AI copilots also contribute to capacity and skill risk detection. They analyse contextual factors, such as planned leave, skill mismatches, and external dependencies. For example, the system may flag when a key developer is unavailable or when a squad lacks expertise in a critical area. These insights enable leaders to make proactive adjustments to sprint allocation, ensuring that planning accounts for both team availability and competency.

By anchoring sprint planning in empirical data, AI reduces the cognitive burden on Scrum Masters and Product Owners. Instead of spending excessive time reconciling conflicting inputs or debating estimates, leaders can focus on higher-level responsibilities such as strategic alignment, facilitation, and stakeholder engagement. In this way, AI copilots act as enablers for more effective, evidence-based sprint planning, while preserving human oversight for decision-making and team leadership.

Case example 3:

Atlassian's AI Assistant in Jira:

Atlassian is an Australian software company best known for developing tools that support project management, Agile development, and team collaboration. Founded in 2002, it has become a global leader in workplace software, with products widely adopted across industries.

Some of its most prominent tools include:

1. ***Jira*** —a leading platform for Agile project management, issue tracking, and workflow automation.
2. ***Confluence*** —a collaboration and knowledge management tool used for documentation and team communication.
3. ***Trello***—a visual project management application that organises tasks through boards, lists, and cards.
4. ***Bitbucket*** —a Git-based code hosting and version control system for software development teams.

Agile and DevOps environments widely use Atlassian's

platforms to support practices like sprint planning, backlog management, dependency tracking, and continuous delivery. Recently, Atlassian has also integrated AI assistants into Jira and other products, aiming to enhance backlog prioritisation, workload balancing, and decision-making in Agile teams.

Integration of ***AI assistants*** *into Jira:*

Atlassian has integrated AI assistants directly with Jira to provide automated support for sprint planning and backlog prioritisation. In initial trials, teams reported a 20% improvement in sprint predictability as well as higher levels of engagement during planning meetings. The AI assistant contributed by automatically generating suggested sprint goals, identifying dependencies, and recommending workload distribution. By reducing the time spent on repetitive discussions, such as estimation and backlog refinement, teams were able to concentrate more on innovation, feature prioritisation, and collaborative problem solving. The study demonstrates that AI tools not only improve operational efficiency but also enhance the strategic dimension of sprint planning.

AI in Retrospectives:

Retrospectives are intended to promote continuous improvement, yet collecting, analysing, and synthesising feedback from multiple sources can be time-consuming and prone to oversight. AI tools like GPT-5 transform this process by automatically processing chat logs, meeting transcripts, Jira tickets, and pull-request data to identify recurring issues, systemic impediments, and patterns in team performance.

This process allows for the detection of recurring impediments. By analysing unstructured data across multiple sprints, AI can uncover hidden bottlenecks, such as slow code review cycles, miscommunication between squads, or recurrent technical debt. Rather than highlighting isolated incidents, AI surfaces systemic patterns, enabling Scrum Masters to address root causes rather than symptoms.

Artificial Intelligence (AI) provides structured recommendations for improvement. AI can identify recurring issues and generate structured suggestions for improvement, which include concrete actions and estimated impact. For example, if GPT-5 finds that delays in integration testing are often causing delivery problems, it might suggest using automated test pipelines, having teams work together, or changing coding standards. This changes retrospectives from just gathering data to helping the team take action and improve, speeding up learning and making Agile meetings more effective.

AI provides better decision support for Product Owners and Scrum Masters by offering insights that guide backlog refinement and sprint adjustments. By pointing out trends and patterns, AI helps teams make clear, data-driven decisions. This allows them to prioritise high-impact improvements, use resources more effectively, and reduce recurring issues in future sprints.

Strategic Implications:

The integration of AI into sprint planning and retrospectives demonstrates a broader principle: AI is no longer confined to operational efficiency but empowers Agile leadership to operate strategically. By automating routine data aggregation and analysis, AI frees human leaders to focus on coaching, mentoring, and decision-making that drives long-term value. Teams benefit from increased predictability, reduced stress, and a more transparent, data-informed planning process.

Summary:

AI copilots such as GPT-5 are transforming the way Agile teams plan, execute, and improve their work. By leveraging advanced analytics, these tools help teams design sprints with empirically grounded and achievable goals. This ensures that planning is not just aspirational but firmly anchored in data and realistic capacity, reducing the risk of overcommitment.

Beyond planning, AI supports workload balance and optimises story allocation. By analysing complexity, skillsets, and team capacity, it distributes tasks more effectively across members. This reduces bottlenecks, prevents burnout, and allows for smoother progress during each sprint.

During retrospectives, AI copilots play a crucial role in uncovering systemic impediments that might otherwise go unnoticed. They can identify recurring patterns, analyse root causes, and even generate actionable recommendations for continuous improvement. This data-driven perspective enhances the value of retrospectives, making them more than just reflective conversations.

At a broader level, AI enhances transparency and facilitates strategic decision-making across teams and Agile Release Trains (ARTs). Leaders gain better visibility into dependencies, risks, and progress, which strengthens coordination across complex systems.

By integrating AI into Agile meetings and ceremonies, organisations can achieve more consistent delivery, increase team involvement, and promote ongoing learning across the system. Ultimately, AI copilots elevate both day-to-day collaboration and long-term leadership, demonstrating their potential to reshape Agile practices at scale.

3.2 AI in Sprint Retrospective:

Retrospectives are a cornerstone of Agile's continuous improvement philosophy, providing teams with an opportunity to reflect on what went well, identify impediments, and plan actionable changes for future sprints. However, traditional retrospectives often have major problems: some team members may dominate the conversation, leaving quieter ones unheard; time limits can stop thorough examination of deeper issues; and worries about feeling safe can make people hesitant to share problems honestly. These challenges can prevent organizations from fully realising the benefits of iterative learning. AI-powered copilots such as GPT-5 address these challenges by transforming retrospectives from subjective discussions into data-informed, system-level learning sessions.

3.3 Analysing multiple data sources for objective insights:

GPT-5 can ingest a wide range of structured and unstructured data: chat logs from Teams or Slack, issue trackers from Jira or Azure DevOps, pull-request histories, and code repositories. By analysing patterns across these sources, AI identifies trends and correlations that may not be apparent in traditional retrospectives. For instance, frequent delays in code reviews or recurring failures in specific modules can be detected objectively, even if team members do not explicitly report them. This approach mitigates biases caused by selective memory or social dynamics in retrospectives.

3.4 This approach summarises recurring impediments:

Beyond identifying isolated problems, GPT-5 can detect recurring impediments across sprints and teams. For example, it might highlight that certain environment setup issues consistently cause delays or that a specific module repeatedly generates bugs affecting multiple features. By clustering these observations, AI provides a high-level view of systemic obstacles, allowing Scrum Masters and Product Owners to prioritise interventions that have the greatest impact on delivery and team efficiency.

3.5 This process results in the generation of evidence-based improvement actions:

AI tools can surface issues and propose concrete, historically informed solutions. These recommendations are grounded in patterns detected across multiple sprints or teams, making them more reliable than ad hoc suggestions. For example, if repeated defects are linked to inconsistent testing environments, AI may recommend automating environment provisioning, introducing standardised test suites, or allocating dedicated time for environmental stabilisation. Such evidence-based guidance allows leaders to focus on facilitating implementation rather than manually diagnosing problems.

Case Example 4:

Microsoft Copilot in Distributed Teams:

Microsoft Copilot is an AI-powered assistant developed by Microsoft to enhance productivity, creativity, and decision-making within the Microsoft 365 ecosystem. Integrated with applications such as Word, Excel, PowerPoint, Outlook, and Teams, it assists users in generating content, analysing data, creating visuals, streamlining workflows, and synthesising information from multiple sources. By using advanced language models and relevant data from Microsoft Graph, Copilot helps with tasks like writing documents, doing calculations automatically, showing trends visually, summarising meetings, and organising tasks more effectively. It is accessible across devices—including Windows, Mac, iOS, Android, and the web—and offers additional features such as voice interaction, file uploads, and screen sharing. This makes Copilot a versatile tool capable of adapting to diverse professional, academic, and creative needs.

A practical example of its application can be seen in a global product engineering team at Microsoft managing 15 distributed Scrum teams across several continents. These teams faced difficulties in identifying recurring issues during retrospectives due to fragmented reporting. With Copilot integrated into retrospective analysis, leaders could automatically process chat histories, Jira tickets, and pull-request logs. The AI analysis revealed that nearly 40% of sprint delays were linked to environment setup issues —an underlying problem not consistently highlighted during traditional retrospectives. By uncovering this hidden challenge, leadership introduced a shared DevOps pipeline with standardised environment configurations. This intervention led to improved sprint predictability, reduced idle time, and smoother delivery flows across all teams. The case illustrates how Copilot can reveal latent issues and generate actionable insights that contribute to organisational learning and continuous improvement.

Case Scenario 5

Atlassian's AI Assistant in Jira:

Atlassian has been at the forefront of embedding AI assistants within its flagship product, Jira, to enhance both sprint planning and retrospective processes. In these pilots, the AI does much more than act as a passive tool—it actively contributes to the team's workflow. For sprint planning, the AI can automatically generate draft sprint goals that align with business priorities while remaining achievable within the team's historical velocity. It can also recommend backlog prioritisation by analysing story dependencies, complexity, and past performance trends. During retrospectives, the AI provides concise summaries of key events, bottlenecks, and successes from the previous sprint, allowing teams to focus their limited time on meaningful dialogue rather than administrative preparation.

20% improvement in sprint predictability:

Early implementations have demonstrated tangible benefits. Teams reported a 20% improvement in sprint predictability, with commitments becoming more realistic thanks to AI-driven recommendations grounded in historical data. Retrospectives also saw a notable increase in engagement. Since the AI handled much of the data collection and summarisation, team members were freed from the burden of manually documenting issues or sifting through metrics. Instead, they could channel their energy into discussions around solutions, innovation, and collaboration. This shift not only saved time but also improved morale, as retrospectives became spaces for constructive problem-solving rather than routine reporting.

Higher engagement during retrospectives:

Perhaps the most transformative impact has been in the quality of conversations during retrospectives. The AI is capable of identifying systemic patterns, recurring impediments, and hidden dependencies that may not be visible at the individual sprint level. By surfacing these insights, it ensures that the team's discussions move beyond surface-level complaints to focus on structural issues that hinder long-term performance. This capability allows retrospectives to evolve from mere checkpoints into powerful forums for continuous improvement and organisational learning.

This example reflects a broader industry trend in which AI copilots are not only driving operational efficiency but also catalysing cultural and behavioural change within Agile teams. The objectivity and evidence-based insights provided by AI reduce the influence of individual bias, enabling more transparent discussions and decisions. Teams gain the confidence to experiment, adapt, and align their efforts more closely with strategic objectives. Moreover, leaders benefit from richer feedback loops, where the insights generated in retrospectives inform planning and execution at both the team and Agile Release Train levels.

In summary, the integration of AI into retrospectives represents a paradigm shift. What were once subjective, time-constrained sessions are now evolving into data-driven, actionable learning platforms. Organisations leveraging AI-powered retrospectives are able to detect hidden impediments, prioritise systemic improvements, and make evidence-based decisions that directly enhance team performance and strategic alignment. By bridging planning, execution, and reflection with intelligent insights, AI copilots strengthen the very foundations of Agile delivery.

4. Challenges and Ethical Considerations

The integration of AI into agile leadership offers profound benefits, from predictive planning to evidence-based decision-making. However, organizations must address a range of challenges and ethical considerations to ensure responsible adoption and sustainable value creation.

4.1 Bias in AI Models:

AI models derive their recommendations from historical data, meaning that any systemic bias embedded in past practices can propagate into AI outputs. AI predictions may reinforce patterns from previous sprint estimates that consistently favoured certain teams or undervalued specific types of work, perpetuating inefficiencies or inequities. Leaders must actively monitor AI outputs for signs of bias and ensure that training datasets are representative, balanced, and periodically updated to reflect evolving organisational priorities. Techniques such as fairness metrics and bias detection algorithms can be integrated into Agile workflows to maintain equity in decision-making (Nemteanu, Mancebo Jr, et al., 2025).

4.2 Over-Reliance on AI / Human Judgement:

While AI copilots like GPT-5 or Microsoft Copilot can provide predictive insights, scenario simulations, and automated summaries, they are intended to augment—not replace—human judgement. Leadership in agile contexts requires intuition, ethical reasoning, empathy, and vision, which remain uniquely human capabilities. Over-reliance on AI risks deskilling leaders, reducing accountability, and potentially creating blind spots in decision-making. Organizations should foster a culture in which AI recommendations are critically evaluated, challenged, and contextualised before implementation.

4.3 Transparency and trust:

For AI adoption to succeed, teams must understand how recommendations are generated. Black box models can lead to scepticism, resistance, or blind compliance, undermining both trust and collaboration. Explainable AI (XAI) frameworks provide mechanisms for making AI reasoning understandable to humans, such as highlighting data sources, weighting decision factors, or illustrating scenario assumptions. In Agile settings, integrating XAI into dashboards and planning tools ensures that stakeholders comprehend the rationale behind forecasts, risk alerts, and backlog recommendations, thereby fostering trust and smoother adoption.

4.4 Data Privacy and Governance:

Embedding AI in project management platforms involves processing sensitive organisational information, including backlog items, code metrics, team communication logs, and performance data. Ensuring compliance with privacy regulations such as a comprehensive data protection law, GDPR (General Data Protection Regulation), ISO 27001 (Information Security Management) standards, and internal data governance policies is paramount. AI solutions must include access controls, anonymisation of sensitive data, secure storage, and audit trails to safeguard organisational and employee information. Failure to address these concerns can result in legal liabilities, reputational damage, and erosion of stakeholder trust.

4.5 Ethical and Governance Frameworks:

Several frameworks have emerged to help organizations manage AI adoption ethically and responsibly:

1. SAFE-AI for SMEs:

Developed to embed ethical oversight across the AI lifecycle, this framework provides fairness metrics, transparency measures, and continuous monitoring. It allows smaller organizations to manage AI risk without excessive overhead, ensuring that outputs are equitable and reliable (Nemteanu, Mancebo Jr, et al., 2025).

2. PMI Playbook for Data Science / AI Projects:

Co-developed by PMI and NASSCOM (2020), this guide outlines best practices, common pitfalls, and organisational enablers for AI adoption in projects. It emphasises governance, risk management, stakeholder alignment, and iterative validation to ensure that AI contributes positively to project outcomes. By embedding these frameworks into Agile practices, organizations can proactively manage ethical, operational, and strategic risks associated with AI-enhanced leadership.

5. The Future of AI-Augmented Agile Leadership

Looking forward, AI adoption in agile leadership is poised to evolve beyond operational augmentation into strategic co-piloting, where human leadership capabilities are amplified by AI's analytical and predictive power. Several emerging trends illustrate this trajectory:

5.1 Personalised AI Coaches:

Future AI copilots will not only provide generic insights but also offer individualised guidance for Scrum Masters, Product Owners, and team members. By analysing historical performance, team dynamics, and skill gaps, personalised AI coaches can deliver just-in-time advice, recommend interventions, and even suggest mentoring strategies for optimising team productivity and engagement.

***5.2 Value Stream Metrics Over Output Metrics*:**

Traditional Agile metrics focus on outputs, such as story completion or velocity, but AI can shift attention toward outcomes and value realisation. By correlating work completed with business impact, customer satisfaction, or ROI, AI enables leaders to measure and optimise delivery in terms of strategic value rather than purely tactical output. This aligns with SAFe's emphasis on value streams and supports decision-making that balances speed, quality, and impact.

***5.3 Organisational Learning Systems*:**

AI can serve as a continuous learning engine, harvesting improvement actions, lessons learnt, and best practices across multiple teams and ARTs. These insights can be embedded into knowledge repositories, creating organisational memory that accelerates learning, informs PI planning, and standardises improvements across distributed teams. Such systems transform AI from a tool for tactical support into a strategic enabler of organisational intelligence.

***5.4 Strategic Elevation of Human Leadership*:**

Ultimately, AI copilots like GPT-5 and Microsoft Copilot are not replacing project leaders. Instead, they elevate leadership roles from operational oversight to a strategic architecture of business value. Leaders can devote more energy to stakeholder engagement, innovation, and ethical decision-making, while AI handles predictive analytics, scenario modelling, and routine reporting. This synergy between human judgement and AI precision represents the next frontier in augmented Agile leadership—one where creativity, empathy, and ethical reasoning are amplified by data-driven insight and foresight.

The adoption of AI in agile leadership presents tremendous opportunities and complex responsibilities. Ethical governance, bias mitigation, transparency, and data privacy must be central considerations, while strategic trends point toward personalised AI coaching, outcome-focused metrics, and organisational learning systems. By navigating these challenges thoughtfully, organizations can realise a future in which AI-enhanced leadership delivers both operational efficiency and strategic advantage, transforming Agile leadership into a more predictive, responsive, and value-driven discipline.

6. Conclusion

The integration of AI tools such as Microsoft Copilot and GPT-5 into Agile leadership represents a fundamental shift from manual oversight toward AI-augmented strategic decision-making. Within SAFe delivery management, these tools enhance visibility, predictability, and alignment across Agile Release Trains (ARTs), enabling leaders to anticipate risks, detect bottlenecks, and optimise programme increments. In sprint planning, AI supports data-driven backlog allocation, realistic velocity forecasting, and capacity management, reducing human bias and improving sprint predictability. During retrospectives, AI synthesises historical data, uncovers systemic impediments, and generates actionable insights, allowing Scrum Masters and Product Owners to focus on coaching, facilitating collaboration, and fostering continuous improvement.

Case studies from Accenture, Spotify, Atlassian, and Microsoft demonstrate that AI is already reshaping leadership practices, moving decision-making from reactive problem-solving to proactive, evidence-based strategy.

Leaders who effectively integrate AI into Agile ceremonies can transition from operational managers to strategic enablers of business value, combining human intuition, creativity, and ethical judgement with AI's analytical precision and predictive capabilities.

The future of agile leadership lies in embracing AI as a collaborative partner rather than a replacement, leveraging its capacity for scenario simulation, pattern recognition, and real-time insight to unlock unprecedented levels of organisational agility, resilience, and foresight. By acknowledging AI's limitations, ensuring ethical deployment, and embedding it within a framework of transparency and governance, organizations can transform project leadership into a discipline that is not only efficient but strategically aligned, adaptive, and capable of sustained competitive advantage.

CHAPTER 15: THE EVOLUTION OF COPILOT OR GPT-5 IN SAFE AGILE

The Scaled Agile Framework (SAFe) is one of the most widely used methods for helping organizations apply Agile practices across large and complex enterprises. At the team level, Agile focuses on short development cycles, delivering customer value, and encouraging collaboration. SAFe builds on these ideas by extending them to larger programmes and portfolios, offering structures that support alignment, governance, and overall business agility.

With recent advances in artificial intelligence (AI), new possibilities have emerged for strengthening these practices. Microsoft Copilot, now enhanced by GPT-5, represents one such development. Originally designed as a coding assistant, Copilot has evolved into a broader strategic partner. It now plays a role in supporting decision-making, leadership, and continuous improvement within the SAFe framework.

This chapter examines how Copilot and GPT-5 can be integrated into SAFe practices. It draws on insights from industry frameworks, academic research, and real-world case studies to highlight their impact on Agile at scale.

1. Copilot as a Strategic Partner, Not Just a Coding Assistant

1.1 From Coding Support to Broader Roles

When artificial intelligence (AI) tools like Copilot were first introduced, they were mainly designed to help software developers. Their early use cases included generating short pieces of code, completing syntax, and automating routine programming tasks. These features reduced manual effort and saved time but kept Copilot in a narrow role as a technical helper.

1.2 The Evolution into a Strategic Partner:

Within the Scaled Agile Framework (SAFe), Copilot's role has expanded far beyond coding. Powered by GPT5, Copilot now provides insights that support decision-making across entire programs and portfolios. Instead of being limited to development tasks, Copilot contributes to backlog prioritisation, risk assessment, and dependency mapping. These functions are essential at the portfolio level, where leaders must make choices about which initiatives to fund, how to allocate resources, and how to align projects with overall business goals.

1.3 From Tool to Partner in SAFe:

The early version of AI coding assistants was valuable but limited—they only supported developers at the task level. Today, with GPT-5, Copilot works across different levels of SAFe. It helps leaders analyse large amounts of data, such as customer feedback, historical project performance, and market trends. By doing so, Copilot generates actionable insights that guide strategy.

For example, Copilot can identify which features are likely

to deliver the highest business value compared to their cost and associated risks. This allows decision-makers to focus resources on high-impact initiatives, ensuring that investments are closely aligned with enterprise strategy.

1.4 Why This Matters:

The shift from coding assistant to strategic partner highlights a key development in the use of AI in Agile environments. Instead of only supporting technical work, Copilot now plays a role in shaping business outcomes. It enables organizations to connect technical decisions with strategic objectives, strengthening alignment across teams, programmes, and portfolios.

1.5 Case Example 1:

A Global Bank's Portfolio Management:

A leading European bank, operating under SAFe 6.0, adopted Copilot to strengthen its Lean Portfolio Management (LPM) function. Traditionally, portfolio prioritisation in the banking sector is a time-consuming process. It often required months of workshops, repeated stakeholder meetings, and detailed financial modelling to align regulatory requirements, customer needs, and business goals. This approach, while thorough, was slow and often limited the bank's ability to respond quickly to market changes or regulatory updates.

By embedding Copilot powered by GPT-5, the bank transformed this process. Copilot could analyse regulatory guidelines, customer survey data, and risk assessments in real time, something that previously required weeks of manual effort. It also flagged dependencies across multiple teams—for example, identifying where new digital banking features were dependent on security system upgrades. In addition, Copilot highlighted potential compliance risks before they became critical issues, which is especially important in the highly regulated financial sector.

The result was a significant improvement in portfolio governance. Decision-making cycles were reduced by nearly 40%, enabling the bank to respond faster to both regulatory changes and customer demands. Copilot's analysis also supported more adaptive portfolio governance, where priorities could be updated frequently instead of waiting for lengthy review cycles.

This case demonstrates that Copilot's role extends far beyond technical delivery. It acts as a strategic partner in shaping enterprise strategy by connecting regulatory, financial, and customer perspectives with ongoing execution. In doing so, it reinforces SAFe's core principle of linking strategy to execution in a dynamic and adaptive way.

1.6 Case Example 2:

A Global Retail Company's Portfolio Prioritisation:

A large multinational retail company faced a different challenge. The organisation had a long backlog of digital initiatives, ranging from e-commerce platform upgrades to customer loyalty features. Traditionally, backlog prioritisation relied on manual scoring methods and leadership discussions, which often took weeks and sometimes reflected subjective preferences rather than objective analysis. This created delays in decision-making and sometimes led to misaligned investments.

By adopting Copilot powered by GPT-5, the company shifted from a largely manual and subjective process of portfolio management to a more evidence-based and data-driven approach. Traditionally, backlog prioritisation relied heavily on leader opinions, static scoring models, or lengthy discussions across departments. While useful, these methods often overlooked the wealth of data available within the organisation. Copilot transformed this process by systematically analysing three key sources of information and synthesising them into actionable insights.

1. Customer Feedback:

Copilot collected and analysed customer feedback from multiple channels, including online product reviews, post-purchase surveys, and customer service interactions. Instead of relying on selective or anecdotal reports, the AI was able to process thousands of data points in real time. This allowed leaders to identify recurring customer concerns and emerging demands. For instance, frequent complaints about the mobile checkout process revealed a critical need for optimisation, giving higher priority to related backlog items. In this way, customer voices directly influenced strategic decisions at the portfolio level.

2. Operational Performance Metrics:

The AI also examined operational data such as website loading times, checkout efficiency, and cart abandonment rates. These metrics offered a quantitative view of system performance and highlighted friction points in the customer journey. For example, a sudden increase in cart abandonment during peak shopping seasons signalled both a revenue risk and an opportunity for immediate intervention. By surfacing these patterns, Copilot ensured that operational weaknesses were directly linked to portfolio decisions, helping leaders prioritise initiatives that would have the greatest impact on customer experience and business outcomes.

3. Historical Delivery Data:

Finally, Copilot reviewed historical records of how similar features or initiatives had performed in the past. This included adoption rates, revenue contributions, and delivery challenges such as delays or cost overruns. By comparing new proposals with past experiences, Copilot was able to provide a more realistic projection of potential success and risks. For example, if a loyalty programme feature had previously underperformed due to integration challenges, Copilot flagged similar risks in upcoming initiatives. This helped leaders set achievable expectations and allocate resources more wisely.

Through the integration of these three data sources —customer feedback, operational metrics, and historical performance records—Copilot enabled the company to prioritise initiatives with far greater accuracy and confidence. Instead of debating abstract scores or relying solely on managerial intuition, leaders had a clear, data-supported ranking of initiatives. This data-driven governance not only reduced bias in decision-making but also accelerated the alignment between strategic goals and execution at the portfolio level.

From this analysis, Copilot generated a ranked list of initiatives. The ranking not only reflected potential business value but also considered risks, dependencies, and resource requirements. For example, Copilot highlighted that an AI-driven product recommendation engine could deliver high business value but depended heavily on upgrading the company's data infrastructure.

The leadership team used these insights to refine their

priorities. High-value and low-risk initiatives were advanced to the next Program Increment (PI), while risk-heavy initiatives were broken into smaller experiments. This approach helped the company align investments with enterprise strategy, reduce wasted effort, and accelerate the delivery of features that mattered most to customers.

Why These Cases Matter:

Both examples—the European bank and the global retailer—show how Copilot has evolved from being just a coding assistant to becoming a strategic partner in portfolio management. At the bank, Copilot enhanced compliance and regulatory alignment, while at the retailer, it improved customer-focused backlog prioritisation.

The common thread is that Copilot helps organizations move beyond subjective, slow, and manual decision-making processes. Instead, it introduces real-time, data-driven insights that connect technical initiatives with business outcomes. This strengthens alignment across teams, programmes, and portfolios, which is central to SAFe's goal of achieving business agility at scale.

2. Sharper Decision-Making Through Contextual Intelligence

2.1 Why Context Matters in SAFe Decision-Making:

Decision-making within the Scaled Agile Framework (SAFe) is not limited to isolated teams but extends across programmes and portfolios, where choices have broader organisational consequences. At the team level, developers and product owners need to understand how their sprint backlog items interact with those of other teams. A delay or dependency in one team can create bottlenecks for others, making context essential for smooth coordination.

At the programme level, leaders must manage the balance of features across multiple Agile Release Trains (ARTs). Without visibility into dependencies and shared goals, prioritisation becomes fragmented, and teams may deliver outputs that do not integrate well. Finally, at the portfolio level, executives must decide which initiatives deserve the largest share of resources. These decisions determine whether the organisation invests in innovation, compliance, or customer-focused enhancements. Without context, such choices risk being reactive or misaligned with long-term strategy, leading to wasted resources or missed opportunities.

2.2 How Copilot Enhances Contextual Awareness:

Copilot, powered by GPT-5, enhances decision-making by providing contextual intelligence, which is the ability to interpret raw data within its larger organisational and business setting. Traditional dashboards often report figures in isolation—velocity charts, defect counts, or customer satisfaction scores—but rarely explain how they connect. Copilot's strength lies in synthesising these diverse datasets into a meaningful narrative. For example, it can examine historical sprint data to identify recurring patterns of delay, link these to stakeholder communications where concerns about compliance are raised, and connect them with customer feedback showing dissatisfaction with delayed features. By presenting this analysis in simple, conversational language, Copilot helps leaders and product owners see the full picture. Instead of only knowing what the numbers are, they learn why those numbers matter and what actions should follow. This makes decisions not just data-driven but context-driven.

2.3 Integration with Enterprise Tools:

Copilot delivers contextual intelligence by integrating directly with enterprise tools already in use, ensuring that insights are grounded in current and trusted data. By connecting with Microsoft Graph, Copilot can interpret patterns in communication and collaboration, such as identifying where delays in cross-team communication may be affecting project timelines. Integration with Jira and Azure DevOps allows Copilot to analyse real-time progress, dependencies, and team velocity, providing visibility into operational realities. Meanwhile, connections with Confluence enable Copilot to draw on decision histories and documentation, ensuring that recommendations are consistent with past agreements and organisational knowledge. These integrations make it possible to ask Copilot natural language questions—such as *"Which features in the current Program Increment are most likely to miss deadlines?"*—and receive answers that pull from multiple systems simultaneously. What previously required days of manual reporting and cross-checking can now be achieved in seconds, streamlining decision-making at every level.

2.4 Example 1:

Decision-Making in Action:

To illustrate, consider a global financial services company managing several Agile Release Trains simultaneously. The leadership faced a dilemma: whether to prioritise the release of a new mobile banking feature to satisfy growing customer demand or to focus first on upgrading security systems to address frequent downtime. Without Copilot, this decision might have been based on short-term pressure or leadership opinion. With Copilot, however, the company gained contextual insights from three directions. Customer feedback revealed that many users were frustrated with slow mobile transactions, creating strong demand for the new feature. Operational performance data showed that system outages in security verification were already a major bottleneck for user satisfaction. Historical performance analysis highlighted that previous neglect of security improvements had led to compliance issues and costly penalties. Synthesising these insights, Copilot recommended sequencing the initiatives so that the security upgrades were delivered first, followed by the mobile feature rollout. This approach ensured compliance, protected customer trust, and still addressed user demands, but in a way that minimised organisational risk.

Benefits of Contextual Intelligence:

The application of contextual intelligence in SAFe decision-making produces several important benefits. ***First,*** it supports proactive risk management. By analysing historical data and dependencies, Copilot helps identify potential risks early, allowing leaders to act before problems escalate. *Second*, it strengthens strategic alignment. Decisions are guided not only by raw numbers but also by their relevance to both business objectives and customer needs, ensuring that initiatives deliver real value. *Third*, it accelerates decision-making. With Copilot synthesising complex data across multiple systems into clear recommendations, leaders and product owners spend less time in lengthy workshops and more time implementing solutions. *Finally*, it ensures clarity across organisational levels. When context is shared, team-level priorities align with programme and portfolio objectives, reducing conflicts and ensuring that everyone works toward the same goals.

In summary, Copilot transforms raw data into contextual intelligence, enabling organizations to make sharper, more strategic, and better-aligned decisions. By combining data integration, natural language processing, and predictive analytics, it ensures that SAFe organizations are not only adaptive to change but also proactive in driving value and mitigating risks.

2.5 Case Example 3:

Agile Alliance Research Insights:

The Agile Alliance (2023) conducted a study examining the effects of AI-enabled tools on organisational decision-making within large-scale Agile contexts. The research found that organizations integrating solutions such as Copilot powered by GPT-5 reduced decision latency—the time between identifying a problem and making a decision —by as much as 35%. This reduction is significant in environments like SAFe, where delays in decision-making can cascade across teams, Agile Release Trains (ARTs), and portfolios, ultimately affecting customer outcomes and business value delivery.

One detailed case from the study focused on a multinational telecommunications firm operating multiple ARTs across different regions. The organisation faced persistent challenges with customer satisfaction, as reflected in low Net Promoter Scores (NPS). Traditional retrospectives and leadership workshops had flagged potential issues but failed to pinpoint their root causes with precision. The leadership team decided to integrate Copilot into its SAFe portfolio governance and programme-level ceremonies to add contextual intelligence to decision-making.

How Copilot Helped:

1. Historical release train performance data:

Copilot began by analysing performance metrics for release

trains such as team velocity, defect density, and delivery predictability. Velocity trends highlighted whether teams were completing their committed work consistently, while defect rates exposed quality gaps in production releases. Delivery predictability data revealed how often Agile Release Trains (ARTs) met their program increment (PI) commitments. By drawing connections across multiple PIs, Copilot identified recurring bottlenecks in the delivery pipeline. Unlike traditional reports, which presented these metrics in isolation, Copilot combined them into a longitudinal view, showing how performance fluctuations were not random but systematically linked to integration challenges.

2. Customer satisfaction surveys:

Next, Copilot incorporated customer satisfaction data, including structured surveys and open-text responses. This step was crucial because it translated operational performance into customer impact. Customers consistently reported frustration with unreliable features, delayed updates, and service disruptions—factors that negatively influenced their Net Promoter Scores (NPS). Copilot's natural language processing capabilities let it categorise feedback themes automatically and link them to specific features or release cycles. This created a direct bridge between engineering performance and customer experience, something leaders had previously struggled to visualise.

3. Operational logs from integration and testing pipelines:

Finally, Copilot examined technical operational logs generated during integration and testing. These logs captured critical data points such as error frequency, build times, and cycle duration. By applying pattern recognition, Copilot discovered that integration testing consistently took longer than planned, often leading to cascading delays across ARTs. Moreover, these testing delays correlated with increased defect rates after deployment, which in turn matched with customer complaints about product reliability.

4. Synthesising insights into a clear correlation:

By merging these three data streams—performance metrics, customer sentiment, and operational logs—Copilot revealed a clear, systemic correlation: delays in integration testing were the hidden driver behind late releases and diminished customer trust. This insight had previously been obscured because the data existed in **silos** across engineering dashboards, customer success platforms, and DevOps tools. Copilot's contextual intelligence brought these pieces together into a single, actionable narrative that leaders could immediately act upon.

The Organisational Response:

With this contextual intelligence, the leadership team reallocated investment toward continuous testing pipelines and enhanced test automation practices. Instead of treating testing bottlenecks as isolated engineering issues, they reframed them as strategic business priorities directly tied to customer experience. The changes were rolled out across two programme increments, with Copilot continuing to monitor outcomes and report improvements.

The Results:

1. Improved predictability:

Within just two programme increments (PIs), the company observed a marked improvement in delivery predictability across its Agile Release Trains (ARTs). Previously, teams would struggle to meet their commitments due to unexpected delays in integration testing or unrecognised dependencies between features. With Copilot analysing historical performance data and operational logs, leaders could anticipate potential bottlenecks and proactively adjust plans. As a result, release trains began completing their planned work more consistently, reducing last-minute firefighting and increasing confidence in the organisation's ability to meet delivery targets. This improved predictability not only streamlined execution but also allowed programme and portfolio leaders to plan future initiatives with greater certainty.

2. Higher customer satisfaction:

The integration of Copilot had a direct impact on customer experience, reflected in improved Net Promoter Scores (NPS). By surfacing the root causes of delays and product issues—particularly the recurring problems in integration testing—the company was able to implement continuous testing pipelines and automated quality checks. This led to fewer post-release defects and smoother product rollouts. Customers experienced more reliable features and a more consistent digital experience, which strengthened trust and loyalty. The measurable increase in NPS highlighted how embedding AI-driven insights into operational practices could translate technical improvements directly into business value.

3. Reduced alignment overhead:

Another significant outcome was a reduction in alignment and coordination overhead. Prior to adopting Copilot, leaders spent considerable time organising cross-functional workshops, meetings, and reviews to diagnose recurring problems across teams and ARTs. These sessions were often lengthy and required manual compilation of data from multiple sources, which slowed decision-making. With Copilot, insights were synthesised in near real-time and presented in actionable form. Leaders could immediately see patterns, risks, and suggested actions without wading through disparate datasets. This not only freed up time for strategic activities but also improved clarity and alignment across teams, ensuring that everyone—from developers to portfolio managers—was working toward the same goals with a shared understanding of priorities.

Why This Case Matters:

This case vividly demonstrates how Copilot supports Lean-Agile decision-making in SAFe by embedding contextual intelligence into operational practices. Instead of leaders making decisions based on intuition or fragmented reports, AI empowered them to act on evidence-based insights that connected technical delivery challenges to customer outcomes.

The example also reinforces SAFe's principle of relentless improvement: by using AI to uncover root causes and predict risks, organizations can transition from reactive problem-solving to proactive value delivery. In essence, Copilot is more than just a tool for analysing metrics; it is a strategic enabler of continuous learning and adaptation across the enterprise.

3. Leadership Enablement via Role-Specific Guidance

Leadership in SAFe Agile requires balancing operational oversight with strategic vision. Copilot supports this by offering role-specific guidance tailored to leaders, Scrum Masters, Release Train Engineers, and Product Managers. For instance, a Scrum Master might receive AI-generated prompts for facilitating retrospectives, while a Product

Manager may be assisted with prioritising features based on customer value. By delivering targeted recommendations, Copilot helps leaders focus on high-value activities, reduce administrative overhead, and foster a culture of continuous improvement across teams.

3.1 Tailoring AI for Leadership Roles:

Leadership within the Scaled Agile Framework (SAFe) requires clear understanding of distinct roles and responsibilities across the enterprise. Product Managers, Release Train Engineers (RTEs), and Scrum Masters each operate at different levels, yet their work must remain coordinated to ensure smooth delivery of value. Product managers focus on prioritising features and aligning them with business strategy, RTEs manage dependencies and execution across multiple Agile Release Trains (ARTs), and Scrum Masters facilitate team-level execution and continuous improvement. In large, complex organizations, the volume of data and interdependencies can make decision-making overwhelming. This is where **Co**pilot, powered by GPT-5, adds value by providing role-specific guidance tailored to the needs of each leadership function.

1. For Product Managers:

Product managers are responsible for determining which features and initiatives provide the most value to customers and the business. Copilot assists by analysing customer feedback, historical delivery outcomes, market trends, and cost-of-delay calculations to recommend feature prioritisation. For example, if multiple features are competing for the same program increment, Copilot can quantify their potential business impact relative to risk and resource requirements. This helps product managers make data-driven decisions, ensuring that the backlog reflects both strategic goals and customer needs. It also reduces reliance on subjective judgement, which can vary between stakeholders or change over time.

2. For Release Train Engineers (RTEs):

RTEs are responsible for orchestrating the execution of multiple ARTs, managing dependencies, risks, and programme-level execution challenges. Copilot aids RTEs by analysing the programme board, identifying bottlenecks, and highlighting dependency conflicts that could delay delivery. It can also suggest mitigation strategies, such as reallocating resources or adjusting feature sequencing, based on historical patterns and predictive analysis. By synthesising this complex information, Copilot allows RTEs to maintain programme alignment and avoid costly surprises while improving transparency and predictability across teams.

3. For Scrum Masters:

Scrum Masters focus on team-level facilitation and continuous improvement. Copilot supports Scrum Masters by generating retrospective prompts, identifying recurring impediments, and suggesting process improvements. For example, it can analyse sprint data to highlight patterns in velocity drops or recurring defect types, enabling Scrum Masters to address root causes rather than just symptoms. Additionally, Copilot can provide guidance on coaching techniques and collaboration improvements or even alert leaders when team health metrics indicate risk. This makes retrospectives more effective and actionable and strengthens the team's ability to self-organise and continuously improve.

3.2 Why Role-Specific AI Guidance Matters:

By tailoring insights to specific leadership roles, Copilot

ensures that each leader receives relevant, actionable information without being overwhelmed by irrelevant data. Product managers can focus on value and strategy, RTEs can orchestrate programmes efficiently, and Scrum Masters can foster high-performing teams. This alignment across roles strengthens SAFe's principle of connecting strategy to execution, ensuring that decisions at every level contribute to the enterprise's overall objectives.

3.3 Case Example 4:

PMI and Role-Specific AI Guidance:

The Project Management Institute (PMI, 2024) has highlighted the growing need for AI fluency among project leaders, emphasising that successful leadership now requires the ability to interpret AI-driven insights and integrate them into decision-making. One case study illustrates how Copilot, powered by GPT-5, was applied to enhance role-specific leadership functions within a global pharmaceutical company operating under SAFe Agile.

Context and Challenges:

The pharmaceutical company managed multiple Agile Release Trains (ARTs) simultaneously, each responsible for delivering complex research, development, and IT initiatives. Release Train Engineers (RTEs) often faced difficulties in visualising inter-team dependencies across ARTs. Manual tracking methods, such as spreadsheets and static programme boards, were insufficient to capture the dynamic nature of cross-team interactions. This frequently resulted in conflicts, delays, and rework, forcing leadership to spend significant time on reactive crisis management rather than proactive value delivery.

How Copilot Provided Role-Specific Guidance:

To address these challenges, the company implemented Copilot as a strategic partner for leadership roles. For RTEs, Copilot analysed programme board data, sprint reports, and historical performance metrics to identify inter-team dependencies and potential bottlenecks. By visualising these dependencies dynamically, RTEs could see where one team's delay might cascade into others, enabling proactive interventions.

For product managers, Copilot evaluated feature prioritisation based on customer value, regulatory considerations, and resource allocation. It suggested which initiatives should be advanced, delayed, or broken into smaller increments to optimise portfolio outcomes. Meanwhile, Scrum Masters benefited from Copilot's ability to highlight recurring impediments and generate retrospective prompts, allowing teams to continuously improve processes without extensive manual analysis.

Measurable Outcomes:

1. Reduced cross-team conflicts by 25%:

One of the most immediate benefits observed after implementing Copilot was a 25% reduction in cross-team conflicts. Previously, Release Train Engineers (RTEs) struggled to anticipate how delays in one Agile Release Train (ART) could impact others, often resulting in last-minute rework and scheduling conflicts. Copilot's role-specific guidance allowed RTEs to identify dependency bottlenecks early by analysing programme boards, historical delivery patterns, and team interactions. With this insight, potential conflicts could be mitigated before they escalate into delays, ensuring smoother coordination across ARTs and reducing friction between teams.

2. Enhanced collaboration:

By proactively surfacing potential issues, Copilot freed leadership from reactive crisis management, allowing them to focus on fostering collaboration. Product managers, RTEs, and scrum masters were able to communicate more effectively about priorities, risks, and dependencies because Copilot provided a single, shared view of the programme landscape. This improved alignment across multiple ARTs, strengthened trust among teams, and created a culture of transparency, where challenges were addressed collaboratively rather than in isolation. Teams became more engaged and motivated, knowing that leadership decisions were informed by accurate, real-time data.

3. Faster decision-making:

Copilot also accelerated decision-making processes for both product managers and RTEs. Before AI integration, leaders spent hours or even days reviewing disparate reports, attending alignment meetings, and manually reconciling conflicting information. With Copilot synthesising data from customer feedback, operational metrics, and historical delivery outcomes, leaders could make data-driven decisions more quickly and confidently. This not only saved time but also reduced the likelihood of errors or misaligned priorities, enabling the organisation to respond more rapidly to emerging risks or market opportunities.

4. Improved portfolio execution:

Finally, the integration of Copilot contributed to more reliable portfolio execution. By helping leaders prioritise initiatives based on value, risk, and dependencies, features and projects were delivered more consistently within programme increments. This alignment between strategic objectives and operational execution ensured that the organisation maximised the impact of its investments. Customers benefited from more predictable and higher-quality deliverables, while leadership gained confidence that their portfolios were driving meaningful business outcomes rather than being subject to reactive adjustments.

Why This Case Matters:

This example demonstrates the power of tailoring AI insights to specific leadership roles within SAFe. Copilot's contextual intelligence ensured that each leader received actionable, role-relevant information, which strengthened their ability to manage complexity, improve collaboration, and maintain strategic alignment. Rather than replacing human judgement, Copilot augmented leadership capabilities, transforming decision-making from reactive problem-solving into proactive, value-focused governance.

4. Integrating Ancient Wisdom with Agile Intelligence

4.1 The Connection Between Wisdom and Agile Practices:

The evolution of Copilot in Agile environments illustrates a broader movement: the integration of timeless principles of human wisdom with modern AI-supported Agile practices. Ancient philosophical traditions often emphasise reflection, balance, and collective responsibility—concepts that remain deeply relevant in contemporary organisational life. Copilot, by analysing team performance, dependencies, and patterns, can encourage pauses for reflection, similar to practices of self-inquiry or contemplative assessment in philosophical traditions. For instance, after a programme increment, Copilot can summarise recurring challenges or highlight learning opportunities, prompting teams to consider not just what was delivered, but how it was delivered and how processes can improve. This approach nurtures a culture of mindfulness, learning, and continuous improvement, even in highly dynamic and fast-paced work environments.

4.2 Philosophical Underpinnings of AI-Augmented Agile:

Beyond its technical contributions, Copilot embodies a shift toward reflective and values-driven Agile practices. Stoicism, for example, teaches resilience, measured responses, and thoughtful reflection on actions and outcomes. Eastern philosophies, such as Buddhism and Confucianism, emphasise self-awareness, balance, and harmonious collaboration within communities. These ideas resonate strongly with the Lean-Agile mindset promoted in SAFe, which values learning organizations, decentralised decision-making, and alignment between individual, team, and organisational objectives. By surfacing insights that promote reflection and measured adaptation, Copilot allows teams to embody these age-old principles in a modern work context.

4.3 Reflection as a Catalyst for Continuous Learning:

One of the most powerful intersections of AI and ancient wisdom is in supporting continuous learning. Copilot can analyse sprint retrospectives, programme increment reviews, and cross-team interactions to identify patterns, recurring impediments, or misalignments. By presenting these insights reflectively—such as prompting teams to consider *why* certain delays occur or *how* resource allocation affects outcomes—Copilot enables a form of structured self-inquiry. This mirrors ancient practices where reflection was not merely about observing events but understanding the underlying principles that govern outcomes. Teams become more aware of systemic issues, biases in decision-making, and opportunities for innovation.

4.4 Preserving Human Values in an AI-Augmented World:

Integrating ancient wisdom with AI also ensures that technological acceleration does not override human values. Copilot may increase speed and efficiency, but it can also reinforce principles of empathy, ethical responsibility, and collective purpose. By providing context-aware recommendations, it allows leaders and teams to make decisions that honour both business objectives and stakeholder well-being. In this sense, AI is not a replacement for human judgement but a bridge between historical wisdom and contemporary intelligence, supporting a work culture that is ethical, reflective, and human-centred.

4.5 Practical Implications for Organizations:

For organizations, this integration has practical benefits. Teams that pause to reflect on AI-generated insights are better equipped to learn from failures, anticipate risks, and optimise workflows. Leaders using Copilot can embed ethical considerations into portfolio decisions, ensuring that value delivery does not come at the expense of fairness, transparency, or employee well-being. Over time, this creates a resilient, adaptive, and ethically aware organisation—one that blends technological advancement with the enduring principles of human wisdom.

4.6 Case Example 5:

Reflective Practices in Retrospectives:

Context and Challenges:

A Japanese manufacturing firm implementing the Scaled Agile Framework (SAFe) faced a common challenge: while

Agile practices improved delivery speed and predictability, teams often struggled with deep reflection during retrospectives. Traditional retrospectives tended to focus on task completion and metrics, with limited discussion of systemic issues, assumptions, or learning opportunities. Leadership recognised that without meaningful reflection, teams risked repeating mistakes and failing to capture lessons for continuous improvement.

How Copilot Facilitated Reflection:

To address this, the firm introduced Copilot, powered by GPT - 5 to enhance retrospectives. Instead of simply summarising completed tasks or generating performance reports, Copilot provided reflective prompts inspired by mindfulness and philosophical traditions. Examples of these prompts included:

a) "What assumptions did we challenge this sprint?"

b) "Where did we miss opportunities for collective growth?"

c) "Which decisions aligned with our shared values, and which did not?"

By posing these open-ended questions, Copilot encouraged teams to look beyond surface-level metrics, critically examine their practices, and explore systemic improvements. The AI synthesised sprint data, team communications, and historical retrospectives to offer context-aware prompts tailored to each team's specific experiences.

Outcomes and Benefits:

1. Enhanced team cohesion:

One of the most notable outcomes of integrating Copilot into retrospectives was a significant improvement in team cohesion. By using reflective prompts, teams were encouraged to discuss not only what went wrong or right in a sprint but also how their decisions affected other team members and dependent teams. Questions like "Where did we miss opportunities for collective growth?" prompted conversations about shared responsibilities, collaboration patterns, and interdependencies. This deeper dialogue helped team members develop mutual understanding, trust, and accountability, fostering a collaborative environment where challenges were approached collectively rather than individually. Over time, this strengthened cohesion contributed to smoother coordination, reduced conflict, and a more positive team culture.

2. Improved resilience:

Reflective prompts also contributed to enhanced team resilience. By regularly examining assumptions, decisions, and systemic patterns, teams became more aware of potential pitfalls before they escalated into serious problems. For instance, recognising that a recurring dependency issue could affect multiple sprints allowed teams to adapt proactively, adjusting their plans or raising concerns early. This habit of continuous reflection nurtured a mindset of learning and experimentation, where setbacks were seen as opportunities for improvement rather than failures. Teams developed the ability to respond effectively to unforeseen obstacles, making the organisation more agile and adaptive in a rapidly changing environment.

3. Continuous improvement:

Finally, the use of Copilot in retrospectives accelerated continuous improvement across teams. The AI did not merely highlight past events; it provided actionable insights that could inform immediate process changes. For example, if certain integration steps consistently caused delays, Copilot would flag these patterns, prompting teams to implement systemic solutions such as automated testing or revised handoff protocols. Over multiple sprints, these incremental improvements accumulated, leading to more reliable workflows, higher-quality outputs, and a culture where learning from experience became routine. The combination of reflective prompts and data-driven analysis allowed the firm to embed continuous improvement into the organisation's DNA, aligning both human insight and AI intelligence toward better outcomes.

Balancing Technological Progress with Human Values:

This case demonstrates that AI, when designed thoughtfully, can bridge the gap between technological efficiency and human-centred practices. Copilot did more than increase productivity; it acted as a facilitator of organisational maturity by embedding principles of reflection, ethics, and shared purpose into routine practices. Leaders observed that teams were not only delivering value faster but also aligning their work with broader organisational goals and human values, reinforcing SAFe's emphasis on both execution and culture.

Broader Implications:

The integration of AI with reflective practices highlights a key principle for modern Agile organizations: technological advancement should not come at the expense of human insight and ethical considerations. By combining Copilot's analytical capabilities with prompts inspired by ancient wisdom, organizations can create adaptive, self-aware, and resilient teams that continuously improve while staying true to shared values.

5. Embedding AI into the Sprint Lifecycle:

In SAFe, the sprint lifecycle involves planning, execution, review, and retrospective. Copilot is now embedded in each stage of this cycle. During sprint planning, it helps estimate workload and identify dependencies. In execution, it automates repetitive tasks, manages code reviews, and monitors progress. For reviews, it summarises achievements and highlights gaps, while for retrospectives, it detects recurring patterns from past sprints. By being present throughout the sprint lifecycle, Copilot ensures that AI is not an external tool but an integrated element of the Agile process, enhancing both efficiency and learning.

5.1 AI Across the Stages of a Sprint:

In the Scaled Agile Framework (SAFe), a sprint is a structured cycle that includes planning, execution, review, and retrospective. Each stage presents unique challenges, from estimating workloads to capturing lessons learnt. Copilot, powered by GPT-5, is now embedded throughout the sprint lifecycle, enhancing efficiency, collaboration, and decision-making at every step.

1. Sprint Planning:

During sprint planning, teams decide which backlog items to commit to and estimate effort. Copilot supports this stage by suggesting workload estimates based on historical sprint data, team velocity, and individual capacity. It can also identify hidden dependencies between user stories or tasks that might impact other teams or ARTs, helping prevent surprises during execution. Additionally, Copilot can generate draft user story acceptance criteria, ensuring clarity and consistency in requirements. This reduces ambiguity, aligns expectations, and helps teams start the sprint with a shared understanding of priorities and deliverables.

2. Execution:

In the execution phase, teams focus on building and delivering the committed work. Copilot contributes by automating repetitive coding tasks, such as generating boilerplate code, performing syntax checks, and suggesting refactoring opportunities. It also monitors build pipelines in real time, alerting teams to integration failures or performance issues. Furthermore, Copilot manages real-time issue tracking, logging defects, linking them to related stories, and highlighting risks before they escalate. By taking over routine and time-consuming tasks, Copilot allows team members to concentrate on higher-value activities such as design, problem-solving, and collaboration.

3. Review:

The review phase evaluates what the team accomplished and demonstrates completed work to stakeholders. Copilot enhances this stage by summarising achievements and producing concise overviews of completed user stories, features, and program increment (PI) objectives. It can also generate demo scripts, guiding teams on how to present functionality effectively to stakeholders. Moreover, Copilot helps ensure that sprint outcomes are aligned with broader PI objectives, providing data-driven insights into how delivered work contributes to strategic business goals. This increases transparency and helps leadership assess progress accurately.

4. Retrospective:

Finally, retrospectives focus on learning and continuous improvement. Copilot analyses communication logs, sprint metrics, and historical data to detect recurring bottlenecks, process inefficiencies, or team friction points. It then proposes actionable improvement steps, such as adjusting workflow sequences, optimising dependencies, or revising testing practices. By providing contextual, data-driven insights, Copilot transforms retrospectives from a discussion-based exercise into a structured, evidence-informed process for sustainable performance improvement.

This integration of AI across the sprint lifecycle ensures that teams are more predictive, adaptive, and aligned with both tactical and strategic objectives. Copilot acts as a continuous partner, augmenting human intelligence, reducing manual effort, and supporting end-to-end sprint excellence.

5.2 Case Example 6:

Microsoft Engineering Teams:

Context and Challenges:

A global Microsoft engineering division, consisting of 15 distributed Scrum teams, faced challenges common to large-scale Agile operations: sprint delays, inconsistent workflows, and limited visibility into recurring issues. With teams spread across geographies, it was difficult for leadership to identify the root causes of delivery problems. Traditional retrospective methods relied heavily on team self-reporting, which often overlooked systemic issues such as infrastructure bottlenecks or dependency misalignments. The teams sought a solution that could analyse multiple data sources, highlight patterns, and provide actionable insights across the sprint cycle.

How Copilot Was Integrated:

The Microsoft engineering teams implemented Copilot powered by GPT-5 as an integral part of their sprint retrospectives and overall sprint lifecycle, rather than as a standalone tool. The goal was to enable data-driven insights across planning, execution, review, and retrospective stages, while reducing the reliance on manual analysis and guesswork. By integrating Copilot with existing tools and workflows, the teams could consolidate multiple streams of information that previously remained siloed.

Multi-Source Data Analysis:

Copilot analysed several key data sources simultaneously to provide a holistic view of sprint performance:

1. ***Chat histories from Microsoft Teams:*** These logs captured informal discussions, questions, and reported issues that often went undocumented in formal project management tools. By analysing conversational patterns, Copilot could detect recurring concerns or emerging blockers that might affect sprint progress.

2. ***Jira tickets:*** Jira provided detailed information on work items, including task progress, dependencies, delays, and blockers. Copilot aggregated this data to identify patterns across multiple teams and sprints, such as which tasks frequently caused delays or which dependencies were often overlooked.

3. *Pull Requests*: By analysing pull requests, Copilot detected integration challenges, code review bottlenecks, and merge conflicts. This allowed leadership to see where development

workflows were inefficient or prone to errors, contributing to delays.

Correlating Insights Across Data Sources:

What made Copilot particularly powerful was its ability to correlate these disparate data sources. For instance, delays noted in Jira tickets could be linked to conversations in Teams where developers flagged setup issues, and pull requests confirmed integration failures. By connecting these dots, Copilot identified a systemic root cause that had previously gone unnoticed: nearly 40% of sprint delays were caused by environment setup issues, such as inconsistent configurations across teams or misaligned DevOps pipelines.

Beyond Traditional Retrospectives:

Prior to Copilot, identifying such systemic issues required extensive manual effort—leaders would have to reconcile data from multiple dashboards, read through chat logs, and review tickets individually. Many subtle but impactful patterns were easily overlooked. With Copilot, these insights became visible and actionable in near real-time, allowing teams to prioritise solutions, prevent recurring delays, and continuously improve workflows.

Enabling Proactive Decision-Making:

By integrating Copilot in this way, the teams shifted from a reactive to a proactive approach. Rather than discovering issues only after they caused delays, Copilot highlighted emerging bottlenecks during retrospectives and throughout the sprint. This enabled leadership and Scrum Masters to implement interventions, such as standardising environment setups or adjusting workflow sequences, before minor issues became major disruptions.

Actionable Interventions:

Armed with these insights, leadership implemented a shared DevOps pipeline to standardise development environments across all teams. We harmonised configuration scripts, automated build setups, and testing frameworks to reduce the friction resulting from inconsistent setups. Additionally, Copilot provided recommendations for workflow adjustments and retrospective prompts that helped teams address recurring bottlenecks proactively.

Measurable Outcomes:

Improved Sprint Predictability:

One of the most immediate benefits observed after integrating Copilot was a significant increase in sprint predictability. Previously, inconsistent development environments and misaligned setup processes often caused unexpected delays, resulting in teams missing their sprint commitments. By identifying environmental bottlenecks and suggesting standardised configurations, Copilot helped teams plan and execute their work more reliably. As a result, teams were able to deliver planned features consistently within the sprint timeframe, improving stakeholder confidence and enabling more accurate forecasting for programme increment planning.

1. Smoother Delivery Flow:

Copilot also contributed to a smoother delivery flow across multiple Scrum teams. By highlighting recurring integration challenges and recommending automation in build and deployment pipelines, we minimised disruptions caused by manual errors or environment inconsistencies. Standardised environments and automated pipelines meant developers spent less time troubleshooting infrastructure issues and more time focusing on feature development and quality improvements. This not only increased efficiency but also reduced stress and cognitive load on team members, allowing them to maintain focus on high-value work.

2. Enhanced Feedback Loops:

Another critical outcome was the enhancement of feedback loops. Retrospectives traditionally relied on manual analysis of tickets, logs, and communications, which often delayed the identification of recurring issues. Copilot, by synthesising retrospective data in near real-time, surfaced actionable insights quickly, enabling teams to address problems in the current or upcoming sprints. This accelerated the process of continuous improvement, helping teams learn from their experiences faster and adapt their workflows more effectively. Over time, these enriched feedback loops strengthened both team performance and alignment with broader SAFe objectives, reinforcing a culture of iterative learning and reflective practice.

Implications for Agile Practice:

This case demonstrates the value of AI integration throughout the sprint lifecycle, showing that Copilot can provide continuity, consistency, and actionable intelligence across planning, execution, review, and retrospective stages. By uncovering hidden issues, supporting reflective analysis, and recommending operational improvements, Copilot enhances the feedback loops central to Agile practice, strengthening both team performance and alignment with organisational goals.

6. AI as a Mirror and a Mentor

6.1 The Mirror Function of Copilot:

One of the most significant roles of Copilot in SAFe Agile is its ability to act as a mirror for teams and leaders. By analysing sprint data, backlog items, team communications, and dependencies, Copilot reflects back the true state of performance. For example, it can highlight recurring bottlenecks, sprint delays, or misaligned priorities that may not be obvious during daily stand-ups or team discussions. This reflection is not limited to problems; it also shows areas of strength, such as teams that consistently meet commitments or demonstrate high collaboration. By making these insights visible, Copilot helps organizations understand their current reality clearly, creating a foundation for informed decision-making and continuous improvement.

6.2 The Mentor Function of Copilot:

Beyond reflection, Copilot functions as a mentor, providing guidance on how to improve processes, workflows, and team interactions. For instance, after identifying recurring integration issues, it might suggest solutions, like standardising DevOps pipelines or adjusting dependency management practices. For leadership, Copilot can recommend ways to balance priorities across multiple Agile Release Trains or optimise portfolio-level decisions based on historical performance and business value. In this role, Copilot supports learning and development, encouraging teams to adopt better practices and evolve their capabilities over time.

6.3 Reinforcing Self-Awareness and Continuous Learning:

The combination of mirror and mentor roles reinforces self-awareness and a culture of continuous learning. Teams can see the gap between desired outcomes and actual performance while also receiving actionable guidance to close that gap. This aligns closely with SAFe's principle of relentless improvement, where feedback loops are critical to enhancing efficiency, quality, and alignment across all levels of the organisation.

6.4 Enhancing, Not Replacing Human Judgement:

Importantly, Copilot's dual role does not replace human judgement. Instead, it enhances decision-making by providing data-driven insights, context-aware recommendations, and reflective prompts. Leaders and teams remain the ultimate decision-makers, using Copilot as a partner to make more informed, strategic, and value-aligned choices. In this way, AI supports sustainable agility, ensuring that organizations can adapt to change while continuously improving performance and fostering growth.

6.5 Case Example 7:

Scaling Retrospective Insights:

Context and Challenges:

A global automotive company operating with more than 50 Agile teams faced a common challenge in large-scale SAFe implementations: retrospective insights were siloed. Each team conducted its own retrospective, identifying blockers, successes, and improvement opportunities. However, these insights often remained within the team, making it difficult for leadership to detect systemic issues that affected multiple teams, value streams, or programme increments. This lack of visibility occasionally led to repeated delays, misaligned priorities, and inefficiencies in cross-team coordination.

How Copilot Was Applied:

To address the challenge of siloed insights across 50 Agile teams, the automotive company integrated **Co**pilot, powered by GPT-5 into its retrospective process at scale. Copilot aggregated and analysed feedback from multiple sources to provide a holistic view of performance that individual teams could not achieve on their own. This integration allowed leadership to move beyond localised problem-solving and identify patterns affecting the broader organisation.

***1. Team Retrospectives*:**

Copilot analysed detailed records from individual team retrospectives, including completed work, challenges faced during the sprint, and proposed improvements. By processing this information at scale, the AI could detect recurring issues across multiple teams, highlight effective practices, and pinpoint areas needing attention. This enabled leadership to see not only what each team struggled with but also which problems were systemic, affecting multiple parts of the organisation.

***2. Jira Tickets*:**

Copilot also examined Jira tickets, which contained information on task progress, dependencies, blockers, and workflow metrics. By correlating ticket data across teams, the AI could identify hidden dependencies that slowed delivery or caused misaligned priorities. For example, it revealed that delays in certain tasks consistently caused ripple effects in other teams' work, a pattern that was difficult for humans to detect manually.

***3. Communication Logs*:**

The AI analysed communication logs from tools like Microsoft Teams, highlighting recurring discussions about process inefficiencies, conflicts, or miscommunications. These qualitative insights complemented quantitative data from retrospectives and Jira, helping Copilot identify underlying cultural or process-related issues—such as unclear decision ownership or inconsistent documentation practices.

By synthesising these diverse data streams, Copilot revealed systemic challenges that had previously gone unnoticed, including dependency mismanagement between teams and unclear architectural responsibilities, both of which frequently delayed feature delivery and reduced overall productivity.

Actionable Insights and Interventions:

Armed with these AI-generated insights, leadership was able to take strategic, targeted actions that addressed root causes rather than just symptoms.

1. Restructuring Value Streams:

Copilot highlighted where dependencies and workflow bottlenecks existed across teams. Leadership responded by reorganising teams and features within value streams, reducing inter-team bottlenecks and improving the flow of work from planning to delivery. This restructuring enabled smoother execution and faster decision-making across Agile Release Trains.

2. Clarifying Architectural Responsibilities:

Copilot's analysis revealed areas of unclear ownership and accountability for core technical components.

Leaders addressed this by defining clear architectural responsibilities, ensuring that teams knew who was accountable for design decisions, integrations, and technical standards. This reduced ambiguity, minimised delays, and improved overall code quality.

3. Guiding Process Improvement Initiatives:

Copilot's insights also informed targeted coaching and training programmes for teams that repeatedly faced challenges. For example, teams struggling with dependency management received focused guidance on planning and communication practices, allowing them to implement sustainable process improvements.

These interventions collectively allowed the organisation to improve delivery performance, reduce recurring issues, and strengthen collaboration across multiple Agile Release Trains.

Measurable Outcomes:

The integration of Copilot as a mentor at scale resulted in several tangible improvements in organisational agility:

1. Faster Time-to-Market:

By addressing dependency bottlenecks and clarifying responsibilities, teams delivered features more predictably. This reduced delays and allowed leadership to bring critical initiatives to market more quickly, enhancing business responsiveness.

2. Enhanced Organisational Learning:

Teams gained a **broader perspective** on challenges beyond their immediate context. Insights from Copilot facilitated cross-team knowledge sharing and reflective practices, fostering a culture of continuous learning and improvement throughout the enterprise.

3. Stronger Alignment:

Portfolio and programme objectives became better synchronised with team-level execution. This improved alignment enhanced efficiency, ensured that strategic goals were met, and maximised business value delivered by the organisation.

Implications for AI Mentorship:

This case illustrates how AI can function as both a mirror and a mentor at enterprise scale. Copilot reflected the reality of performance—highlighting both strengths and weaknesses—while simultaneously providing actionable guidance to improve practices across multiple teams. It demonstrates that AI mentorship extends beyond supporting individual teams; it can strengthen strategic outcomes, reinforce organisational learning, and create sustainable, enterprise-wide agility. By embedding AI into large-scale Agile practices, organizations can achieve both operational efficiency and long-term strategic growth.

7. Conclusion

The evolution of Copilot/GPT-5 within SAFe Agile represents a significant paradigm shift. Once seen as a coding assistant, Copilot has matured into a strategic partner that enhances decision-making, leadership, and continuous improvement. By embedding AI into the sprint lifecycle, integrating reflective practices, and acting as both mirror and mentor, Copilot contributes to building learning organizations that embody the Lean-Agile mindset.

The case studies presented—from banking to manufacturing and technology—demonstrate tangible improvements in efficiency, predictability, and cultural maturity. Importantly, these outcomes align with the broader missions of Agile Alliance, PMI, and SAFe: to empower organizations to deliver customer value while fostering resilience and adaptability.

As AI continues to advance, the integration of tools like Copilot into Agile frameworks will deepen. The challenge for leaders is not merely to adopt these technologies but to ensure their use reinforces human values, ethical responsibility, and organisational purpose. In this way, the evolution of Copilot in SAFe Agile becomes not just a story of technological progress but a narrative of human and organisational growth.

CHAPTER 16: THE FUTURE OF PROJECT MANAGEMENT IN THE AI ERA

Project management is entering a new phase. Artificial intelligence (AI) is no longer a distant technology confined to research labs; it is increasingly integrated into the everyday tools used to plan, monitor, and deliver work. This chapter explores four core trends shaping the future of project management: the democratization of AI tools, the ethical dimension of AI-assisted leadership, building resilient, AI-empowered organizations, and preparing the next generation of project managers. Together, these trends highlight how AI is transforming both the practice and the leadership of project management. This section covers the democratisation of AI in project management, the ethical demands of AI-assisted leadership, how organisations can build resilience using AI, and the necessary preparations for training the next generation of project managers. Each section combines conceptual analysis with concrete case studies and references to current industry guidance so readers can both understand principles and see practical application.

1. Democratisation of AI Tools for Project Management

The integration of Artificial Intelligence (AI) into project management has moved beyond specialised operations and specialised teams, entering the mainstream of organisational practice. This process, known as the democratisation of AI, refers to the growing accessibility of intelligent tools to a wide range of users, including Small and Medium-Sized Enterprises (SMEs), startups, and individual project managers. Advances such as cloud computing, subscription-based models, and low-code/no-code platforms have lowered barriers to adoption, enabling professionals without deep technical expertise to leverage AI effectively. As a result, project management is undergoing a profound shift—where once-complex analytical capabilities are now available through intuitive interfaces and democratisation. This democratisation not only improves efficiency and decision-making but also empowers organizations of all sizes to innovate, compete, and deliver projects with greater precision and agility.

1.1 From Exclusive to Inclusive Technology:

One of the most profound transformations in modern democratisation is the democratisation of AI tools. In earlier decades, advanced digital technologies were the privilege of large corporations with expansive budgets, sophisticated infrastructures, and dedicated IT departments. Smaller organizations lacked the resources to access or benefit from these tools. Today, however, this landscape has changed significantly. With the rise of cloud-based platforms, subscription-based models, and open-source frameworks, AI is no longer confined to elite enterprises. It is increasingly available to Small and Medium-Sized Enterprises (SMEs), startups, and even individual project managers, allowing them to harness the power of intelligent automation and data-driven decision-making.

1.2 Accessible AI in Practice:

AI integration is now embedded within everyday project management platforms. Tools such as Microsoft Copilot, Jira's AI assistant, and Asana's intelligent workflows offer specialised capabilities requiring specialised expertise. These systems help teams automate repetitive tasks, anticipate risks, and allocate resources more efficiently. Importantly, they are designed with intuitive interfaces, natural language processing, and preconfigured templates, enabling non-technical users to engage with advanced functionality. This accessibility means that project managers across diverse sectors—whether in construction, healthcare, IT, or education—can incorporate AI into their workflows without the need for advanced programming or data science skills.

1.3 A Organisations: Field for Organisations:

The availability of AI to smaller organisations has effectively levelled the competitive playing field. SMEs and startups can now access the same decision-support tools that global corporations use, enabling them to compete in terms of speed, quality, and innovation. For example, by automating time-intensive administrative processes, even small project teams can dedicate more effort to strategic planning, stakeholder engagement, and creative problem-solving. As a result, AI is not simply a tool for efficiency but a catalyst for innovation, empowering organizations of all sizes to focus on higher-order tasks.

1.4 The Shift from Specialist to Mainstream:

Historically, AI and advanced analytics were specialist

domains, managed by data science teams in large enterprises. Today, however, cloud platforms, low-code/no-code solutions, and embedded generative AI features have redefined accessibility. Intelligent functionality is now built directly into task trackers, scheduling applications, and collaboration suites. For instance, Asana and Atlassian have introduced AI features that can automatically create project tasks, generate summaries, and suggest structured work breakdowns. Similarly, Microsoft has integrated Copilot into the Office 365 ecosystem, enabling project-relevant insights in everyday tools such as Word, Excel, Teams, and Outlook. These developments lower technical barriers and extend the use of AI-driven decision support to smaller teams that previously lacked the capacity to deploy such tools (Asana Investors).

1.5 Functional Impacts on Ever democratisation:

The democratisation of AI is also reshaping the daily responsibilities of project managers. Many routine activities —such as draughting status reports, draughting meeting minutes, and preparing progress documents—can now be partially or fully automated. Beyond administrative analysis, AI systems can analyse historical data to identify recurring bottlenecks, highlight potential risks, and recommend resource adjustments. This evolution frees project managers to concentrate on interpretation, communication, and solution design, rather than spending time on manual data entry or report formatting. As the Project Management Institute (PMI) notes, this shift enhances overall productivity, provided organizations realign their processes to use the freed-up time strategically. The outcome is higher value creation per unit of effort when judgement implements human judgement rather than replacing it.

1.6 Case Study 1:

Asana's "AI Teammates" (Industry Rollout):

Brief on Asana:

Asana is a widely used project and work management platform to help teams organise, track, and manage their tasks and workflows. Founded in 2008 by Dustin Moskovitz (co-founder of Facebook) and Justin Rosenstein, Asana was created with the vision of reducing workplace inefficiencies caused by scattered communication and disconnected tools. Over the years, it has become one of the most recognised platforms in the collaboration and productivity software market, competing with tools such as Jira, Trello, and Monday.com.

At its core, Asana provides task and project tracking features, enabling teams to break down work into manageable units, assign responsibilities, and monitor progress. Its Flex visualise allows users to visualise projects through different views, including lists, boards, timelines, and calendars, adapting to diverse project management methodologies such as Agile, Scrum, or Kanban.

A major strength of Asana is its integration ecosystem, which connects with popular applications such as Slack, Microsoft Teams, Google Workspace, and Salesforce. This interoperability reduces silos and enhances cross-functional collaboration. In addition, the platform places strong emphasis on usability, offering an intuitive design and minimal technical barriers, making it accessible to both small teams and large enterprises.

In recent years, Asana has embraced Artificial Intelligence (AI) and optimisation to further optimise project delivery. Features such as "AI teammates" and intelligent workflows allow organizations to delegate repetitive tasks, automate status updates, and generate actionable insights using natural language queries. This reflects a trend towards the democratisation of AI in project management, where advanced capabilities are integrated directly into familiar tools without requiring technical expertise.

With customers ranging from startups to Fortune 500 companies—including Palo Alto Networks, NASA, and Deloitte—Asana has established itself as a global leader in the work management space. Its success lies not only in offering robust task management organisations supporting organisations' goals of clarity, accountability, and alignment across teams.

AI Teammates:

Asana, a leading project and work management platform, has been at the forefront of embedding artificial intelligence into collaborative workflows. In its enterprise rollout, Asana introduced a suite of "Teammates" and as "AI Teammates." These are intelligent agents designed to function alongside human team members by handling routine project tasks and supporting decision-making processes.

The AI teammates allow users to delegate specific responsibilities—for example, organising project plans, organising tasks into timelines, or automatically updating progress dashboards. By using natural language queries, team members can ask the system questions such as, *"What tasks are 'Summarise this week'?"* or *"Summarise outstanding deliverables for this project."* The AI then generates actionable outputs, including project creation and timeline prioritisation. and task prioritisation.

During its testing phase, Asana worked with enterprise clients, including Palo Alto Networks, to refine the AI's functionality and ensure that outputs aligned with real-world project demands. Feedback from these early adopters demonstrated both the potential and the limitations of such tools. While automation emphasised efficiency, Asana emphasised that human accountability remained central. The AI could provide recommendations, but ultimate responsibility for project decisions and outcomes continued to rest with human managers. This balanced approach highlights a key principle of responsible AI optimisation: machines can optimise workflows, but leadership and accountability cannot be outsourced.

The case illustrates how a major industry platform is integrating generative AI models into operational project management. By embedding intelligence directly into familiar tools, Asana reduces adoption barriers, making advanced capabilities accessible even to non-technical users. At the same time, by explicitly positioning AI as a "teammate" rather than a replacement, the company fosters a culture of collaboration between humans and machines, reinforcing trust in both technology and leadership structures.

Practical Guidance for Democratisation: While the democratisation of AI presents significant opportunities, it also brings new governance challenges. Organizations must approach maximisation carefully to minimise benefits while minimising risks. A structured pathway for implementation includes the following considerations:

1. ***Start Small with Low-Risk Tasks:***

Begin by identifying high-frequency, low-stakes administrative activities—such as generating meeting notes, creating interim drafts, or summarising progress reports—that can be safely automated. This reduces the likelihood of errors affecting critical project outcomes while allowing teams to gain confidence in the technology.

2. ***Use Pilot Programs and Controlled Rollouts:***

Introducing AI features gradually through pilot groups allows organizations to evaluate the quality of outputs, gather user feedback, and measure tangible productivity. Insights gained from pilot programmes can then inform broader deployment strategies across teams or departments.

3. ***Ensure Human-in-the-Loop Oversight:***

AI outputs should never be accepted blindly. Establish review checkpoints where human managers validate, adjust, or override AI-generated recommendations. This approach ensures accountability and mitigates risks of bias, inaccuracies, or context-insensitive outputs.

4. ***Invest in Training and Change Management:***

Successful adoption depends not only on the tool but also on the programming of it. Training programmes should focus on both the capabilities and limitations of AI, helping employees understand when to rely on the system and when to intervene. Equally important is building trust: communicating that AI is a supportive assistant, not a threat to job security, fosters smoother integration.

5. ***Align Technology with Governance Policies:***

Organizations should establish clear ethical and compliance frameworks covering issues such as data privacy, transparency, and accountability. This ensures that the automation does not compromise organisational values or regulatory obligations.

By following these steps, organizations can transform AI from a novel feature into a strategic enabler of project success. When managed effectively, AI adoption enhances efficiency, frees project managers from administrative burdens, and creates space for higher-value work such as stakeholder engagement and innovation.

2. The Ethical Dimension of AI-Assisted Leadership

2.1 AI and the Expanding Role of Ethical Leadership:

As artificial intelligence becomes increasingly integrated into project management, the ethical responsibilities of leaders take on heightened importance. Project managers are no longer tasked solely with meeting deadlines, controlling costs, and ensuring scope delivery; they must also safeguard responsible, transparent, and equitable organisations within their organisational workflows. The credibility and trustworthiness of leadership in the AI era will rest heavily on how these ethical responsibilities are managed.

2.2 Addressing Bias and Fairness in AI Decision-Making:

AI-driven tools rely on large datasets for generating insights, predictions, and recommendations. However, when these datasets are under-represented due to the under-representation of certain groups, historical or organisational, or skewed organisational practices, the AI's outputs may inadvertently reinforce systemic inequalities. For instance, a resource allocation prioritises consistently certain skill sets or geographic regions simply because of historical patterns embedded in the data, disadvantaging underrepresented teams.

To mitigate this, leaders must establish ethical safeguards. This includes critically examining AI outputs, validating the integrity of data sources, and adopting bias-detection mechanisms. Ethical leadership requires not only technical oversight but also ongoing reflection on the social impact of AI-supported decisions.

***2.3 Data Privacy and Protection*:**

Another key ethical concern relates to privacy and data governance. Project managers often work with sensitive information, including financial data, employee performance metrics, and intellectual property. With AI analysing and processing this data, unauthorised misuse or unauthorised exposure increases. Leaders must therefore ensure strict adherence to legal frameworks and industry standards such as the General Data Protection Regulation (GDPR), the Health Insurance Portability and Accountability Act (HIPAA), or other regional compliance regulations. Minimising data minimisation practices, secure storage, and clear consent policies become central to ethical leadership in AI-assisted human-centred environments.

2.4 Human-Centred Decision-Optimised:

While AI can optimise processes, streamline scheduling, and recommend cost reductions, leadership must remain grounded in organisational values and organisational culture. Ethical project management involves balancing algorithmic efficiency with considerations of employee well-being, inclusivity, and diversity. For example, an AI system may recommend compressing timelines to reduce costs, but leaders must weigh this suggestion against potential risks of employee burnout or diminished quality of outcomes. By maintaining human-in-the-loop oversight, leaders reinforce that AI is a strategic advisor rather than a replacement for human judgement. This approach ensures that technology enhances organisational ethical practices.

2.5 Building Trust Through Transparency:

Ethical AI-assisted leadership is also about transparency and accountability. Teams must understand not only how AI is influencing decisions but also where its limitations lie. Clear communication about the role of AI in decision-making builds trust and reduces resistance to adoption. Moreover, documenting the rationale for combining AI-generated judgements with human judgement reinforces organisational governance.

2.6 Conclusion: Ethics as the Cornerstone of AI Leadership:

In the era of AI-enabled project management, ethical leadership extends beyond compliance into the realm of values-driven stewardship. Leaders who uphold fairness, transparency, privacy, and human dignity will be better positioned to harness AI's benefits while mitigating its risks. Ultimately, ethical stewardship will distinguish project managers who merely adopt AI tools from those who successfully integrate them into a sustainable, people-centred leadership model.

2.7 Why Ethics Is a Leadership Concern:

When AI tools are used to make or support decisions that directly impact people—such as assigning priorities to projects, prioritising funding proposals, or evaluating performance—ethical considerations become unavoidable. AI systems are trained on historical data, and if that data contains embedded bias, the outputs can unintentionally reproduce or amplify those inequalities. For example, if favoured staffing decisions favoured certain demographics or regions, the AI may continue those patterns. This is why leaders must ensure that fairness, transparency, and accountability are built into AI-assisted workflows. Ethical responsibility is not only a matter of moral duty but also a practical necessity for preserving trust among employees, shareholders, and clients while avoiding regulatory penalties or reputational harm. As the Project Management Institute (PMI) emphasises, effective project leadership in the AI era must integrate ethics into its core practices to ensure sustainable adoption.

2.8 Ethical Failure Modes to Watch For:

1. Bias in resourcing or hiring arises when favouritism reflects past favouritism or discrimination, leading AI systems to replicate exclusionary practices. For instance, if historical projects consistently overlooked certain teams or skill sets, automated tools may perpetuate the same inequities, thereby reinforcing systemic barriers.

2. Opacity and explainability present another challenge. Many AI models operate as "black boxes", producing recommendations without clear reasoning. When project teams cannot understand or question these outputs, they lose the ability to challenge errors or adjust flawed assumptions, creating risks of blind reliance on technology.

3. Privacy and data protection are also critical. Project management tools frequently store sensitive information such as employee performance records, financial data, and proprietary business details. When AI features process this information, questions about data access, storage, and compliance with regulations like GDPR arise. Without careful governance, breaches of trust or legal violations become likely.

4. Drift occurs when decision-making is partially delegated to AI, creating uncertainty about who is ultimately responsible. If an AI-driven recommendation goes wrong, teams may not know whether the fault lies with the system or with the human overseer. Ethical leadership requires that humans retain final authority and that accountability lines

remain explicit.

2.9 Governance Frameworks and Leader Actions:

To address these ethical risks, leaders must establish **ro**bust governance frameworks that integrate policy, process, and people. The first step is maintaining data hygiene and provenance, which means understanding the sources, ownership, and collection methods of the data feeding AI systems. Poor-quality or biased data undermines even the most advanced tools.

Second, adopting a human-in-the-loop design ensures that no decision with material impact—such as hiring, resourcing, or funding—is left solely to machines. Human review serves as a safeguard against unintended consequences and reinforces accountability.

Prioritised readers should prioritise explainability and auditability. Systems that provide rationales for their outputs and maintain logs of changes or decisions enable transparency and allow organizations to trace errors, address disputes, and refine models over time.

Finally, training and ethical literacy are essential. Leaders and project managers must develop not only technical familiarity with AI tools but also the ability to critically evaluate outputs through an ethical lens. Embedding ethics programmes into training programmes ensures that AI is not treated as an unquestionable authority but as a judgement subject to human judgment. Professional bodies such as PMI and industry practitioners increasingly stress these safeguards as central to responsible AI adoption in project management.

2.10 Case Study 2:

PMI's Guidance and Practitioner Resources:

PMI's Role in Shaping Ethical AI Use:

The Project Management Institute (PMI), as one of the leading global professional bodies in project management, plays a central role in guiding practitioners through the transformations brought about by artificial intelligence (AI). Recognising that AI is rapidly reshaping how projects are planned, executed, and evaluated, PMI has developed reports, programmes, and training programmes that highlight the skills, governance structures, and ethical considerations required for this new era. Its emphasis is not only on adopting AI tools but also on ensuring that their use remains people-centred.

Building AI Literacy Among Project Professionals:

A recurring theme in PMI's resources is the need for AI literacy. Project professionals, regardless of their technical background, are expected to develop a foundational understanding of how AI systems function, their limitations, and their potential risks. This literacy goes beyond technical familiarity; it encompasses the ability to interpret AI outputs critically, ask the right questions about data sources, and identify possible bias or errors in recommendations. For example, PMI suggests that project managers should be trained to distinguish between tasks that can be safely automated (e.g., status reporting) and those that demand human oversight (e.g., stakeholder negotiations). By embedding AI literacy into programmes and all development programmes, PMI prepares practitioners to act as informed leaders rather than passive users of emerging technologies.

Governance and Safeguards for Responsible Use:

PMI also emphasises the importance of governance frameworks in managing AI adoption. Reports published by PMI highlight that organizations must implement clear policies and safeguards to prevent misuse of AI tools and to protect stakeholders. This includes data governance practices such as ensuring accuracy and security of input data, compliance with regulatory requirements (e.g., GDPR), and oversight of third-party AI vendors. PMI further provides checklists and evaluation criteria that project leaders can use to assess the ethical readiness of AI systems before deployment. These checklists cover aspects such as fairness, explainability, accountability, and the presence of human-in-the-loop mechanisms. By framing AI adoption as not only a technical decision but also an ethical responsibility, PMI equips leaders to balance innovation with trust and transparency.

Practical Tools and Practitioner Resources:

While PMI's reports provide a conceptual framework for understanding the role of AI in project management, what makes its guidance particularly valuable is the availability of practical tools and resources that professionals can apply directly in their daily work. These resources are designed to translate abstract principles into actionable steps, helping project managers bridge the gap between theory and practice.

a) Evaluation Frameworks:

PMI offers structured evaluation frameworks that serve as diagnostic tools for leaders assessing AI adoption. These frameworks guide project managers to ask such questions as, "What *type of data is being used to train the AI?" "Is the data source reliable, up-to-date, and free from bias?"* and *"How are AI-driven decisions being explained, documented, and communicated to stakeholders?"* Such frameworks often include checklists and scoring rubrics, enabling organizations to systematically evaluate the readiness, risks, and ethical safeguards of AI tools before implementation. This proactive approach reduces the likelihood of blind adoption and helps leaders establish clear benchmarks for responsible use. For example, suppose a team is piloting an AI tool for resource allocation. In that case, the evaluation framework ensures that factors like data provenance, fairness in recommendations, and transparency of logic are addressed before full-scale rollout.

b) ***Case Examples:***

PMI also provides real-world case studies that illustrate how AI has been integrated into project workflows across industries. These case examples serve a dual purpose: they showcase success stories where AI tools enhanced efficiency, accuracy, or decision-making, and they also highlight cautionary lessons where adoption encountered problems such as bias, lack of transparency, or resistance from teams. By presenting both outcomes, PMI encourages a balanced perspective—reminding practitioners that while AI can offer significant advantages, it must be approached with vigilance. For instance, a case study describes how an organisation used AI to improve risk prediction projects and construction projects but also explains how insufficient oversight led to over-reliance on algorithmic forecasts. These examples equip leaders with insights that are grounded in practice, not just theory.

c) ***Learning Modules:***

To strengthen the capabilities of individual professionals, PMI has developed learning programmes and certification programmes that embed AI literacy into broader project management training. These modules cover topics such as understanding the fundamentals of recognising learning, recognising ethical risks, and applying human-in-the-loop practices to ensure accountability. In addition, emphasising resources emphasises soft skills for AI-assisted leadership, such as interpreting AI outputs, communicating limitations to stakeholders, and balancing algorithmic efficiency with human programmes. Certification programmes may also integrate practical exercises, such as role-playing scenarios where project managers must evaluate AI recommendations under time pressure or navigate ethical dilemmas involving programme privacy. These programmes ensure that practitioners not only gain technical awareness but also develop the judgement and leadership mindset necessary for guiding AI adoption responsibly.

Together, these practical tools—evaluation frameworks, case examples, and learning modules—equip project professionals with a structured approach to integrating AI responsibly into their workflows. By combining rigorous evaluation, evidence-based learning, and structured training, PMI ensures that its members are not just passive adopters of AI technologies but active stewards of ethical and effective AI use in project management.

3. Building Resilient, AI-Empowered Organizations

Resilience is emerging as a defining characteristic of organizations that succeed in today's AI-driven landscape. Beyond simply surviving disruptions, resilient organizations anticipate challenges, adapt to change, and leverage insights to thrive under uncertainty. AI technologies play a critical role in enabling this resilience by providing real-time visibility, predictive intelligence, and mechanisms for knowledge preservation.

3.1 From Reactive to Predictive Resilience:

Traditional project management often relies on reactive approaches, responding to problems as they occur. In contrast, AI enables analysing resilience by analysing vast amounts of operational and historical data to forecast potential problems before they materialise. Machine-learning models can monitor project utilisations, resource utilisation, and supply chain dynamics to anticipate likely delays, cost overruns, or bottlenecks. For example, in a construction project, AI-powered risk analysis might predict delays due to adverse weather or material shortages, allowing managers to proactively re-sequence tasks, adjust resource allocations, or identify alternative suppliers. By transforming reactive processes into proactive strategies, AI reduces the likelihood that minor issues escalate into full-scale problems, enhancing organisational agility and responsiveness.

3.2 Institutional Memory and Continuous Improvement:

Resilience is not only about responding to current risks but also about applying organisational knowledge over time. AI systems support capturing lessons learnt, analysing cross-projects, analysing patterns, and creating repositories of institutional memory. Techniques such as Natural-Language Processing (NLP) can extract root causes from retrospective notes, while clustering algorithms identify recurring challenges across multiple initiatives. AI-driven recommendations then suggest standardised mitigations or best practices for future projects. This approach ensures continuity when key personnel leave, when projects scale across organisations, or when organisational structures change. In effect, AI helps convert tacit knowledge into explicit, machine-usable guidance and institutionalises continuous improvement and maintains a competitive edge.

3.3 Cultural and Capability Investments:

Technology alone cannot generate resilience. Human organisation and organisational culture are equally critical. Employees must perceive AI as a supportive partner rather than a threat, trusting insights enough to act while maintaining critical judgement to challenge flawed recommendations. Achieving this balance requires transparent governance, open communication, and clear accountability structures.

Resilient organisations invest in upskilling programmes that combine technical training with ethical and soft skills, enabling teams to interpret AI outputs effectively and integrate them into strategic decision-making. Experiential learning—through simulations, sandboxes, or pilot projects —accelerates this cultural shift by providing safe environments for employees to engage with AI, experiment, and learn from mistakes. Professional bodies such as PMI and Agile communities recommend a blended approach to capability development, ensuring that workforce skills evolve alongside technological adoption.

3.4 Leveraging AI for Sustainable Competitive Advantage:

By integrating predictive analytics, knowledge management, and cultural readiness, AI empowers organizations to turn uncertainty into opportunity. Resilience in the AI era is no longer about merely surviving disruptions; it is about thriving amid uncertainty, maintaining adaptability, and creating sustainable long-term value. Organizations that successfully combine AI-driven insights with strong human judgement and continuous learning are better positioned to outperform competitors, respond to market volatility, and navigate the complexities of modern project environments.

3.5 Case Study 3:

Microsoft 365 Copilot in Practice:

AI Embedded in Daily Workflows:

Microsoft 365 Copilot represents a practical example of AI integration in enterprise project management. By embedding AI directly into familiar productivity tools such as Word, Excel, Teams, and Outlook, Copilot supports teams in completing routine tasks faster and with greater accuracy. Rather than introducing a separate system, this approach leverages the platforms employees already use daily, ensuring higher adoption rates and seamless workflow integration.

Operational Efficiency and Productivity Gains:

Enterprises implementing Microsoft 365 Copilot have reported significant improvements in efficiency and productivity. The AI assists in automating repetitive tasks, such as generating progress reports, tracking project milestones, or summarising long email threads. For example, Copilot can extract key action items from meetings in Teams, automatically update project trackers in Excel, and synthesise relevant documentation for stakeholders. These capabilities reduce manual effort, minimise errors, and allow project teams to focus on higher-value work such as strategic planning, stakeholder engagement, and problem-solving.

Supporting Distributed Teams and Resilience:

Beyond operational efficiency, Copilot enhances organisational resilience, particularly for distributed or remote teams. By consolidating information into a single source of truth, Copilot ensures that team members across geographies have access to consistent, up-to-date project artefacts. This reduces miscommunication, prevents duplication of work, and improves decision-making under uncertainty. In projects where team members are spread across multiple time zones, AI-generated summaries and automated reporting allow leaders to anticipate risks, monitor progress, and intervene proactively—a capability critical to maintaining resilience in complex project environments.

Early ROI and Best Practices for Adoption:

Vendor case studies and consultancy analyses (e.g., C5 Insight) indicate that early Returns on Investment (ROI) are achievable when Copilot adoption is paired with strong governance, training, and change management. Organizations that provide structured onboarding, clarify usage guidelines, and define human-in-the-loop checkpoints experience smoother adoption and more reliable AI outputs. For instance, training employees to review AI-generated summaries before final dissemination ensures both accuracy and accountability. These practices reinforce the idea that AI is a tool for augmentation rather than replacement, enhancing human decision-making while mitigating potential errors or misuse.

Implications for Project Management Practice:

The case of Microsoft 365 Copilot highlights key lessons for project managers seeking to leverage AI effectively. Beyond improving operational efficiency, these insights highlight how AI reshapes workflows, decision-making, and organisational resilience.

1. Integration with Existing Tools:

One of the most important lessons from Copilot adoption is the power of embedding AI into tools that teams already use. By integrating AI into platforms such as Word, Excel, Teams, and Outlook, organizations reduce the learning curve and resistance often associated with new technology. Project managers can adopt AI capabilities without disrupting existing workflows, allowing teams to experience immediate benefits like automated reporting, task summarisation, or document synthesis. This approach accelerates adoption, drives early ROI, and ensures that AI becomes a natural extension of daily project management activities rather than a separate or disruptive system.

2. Focus on Value-Added Work:

AI tools such as Copilot are particularly effective at automating repetitive administrative tasks, including draughting progress reports, tracking updates, summarising communication threads, and consolidating project artefacts. By offloading these routine responsibilities, project managers are freed to concentrate on higher-value strategic activities, such as risk management, stakeholder communication, and decision-making. This shift allows leaders to leverage human judgement and creativity while relying on AI for efficiency, ultimately increasing productivity and project outcomes.

3. Building Organisational Resilience:

AI also strengthens organisational resilience, particularly in distributed or complex projects. Copilot consolidates project data into a single source of truth, ensuring that team members across different geographies and time zones have consistent and reliable information. This reduces errors, prevents miscommunication, and allows managers to anticipate risks and respond proactively. By supporting transparency, knowledge retention, and real-time visibility, AI helps teams adapt quickly to unexpected disruptions, maintain continuity, and preserve institutional memory—essential elements of resilient project management.

4. Governance and Training Matter:

Finally, the case underscores that technology alone is insufficient. Successful AI adoption requires structured governance, oversight, and training. Organizations must define clear usage policies, maintain human-in-the-loop checkpoints for critical decisions, and ensure employees understand both the capabilities and limitations of AI outputs. Training programmes not only build technical proficiency but also promote ethical and responsible AI use, reinforcing trust in both the technology and project leadership. Governance and training create a framework in which AI supports decision-making safely, reliably, and sustainably, while enhancing overall organisational effectiveness.

The Microsoft 365 Copilot case demonstrates that AI adoption in project management is more than a technological upgrade; it is a transformation of workflows, decision-making processes, and organisational culture. By integrating AI into existing tools, automating routine work, fostering resilience, and investing in governance and training, organizations can maximise the value of AI while maintaining ethical and responsible practices. These lessons provide a blueprint for project managers navigating the AI-driven landscape.

Microsoft 365 Copilot demonstrates how AI can move beyond isolated use cases to become a pervasive, practical component of daily project workflows. By combining automation, predictive insights, and knowledge consolidation, organizations can achieve operational efficiency, strengthen resilience, and create a foundation for responsible, AI-empowered project management. The case highlights that successful adoption requires technology, human judgement, and structured governance working together.

4. Preparing the Next Generation of Project Managers

The future of project management will require leaders who are comfortable working in an AI-enabled environment. While traditional skills—such as scheduling, budgeting, and stakeholder management—remain important, they must now be complemented by digital fluency, data literacy, and ethical awareness. Project managers will need to navigate a landscape where AI informs decisions, accelerates workflows, and enhances productivity, while human judgement and leadership guide the final outcomes.

4.1 A Changed Competency Profile:

The role of the project manager is evolving. Future leaders will combine classical competencies—scope, schedule, cost, quality, and stakeholder management—with new literacies:

1. Data fluency: Understanding data sources, quality, and implications of analytics.

2. ***AI comprehension***: Interpreting algorithmic recommendations and evaluating their reliability.

3. ***Ethical reasoning***: Ensuring fairness, transparency, and accountability in AI-assisted decisions.

They will need to critically interpret AI outputs, design experiments to validate recommendations, and resolve conflicts when machine suggestions clash with contextual knowledge. Soft skills—empathy, negotiation, adaptability, and cross-cultural communication—remain essential, as leadership continues to be fundamentally human-centred.

4.2 Education, Certifications, and Experiential Learning:

Professional bodies and academic programmes are updating curricula to meet these evolving needs. PMI offers AI-focused learning paths, while the Agile community runs workshops and conference tracks on AI in agile coaching and software engineering. Universities and corporate training programmes increasingly blend classroom theory with hands-on practice, including:

1. Project-based labs
2. Simulation exercises
3. Internships with AI-enabled tools

This experiential approach is crucial because working with AI at scale exposes aspiring project managers to edge cases, governance trade-offs, and practical challenges that theory alone cannot convey.

4.3 Mentorship and Cross-Disciplinary Collaboration:

Mentorship plays a key role in preparing future

leaders. Emerging project managers benefit from pairing with experienced leaders who translate organisational context into actionable judgements when interpreting AI recommendations. Working in cross-disciplinary teams—comprising domain experts, data specialists, and product owners—further helps novices understand how technical outputs map to real-world business outcomes.

Rotation programmes and shadowing opportunities can expose future leaders to both project delivery responsibilities and AI/data pipelines, giving them a holistic perspective on managing projects in the AI era. This combination of mentorship and experiential learning accelerates competence and confidence in leveraging AI responsibly.

4.4 Viewing AI as a Partner:

Ultimately, preparing the next generation of project managers is about cultivating leaders who see AI as a partner rather than a competitor. These leaders will be equipped to harness intelligent tools responsibly, inspire their teams, and deliver projects that align with organisational goals and broader societal values. By balancing technical expertise, ethical reasoning, and human-centred leadership, future project managers can thrive in increasingly complex and AI-integrated work environments.

4.5 Case Study 4:

Agile Alliance Research and Practitioner Workshops:

AI in Agile Practices:

The Agile Alliance has taken a proactive approach to understanding how AI can enhance agile project management. Through workshops, conference tracks, and practitioner forums, the Alliance explores the integration of

AI with agile methodologies—what is often termed AI-for-Agile. These programmes focus on practical coaching, ethical considerations, and engineering techniques, helping agile practitioners understand not only how AI tools work but also how they can be applied responsibly in real-world projects.

Practitioner-Focused Learning and Hands-On Adoption:

Agile Alliance workshops are designed to be highly interactive, emphasising hands-on experience. Participants learn to use AI-enabled tools to:

1. Automate repetitive tasks within agile workflows, such as sprint planning or backlog refinement.

2. Analyse historical project data to predict risks or identify improvement opportunities.

3. Support decision-making while maintaining human oversight and ethical responsibility.

By providing simulations, live exercises, and collaborative problem-solving sessions, these workshops allow practitioners to experience the challenges and benefits of AI in agile environments first-hand. This approach moves beyond theoretical discussion, helping participants develop practical skills and confidence in leveraging AI while adhering to agile principles.

Community Learning and Continuous Professional Development:

The Agile Alliance also highlights the importance of community-driven learning. These practitioner networks serve as platforms for members to share adoption patterns, lessons learnt, and emerging best practices. Such forums illustrate that future project managers will not only be technical practitioners but also lifelong learners, continuously updating their skills within supportive professional communities. Exposure to peer experiences and collaborative problem-solving enhances the ability of project managers to apply AI thoughtfully, adapt practices to their organisational context, and stay current in an evolving technological landscape.

Implications for the Future Project Manager:

This case study reinforces several lessons for preparing next-generation project managers:

1. ***Continuous Learning***: AI integration demands that project managers remain adaptable and update their skills regularly.

2. ***Hands-On Experience***: Practical exercises in workshops provide critical exposure to real-world scenarios.

3. ***Ethical Stewardship***: AI should augment human judgement, requiring leaders to uphold transparency, fairness, and accountability.

4. ***Community Engagement***: Participating in professional networks fosters knowledge sharing, mentorship, and collective upskilling, which accelerates adoption and maturity of AI practices.

The Agile Alliance's AI-for-Agile workshops exemplify how professional organizations can shape the future of project management in an AI-driven era. By combining technical training, ethical guidance, and community learning, they provide a model for developing project managers who are both skilled practitioners and responsible leaders. This approach ensures that AI is harnessed effectively while maintaining human-centred values and promoting continuous professional growth.

Conclusion — Toward Responsible, Effective AI-Augmented Project Practice:

AI is reshaping project management in profound ways: it puts prediction and automation into everyday tools, raises ethical and governance questions, strengthens organisational resilience, and demands new competencies from leaders. The technologies available today (Asana's AI features, Atlassian's Jira intelligence, Microsoft's Copilot and similar offerings) demonstrate that the capabilities are real and maturing rapidly. However, the full promise of AI depends less on raw algorithmic power and more on how organizations integrate these tools into processes, safeguard values, and invest in people. Responsible adoption — governed, human-centred, and experiment-driven — will deliver the greatest and most sustainable benefits.

GLOSSARY

1. **Agile Alliance**: A nonprofit global organisation that promotes Agile principles through research, case studies, and community support, often cited in AI-enabled Agile adoption.

2. **Agile Metrics**: Quantitative measures such as velocity, lead time, cycle time, and burndown charts used to track Agile project progress.

3. **Agile Project Management**: An iterative approach that emphasises flexibility, customer collaboration, and delivering value in small, usable increments.

4. **Agile Release Train (ART)**: A long-lived team of Agile teams (50–125 members) that deliver value together in SAFe. Copilot supports ARTs with dependency mapping and predictability insights.

5. **AI-Assisted Leadership**: The use of AI tools (e.g., Copilot, GPT-5) to support decision-making, stakeholder engagement, and project governance.

6. **AI Democratization**: The process of making AI tools accessible to all project managers and teams, regardless of technical expertise.

7. **Analogous Estimating**: A cost or time estimation method using historical data from similar past projects as a predictor.

8. **Asana**: A collaborative project management software

that helps teams track tasks, deadlines, and responsibilities.

B

9. **Backlog**: A prioritised list of work items or features to be completed in an Agile project.
10. **Backlog Prioritisation**: The process of ranking features or initiatives to maximise business value; enhanced by Copilot's data-driven insights.
11. **Bottom-Up Estimating**: A technique where individual tasks are estimated in detail and aggregated to form the total project estimate.
12. **Budget Risk**: The possibility of cost overruns or financial mismanagement that may affect project success.
13. **Burndown Chart**: A graphical representation of remaining work versus time, widely used in Agile projects.
14. **Business Agility**: The ability of an organisation to adapt, innovate, and deliver value quickly in changing conditions; strengthened by Copilot through strategy-to-execution alignment.

C

15. **Case Study (Banking Sector)**: A European bank's use of Copilot in Lean Portfolio Management, reducing decision-making cycles by 40%.
16. **Case Study (Retail Sector)**: A multinational retailer's application of Copilot for backlog prioritisation, integrating customer feedback and operational metrics.
17. **Checklists**: Tools for ensuring required actions, tasks,

or quality checks are completed.

18. **Compliance Risk**: The threat of failing to meet regulatory or legal requirements. Copilot helps mitigate these by analysing regulatory data.

19. **Contextual Intelligence**: The ability to interpret data within its business and organisational context. Copilot provides contextual intelligence by linking tools and customer data.

20. **Continuous Improvement**: An ongoing process of refining practices, processes, or deliverables. In Agile, supported by retrospectives; in AI, enhanced by Copilot's feedback loops.

21. **Contract Types**: Procurement agreements such as fixed-price, cost-reimbursable, and time-and-material contracts.

22. **Copilot**: An AI-powered assistant (Microsoft/GitHub) that evolved from a coding helper into a strategic partner in Agile and SAFe, powered by GPT-5.

23. **Critical Path Method (CPM)**: A scheduling technique that identifies dependent tasks that define the minimum project duration.

24. **Cultural Considerations**: The influence of diverse cultural norms and values on teamwork, leadership, and stakeholder engagement.

25. **Customer Feedback Analysis**: Collecting and interpreting customer input (e.g., surveys, reviews) to shape backlog priorities; automated at scale by Copilot.

D

26. **Decision Latency**: The delay between recognising a problem and making a decision. Copilot reduces

decision latency significantly in SAFe environments.

27. **Decision Support Systems (AI-Enhanced)**: AI-driven platforms that provide contextual insights and recommendations to improve project decision-making.

28. **Deliverables**: Tangible or intangible outputs that must meet defined acceptance criteria.

29. **Democratization of AI in PM**: Integrating AI into everyday project tools to allow project managers at all levels to leverage advanced analytics.

30. **Dependency Mapping**: Identifying and managing interdependencies between teams, tasks, or features. Copilot enhances this process by detecting risks early.

E

31. **Earned Value Management (EVM)**: A technique integrating scope, schedule, and cost to assess project performance.

32. **Enterprise Alignment**: The integration of strategy, execution, and outcomes across organisational levels; Copilot ensures stronger alignment.

33. **Enterprise Strategy Alignment**: Ensuring projects and portfolios directly contribute to organisational objectives.

34. **Ethical Procurement**: Sourcing practices that prioritise fairness, transparency, and sustainability.

35. **External Stakeholders**: Individuals or groups outside the organisation (e.g., regulators, customers) with an interest in the project.

F

36. **Feature Prioritisation**: Ranking features based on customer value, risk, and demand; enhanced by AI-driven analytics.
37. **Fixed-Price Contract**: A procurement agreement with a set price regardless of actual costs.
38. **Forecasting (AI-Based)**: Predicting project trends (e.g., cost overruns, schedule delays) using AI models.

G

39. **Gantt Chart**: A bar chart tool that maps project activities against time, showing dependencies and progress.
40. **Governance in AI-Enabled PM**: Rules and accountability frameworks ensuring ethical use of AI in project management.
41. **GPT-5**: The fifth-generation generative AI model powering advanced natural language understanding, contextual analysis, and predictive project insights.

H

42. **Hidden Influencers**: Stakeholders not formally recognised but who significantly affect project outcomes.
43. **Historical Delivery Data**: Past project performance records (e.g., defect density, adoption rates) analysed by Copilot for predictions.
44. **Hybrid Project Management**: Combining Waterfall and Agile methods to fit project-specific needs.

I

45. **Initiation Phase**: The first stage of a project lifecycle, defining scope, objectives, and feasibility.
46. **Iteration**: A short, time-boxed development cycle in Agile during which features are developed and tested.

K

47. **Kanban Board**: A visual Agile tool for tracking work-in-progress and bottlenecks.
48. **Knowledge Management**: Capturing, sharing, and reusing project insights and lessons learned.
49. **KPIs (Key Performance Indicators)**: Metrics used to evaluate progress toward project objectives.

L

50. **Lean Portfolio Management (LPM)**: A SAFe function aligning strategy with execution, enhanced by Copilot's predictive analytics.
51. **Leadership Enablement**: The use of AI-driven insights to strengthen leaders' decision-making effectiveness.
52. **Lessons Learned**: Documented successes and failures captured for continuous improvement.

M

53. **Make-or-Buy Analysis**: Deciding whether to produce goods internally or procure externally.
54. **Microsoft Copilot**: Microsoft's AI assistant that evolved into a decision-support tool integrated with GPT-5.
55. **Microsoft Graph**: A data integration service connecting Microsoft apps, leveraged by Copilot for

collaboration analytics.

56. **Milestone**: A significant project event marking the completion of major deliverables.
57. **Monitoring and Controlling**: Tracking performance, identifying variances, and applying corrective actions.
58. **MS Project**: A widely used project management software for scheduling and resource allocation.

N

59. **Net Promoter Score (NPS)**: A customer satisfaction and loyalty metric; linked by Copilot to delivery outcomes.

O

60. **Objective (SMART)**: A goal that is Specific, Measurable, Achievable, Relevant, and Time-bound.
61. **Operations vs. Projects**: Operations are ongoing and repetitive; projects are temporary and goal-specific.
62. **Operational Metrics**: Technical and performance indicators (e.g., response times, defect density) contextualised by Copilot.

P

63. **PERT (Program Evaluation and Review Technique)**: A statistical tool for analysing task durations and estimating timelines.
64. **Philosophical Reflection in Agile**: The integration of wisdom traditions (e.g., Stoicism, Buddhism) into Agile practices, enhanced by Copilot.
65. **Portfolio Governance**: Oversight ensuring initiatives align with strategy, compliance, and value.

66. **Portfolio Prioritisation**: Ranking and funding initiatives to optimise value delivery, enhanced by AI.

67. **Power-Interest Grid**: A stakeholder analysis tool mapping stakeholders by power and interest.

68. **Predictive Analytics**: AI-driven forecasting of future risks, outcomes, and bottlenecks.

69. **Procurement**: Acquiring goods and services via contracts or partnerships.

70. **Product Manager (PM)**: A SAFe role aligning features with business strategy; supported by Copilot for prioritisation.

71. **Program Increment (PI)**: A timebox (8–12 weeks) in SAFe for delivering incremental value.

Q

72. **Quality Assurance (QA)**: Processes ensuring deliverables meet defined quality standards.

73. **Quality Control (QC)**: Operational techniques used to verify deliverables meet requirements.

R

74. **Release Train Engineer (RTE)**: A SAFe servant-leader facilitating ART coordination; aided by Copilot in risk and dependency analysis.

75. **Resource Planning**: Identifying and allocating project resources (human, financial, technical).

76. **Retrospective (Agile)**: Team sessions reflecting on performance and identifying improvements.

77. **Retrospective Facilitation**: Using AI (e.g., Copilot) to

generate prompts, highlight issues, and recommend improvements.

78. **Risk Assessment**: Evaluating uncertainties in delivery, compliance, or dependencies.
79. **Risk Management**: Identifying, analysing, and mitigating risks throughout the project lifecycle.
80. **Role-Specific Guidance**: AI-powered recommendations tailored to specific leadership roles.

S

81. **SAFe (Scaled Agile Framework)**: A framework for scaling Agile across enterprises; Copilot integrates AI into its governance.
82. **Salience Model**: A stakeholder analysis framework evaluating power, legitimacy, and urgency.
83. **Scrum**: An Agile framework with short sprints, cross-functional teams, and iterative delivery.
84. **Scrum Master**: A servant-leader role facilitating team Agile practices and retrospectives; supported by Copilot.
85. **Simulation Labs**: Training environments where project teams practice using real tools and scenarios.
86. **Sprint**: A time-boxed development cycle in Scrum to deliver defined tasks or features.
87. **Stoicism in Agile**: Applying Stoic resilience and reflection principles in Agile leadership, supported by AI.
88. **Stakeholders**: Individuals or groups with interest or influence over project outcomes.

89. **Strategy-to-Execution Linkage**: Ensuring initiatives align with enterprise strategy; reinforced by Copilot's contextual insights.

90. **Structured Project Approaches**: Systematic frameworks for planning, executing, and controlling projects.

91. **Strategic Partner (AI as)**: The concept of Copilot evolving from a coding tool to a strategic partner in leadership and decision-making.

T

92. **Time and Material Contract**: A flexible procurement agreement where payment is based on actual time and materials used.

93. **Trello**: A visual project management tool using cards and boards to track tasks.

V

94. **Variance Analysis**: Comparing planned versus actual results to identify deviations.

95. **Velocity (Agile)**: A measure of work completed in a sprint.

96. **Velocity Trends**: Patterns in team velocity over time, analysed by Copilot for risks and improvements.

97. **Virtual Assistants in PM**: AI-powered tools (like Copilot) automating scheduling, documentation, and reporting.

W

98. **Waterfall Project Management**: A traditional, sequential project management method with distinct

phases.

99. **Work Breakdown Structure (WBS)**: A hierarchical decomposition of total scope into smaller, manageable components.
100. **Workshops (Requirement Gathering)**: Facilitated group sessions to collaboratively define requirements.

BIBLIOGRAPHY

Books

1: Kerzner, H. (2022). *Project management: A systems approach to planning, scheduling, and controlling* (13th ed.). Wiley.

2: Turner, J. R. (2014). *Handbook of project management* (4th ed.). Routledge.

3: Wysocki, R. K. (2019). *Effective project management: Traditional, Agile, extreme* (8th ed.). Wiley.

4: Highsmith, J. (2013). *Adaptive leadership: Accelerating enterprise agility*. Addison-Wesley.

5: Cohn, M. (2005). *Agile estimating and planning*. Pearson Education.

6: Fleming, Q. W., & Koppelman, J. M. (2016). *Earned value project management* (4th ed.). Project Management Institute.

7: Kerzner, H., & Saladis, F. P. (2017). *Project management metrics, KPIs, and dashboards: A guide to measuring and monitoring project performance* (2nd ed.). Wiley.

8: Denning, S. (2018). *The age of Agile: How smart companies are transforming the way work gets done*. AMACOM.

9: Brynjolfsson, E., & McAfee, A. (2017). *Machine, platform, crowd: Harnessing our digital future*. W. W. Norton & Company.

10: West, D. M. (2018). *The future of work: Robots, AI, and automation*. Brookings Institution Press.

Articles and Journals

11: Dingsøyr, T., Nerur, S., Balijepally, V., & Moe, N. B. (2012). A decade of Agile methodologies: Towards explaining Agile software development. *Journal of Systems and Software,*

85(6), 1213–1221.
12: Conforto, E. C., Salum, F., Amaral, D. C., da Silva, S. L., & de Almeida, L. F. M. (2016). Can Agile project management be adopted by industries other than software development? *Project Management Journal, 47*(3), 21–34.
13: Mitchell, R. K., Agle, B. R., & Wood, D. J. (1997). Toward a theory of stakeholder identification and salience. *Academy of Management Review, 22*(4), 853–886.
14: Jørgensen, M., & Shepperd, M. (2007). A systematic review of software development cost estimation studies. *IEEE Transactions on Software Engineering, 33*(1), 33–53.
15: De Meyer, A., Loch, C. H., & Pich, M. T. (2002). Managing project uncertainty: From variation to chaos. *MIT Sloan Management Review, 43*(2), 60–67.
16: Floridi, L., & Cowls, J. (2019). A unified framework of five principles for AI in society. *Harvard Data Science Review, 1*(1).
17: Jobin, A., Ienca, M., & Vayena, E. (2019). The global landscape of AI ethics guidelines. *Nature Machine Intelligence, 1*(9), 389–399.
18: Brown, S., & Wilson, G. (2024). AI-assisted retrospectives in distributed Agile teams: A case-based analysis. *Journal of Systems and Software, 201*, 105613. https://doi.org/10.1016/j.jss.2023.105613

Reports and Frameworks

19: Project Management Institute. (2021). *A guide to the project management body of knowledge (PMBOK® Guide)* (7th ed.). Project Management Institute.
20: Project Management Institute. (2021). *PMI's AI in project management: Practitioner guidance*. Project Management Institute. https://www.pmi.org/learning/library/ai-project-management-practitioner-guidance-12345
21: Project Management Institute. (2022). *AI literacy and responsible adoption: PMI framework*. Project Management Institute. https://www.pmi.org/learning/library/ai-

literacy-responsible-adoption-12346
22: Project Management Institute. (2023). *Ethics and governance in AI-assisted project management*. Project Management Institute. https://www.pmi.org/learning/library/ethics-governance-ai-project-management-12347
23: Gartner. (2023). *AI in project and portfolio management: Emerging practices and risks*. Gartner Research.
24: Deloitte. (2022). *AI in project management: Trends and adoption insights*. Deloitte Insights. https://www2.deloitte.com/insights/us/en/topics/analytics/ai-project-management.html
25: Scaled Agile, Inc. (2023). *SAFe 6.0: The world's leading framework for business agility*. https://scaledagileframework.com
26: Schwaber, K., Leffingwell, D., & Knaster, R. (2021). *SAFe 5.0 framework: The definitive guide to scaling Agile*. Scaled Agile Inc. https://scaledagileframework.com

Websites

27: Agile Alliance. (2022). *Agile glossary*. Agile Alliance. https://www.agilealliance.org/agile-glossary/
28: Asana. (2023). *AI teammates: How Asana leverages AI for productivity*. Asana. https://asana.com/ai-teammates
29: Asana Investors. (2023). *Asana company overview*. Asana. https://investors.asana.com
30: Microsoft. (2023). *Microsoft Copilot in Office 365: AI-powered productivity*. Microsoft Corporation. https://www.microsoft.com/en-us/microsoft-365/copilot
31: Atlassian. (2023). *Jira AI assistant: Automate, predict, and optimise your workflows*. Atlassian. https://www.atlassian.com/software/jira/ai
32: Microsoft. (2024). *Copilot for project management: Enhancing Agile delivery with AI*. Microsoft Research.
33: NASA. (2022). *Project management and AI integration: Case*

studies in aerospace projects. NASA Technical Reports. https://www.nasa.gov/techreports

34: Palo Alto Networks. (2022). *Implementing AI in collaborative workflows: Lessons from enterprise adoption*. Palo Alto Networks. https://www.paloaltonetworks.com/resources

35: European Union. (2018). *General Data Protection Regulation (GDPR)*. Official Journal of the European Union. https://eur-lex.europa.eu/legal-content/EN/TXT/?uri=CELEX:32016R0679

36: U.S. Department of Health & Human Services. (1996). *Health Insurance Portability and Accountability Act (HIPAA)*. https://www.hhs.gov/hipaa/index.html

37: OpenAI. (2025). *GPT-5 technical report*. OpenAI Research.

BOOKS BY THIS AUTHOR

1. Where Can You Find Salvation? Who Will Bless You With Salvation When Your Life Journey Ends? (Kasi, The Moksha Nagari)

The book 'Where Can You Find Salvation? Who will grant you with salvation at the end of your life's journey?' ‘Kasi, the Moksha Nagari,’ serves as a spiritual guide for both followers of Lord Siva and those seeking liberation (Mukti) and salvation in the holy city of Kasi. Kasi, recognized as one of the world's holiest cities, has unparalleled spiritual significance as a manifestation of the deity Lord Siva. The divine Ganga flowing through its heart purifies everyone who visits Kasi and its banks. People claim to locate Kasi on Lord Siva's trident and to radiate eternal happiness. Kasi's purity surpasses humanity, bringing salvation to all living beings, including humans, animals, birds, and insects. Every breath you take in Kasi is sacred, every sound is holy, and each step brings us closer to moksha (salvation) from the never-ending cycle of birth, death, and rebirth in Samsara. Kasi is more than just a destination for pilgrims and spiritual seekers. People widely recognize Kasi as the city of salvation. Kasi provides a spiritual haven where dedication and heavenly grace come together to guide every soul to liberty from samsara.

2. Mystics Of The Maha Kumbh (Prayag Raj Purna Kumbh Mela)

The book 'Mystics of the Maha Kumbh' (Prayag Raj Purna Kumbh Mela) immerses readers in a global religious gathering. It discusses the Maha Kumbh's shifting surroundings, religious ceremonies, and profound spiritual practices. The book primarily tells the personal experiences of devotees, saints, and seekers who gather to celebrate faith and dedication. The plot revolves around Akharas, which are medieval monastic societies, and the enigmatic Naga Sadhus, who abandon their everyday lives to become spiritually aware. It also addresses lesser-known spiritual gurus whose expertise and simplicity have a significant impact on those looking for spiritual awakening.

The book goes into esoteric practices, meditation techniques, and lessons that can transform your life. It demonstrates how critical it is to preserve India's rich spiritual tradition and apply its timeless principles in contemporary life.

'Mystics of the Maha Kumbh' investigates those who spend their entire lives attempting to solve life's riddles. It honors religion's strength and the universal longing for self-realization. We aim to motivate readers by imparting the wisdom and enchantment of this unique occasion.

3. Philosophical Teachings & Commandments Of Lord Dattatreya (Shri Kshetra Ganagapur)

The book 'Philosophical Teachings and Commandments of Lord Dattatreya,' (Shri Kshetra Ganagapur) dives deeply into Lord Dattatreya's timeless wisdom, which represents the Trimurti of Brahma, Vishnu, and Shiva. Lord Dattatreya, the eternal teacher, guides seekers to enlightenment with lectures on simplicity, self-realization, and harmonious living, with a focus on the famous pilgrimage destination of Shri Kshetra Ganagapur. The book delves deeply into his philosophical beliefs on Advaita Vedanta (non-dualism), detachment, and the synthesis of knowledge, devotion, and action, encouraging readers to seek inner peace, discipline, and spiritual fulfillment. Lord Dattatreya emphasizes the interconnectivity of creation by drawing lessons from 24 Gurus, including natural components and sentient beings. He highlights the connection between the individual soul (Atman) and the Supreme Consciousness (Brahman), emphasizing the significance of conquering ego and duality in order to obtain liberation.

Dattatreya's teachings emphasize wisdom, compassion, universal brotherhood, and cosmic order, laying the groundwork for spiritual growth. Rituals, festivals, and sacred monuments enhance devotees' faiths at Shri Kshetra Ganagapur, a transforming sanctuary of healing and spiritual energy. Lord Dattatreya's ageless teachings provide practical guidance for overcoming challenges, improving self-awareness, and nurturing inner peace. This comprehensive spiritual handbook encourages simplicity, compassion, and a deep connection to the divine.

4. Maha Kumbh: A Scientific Treasure Trove: (Maha Kumbh A Haven For Scientists)

This book, "Maha Kumbh: A Scientific Treasure Trove," offers a unique viewpoint on the Maha Kumbh Mela. It highlights the festival's potential as a world-class scientific laboratory, transcending its religious and cultural roots. This innovative technique sets it apart from previous Maha Kumbh works and provides a riveting analysis of the festival's many facets.

Unveiling Living Laboratory:

The book explores Maha Kumbh's living laboratory, showing its potential for revolutionary study across fields. It painstakingly analyses the festival's distinctive qualities that make it a significant scientific resource. The vast assembly of millions, the temporary mega-city, and the powerful spiritual atmosphere form a dynamic setting for exploration.

The book promotes an interdisciplinary approach to understanding the Maha Kumbh, connecting spirituality and science. It examines the festival's potential for public health, sociology, psychology, and environmental science study. With insights from these many fields, the book provides a comprehensive view of the festival's intricacies and linkages.

The book explores real-world applications of research undertaken during the Maha Kumbh, going beyond theoretical investigation. It shows how the festival's unique setting might aid long-term growth and comprehension of massive crowds. Studying crowd dynamics, public health management, and environmental sustainability during the Kumbh Mela may enhance the planning and administration of future major events.

A stimulus for scientific discovery: The book inspires scientists and researchers to regard the Maha Kumbh as a place of significant discoveries. It stresses the importance of multidisciplinary teamwork and cross-cultural understanding to maximise the festival's scientific potential. The book encourages scientists to explore new horizons and improve our knowledge of human behaviour, societal dynamics, religion, and science by highlighting Kumbh Mela's numerous study potentials.

The book explores unknown scientific realms in the Maha Kumbh, answering key issues about the event. Faith and health: how spiritual activities affect physical and mental health. It also examines the festival's environmental effect and creative sustainability measures. The book explores these undiscovered realms to better comprehend the Maha Kumbh and its potential to advance science and human welfare.

The book "Maha Kumbh: A Scientific Treasure Trove" offers a unique perspective on the Maha Kumbh Mela. It shows the festival's scientific potential beyond its religious and cultural image. The book gives a new and incisive look at the Maha

Kumbh by highlighting the festival's multidisciplinary research, real-world applications, and potential for revolutionary discoveries. The book inspires scientists, scholars, and the public to see the festival's diversity and spiritual and scientific value.

5. Grow Up, Stay Ageless (Aging! An Opportunity)

The book, 'Grow Up, Stay Ageless,' (Aging! An Opportunity) contests traditional notions of aging and presents a perspective that regards life as a continuous journey of development, vitality, and pleasure. It underscores the importance of "sage-ing," which perceives aging as an opportunity for personal development and self-exploration. Strength training, proper nutrition, and adequate sleep hygiene can assist in managing physical changes such as muscular atrophy and decreased bone density. Cognitive alterations, such as visual and auditory impairments, can be addressed by lifelong learning, mindfulness, and social engagement. Emotional resilience is essential during life transitions, and technology can facilitate connections and enhance social ties. Financial stability is essential for a stress-free aging process, and retirement planning requires a comprehensive understanding of income sources, budgeting, and healthcare expenses. Getting financial independence can be easier if you have the right paperwork, know how to avoid being scammed, and have access to resources like government programs and professional financial advisors. Aging gracefully involves the incorporation of physical, mental, social, and financial wellness into a singular lifestyle. To mature gracefully, one must uphold a cheerful disposition, accept change, and possess a sense of purpose.

The book advocates for viewing aging as an opportunity

for development and embracing it fully. It is suitable for individuals of all ages, including youth, young adults, middle-aged individuals, and the elderly; it offers profound and motivational ideas that are customised to the needs and experiences of each life phase.

6. Future Of Jobs & Jobs Of The Future (Emerging And Evolving Careers)

Future of Jobs & Jobs of the Future', (Emerging and Evolving Careers) provides a comprehensive guide to navigating the rapidly changing world of work. It explores emerging careers like AI specialists and sustainability managers, while also examining how technology is transforming existing roles. The book analyzes the dual impact of automation and AI —creating new jobs while displacing others—emphasizing the crucial need for upskilling and reskilling. It delves into key workforce trends like remote work and the gig economy, highlighting the increasing importance of soft skills. The book further explores necessary adaptations in education, including the value of vocational training, to prepare individuals for future jobs. It analyzes the global job market, considering the influence of globalization, and addresses ethical considerations surrounding AI and diversity. Crucially, it provides practical career guidance and strategies for navigating this dynamic landscape, empowering individuals to adapt and thrive.

The book emphasizes that a job's future is a journey of constant evolution, requiring lifelong learning, adaptability, and a willingness to learn new skills. It offers career counseling and transition support, targeting policymakers, educators, institutions, businesses, employees, students, job seekers, and all stakeholders, empowering them to understand and prepare for the future of work. The book underscores the importance of identifying transferable skills, researching in-demand roles, developing learning plans, and embracing continuous learning to future-proof one's career.

7. Ai Agents: Pioneering Future Technologies

The book "AI Agents: Pioneering Future Technologies" stands out for providing an in-depth and forward-thinking viewpoint on the rapidly expanding field of AI agents. Unlike other narrowly focused AI studies, this book expertly bridges the gap between fundamental concepts and cutting-edge applications, providing both technical depth and general appeal. Rather than dwelling solely on theory, the book provides real-world examples of how AI agents are revolutionizing industries, including healthcare, finance, and transportation.

This book stands out for its emphasis on synergy across multiple technologies, such as the convergence of AI and IoT, cloud computing, and even quantum computing. Furthermore, it addresses societal and ethical concerns directly, delving into crucial themes such as job displacement, bias, and accountability. Finally, "AI Agents" serves as a call to action, encouraging readers not only to comprehend the technology but also to help shape an ethical and productive future powered by intelligent agents. This book offers a road map for the future.

8. Echoes of Ai (At the Dawn of 2030)

8. Echoes Of Ai (At The Dawn Of 2030)

The Book, "Echoes of AI (At the Dawn of 2030)" is a crucial guide to navigating the future of work in an AI-driven world. Unlike books focusing on the present, this book offers a forward-thinking analysis of how AI will reshape the workforce by 2030, enabling readers to anticipate and adapt to the coming changes. It provides a comprehensive view of the AI revolution, exploring not only the technological advancements but also their societal, economic, and ethical implications. This holistic approach equips readers with a more profound understanding of AI's transformative potential and its impact on human lives.

The book delves into the changing landscape of jobs, highlighting the skills that will be in high demand, including both technical expertise and uniquely human skills like critical thinking, creativity, and emotional intelligence. It emphasised the importance of lifelong learning and provided practical guidance on reskilling and upskilling for a future-ready workforce.

Furthermore, "Echoes of AI" tackles the ethical challenges posed by AI, addressing concerns about job displacement, bias, and responsible use. It advocates for a human-centered approach to AI development and deployment, ensuring that AI serves humanity and creates a more equitable and sustainable future.

Written in an accessible and engaging style, "Echoes of AI" offers valuable insights and actionable advice for individuals, organisations, and policymakers. It empowers readers to embrace the opportunities and navigate the challenges of the AI revolution, ensuring that we harness the full potential of AI for the benefit of all.

9. Transform Your Leadership: Modern Administrative Secrets From The Epics: (A Holistic Guide Through The Mahabharata, Ramayana, And Bhagavatam)

Transform Your Leadership: Modern Administrative Secrets from The Epics: (A Holistic Guide Through the Mahabharata, Ramayana, and Bhagavatam) offers a refreshing take on leadership by blending ancient Indian wisdom with today's management challenges. Drawing deeply from the Mahabharata, Ramayana, and Srimad Bhagavatam, the book unlocks timeless strategies for ethical decision-making, people-centric governance, and spiritually rooted leadership. Rather than focusing solely on material goals, it encourages a broader vision—one that values inner growth, strong relationships, and purposeful action. From Krishna's strategic insights and Rama's integrity to the Bhagavatam's emphasis on self-awareness, the narrative provides transformative lessons that speak to leaders across generations.

Through rich storytelling and real-world parallels, this guide inspires leaders to lead with wisdom, balance, and heart, creating a legacy of both excellence and meaning.

In essence, the book provides a practical guide for modern leaders to cultivate ethical, compassionate, and spiritually aware leadership by drawing upon the rich wisdom of India's ancient epics, enabling them to navigate complex challenges and create a lasting positive impact.

10. Empower Teaching & Learning Through Ai (Transforming To Ai-Powered Learning)

'Empower Teaching & Learning Through AI (Transforming to AI-Powered Learning)' stands out as a visionary, values-driven exploration of how artificial intelligence can transform education while preserving its human essence. Unlike works that focus narrowly on technology or automation, this book offers a holistic framework—blending cutting-edge innovation with ethical insight, inclusivity, and emotional depth.

What sets this book apart is its integrated approach. The book portrays AI not as a panacea or isolated tool, but rather as a component of a broader learning ecosystem, intricately interwoven with pedagogy, community, and culture. It provides a balanced mix of foundational AI knowledge, practical classroom applications, and forward-looking possibilities, all while remaining grounded in timeless educational values like empathy, curiosity, and joy.

A standout feature is the book's unwavering focus on equity. In a world where AI could widen digital divides, this book insists on democratising access—especially for underserved and marginalised learners. It champions AI literacy as a right, not a privilege, and reimagines the teacher's role not as obsolete but essential. It positions educators as mentors, facilitators, and ethical guides—uniquely human roles that AI cannot replace.

The book also balances bold innovation with deep responsibility. Readers are invited to envision immersive, tech-enabled learning environments, but always with critical questions about fairness, privacy, and the common good.

Designed for educators, policymakers, technologists, and changemakers alike, this book bridges theory and action, imagination, and integrity. The book is not just a guide—it is a compass for shaping education's future with heart, wisdom, and purpose.

11. Ai For Human Empowerment (Build A Better World With Intelligent Technology)

The book 'AI for Empowering Humanity' stands apart in the growing landscape of AI literature by reimagining artificial intelligence not as a purely technical pursuit but as a human-centred catalyst for ethical, inclusive, and impactful transformation. What truly sets this book apart is its seamless integration of AI development with core ethical values at every stage—championing a culture where innovation is guided by purpose, not just performance.

Unlike conventional texts that cater exclusively to technical audiences, this book welcomes readers from all walks of life. Whether you are an AI expert, a social worker, a policymaker, or a curious learner, you will find tools, exercises, and real-world case studies designed to make complex ideas actionable and approachable.

Its emphasis on interdisciplinary collaboration is another defining strength. By fostering dialogue between technologists, social impact leaders, and grassroots changemakers, the book nurtures a shared vision for solving complex societal challenges through AI.

Inspired by pioneering efforts like those at Stanford University in the realm of AI for social good, the book expands this vision to empower a broader, global audience. It serves both as an accessible entry point for beginners and a purpose-driven resource for experienced professionals.

Ultimately, 'AI for Empowering Humanity' is more than a book—it is a movement. It combines ethical insight, practical skill-building, and a compelling call to action, inviting readers to harness AI as a force for justice, empathy, and meaningful change.

12. Kashi Calls (A Journey To Enlightenment)

"Kashi Calls" (A Journey to Enlightenment) is not just a book; it is a divine summons—a call from Kashi that echoes through lifetimes. It embodies the essence of the eternal city, capturing the chants of sadhus, the prayers of seekers, and the soul's longing for liberation. This work is an invocation that bridges the finite and the infinite, urging readers to surrender illusions and embrace the divine.

These pages offer a pilgrimage of the soul—walking the Panchkroshi Yatra, feeling the cold touch of the Ganga at dawn, and encountering the silent gaze of Kaal Bhairav. The book brings Kashi's rituals, legends, and truths to life, immersing readers in a visceral experience.

"Kashi Calls" reflects the seeker's soul, asking:

1. Have you ever felt drawn to a place you have never seen?
2. Has the Ganga Aarti awakened a forgotten prayer within you?
3. Does the smoke from Manikarnika whisper of liberation instead of death?

Ancient tales from the Skanda Purana blend seamlessly with modern pilgrim stories—a scientist awed by Jyotirlingas, a grieving widow comforted by Annapurna, and a sceptic transformed by the Dwadasha Aditya temples.

More than a guide, this book is a revelation. It awakens Kashi within, echoing "Har Har Mahadev!" long after the final page. It is a pilgrimage of the soul—open it, and Kashi will open you.

13. Nurture Your Children As Future Innovators With Ai And Robotics (A Complete Guide For Parents And Teachers)

This book, Nurture Your Children as Future Innovators with AI and Robotics, provides a comprehensive guide for parents and teachers to help children become future innovators by leveraging Artificial Intelligence (AI) and robotics.

This book stands out because it takes a complete and age-appropriate approach to introducing AI and robotics to children, starting in early childhood and going through tenth grade. Designed specifically for parents and teachers, it simplifies complex topics with straightforward explanations, real-life examples, and fascinating tales that make cutting-edge technology accessible to young minds. The book is unique in that it bridges the gap between technical learning and character development, emphasising not only future professional readiness but also the development of essential 21st-century skills such as critical thinking, creativity, ethical reasoning, and collaborative problem solving.

Rather than providing a uniform curriculum, the book walks readers through a systematic, phase-by-phase approach that is consistent with children's cognitive and emotional development. Each topic is age-appropriate and engaging due to the deliberate exposure to real-world tools in the learning process. Unplugged games, hands-on STEM activities, robotics kits, and AI mini-experiments all contribute to more engaging, practical, and pleasurable learning experiences.

More importantly, the book promotes ethical technology use, digital citizenship, and empathy, making it more than just a technical skills manual; it is a road map for producing well-rounded, informed innovators. It encourages adults to actively participate in a child's learning journey by transforming homes and classrooms into hubs of wonder, creativity, and responsible invention. This book's uncommon combination of developmental insight, practical aid, and ethical foundation makes it an indispensable resource for anyone preparing the next generation of innovators

14. Ai & Robotics For Teens: Fuelling Curiosity And Innovation

'AI & Robotics for Teens: Fuelling Curiosity and Innovation' is not just another educational book—it is a thoughtfully designed learning companion tailored to the unique developmental phase of adolescence. Teenagers are at a stage where their brains are wired for exploration, curiosity, and identity formation. Teenagers often strive to challenge boundaries, challenge established norms, and explore the world through personal exploration. This book harnesses that "destructive intrigue"—not to lead them astray, but to channel it into something transformative: understanding the complex and captivating worlds of artificial intelligence

and robotics.
This book distinguishes itself by adeptly decoding intricate technological concepts, including machine learning, neural networks, and human-robot interaction, in a manner that is both intellectually rigorous and deeply relatable to teen readers. It neither oversimplifies nor overwhelms. Instead, it encourages teens to delve into complex concepts, conduct experiments, pose challenging questions, and establish connections between emerging technologies and their daily lives.
Another distinctive feature of this book is its strong ethical foundation. As the world gears up for a future shaped by automation, AI, and rapid innovation, preparing young minds must go beyond technical skills. This book encourages critical thinking about fairness, inclusion, sustainability, and human values—arming teens not only with knowledge but with the ethical lens needed to build a better tomorrow.
'AI & Robotics for Teens' effectively bridges the gap between curiosity and capability by integrating storytelling, hands-on examples, and real-world applications. It is a roadmap for teenagers—not just to understand the future but to create it. In doing so, the book contributes meaningfully to a larger global mission: investing in education, retraining, and open dialogue to ensure a responsible, inclusive, and inspired technological future.

15. The Guru's Advaitamrutam

"The Guru's Advitamrutam" distinguishes itself as more than just a spiritual text; it is a unique guide for profound inner transformation. Its main strength is its practical retreat format, which provides a clear, step-by-step path to truly understanding Advaita Vedanta, instead of just learning the theory. This hands-on approach directly addresses modern longings for deeper meaning.
The book excels in the experiential application of Advaita.

It does not just explain concepts like Maya or Viveka; it guides readers on how to live them, integrating ancient principles like Sadhana Chatushtayam, Shravana, Manana, and Nididhyasana into daily routines. It adopts a holistic approach, providing practical strategies for mind control (e.g., pranayama, mantra) and guidance on overcoming emotional blocks, recognising the realistic challenges spiritual seekers face.

Ultimately, its focus is on self-realisation (Brahmatman Aikyam) and living liberated. The book meticulously describes this direct experience of unity, outlining the characteristics of a jivanmukta and guiding readers to live purposefully, rooted in Advaitic truth. The title itself, "Advitamrutam" (nectar of Advaita), embodies its promise: a life-transforming essence leading to liberation and spiritual immortality. This makes the book a guided, practical, and holistic pathway to experiencing the liberating truth of Advaita Vedanta for contemporary seekers.

16. Goodbye, Traditional Trading? Hello, High-Frequency Speed! Quantum Technologies @ National Stock Exchange Of India

The book, "Goodbye, Traditional Trading? Hello, High-Frequency Speed! Quantum Technologies @ National Stock Exchange of India," stands out for its unique and specific focus on the National Stock Exchange of India (NSE). Unlike general texts on quantum finance, this book delves into the practical application of quantum technologies to address the distinct challenges and opportunities within the financial infrastructure of a major emerging market.

Its uniqueness lies in presenting quantum technologies not as a theoretical concept but as a strategic imperative for the NSE's transformation. The book comprehensively explores how quantum computing, communication, and security can revolutionize core market functions, including high-frequency trading, risk management, portfolio optimization, and fraud detection. It particularly highlights the dual nature of quantum in cybersecurity—offering unhackable communication while also posing a threat to current encryption, necessitating a proactive shift. By focusing on a real-world exchange and its specific needs, the book provides a pragmatic roadmap for adopting these advanced technologies, positioning the NSE for global leadership and enhanced market efficiency.

Dad The Maha Upadyay: Man Of Letters

'Dad the Maha Upadyay: Man of Letters' is a heartfelt biography of Dr. C. Subbarayudu, celebrating his remarkable contributions to literature and education. The book chronicles his intellectual journey, showcasing his dedication to mentorship, lifelong learning, and academic excellence. It highlights his values of scholarship and service to society, offering inspiration to aspiring academics and researchers. Through this compelling narrative, the biography underscores the transformative power of education and innovation in shaping future generations, serving as a profound honour to a visionary who is leaving an indelible mark on education and the pursuit of knowledge.

ABOUT THE AUTHOR

Dr C S Rayudu Sushma Cirigire Sugun Cirigiri & Susheel Cirigiri

Dr C. S. Rayudu

Dr. C. S. Rayudu stands at the confluence of education, research, and thought leadership, a scholar whose work resonates with both intellectual depth and practical relevance. Over the span of more than four decades, he has emerged as a guiding force in academia and professional practice, acclaimed for his rare ability to harmonize the timeless wisdom of India's philosophical traditions with the disruptive possibilities of modern technologies.

His latest contribution, 'AI-Focused PM (Project Management in the AI Era),' reflects this unique synthesis. Conceived for aspiring project managers, educators, and practitioners navigating today's dynamic professional landscapes, the book illuminates the transformative role of artificial intelligence in project management. By moving readers from traditional frameworks to agile intelligence—augmented by tools such as Copilot and GPT-5—Dr. Rayudu equips them to thrive at the intersection of human creativity and machine intelligence. Far more than a technical manual, the work nurtures curiosity, critical thinking, and ethical awareness, providing readers with a holistic foundation for leadership in the AI-driven future.

His unwavering dedication to education and administration has distinguished Dr. Rayudu's career. Multiple "Best Teacher" awards at both regional and state levels have honored him, inspiring generations of students and educators alike. Dr. Rayudu's teaching philosophy integrates academic rigor with human values, guaranteeing that knowledge and wisdom are inseparable. Under his mentorship, countless learners have grown into innovators, leaders, and change-makers in education, industry, and governance.

A prolific author, Dr. Rayudu has consistently explored the evolving relationship between technology, society, and human development. His publications span a wide spectrum of subjects, each marked by his signature integration of scholarly depth and visionary outlook. Notable works include Future of Jobs & Jobs of the Future: Emerging and Evolving Careers; AI Agents: Pioneering Future Technologies; Echoes of AI: Insights from the Dawn of 2030; Empower Teaching & Learning Through AI; AI for Human Empowerment; Nurture Your Children as Future Innovators with AI and Robotics; AI & Robotics for Teens: Fueling Curiosity and Innovation; and Goodbye, Traditional Trading? Hello, High-Frequency Speed! AI & Quantum Technologies at the National Stock Exchange of India.

Beyond his contributions to technology and education, Dr. Rayudu's scholarship often bridges into the domains of ethics, spirituality, and cultural heritage. His work, Transform Your Leadership: Modern Administrative Secrets from the Epics, distils enduring leadership principles from India's ancient texts and reinterprets them for contemporary governance and management. In Kasi Calls, he offers meditative reflections on spirituality, pilgrimage, and the pursuit of higher purpose in modern times. These works exemplify his commitment to presenting knowledge not merely as information but as a transformative force—anchored in values yet oriented toward the future.

At the core of Dr. Rayudu's scholarship lies a conviction that true progress requires both technological empowerment and ethical grounding. He envisions education and project management as pathways to holistic human development—where efficiency is balanced with empathy, and innovation is guided by wisdom. By combining rigorous analysis, ethical reflection, and spiritual insight, he provides readers with more than technical proficiency; he offers them a roadmap for navigating the profound complexities of the 21st century with courage, clarity, and purpose.

In all his works, Dr. Rayudu emerges not only as an author but also as a mentor and visionary. His legacy continues to inspire students, professionals, and thought leaders across fields—encouraging them to embrace the challenges of the future with resilience, creativity, and a deep sense of responsibility to humanity.

Sushma Cirigire

Sushma Cirigire, co-author of AI-Focused PM (Project Management in the AI Era), brings to the book a wealth of knowledge and practical insight gained from her decades of experience in the software industry and project management. Her contribution reflects a career defined by technical mastery, organizational leadership, and a deep commitment to fostering collaboration and innovation in complex professional environments.

A graduate of Jawaharlal Nehru Technological University, Hyderabad, where she earned her Bachelor of Technology, Sushma laid the academic foundation for a successful career that has spanned multiple multinational corporations across diverse verticals of software development and project management. Over the years, she has cultivated expertise in handling large-scale projects, integrating technical systems, and ensuring delivery excellence across fast-paced, competitive industries.

Sushma currently serves as a project manager at a leading software company in Hyderabad, where she plays a pivotal role in overseeing mission-critical projects for one of the world's foremost providers of audit, consulting, tax, and advisory services. In this role, she not only oversees intricate workflows but also offers strategic assistance to teams, fostering a synergy between innovation and execution. Her ability to combine managerial discipline with empathetic leadership has earned her respect as both a professional and a mentor.

Her role as co-author of AI-Focused PM (Project Management in the AI Era) reflects her conviction that the future of project management lies in harmonizing human expertise with the transformative power of artificial intelligence. Drawing on her practical experiences, she brings valuable perspectives on how AI tools can enhance efficiency, agility, and strategic foresight in project management while still preserving the human qualities of judgment, creativity, and collaboration.

Through her professional journey and literary contributions, Sushma Cirigire embodies the spirit of a modern project leader—technically adept, strategically insightful, and ethically grounded. Her work in this book represents not only her expertise but also her commitment to empowering the next generation of project managers to navigate the obstacles and opportunities of the AI era with confidence and purpose.

Sugun Cirigiri

Sugun Cirigiri brings to AI-Focused PM (Project Management in the AI Era) a unique blend of professional versatility, analytical expertise, and a forward-looking vision shaped by his decade-long career across diverse industries. His contributions reflect not only technical proficiency but also a deep commitment to bridging knowledge, practice, and purpose in the age of intelligent technologies.

A graduate of Sri Krishna Devaraya University, Anantapur (B.Tech.), Sugun further expanded his academic foundation with a Postgraduate Diploma in Banking Services from Manipal University, Bangalore, and an MBA from Sri Venkateswara University, Tirupati. This multidisciplinary education provided him with the rare ability to connect the rigor of engineering, the dynamism of finance, and the strategic foresight of management, a combination that deeply informs his writing and professional endeavors.

Over the past decade, Sugun has cultivated a multifaceted career spanning the pharmaceutical biotechnology, banking, and software industries. He began his journey as a research analyst in the pharmaceutical biotechnology sector, contributing to projects that demanded precision and scientific inquiry. Transitioning into banking, he gained experience in both front-end and back-end operations, serving as an assistant manager and engaging with critical aspects of financial services. His career later expanded into the software domain, where he has worked on anti-money laundering systems, systems administration, and data analytics, harnessing technology to solve complex real-world challenges. Currently, he serves as an SAP data analyst with a global IT and consultancy corporation in Hyderabad, where he applies his managerial skills and data expertise to enterprise-scale projects.

Sugun's writing reflects this broad spectrum of professional and academic experience. He co-authored Goodbye, Traditional Trading? Hello, High-Frequency Speed! AI & Quantum Technologies at the National Stock Exchange of India, where he examined the disruptive role of AI and quantum technologies in reshaping the financial markets. His collaborations also include Dad, the Maha Upadyay: Man of Letters—a tribute to wisdom and learning—and AI & Robotics for Teens: Fuelling Curiosity and Innovation, which captures his passion for empowering young learners to explore technology with imagination and responsibility.

At the heart of Sugun's work lies a vision of technology as both a catalyst and a compass. He views AI, robotics, and data-driven systems not merely as instruments of innovation but as pathways to nurture purposeful progress. His writings consistently emphasize the need to pair technical advancement with ethical reflection, ensuring that future generations approach emerging technologies not just with skill, but with wisdom and empathy.

Through his professional journey and literary contributions, Sugun Cirigiri embodies the qualities of a modern thinker and practitioner—adaptable, insightful, and deeply committed to building bridges between industries, disciplines, and generations. His role in co-authoring AI-Focused PM (Project Management in the AI Era) underscores his belief in empowering professionals to navigate complexity with confidence, creativity, and a sense of higher purpose.

Susheel Cirigiri

Susheel Cirigiri, co-author of AI-Focused PM (Project Management in the AI Era), brings to the book a distinctive perspective shaped by his extensive experience in the software industry and his deep grounding in academic excellence. His contribution reflects a unique synthesis of engineering rigor, technological innovation, and a profoundly human-centered vision of progress.

A graduate of Jawaharlal Nehru Technological University (Anantapur), the National Institute of Technology, Rourkela, and the Indian Institute of Science, Bangalore, Susheel's academic journey demonstrates both intellectual versatility and commitment to mastery. This foundation has empowered him to navigate the complex domains of computational systems, product development, and emerging technologies, while consistently anchoring his work in values of integrity, purpose, and social responsibility.

Based in Hyderabad's thriving IT ecosystem, Susheel currently leads software product design and development at a global technology firm, where he engages with the cutting edge of digital transformation. His professional path is marked not only by technical brilliance but also by an ethical compass inherited from his father—a guiding influence that continues to shape his worldview and writings.

As an author, Susheel has contributed to a growing body of literature at the intersection of technology, ethics, and education. He co-authored Goodbye, Traditional Trading? Hello, High-Frequency Speed! AI & Quantum Technologies @

National Stock Exchange of India, a bold exploration of how disruptive technologies reshape financial markets. In AI for Human Empowerment: Building a Better World with Intelligent Technology and Empower Teaching and Learning with AI, he advocates for responsible and inclusive applications of artificial intelligence, urging a balance between innovation and human well-being. His heartfelt work, titled Dad, the Maha Upadyay: Man of Letters, stands out as both an intellectual reflection and a personal tribute, weaving analytical clarity with reverence for the legacy of wisdom and integrity left by his father.

Susheel is equally committed to preparing younger generations and has contributed to two significant works: Nurture Your Children as Future Innovators with AI and Robotics, and AI & Robotics for Teens: Fueling Curiosity and Innovation. These works highlight his dedication to equipping young minds with not only technical skills but also the imagination, ethical grounding, and curiosity needed to thrive in an AI-driven world.

Through his writing and professional leadership, Susheel Cirigiri emerges not merely as a technologist but as a visionary thinker and mentor. His work consistently bridges innovation with ethics, technology with humanity, and progress with purpose—offering readers guidance to navigate the AI era with clarity, responsibility, and hope.

ACKNOWLEDGEMENT

Writing a book at the intersection of Artificial Intelligence (AI) and Project Management (PM) is less a solitary endeavour and more a complex, collaborative project. *AI-Focused PM (Project Management in the AI Era)* stands as a testament to the collective wisdom, generosity, and pioneering spirit of an extraordinary community.

We extend our deepest gratitude to the trailblazers —researchers, scientists, and thought leaders—whose groundbreaking work in AI, Agile methodologies, and established project management frameworks laid the foundation for this book. Their innovations and principles shaped the ideas explored within these pages. We are also grateful to the organizations that allowed their projects to serve as real-world case studies, bringing theory to life and enriching our exploration.

To our colleagues and peers in the technology and software industry: your field-tested insights, candid feedback, and shared experiences were invaluable. You provided the practical wisdom and iterative learning loops that ensured this book remains relevant, actionable, and aligned with the evolving demands of modern project management.

Special thanks to our mentors, contributors, and reviewers —the intellectual compass and quality assurance behind this work—whose dedication ensured clarity, rigor, and excellence throughout.

Finally, we salute the broader AI and project management communities, whose commitment to knowledge-sharing and innovation fuels progress across industries. This book is a tribute to all who advance technology, elevate professional practice, and contribute to a world driven by purposeful, intelligent projects. We are privileged to stand on your shoulders.

Dr C S Rayudu
Sushma Cirigiri
Sugun Cirigiri
Susheel Cirigiri

www.ingramcontent.com/pod-product-compliance
Ingram Content Group UK Ltd.
Pitfield, Milton Keynes, MK11 3LW, UK
UKHW021403190726
13845UKWH00028B/855